I

[

PICTURED STORY
OF
ENGLISH LITERATURE

BRITISH MUSEUM READING ROOM

PICTURED STORY
OF
ENGLISH LITERATURE

FROM ITS BEGINNINGS
TO THE PRESENT DAY

by

J. W. CUNLIFFE

D. LIT. (UNIVERSITY OF LONDON),
LITT. D. (COLUMBIA UNIVERSITY)

PROFESSOR OF ENGLISH AND DIRECTOR EMERITUS OF THE
SCHOOL OF JOURNALISM OF COLUMBIA UNIVERSITY
IN THE CITY OF NEW YORK

STUDENT'S EDITION

D. APPLETON-CENTURY COMPANY
INCORPORATED
NEW YORK   LONDON

PREFACE

To tell again the oft-repeated story of English literature may seem to call for an apology, however practised the pen of the author and however prolonged his study of the subject may be. But in the field of illustration there is still ample opportunity for the adventurous. The current handbooks are for the most part accurate in their facts and sincere in their opinions; but where illustrations are used, the choice often seems to a discerning eye to have been based mainly on what was at hand or at least easily obtainable; the reader has been asked to accept without question any pictorial representation of a person, place, or scene, however fanciful or void of historical authority. It seemed, therefore, to the present writer and publishers that there was an opening for a readable account of the growth of English literature with illustrations which would enable the reader to see what the great writers and the books they wrote really looked like, and what, so far as can be ascertained, were the surroundings in which they moved. The undertaking has been made much easier by the establishment, at the Bodleian Library in Oxford and at the British Museum and the National Portrait Gallery in London, of photographic studios for the dissemination of accurate reproductions of the priceless treasures they preserve, and by the recent improvements in the United States of methods of photographic reproduction for book illustration. Among the wealth of material thus placed at his disposal, the author has done his best to choose, within the necessary limits of space, what is most significant, and the original manuscripts, books, portraits, and prints which form the sources for the illustrations have been briefly indicated. It is hoped that the reader may experience as much pleasure in finding them here as the author had in looking for them—chiefly in the excellently organized Print Room of the British Museum and in the London print-shops.

ACKNOWLEDGMENTS

The author wishes to acknowledge with many thanks permission from Mrs. J. M. Scott Moncrieff to use the translation from the poem *Deor* by her son, Charles Scott Moncrieff; from Professor Oliver Elton, and the Clarendon Press, Oxford, to use Mr. Elton's translation of a page from *Judith;* and from George Routledge & Sons, Ltd., London, for permission to use the translation of the *Cædmon* Hymn by Dr. Charles W. Kennedy, of Princeton University.

Acknowledgments for the reproduction of facsimiles and photographs are made in detail in the notes on the illustrations.

CONTENTS

NOTES ON THE ILLUSTRATIONS   xi

   I   THE HEROIC AGE   1

  II   THE AGE OF ROMANCE   11

 III   THE INVENTION OF PRINTING   21

  IV   THE ELIZABETHANS   31

   V   THE FIGHT FOR FREEDOM   69

  VI   COFFEE-HOUSES, CLUBS, AND PERIODICALS   107

 VII   THE RISE OF THE MODERN NOVEL   143

VIII   THE ROMANTIC REVIVAL   173

  IX   THE VICTORIAN AGE   261

   X   THE TWENTIETH CENTURY   385

INDEX OF THE ILLUSTRATIONS   425

INDEX OF NAMES AND TITLES   427

NOTES ON THE ILLUSTRATIONS

Abbreviations:

B.M. Phg.—Photograph supplied by the British Museum Photographic Service.

B.M.Fl. Phg.—Photograph supplied by R. B. Fleming & Co. from material in the British Museum.

N.P.G. Phg.—Photograph supplied by the Photographic Service of the National Portrait Gallery.

BRITISH MUSEUM READING ROOM   *Frontispiece*

Reproduced by permission of the Trustees of the British Museum, to whose staff the author is indebted for many courtesies. The Reading Room was built in 1857 in accordance with a design made by the principal librarian; the dome is 140 feet in diameter and 106 feet high; above the zone of the stacks and galleries runs an ornamental band bearing the names of the leading English writers: Chaucer, Caxton, Tyndale, Spenser, Shakspere, Bacon, Milton, Locke, Addison, Swift, Pope, Gibbon, Wordsworth, Scott, Byron, Carlyle, Macaulay, Tennyson, Browning. On the floor are seats for 458 readers, a central daïs for the operating staff, and the general catalogue of over a thousand volumes, around which there is a constant stream of researchers. The Library is the Mecca of students of English literature from all over the world. Under the Copyright Act of 1842 and subsequent statutes it is entitled to receive and is bound to preserve a copy of every book published in Great Britain. There are between four and five million books on the shelves, accessible either in the Reading Room or in the North Library, which is reserved for the examination of rare books; manuscripts and prints are housed in other parts of the Museum, and the newspaper files are in a special building at Colindale, Hendon. The literary treasures accumulated by the Museum since its foundation in 1753 are beyond any flight of fancy and are freely open to scholars without restriction of race or nationality.

PAGE

EXETER CATHEDRAL CHAPTER-HOUSE   XXXiv

Reproduced from Plate 99 in Winkles's "Cathedrals," Vol. II, 1838, drawn by R. Garland, engraved by R. Winkles. The MS. of the Exeter Book is probably older than any part of the cathedral building as it now stands; but the chapter-house, in which it is still shown to the curious or learned visitor, is of a respectable antiquity, dating, as to its lower part, from the thirteenth century, and as to its upper part, from the fifteenth.

FRANKS CASKET   3

B.M. Phg. of Franks Casket, so called from Sir Augustus Wollaston Franks, formerly Keeper of the British Museum, who discovered the casket in 1856 in the store of a well-known dealer in antiquities at Paris and after buying it, presented it to the Museum. He traced the casket back to Professor Mathieu of Clermont Ferrand, who said that it was found in the house of a middle-class family of Auzon in the department of Haute-Loire. The ladies had been using it as a work-box and kept their needles and thread in it. It was mounted in silver. When the mountings were removed the box fell to pieces and some of it got lost, but the missing right side was discovered some years later in a museum in Florence, where it still remains. In 1870 W. Arndt discovered a plaster cast of the casket in the sacristy of a church in Clermont; it is now thought that the casket itself had long ago belonged to St. Julian's at Brioude, the district in the department of Haute-Loire in which Auzon is situated.

THE BODLEIAN LIBRARY   6

The Bodleian, Oxford, is the oldest public library in Europe, and next to the British Museum, the largest in Great Britain. It contains well over 1,250,000 books and over 40,000 MSS. and has the right to a copy of every book published in Great Britain. The nucleus of the collection was formed in 1439 with the gift of 129 valuable books by Humphrey, Duke of Gloucester, and the promise of £100 toward the upkeep of the library, the remainder of his books and MSS. to be given on his death. But he died intestate and difficulties arose. The contents of Duke Humphrey's library were dispersed in the reign of Edward VI, and now only three books of the original collection remain in the Bodleian, though others are to be found in libraries of some of the Oxford colleges and of the British Museum. In February, 1597, Sir Thomas Bodley met the expense of restoring the original room; on November 8, 1603, the library was formally opened, and in 1604 James I granted letters patent in Bodley's name. In 1610 the original room was found to be too small and an east wing was begun which was completed by 1612. In 1611, as his health was failing, Bodley began to endow the library, and on his death he made the university his chief heir, establishing a further endowment, which provided for the acquisition of noteworthy books and manuscripts, many of them unique. An effort is now being made to raise further funds for the accommodation of the books and MSS. accumulated in large numbers in modern times.

WHITBY ABBEY, YORKSHIRE   6

According to the contemporary history of the Venerable Bede, this abbey was founded about the middle of the seventh century for men and women of the Benedictine Order; it flourished for about two hundred years, when it was plundered and laid waste by the Danes. In the reign of William the Conqueror the monastery was refounded as a Benedictine priory and was made an abbey by Henry I. In the reign of Henry VIII the yearly revenues amounted to about £500. It was surrendered to the Crown in 1540 and passed into private hands. Our view, which represents the northwest aspect, was drawn in 1775, and the engraving by S. Hooper bears the date of January 20, 1776.

GEOFFREY'S WINDOW   10

This old window, which may still be seen at Monmouth, is associated with the name of Geoffrey; it is now part of a building used as a national school.

SUMER IS ICUMEN IN   14

A modern transcription of this song is given in our text. The instructions to the singers state that it is to be sung by at least four men, two of whom sing the foot, or refrain. One begins, accompanied by those who sing the foot. When the first singer has reached the first note after the cross, the second joins in. Each in turn pauses at the places marked for a pause for the space of one long note. The singers of the refrain repeat it as often as necessary, one making a pause at the end and the other a pause in the middle.

JOHN GOWER   17

An engraving done by the well-known eighteenth-century artist George Vertue, in the year 1727, as the inscription at the foot of it indicates. The titles of the three books appear also in the monument to Gower in Southwark Cathedral, of which a view is given in the lower part of the print.

CHAUCER   19

This portrait of Chaucer is contained in an early fifteenth-century manuscript of a poem by his disciple Thomas Occleve. The manuscript is in the MS. Department of the British Museum, which supplied the reproduction.

LINDISFARNE GOSPEL   24

(B.M. Phg.) The beginning of the Gospel of St. John in a manuscript containing the four Gospels in the Latin Vulgate version, written about the end of the seventh century.

RICHARD II'S BIBLE   24

(B.M. Phg.) A MS. executed about the end of the fourteenth century, probably for Richard II. The decorated initial represents (beginning from the left): first, the birth of Moses; then, in the center, the placing of the baby Moses in the river Nile; and finally, on the right, the finding of the baby in "the ark among the flags," by the daughter of Pharaoh, as recounted in Exodus II, 1-10.

WYCLIFFITE BIBLE   24

This is a B.M. MS. of the first translation of the Bible into English, made about 1380-84 under the orders of the first Protestant reformer, John Wycliffe, though probably not actually done by him. The passage represented is the beginning of the first chapter of the Gospel according to St. John.

FIRST PRINTED ENGLISH BIBLE   26

(B.M. Phg.) A British Museum copy of the translation by Tyndale and Coverdale, of which particulars are given on the opposite page. The passage is from the beginning of the first chapter of Genesis.

FIRST "GREAT BIBLE"   26

The first of the "Great Bibles" issued for use in English churches, 1539-41. The printing was done mainly at Paris, but was completed in England. The copy from which the photograph is taken is again in the British Museum, and the same passage has been chosen for reproduction.

AN EARLY CAXTON   26

(B.M. Phg.) The first dated book printed in England. The passage runs as follows: "Here endeth the book named the dicts or sayings of the philosophers imprinted by me, William Caxton, at Westminster in the year of Our Lord, 1477, which book is lately translated out of French into English by the noble and puissant lord, Lord Anthony, Earl Rivers, Lord of Scales and of the Isle of Wight, Defender and Director of the Apostolic Seat of our Holy Father the Pope in this realm of England, and Governor of my Lord Prince of Wales; and it is so that at such time as he had accomplished this said work it pleased him to send it to me in certain quires to oversee. . . ."

HENRY VIII (B.M. PHG.)

CARDINAL WOLSEY (B.M. PHG.)

SIR THOMAS MORE (B.M. PHG.)

THOMAS CROMWELL (B.M. PH.G.)

28

All four of these portraits of leading personages in the English Protestant Reformation are from the British Museum Series.

WILLIAM TYNDALE 30

This print of the Protestant reformer and translator of the Bible represents him in skullcap with ruff and gown. It appeared first in the French translation by Simon Goulard of Beza's *Icones*, 1581.

AN EARLY PRINTING-OFFICE 30

This interesting woodcut was made by the well-known sixteenth-century engraver, Jost Amman or Judocus Ammanus, who was born in Zurich about 1539 and died at Nuremberg in 1591. It appeared in 1568 as part of a series of illustrations of various trades and professions, with accompanying verses by Hans Sachs. It represents in embryo the equipment of a modern printing-office: the compositor at his case, the type on the press, and the machinery by which sheets are printed and laid aside, to be gathered together into a book.

GASCOIGNE PRESENTING HIS WORK TO QUEEN ELIZABETH 32

(B.M. Phg.) A description of the drawing is given in our text.

SPENSER 34

An engraving by J. Thomson from a portrait formerly in the possession of the Earl of Kinnoull.

FAERIE QUEENE, TITLE-PAGE, FIRST EDITION, 1590 (B.M. PHG.) 36

FAERIE QUEENE, DEDICATION, SECOND EDITION, 1596 (B.M. FL. PHG.) 36

The dedication runs: "To the most high, mighty and magnificent empress, renowned for piety, virtue, and all gracious government, Elizabeth, by the Grace of God Queen of England, France and Ireland and of Virginia, Defender of the Faith, etc., her most humble servant Edmund Spenser doth in all humility dedicate, present and consecrate these his labours to live with the eternity of her fame." The dedication of the first edition is simpler in character and styles Elizabeth "Queen of England, France and Ireland" but without any mention of Virginia, the words "and Virginia" being added in the second edition.

PAGE

SIR PHILIP SIDNEY   36

Engraved by H. Robinson from the portrait ascribed to Sir Antonio More;
formerly in the collection of the Duke of Bedford, now in the National
Portrait Gallery.

SIR WALTER RALEIGH   36

An engraving by J. Posselwhite, from a portrait belonging to the Duchess
of Dorset.

SWAN THEATER ABOUT 1596   41

(Fl. Phg.) This is the earliest drawing known of the interior of an Elizabethan theater. It was discovered in 1888 in the Commonplace Book of
Arand van Buchell (1565-1641), in the library of the University of Utrecht.
Van Buchell's friend De Witt had apparently sent him this drawing, together
with an account of a visit to London about 1596. It is useful as a confirma-
tion of the accepted view of the shape of the Elizabethan stage as described
in our text.

SHAKSPERE'S BIRTHPLACE   43

This view of the birthplace of Shakspere, now an object of pious pilgrimage
for numerous tourists, is taken from an old print showing the house as it
stood before the restoration of 1864, when it was still used as a butcher's
shop. The building on the right of the engraving is the old Swan and
Maidenhead Inn.

SHAKESPERE'S BIRTHPLACE RESTORED   43

The house is small and plain, with a modest living-room and kitchen below,
from which one mounts by a staircase to a bedchamber, where, presumably,
Shakspere was born.

STRATFORD CHURCH   45

Stratford-upon-Avon in Warwickshire, with the Church of the Holy Trinity,
in which Shakspere was baptized and buried. There we see in the register
of baptisms under the date of April 26, 1564: "Gulielmus filius Johannes
Shakespere," plainly written in Elizabethan script; and in the register of
burials, April 25, 1616: "Will: Shakspeare Gent."

ANNE HATHAWAY'S COTTAGE   45

This charming Elizabethan cottage, which may be reached from Stratford
by an easy and pleasant walk through a field path, is one of the best authen-
ticated and best preserved of Shaksperean relics. Sir Sidney Lee says in
his *Life* of Shakspere that it "undoubtedly once formed part of Richard
Hathaway's farmhouse, and, despite numerous alterations and renovations,
still preserves the main features of a thatched farmhouse of the Elizabethan
period." It remained in the Hathaway family till 1838 and now belongs to
the Birthplace Trustees.

EARLY SHAKSPERE QUARTOS   48

These early editions of Shakspere's plays, which were sold for sixpence
each and are now extremely costly, are often of very great value in deter-
mining the text. It will be noticed that in the title-pages here reproduced
from copies in the British Museum, Shakspere's name is not mentioned in
the case of *Romeo and Juliet* and of *Henry IV;* also that Shakspere's
company is variously described, for *Romeo and Juliet* as "Lord Hunsdon's
Servants," for *Richard III*, as "the Lord Chamberlain's Servants," and

for *Hamlet* as "the King's Servants." George Carey, Lord Hunsdon, became Lord Chamberlain in 1597; and the company of actors which had enjoyed his patronage were appointed "the King's Servants" by letters patent dated May 19, 1603.

GLOBE THEATER 1616

50

(B.M. Phg.) This view of the exterior of the Globe Theater with its flag waving and the traffic of the Thames in the background is taken from Visscher's map of London, 1616, of which the British Museum has an excellent copy. The first Globe Theater was ready for occupation by the Lord Chamberlain's men by the beginning of the autumn season of 1599 and was used by them for the performance of Shakspere's and other plays until it was burnt down in 1613. As it was the leading London theater at that time, it was immediately rebuilt and a new theater was opened in 1614. It is this second theater which is shown in our illustration. It will be seen that the second theater is octagonal in shape; the shape of the first Globe was cylindrical. It was probably the first Globe that was described by Shakspere in the opening chorus of *Henry V* as "this wooden O," on account of its round shape.

SHAKSPERE'S BUST

54

The bust on the monumental tomb erected by Shakspere's family in Trinity Church, Stratford, is probably the best guide we have to his personal appearance; it is not very well carved, but the deficiency in lines was partly made up for by the addition of color, at one time obliterated, but now restored. "As it now appears, the poet is wearing a doublet of scarlet with many buttons, under a black cloak, having a white collar turned down from the neck and turned-back white cuffs. The right hand holds a quill pen, while the left rests on a sheet of paper, above a cushion of crimson and green with gilt tassels." The sculptor was a well-known tomb-maker of the time, Geraert Janssen, otherwise called Gerard Johnson. The tomb has a prominent place in the church chancel, given to it, no doubt, not because of Shakspere's eminence as a dramatist but because, as the owner of New Place and a man of wealth, he was a leading citizen of Stratford-on-Avon. Our illustration is from an engraving by W. T. Fry.

FIRST FOLIO TITLE-PAGE

55

(Fl. Phg. from B.M. copy.) The folio edition of Shakspere's collected plays, published seven years after his death, remains the best authority for the text of most of the plays, and the only authority for that of some of them of which no quarto editions are extant. The portrait and the bust are the only representations of Shakspere's physical appearance for which contemporary authority can be established. The British Museum is fortunate in the possession of more than one copy of the folio; that from which our illustration is made shows the portrait in what is considered its more finished though not its earliest state, after the mustache and the left side of the collar have been touched up by the printer.

BEAUMONT AND FLETCHER ⎫
BEN JONSON   ⎬
CHAPMAN   ⎭

57

The portraits of Beaumont, Fletcher, and Chapman are taken from prints prefixed to early editions of their works; that of Jonson is from an engraving by E. Scriven after a portrait by Gerard Honthorst (1590-1653).

PAGE

BACON   60

An engraving by J. Cochran from a portrait by Paul van Somer (1576-1621), formerly belonging to the Earl of Verulam and now in the National Portrait Gallery. Bacon is represented in the robes which he was entitled to wear as Lord Chancellor not very long before his disgrace and downfall. It may therefore be dated from 1618 or thereabouts.

THE INSTAURATIO MAGNA, TITLE-PAGE, FIRST EDITION   64

Bacon's great philosophical work, which he presented to the King just before his fall from office in 1621, bore this title, describing him as still Lord Chancellor. The Latin motto may be translated: "Many shall run across the sea and knowledge shall be increased." As explained in the text, the *Novum Organum* upon which Bacon's fame rests was regarded by him as merely a part of the larger scheme outlined in the *Instauratio,* which he left uncompleted at his death.

QUEEN ELIZABETH   67

An engraving by W. T. Fry from a portrait by Zucchero belonging to the Marquis of Salisbury.

MILTON AGED TEN   72

Drawn and etched by Cipriani from a portrait painted by Cornelius Janssen Van Ceulen in 1618.

MILTON'S POEMS (1645), TITLE-PAGE   74

(B.M. Fl. Phg.) The Latin motto may be translated: "Crown his brow with bay lest an evil tongue should hurt the future poet."

MILTON AT SIXTY-TWO   76

An engraving by G. Vertue

AREOPAGITICA, TITLE-PAGE, FIRST EDITION   79

(B.M. Fl. Phg.) The translation of the motto from Euripides reads:
This is true liberty when free-born men
Having to advise the public may speak free;
Which he who can, and will, deserves high praise.
Who neither can nor will, may hold his peace.
What can be juster in a State than this?

PARADISE LOST, TITLE-PAGE, FIRST EDITION (B.M. FL. PHG.)   84

JOHN BUNYAN   88

Engraved by J. Rogers from a portrait painted by Thomas Sadler in 1685, now in the National Portrait Gallery.

THE PILGRIM'S PROGRESS, TITLE-PAGE, FIRST EDITION (B.M.
     PHG.)   91

PAGE

ELSTOW CHURCH AND BELFRY   94

(B.M. Phg.) From an old print (1803), drawn by T. Hearne and engraved by William Byrne.

BUNYAN'S BIRTHPLACE AT ELSTOW   94

Drawn and engraved for Dugdale's *England and Wales* (1819).

DRYDEN   96

An engraving by M. Van der Gucht from a portrait by Sir Godfrey Kneller, prefixed to Vol. II of Dryden's *Virgil* (1709).

DONNE   98

An engraving by J. W. Cook after the frontispiece to Donne's *Poems* (1633).

HERRICK   102

From an engraving published by W. Marshall (1647).

MARVELL   102

An etching by I. B. Cipriani (1760) from a portrait painted in 1660.

LOVELACE   105

An engraving by W. C. Edwards from a painting by Dobson in Dulwich College.

SUCKLING   105

From a panel by Theodore Russell after Van Dyck.

DORSET   105

Drawn from the original at Knowle, by O. Humphrey (1806).

A LONDON COFFEE-HOUSE   108

The frontispiece to the fourth part of *Vulgus Britannicus or the British Hudibras* (1710), with the caption "The Coffehous Mob." The engraving represents the interior of a coffee-house, at the beginning of the eighteenth century. "Many gentlemen sit at the sides and ends of an oblong table, on which are newspapers, tracts, tobacco-pipes, and a lighted candle for the use of the smokers, one of whom sits with his back towards us; a boy pours coffee into a cup, a visitor standing on the floor drinks from a cup, a young woman sits behind an enclosed counter, or bar, as in similar places on the Continent at the present time [1872], with two lighted candles before her. A quarrel has occurred between two guests, one of them dashes the contents of his cup in the face of the o her. A second table is behind the first."—B.M. Catalogue of Prints and Drawings, Personal and Political Satires, No. 1539.

AUCTION MART COFFEE-ROOM   108

This more peaceful scene, representing the development of the coffee-house on its commercial side, is reproduced from Plate No. 34 of R. Ackerman's *Repository of Arts* (1811).

PAGE

LONDON GAZETTE   110

A B.M. Phg. of the heading and first few lines of the *Gazette,* which is still published as the official organ of the British Government. It was first printed at Oxford in 1665, when Charles II was holding his court there.

DEFOE'S REVIEW, TITLE, FIRST ISSUE (B.M. PHG.)   110

DEFOE   112

Engraved by J. Thomson from the print by M. van der Gucht after a portrait by Taverney, which formed the frontispiece to Defoe's *Jure Divino* (1706). The Dictionary of National Biography lists this as "probably the best portrait," but Freeman O'Donoghue (B.M. Catalogue of British Portraits) expresses the opinion that "none of the engravings of Defoe have any claim to authenticity."

ROBINSON CRUSOE, FRONTISPIECE, FIRST EDITION (B.M. PHG.)   114

STEELE   118

Engraved by J. Rogers from a painting by Sir Godfrey Kneller.

ADDISON   118

An engraving by S. Freeman from a portrait by Sir Godfrey Kneller.

TATLER, TITLE   118

(B.M. Phg.) Isaac Bickerstaff was a pen-name Steele borrowed from Swift. The Latin motto suggests that the paper is concerned with every form of human activity.

SPECTATOR, TITLE   118

(B.M. Phg.) The Latin motto suggests that the purpose of the editors is not "to draw smoke from fire but to bring light out of darkness."

SWIFT   122

Engraved by B. Holl from the picture in the Bodleian Library.

GULLIVER'S TRAVELS, TITLE-PAGE, FIRST ISSUE (B.M. PHG.)   124

STELLA   ⎫
                ⎬   126
HESTER VANHOMRIGH ⎭

Photographs from pictures belonging to G. Villiers Briscoe.

JOURNAL TO STELLA   126

A B.M. Phg. of the original in the MS. Department; the letter is dated March 8, 1711-12, postmarked March 22, and endorsed by Stella as received March 30. The address, written on the back of the letter by Swift, after it had been folded and sealed, reads: "To Mrs. Johnson, at her Lodgings over against St. Mary's Church, near Capel Street, Dublin, Ireland."

PAGE

POPE 132

This, the only full-length portrait of Pope ever made (for he objected to the exhibition of his deformities), was done by William Hoare of Bath, without Pope's knowledge, while the latter was conversing with Ralph Allen, the patron of Fielding and the original of Squire Allworthy in *Tom Jones*. Pope and the painter were both Allen's guests at his house at Prior Park, and Hoare sat at the end of the long gallery while he made the drawing.

MARTHA BLOUNT 136

Engraved by C. Ricart from a drawing by Gardner of the original picture in the Blount collection at Maple Durham.

LADY MARY WORTLEY MONTAGU 136

From a miniature by Zincke, belonging to the Earl of Wharncliffe. The Oriental costume is doubtless associated with her husband's ambassadorship at Constantinople.

POPE'S VILLA AT TWICKENHAM 136

Drawn and engraved by W. Cooke for *The Beauties of England and Wales* (1807).

ARBUTHNOT 140

Fron. an old print.

BOLINGBROKE 140

Engraved by H. Wallis from a canvas of the French school, artist unknown, now in the National Portrait Gallery.

CONGREVE 140

An engraving from a portrait by Sir Godfrey Kneller, now in the National Portrait Gallery.

GAY 140

An engraving from a portrait by William Aikman.

RICHARDSON 142

N.P.G. Phg. of a portrait by Joseph Highmore.

CLARISSA, TITLE-PAGE, FIRST EDITION (B.M. PHG.) 146

FIELDING 150

An engraving by J. Basire, from a sketch by Hogarth.

TOM JONES, TITLE-PAGE, FIRST EDITION (B.M. PHG.) 152

SMOLLETT 155

Engraved by G. Phillips from a portrait by Sir Joshua Reynolds.

PAGE

STERNE   155
  Engraved by W. J. Alais from a portrait by Sir Joshua Reynolds.

RODERICK RANDOM, TITLE-PAGE, FIRST EDITION (B.M. PHG.)   155

TRISTRAM SHANDY, TITLE-PAGE, FIRST EDITION (B.M. PHG.)   155

JOHNSON   158
  Engraved by R. Page from a portrait by Sir Joshua Reynolds, now in the
  National Portrait Gallery.

BOSWELL   158
  Engraved by S. Freeman from a portrait by Sir Joshua Reynolds, now in the
  National Portrait Gallery.

GOLDSMITH   158
  Engraved by S. Freeman from a portrait by Sir Joshua Reynolds, now in the
  National Portrait Gallery.

BURKE   158
  Engraved by C. E. Wagstaff from a portrait by Sir Joshua Reynolds, now
  in the National Portrait Gallery.

BOSWELL'S LIFE OF JOHNSON, TITLE-PAGE, FIRST EDITION
  (B.M. PHG.)   160

ADAM SMITH   162
  Engraved by R. C. Bell from a medallion by James Tassie, done during
  Smith's lifetime.

WEALTH OF NATIONS, TITLE-PAGE, FIRST EDITION   162

FANNY BURNEY   166
  Engraved by C. Turner from a portrait by Edward Francesco Burney.

JANE AUSTEN   168
  The American engraving (1878) of a family portrait.

MARIA EDGEWORTH   171
  Engraved by K. Mackenzie from a portrait by W. M. Craig (1808).

MORAL TALES, TITLE-PAGE, FIRST EDITION (B.M. PHG.)   171

GRAY   174
  Engraved by W. Greatbatch from a portrait by John Giles Eccardt, formerly at Strawberry Hill and now in the National Portrait Gallery.

PAGE

ETON   176

Engraved by J. Smith from a drawing by E. Dayes.

STOKE POGES CHURCHYARD   176

Engraved by W. Byrne from a drawing by A. Tendi. Gray's tomb may be
seen in the background.

COWPER   179

Engraved by Caroline Watson (1805) from a pastel by Romney (1792) now
in the National Portrait Gallery.

COWPER'S HOUSE AT WESTON, BUCKS.   182

Engraved by J. Storer from a drawing by John Greig.

WILLIAM BLAKE   184

N.P.G. Phg. of the portrait by Thomas Phillips.

MOSSGIEL   189

Engraved by R. Sands from a drawing by D. O. Hill.

DUMFRIES   189

Engraved by F. J. Havell from a drawing by W. H. Bartlett.

FIRST (KILMARNOCK) EDITION OF POEMS BY BURNS, TITLE-
PAGE (B.M. PHG.)   191

BURNS   193

Engraved by Ryall from a portrait by Nasmyth; the frontispiece to the
Edinburgh edition.

WORDSWORTH'S SCHOOL, HAWKSHEAD   196

From a photograph.

WINDERMERE AND ESTHWAITE WATER   196

Engraved by J. Engleheart from a drawing by G. Pickering. Esthwaite
Water is the smaller lake to the spectator's right. The view is from the
upper end of Windermere, with Ambleside in the foreground.

COLERIDGE AT TWENTY-THREE   202

N.P.G. Phg. of the portrait by Peter Vandyke (1795).

WORDSWORTH   202

Print by Wittman, Paris, after a portrait ascribed to William Shuter.

PAGE

TITLE-PAGE OF THE FIRST EDITION OF LYRICAL BALLADS   202

Photographed from a copy formerly belonging to Robert Southey and containing annotations with his initials, now in the British Museum.

TITLE-PAGE OF LYRICAL BALLADS, SECOND EDITION   202

TINTERN ABBEY   204

From a contemporary print by S. Hooper, published in 1784.

LINES WRITTEN A FEW MILES ABOVE TINTERN   204

A B.M. Phg. from the first edition of *Lyrical Ballads.*

DOVE COTTAGE   206

A B.M. Phg. of the sketch by Gordon Home, used by permission of A. & C. Black, Ltd., London.

GRASMERE   206

Drawn by G. W. Pettit and engraved by W. Banks, Edinburgh.

RYDAL MOUNT   208

From an old print.

RYDAL WATER   208

Drawn by W. Westall, engraved by E. Finden.

WORDSWORTH   210

Drawn and engraved by D. Maclise for *Fraser's Magazine* (1832).

COLERIDGE   214

A companion drawing to the above.

KESWICK BRIDGE AND GRETA HALL   216

Drawn by W. Westall, engraved by E. Francis.

NEWSTEAD ABBEY   218

Drawn by T. Allom, engraved by D. Buckle. Byron's most characteristic contribution to the interest of this ancient pile is the inscription to his favorite dog, buried on the site of the altar; it reads as follows:

Near this spot
Are deposited the remains of one
Who possessed Beauty without Vanity,
Strength without Insolence,
Courage without Ferocity
And all the Virtues of Man without his Vices.
This praise, which would be unmeaning flattery
If inscribed over human ashes,
Is but a just tribute to the memory of BOATSWAIN, a dog
Who was born at Newfoundland, May 1803,
And died at Newstead Abbey
November 18, 1808.

PAGE

HARROW   220

> Drawn by C. Stanfield, engraved by E. Finden, and published by J. Murray, 1837. The stone on which a boy is kneeling is not that of Byron's grave but one on which he was fond of reclining to read or to enjoy the view; it is still associated, at the famous school, with Byron's name.

TRINITY COLLEGE, CAMBRIDGE   220

> Drawn by J. A. Bell, engraved by J. Le Keux. This view of the great Cambridge college, associated with the names of some of the most distinguished alumni of the university, from Isaac Newton to Sir J. J. Thomson, was taken from St. John's College, Old Bridge, and published in 1837.

HOURS OF IDLENESS

ENGLISH BARDS AND SCOTCH REVIEWERS

CHILDE HAROLD'S PILGRIMAGE   222

DON JUAN

> These title-pages of Byron first editions are all done by the British Museum Photographic Service. Each has an interest of its own, the first for its classical quotations and its reference to Byron's youth; the second for its aggressive attitude to the poets and critics of the time; the third for its French quotation: "The universe is a kind of book, of which one has read only the first page when one has seen only one's own country. I have turned over a very large number of these pages and have found them all equally bad. This experience has not been unfruitful. I used to hate my own country. I have been reconciled to it by every impertinence of the various peoples with whom I have lived. If I had received no other advantage from my travels than this, I should regret neither the expense nor the fatigue incurred." The fourth title-page, with its brief motto from the *Ars Poetica* of Horace, "It is difficult to give a new turn to ancient commonplaces," is the simplest of all.

BYRON   224

> Painted by G. Sanders in 1807, when Byron was nineteen; engraved by Edward Finden and published by John Murray in 1835, in Finden's *Illustrations of Byron's Life*.

LADY CAROLINE LAMB   226

> Engraved by W. Finden from an original in the possession of John Murray, by whom it was published in 1837.

LADY BYRON   226

> Also published by Murray in 1832; painted by W. J. Newton and engraved by W. H. Mote.

BYRON IN 1814   228

> An engraving by H. B. Hall from the original picture by Thomas Phillips, formerly in possession of John Murray and now in the National Portrait Gallery.

PAGE

MAGDALEN COLLEGE AND BRIDGE 234

Drawn by F. Mackenzie, engraved by J. LeKeux; published in 1833 by J. H. Parker, Oxford. Magdalen Bridge is associated with Shelley by an incident related by his friend Hogg. Shelley when an undergraduate met a young woman on the bridge with a baby in her arms. He took it from her and gazing earnestly into its eyes asked, "Will your baby tell us anything about pre-existence?" She explained that as the child could not yet speak, it could not tell anybody about anything. "How provokingly close are these new-born babes!" he ejaculated; "but it is not the less certain, notwithstanding the cunning attempts to conceal the truth, that all knowledge is reminiscence: the doctrine is far more ancient than the times of Plato, and as old as the venerable allegory that the Muses are the daughters of Memory; not one of the nine was ever said to be the child of Invention!"

HIGH STREET, OXFORD 234

This street, said to be the most beautiful thoroughfare in England, leading down from Magdalen Bridge to the Carfax, which is the center of the city, must have been often trodden by Shelley, who was a student at University College, seen on the spectator's left. The university church, St. Mary's, where Newman preached, is seen on the opposite side of the street.

SHELLEY 236

Engraved by Wm. Finden from the original picture by Amelia Curran, formerly in the possession of Mary Godwin Shelley, and bequeathed by Shelley's daughter-in-law, Jane, Lady Shelley, to the National Portrait Gallery. This is the only painting of Shelley by an artist who was in personal contact with him. George Clint (1770-1854), who was an A.R.A. and as an artist much more skilled than Miss Curran, made a second canvas (also in the National Portrait Gallery) based on her portrait and a drawing by Shelley's friend, E. E. Williams, which has since been lost. From Clint's oil painting was made the crayon drawing known as the Oxford portrait, now in the Bodleian Library. Mr. Roger Ingpen, the recognized authority on Shelley, stated to the author that the portrait here reproduced is the one which has the best claim to be considered an accurate likeness.

MARY GODWIN SHELLEY 238

From a portrait painted by R. Rothwell in 1841.

SHELLEY'S VILLA AT LERICI 242

(B.M. Phg.) This view of Villa Magni, Shelley's residence on the Gulf of Spezia, and the yacht in which he sailed on his last voyage, was drawn by Captain Roberts, an old naval friend of Shelley's friend E. J. Trelawny, who published this and the following sketch as woodcuts in his *Recollections of the Last Days of Shelley and Byron* (1858) and in *Records of Shelley* (1878).

THE BURNING OF SHELLEY'S BODY 242

(B.M. Phg.) This woodcut was made from a sketch drawn by Trelawny's daughter on the scene of the burning, the coast near Viareggio, about twenty-two miles equidistant from Leghorn and Lerici. The figures in the foreground are those of Trelawny and Byron and two Italian coastguardsmen; Leigh Hunt stayed in the carriage in the background.

PAGE

PROTESTANT CEMETERY AT ROME   244

An etching by A. Evershed (1876) from the painting by W. B. Scott. The
Tomb of Shelley is the prone slab to the right. That of Keats is an upright
stone not far away. The pyramid in the background is the ancient Roman
tomb of Caius Cestius.

KEATS, PORTRAIT AND FACSIMILE   248

The portrait is taken from the plate in Leigh Hunt's *Byron and His Contemporaries* (1828), which is based upon a crayon drawing. The facsimile
of the first draft of Keats's "last sonnet," *Bright Star, Would I Were Steadfast as Thou Art,* which is in the poet's own handwriting, is reproduced
by permission of Dodd, Mead & Co., Inc., from *The John Keats Memorial
Volume* (1921).

CHARLES LAMB   250

From Daniel Maclise's *Gallery of Illustrious Literary Characters* (1830-38),
originally published in *Fraser's Magazine.*

HAZLITT   252

From an original miniature on ivory painted by his brother when he was
thirty years of age.

DE QUINCEY   252

N.P.G. Phg. of the portrait painted in 1845 by Sir John Watson Gordon.

SIR WALTER SCOTT   254

Engraved by H. T. Ryall from a portrait by J. P. Knight.

ABBOTSFORD   258

Drawn by R. Westall, engraved by Edward Finden.

QUEEN VICTORIA IN 1837 (N.P.G. PH.G.)   262

QUEEN VICTORIA IN 1897   264

MACAULAY   268

Engraved by D. J. Pound from a photograph by Maull and Polyblank.

MALTHUS, ESSAY ON POPULATION, TITLE-PAGES   273

It will be noticed that the title of the second edition (quoted also in our
text) is much more significant and comprehensive than that of the first.

JOHN STUART MILL   276

N.P.G. Phg. of the portrait by G. F. Watts.

PAGE

CARLYLE'S HOUSE IN CHELSEA 278

The house in Cheyne Row, Chelsea (now No. 24 but then No. 5) is preserved as a national memorial to the genius of Carlyle, who lived there for nearly fifty years, did his most mature work in its "sound-proof room," to which he escaped from the noise and bustle of the metropolis, met the leading men of his time, and exhorted and inspired his generation to a life of high-minded labor.

FRONT DOOR OF CARLYLE'S HOUSE ON CHEYNE ROW ⎫
THE SOUND-PROOF ROOM ⎬ 278
THE GARDEN DOOR ⎭

All these views are from *The Homes and Haunts of Carlyle*, published in 1895 by the *Westminster Gazette*.

CARLYLE IN 1865 280

Engraved by Joseph Brown from a photograph by Elliott and Fry.

RUSKIN AS A YOUNG MAN 282

From the painting by Sir John Millais.

RUSKIN IN OLD AGE 284

NEWMAN 286

An engraving by Joseph Brown from a photograph taken in Newman's old age.

DICKENS 288

Engraved by Finden from a portrait by Daniel Maclise. Published by Chapman and Hall in 1839.

SKETCHES BY BOZ, TITLE-PAGE (SECOND SERIES) 290

The design of the balloon carrying aloft the author and publisher took the fancy of Dickens, who wrote in the preface to the first edition (1836): "In humble imitation of a prudent course, universally adopted by aeronauts, the Author of these volumes throws them up as his pilot balloon, trusting it may catch some favorable current, and devotedly and earnestly hoping it may *go off well*—a sentiment in which his Publisher cordially concurs . . . His object has been to present little pictures of life and manners as they really are; and should they be approved of, he hopes to repeat his experiment with increased confidence, and on a more extensive scale."

PORTRAITS BY CRUIKSHANK 292

This drawing by Cruikshank first appeared as an additional illustration in the "new and complete" edition of *Sketches by Boz* published in 1839 by Chapman and Hall, who are supposed to be represented by the two stout gentlemen in front of the procession; Dickens, with his youthful, beardless face, is in the center of the engraving, also leading the children in; and on the spectator's right is Cruikshank himself, wand in hand. The title of the new edition reads: "Sketches by Boz Illustrative of Everyday Life and Everyday People, with forty illustrations by George Cruikshank. New Edition, complete. London: Chapman and Hall, 186, Strand, 1839." The "Advertisement" is dated London, May 15, 1839, and runs: "The following pages contain the earliest productions of their Author, written from time to time to meet the exigencies of a Newspaper or a Magazine. They were originally published in two series; the first in two volumes, and the second in one. Several editions having been exhausted, both are now published together in one volume, uniform with the *Pickwick Papers,* and *Nicholas Nickleby.*"

DICKENS, HIS WIFE, AND HER SISTER   294

Drawn by Maclise in 1842 and engraved by C. H. Jeens. The sister kept house for Dickens at Gadshill Place and was referred to in his will as the best friend he had ever had.

DICKENS READING *THE CHIMES* TO HIS FRIENDS   296

Drawn by Maclise in 1844 and engraved by Edward Stodart.

DICKENS IN 1868   298

Engraved by J. C. Armytage from a photograph taken in the United States during the last visit.

GADSHILL PLACE, KENT ·   300

When Dickens was a small boy, living in Chatham, some twenty miles from London, his spendthrift but affectionate father took him for a walk to a neighboring mansion called Gadshill Place, and as they gazed upon it, remarked meditatively, "If you were to be very persevering and to work very hard, you might some day come to live in it." And one day, nearly half a century later, after working very hard, Dickens bought that house, and lived in it till the day of his death.

THE EMPTY CHAIR   300

A sketch made at Gadshill Place of the great novelist's chair and writing-desk, after his death.

OLD PORCH, CHARTERHOUSE   302

Drawn by J. P. Neale, engraved by Owen for *The Beauties of England and Wales* (1815).

PENSIONERS' HALL, CHARTERHOUSE   302

Drawn by Thomas R. Shepherd, engraved by J. Rogers for *The Temple of the Muses* (1830).

THACKERAY   304

An engraving by H. W. Smith.

ANTHONY TROLLOPE   309

From a contemporary caricature, representing the novelist as sitting upon a pile of his volumes of stories of clerical life, with the caption, "to parsons gave up what was meant for mankind."

PAGE

KINGSLEY 312

Engraved by C. H. Jeens from a photograph.

CHARLES READE 312

FACSIMILE OF A LETTER FROM CHARLOTTE BRONTË 314

Last page of a letter written by Charlotte Brontë to her friend Ellen Nussey, and dated Haworth, August 25, 1852. The passage with its context reads: "The evils that now and then wring a groan from my heart lie in my position—not that I am a *single* woman and likely to remain a *single* woman, but because I am a *lonely* woman and likely to be *lonely*. But it cannot be helped, and therefore *imperatively must be borne,* and borne, too, with as few words about it as may be. I write this just to prove to you that whatever you would freely *say* to me, you may just as freely write. Understand that I remain just as resolved as ever not to allow myself the holiday of a visit from you till I have done my work. After labour, pleasure; but while work was lying at the wall undone, I never yet could enjoy recreation."

CHARLOTTE BRONTË 316

Engraved by J. C. Armytage from a portrait in chalks (1850) by George Richmond, afterward bequeathed to the National Portrait Gallery by her husband, the Rev. A. B. Nicholls, to whom she was married not very long before her death. The engraving was published by Smith Elder & Co. in 1857.

EMILY BRONTË 316

N.P.G. Phg. from the painting by her brother, Patrick Branwell Brontë (about 1845).

ANNE BRONTË 316

From a pencil drawing by her sister Charlotte.

MRS. GASKELL 316

From a drawing in chalks on toned paper (1851) by George Richmond, bequeathed by her daughter, Margaret Emily Gaskell, to the National Portrait Gallery.

COVENTRY 318

A B.M. Phg. from an engraving in *Scenes from "George Eliot"* by S. Parkinson (1888).

GEORGE ELIOT 320

N.P.G. Phg. of a drawing in chalks on buff paper (1865) by Sir Frederick W. Burton. Presented, after George Eliot's death, by her husband, J. W. Cross, to the National Portrait Gallery.

TENNYSON 324

N.P.G. Phg. of the picture by Samuel Lawrence, regarded as the best portrait of Tennyson in his youth.

PAGE

SOMERSBY CHURCH   326

    Engraved by J. Storer from a drawing by the Rev. W. Horner for *The Antiquarian and Topographical Cabinet* (1811).

SOMERSBY RECTORY   326

    A B.M. Phg. from the drawing in crayon by A. Forestier in R. G. Ambler's *Alfred Lord Tennyson,* published by T. C. and E. C. Jack, by whose permission it is here reproduced.

TENNYSON IN OLD AGE   330

    From a photograph by Mayall.

BROWNING AT FORTY-SEVEN   333

    N.P.G. Phg. of a companion portrait to the following, done at Rome in 1859.

ELIZABETH BARRETT BROWNING   335

    An N.P.G. Phg. of a drawing in chalk on paper (1859) by Field Talfourd.

BROWNING LETTER IN FACSIMILE   337

    (B.M. Phg.) The page of a letter from Browning in answer to an admirer who drew his attention to the charge of wilful obscurity, often made against him. The poet's reply reads: "I can have little doubt that my writing has been in the main too hard for many I should have been pleased to communicate with; but I never designedly tried to puzzle people, as some of my critics have supposed. On the other hand, I never pretended to offer such literature as should be a substitute for a cigar or a game of dominoes to an idle man. So, perhaps, on the whole I get my deserts, and something over—not a crowd, but a few I value more."

BROWNING IN OLD AGE   340

    From a photograph taken not long before Browning's death.

PALAZZO REZZONICO, VENICE (PHOTOGRAPH)   342

RUGBY SCHOOL ⎱
RUGBY CHAPEL ⎰   344

    Engraved from photographs by R. Preston.

MATTHEW ARNOLD (PHOTOGRAPH)   346

DANTE GABRIEL ROSSETTI   348

    N.P.G. Phg. of a drawing in pencil on paper by himself, bearing the date March, 1847, when he was eighteen.

DANTE GABRIEL ROSSETTI IN 1855   350

    Another self-portrait.

PAGE

CHRISTINA ROSSETTI AND HER MOTHER   350

N.P.G. Phg. of a drawing by D. G. Rossetti in chalk on paper (1877).

WILLIAM MORRIS (PHOTOGRAPH)   350

SWINBURNE (PHOTOGRAPH)   350

HUXLEY   355

N.P.G. Phg. of the portrait by his son-in-law, the Hon. John Collier.

DARWIN   357

N.P.G. Phg. of the portrait by Collier.

MEREDITH   359

N.P.G. Phg. of the portrait by G. F. Watts, presented to the National Portrait Gallery on Meredith's death in accordance with the artist's will.

FACSIMILE OF A LETTER FROM MEREDITH   361

A letter sent with flowers to Miss Buckston Browne (Mrs. Lett). It reads: "Box Hill, Dorking, Feby 20th. Miss Nellie! We violets are modest flowers, but not the Queenly Rose is surer of welcome where she appears. So, pray withhold acknowledgments of our transmission to you, and we shall be flattered the more by knowing you pleased *of course.*"

HARDY   363

N.P.G. Phg. from a drawing in pencil on white paper (1919) by William Strang.

HARDY FACSIMILE   365

A facsimile page of the original MS. of *Winter Words* (1927), reproduced in Mrs. Hardy's *The Later Years of Thomas Hardy,* by permission of Macmillan & Company, Limited, London, and of The Macmillan Company, New York.

BUTLER   367

N.P.G. Phg. of the portrait (1896) by Charles Gogin.

15, CLIFFORD'S INN   367

From a photograph by Emery Walker, Ltd., Clifford's Inn, Fleet Street, London, E.C. 4.

GILBERT   369

A B.M. Phg. of a contemporary drawing.

SULLIVAN   369

From a contemporary lithograph.

PAGE

H. A. JONES (B.M. PHG.)
369

A. W. PINERO (PHOTOGRAPH)
369

WALTER PATER (B.M. PHG.)
371

OSCAR WILDE
371
From a contemporary drawing.

R. L. STEVENSON
373
N.P.G. Phg. of the bronze relief of 1887 by Augustus St. Gaudens.

R. L. STEVENSON
375
N.P.G. Phg. of a sketch in oils on canvas by Sir William Blake Richmond, given to the National Portrait Gallery by the artist.

GISSING
377

CONRAD
377
A photograph reproduced by permission of Doubleday, Doran & Company, New York.

BARRIE
377
A photograph reproduced by permission of Charles Scribner's Sons, New York.

KIPLING
377
A photograph (copyright, Elliott and Fry) reproduced by permission of Doubleday, Doran & Company, New York.

BERNARD SHAW
386
A sketch from life, by Edmund J. Sullivan, January 17, 1929.

W. B. YEATS
396
A photograph, reproduced by permission of The Macmillan Company, New York.

J. M. SYNGE
396
A portrait by James Paterson (Edinburgh, 1906), reproduced by permission of John W. Luce & Co., Boston, Mass.

GEORGE MOORE
396
From a painting by J. B. Yeats. The photograph is used by courtesy of Horace Liveright, Inc., Publishers, New York City.

PAGE

SEAN O'CASEY 396

> From a portrait by Evan Walters, the frontispiece to *The Silver Tassie* (1928), published by Macmillan & Company, Limited, London, and The Macmillan Company, New York, by whose permission it is here reproduced.

H. G. WELLS 400

> A photograph reproduced by permission of The Macmillan Company, New York.

ARNOLD BENNETT 400

> A photograph (copyright, Howard Coster) reproduced by permission of Doubleday, Doran & Company, New York.

JOHN GALSWORTHY 400

> A photograph reproduced by permission of Charles Scribner's Sons, New York.

D. H. LAWRENCE 400

> A photograph reproduced by courtesy of Alfred A. Knopf, Inc., New York.

JOHN MASEFIELD 410

> A photograph reproduced by permission of The Macmillan Company, New York.

RUPERT BROOKE 410

> (N.P.G. Phg.) A posthumous drawing made, from photographs and descriptions, by J. Havard Thomas for the memorial in Rugby School Chapel.

MAY SINCLAIR 410

> A photograph reproduced by permission of The Macmillan Company, New York.

VIRGINIA WOOLF 410

ALDOUS HUXLEY 417

> A photograph reproduced by permission of Doubleday, Doran & Company, New York.

LYTTON STRACHEY 419

EXETER CATHEDRAL CHAPTER-HOUSE

CHAPTER I

THE HEROIC AGE

Britain, which Julius Cæsar visited but "made not here his boast of *came, and saw, and overcame,*" fell under the dominion of his successors and became part of the Roman Empire. It was only when that empire was stricken to the heart that the withdrawal of the Roman legions and the Roman fleet left the island a prey to those hardy seafarers who called themselves by various names but later agreed in describing their language as English. When the first English-speaking folk took possession of Britain, they found there a civilization which was both classical and Christian, and their association with it was renewed by Roman missionaries. The words *church, bishop, dean,* and *priest* have been so worn down by more than a thousand years of use that we hardly recognize in them to-day their Greek and Roman originals; but they still bear witness to the conversion of our heathen forefathers to an Oriental religion which had enshrined its records in the Greek language and had been transformed by Roman organization.

The oldest English literature exhibits this threefold strand of interwoven threads: (1) A Teutonic folklore shot through or overlaid with (2) classical culture and (3) Christian teaching. It is hard now to find the heathen English element in its native purity, but we may take as an example of it a short lyric in alliterative verse, with a refrain, called *The Song of Deor*. This is preserved in a manuscript named *The Exeter Book* because it has for over eight hundred years been part of the Library of Exeter Cathedral, to which it was presented by Leofric (d.1072), Edward the Confessor's trusted counselor and personal friend, and the first Bishop of Exeter.

In this perhaps the earliest of English elegies the poet persuades himself into a stoical acceptance of his personal misfortunes by recalling the ills suffered and overcome by his heathen ancestors. The first example that occurs to him is a familiar figure in Teutonic folklore and old English literature, Wayland the Smith. This wonder-working craftsman of Northern European mythology was hamstrung and robbed of his magic ring by King Nithhad, to prevent his running away. In revenge Wayland killed Nithhad's two sons and gave the king drinking-cups made out of their skulls. Beaduhild, Nithhad's daughter, to whom Nithhad gave the ring, broke it and brought it to Wayland to mend; Wayland drugged and violated her. Then, with the help of the ring, he made himself wings from the feathers of birds and flew away.

Of these woes sings the poet DEOR (he tells us his name in the last stanza), as follows:

> Wayland among the Wurmas/wandered in exile,
> A single-minded earl/he suffered hardship,
> He had for his comrades/care and longing,
> Winter-cold wretchedness;/woe he often found,
> When Nithhad him/with need constrained,
> Bitter sinew-cutting/of a better man.
>   That overpassing,/this also may.
>
> To Beaduhild was not/her brothers' death
> As sore in her soul/as herself's own plight,
> For clearly she/conceived had
> That she was mothering;/nor might she ever
> With certainty think/how that should be.
> We have heard, we many,/of Hilda's raping.
>   That overpassing,/this also may.
>
> Was deep beyond plumbing/the passion of the Geat.
> So that sorrow of love/his sleep all stole.
>   That overpassing,/this also may.
>
>   (Translation by Charles Scott Moncrieff.)

Nithhad, sleepless from sorrow and love of his children; Beaduhild, embittered by a shameful wrong; Wayland, maimed but triumphant, all survived and overcame their woes, says the poet: "Why should not I?" He applies the lesson to his own misfortunes and to the common lot.

The manuscript from which the above lines are translated is in "a fair and rather fine hand of the tenth century" (Thorpe), but the poem was probably composed some two hundred years earlier, about the time when an eighth-century English artist, not in pen and ink but with carving in whalebone, set forth by his craft the story of Wayland the Smith. This carved box is now in the British Museum and is known as the Franks Casket; it is one of the most precious treasures of Anglo-Saxon antiquity, and has had strange adventures. From Northumbria it found its way somehow to the neighborhood of Clermont-Ferrand, about 135 miles south of Paris. The story of its recovery is told in the *Notes on the Illustrations*. The reproduction given below shows the left half of the front panel:

On the extreme left of this photograph we see Wayland at his anvil; on the anvil lies the head of one of the sons of Nithhad; below the anvil lies the headless body. Wayland is at work, making a cup out of the skull. The princess Beaduhild, accompanied by an attendant, is offering him the ring, which leads to her doom. Wayland's brother is seizing the birds that are to furnish wings for Wayland's flight.

On the right half of the front panel, which is not shown in our reproduction, are the three Magi bearing their gifts to the infant Christ, so that even in this ancient relic we have the combination of heathen and Christian elements to be noted in the oldest English literature.

The longest, the noblest, and possibly, in its original form, the oldest literary example of this mingling of native English folklore with Romanized Christian elements, is the _Beowulf,_ a poem of over three thousand lines, written (like the lyric above quoted) in alliterative verse, depending for metrical effect upon the stressed recurrence of the same initial consonants or different initial vowels, in a line broken by a strong cæsura. It tells the heroic exploits and death of Beowulf, who fought with sea monsters on the coast of Denmark—so it is judged from the description of the scenery. The legendary stories upon which the poem is founded were doubtless carried from Denmark or the neighboring coast in the memories of the gleemen who sang or recited them to their seafaring comrades, but in its present structure the poem is thought to have been written in Northumbria about the beginning of the eighth century. As the center of power in the island moved from North to South and the center of Old English cultivation moved with it, the poem was rewritten, first in the Mercian and then in the West Saxon dialect—the latest version probably in the time of King Alfred, who died at the beginning of the tenth century. The manuscript which has come down to us was copied out, so scholars say, about the year 1000. It bears on the top of its first page the signature of Laurence Nowell, Dean of Lichfield in the sixteenth century and the maker of an Anglo-Saxon dictionary; from his hands it passed into those of a

famous Elizabethan antiquary, Sir Robert Cotton, and so into
the British Museum Library.

In the same manuscript (Cotton Vitellius A XV) we have
the *Judith,* a remarkable fragment in which an Old Testament
story (in the Apocrypha) is poetically rendered in a form which
breathes the traditional spirit of English folklore. The Jewish
heroine frees her people by the slaughter of the Assyrian leader
Holofernes, who has been led by her beauty to invite her to
share his victorious revels. The following passage is taken by
permission from Professor Oliver Elton's translation, and reproduces admirably the spirit of the original, though it makes no
attempt to reproduce in detail the alliterative measure in which
the poem was written:

> And hard she haled by the hair the idolater
> Deadly and hateful, and dragged him disdainfully
> Forth to her fealty, to fall at her mercy.
> And the sword of the maiden with sinuous tresses
> Flickered and fell on the furious-hearted
> Bane of his foes, bit into his neck-bone.
> And drunken he lay there, drowned in a stupor,
> And life in him lingered, though large was his wound.
> And she smote with the strength of her soul once more
> At the heathenish hound, and the head rolled over
> Forth on the floor; and the filthy carrion
> Lay on the bed without life; but the spirit had
> Fared away far in the fathomless underworld,
> To be hampered in hell-pains and humbled eternally,
> Wreathen with serpents in regions of torment,
> Fettered and fast in the flame of perdition.
> He has done with our life; nor dare he have hope
> In the heart of the dark habitation of dragons
> Thence to depart, but he there must abide
> In that dwelling of dimness, undawned on of joy,
> Ever and ever for infinite ages.

Another important collection of old English religious poems
is the Bodleian Library manuscript, given in 1630 by Archbishop Ussher to Lord Arundel's librarian, whose name was
DuJon—or, in Latin, Junius. It is properly described as "Junius

THE BODLEIAN LIBRARY

WHITBY ABBEY

XI," but is usually called the Cædmon MS., owing to the identification of the author of some of the poems of CÆDMON, a monk of Whitby in Yorkshire under the Abbess Hilda between 658 and 680.

The story of Cædmon is told in Latin by the Venerable Bede (673-735) in his *Ecclesiastical History,* which was translated by Thomas Stapleton in the time of Elizabeth (to whom the edition of 1565 is dedicated), and more recently by A. M. Sellar. The twenty-fourth chapter of Book IV tells us that there was in Whitby Abbey a brother endowed by God with the gift of making poetry so that he turned the stories of Scripture into English verse of great sweetness and religious power. "By his songs the minds of many were often fired with contempt of the world and desire of the heavenly life." Until an advanced age he wore the secular habit and never learned anything of versifying; for this reason sometimes at a feast, when men made merry by singing in turn, if he saw the harp coming toward him he would rise from table and return home. Once, having gone from the dining-hall to the stable where he had to take care of the cattle that night, as he slept one stood by him and, calling him by name, said, "Cædmon, sing me something." He answered, "I cannot sing, and for this cause I left the feast." The reply came: "Nevertheless, thou must sing to me." "What must I sing?" he asked. "Sing the beginning of Creation," said the other. Straightway Cædmon began to sing verses to the praise of God the Creator, of which the purport was after this manner: "Now must we praise the Maker of the heavenly kingdom, the power of the Creator, and His counsel, the deeds of the Father of glory; how He, being the Eternal God, became the Author of all wondrous works, Who, being the Almighty Guardian of the human race, first created heaven for the sons of men to be the covering of their dwelling-place, and next the earth."

The poem of which Bede's version is given above is now known as *Cædmon's Hymn* and is given in Northumbrian in a manuscript of the *Ecclesiastical History* preserved in the Cambridge University Library. This Northumbrian version is accepted by some scholars as Cædmon's Hymn in its original form; if so, it goes back to the seventh century and is one of our oldest examples of English verse. It is translated by Dr. C. W. Kennedy of Princeton University as follows:

> Praise we the Lord/of the heavenly kingdom,
> God's power and wisdom,/the works of His hand;
> As the Father of glory,/Eternal Lord,
> Wrought the beginning/of all His wonders!
> Holy Creator!/Warden of men!
> First for a roof/o'er the children of earth,
> He established the heavens/and founded the world,
> And spread the dry land/for the living to dwell in.
> Lord Everlasting!/Almighty God!

With this, the version of Cædmon's Hymn in West Saxon given by KING ALFRED in his translation of Bede's *Ecclesiastical History* is in substantial agreement. This translation links Alfred, not only with Northumbrian poetry but with the Northumbrian learning, of which the most notable ornaments were the Venerable Bede and his successor Alcuin (735-804), who became minister to Charlemagne. The main purpose of the translations which Alfred made or commanded was to bring the classics of his time within the reach of every free man among the English-speaking folk. "While they have no other necessary occupation," he wrote, "let all our youth be set to learning until they can read English well; afterwards let them study Latin if they would go further in their education and fit themselves for higher office."

It is in the Anglo-Saxon Chronicle, which was started in Alfred's time and probably at his instigation, that we find the last Old English poems preserving the traditional meter and the traditional spirit. Under the date 937 the Chronicle inserts a poem commemorating the battle of Brunanburgh, which has been rendered into modern verse by the collaboration of Tennyson and his son. A later poem, *The Battle of Maldon* (991), records the heroic but unavailing courage of the English leader Byrhtnoth against the Danes, who were at this time extending their power and influence; the Danish Canute became in 1017 ruler of all England. Hated as were the invaders, they were closely allied in language and tradition with the people they conquered. Canute is named by one of the chroniclers as author of a little lyric which is of interest not merely for its royal origin but as illustrating the state of the English language and of English poetry at the time:

> Merie sungen ðe muneches binnen Ely
> Ða Cnut ching reu ðer by;
> Roweð cnichtes noer ða land,
> And here we þes muneches sæng.

> Merrily sang the monks in Ely
> When Cnut King rowed thereby;
> Row, knights, near the land,
> And hear we these monks' song.

GEOFFREY'S WINDOW

CHAPTER II

THE AGE OF ROMANCE

The principal effects of the Conquest of England by William of Normandy (1066) were (1) to establish the feudal system of land tenure and military service, with its recognized ranks of princes and vassals, knights and squires, lords and serfs; (2) to bring England into closer relations with Continental Europe and especially with France; (3) to make French the language of polite society and of the law-courts up to 1362; (4) to introduce many French words into written and spoken English; (5) to break down gradually the Old English system of alliterative verse and to substitute for it the French system of rime; and (6) to make romances translated or copied from the French the prevalent form of polite and ultimately of popular literature.

About the end of the twelfth century French romance became supreme all over Europe with its three "matters" or themes: (1) Rome, including all antiquity, the tales of Thebes and Troy and of Alexander the Great; (2) France, the exploits of Charlemagne and his twelve "peers"; (3) Brittany, the adventures of King Arthur and the Knights of the Round Table. Adventures were what English readers wanted, "slaughter of Saracens, fights with dragons and giants, rightful heirs getting their own again, innocent princesses championed against their felon adversaries," and they were especially interested in the romances of King Arthur, for he was in a manner of speaking their own. As early as 1136 Geoffrey of Monmouth, a monk gifted with a riotous imagination, completed a Latin history of the kings of Britain, which won for him, even among his credulous contemporaries, the title of a shameless liar. But his lies provided some famous stories, as elaborated in French by Wace of Jersey (1155) and in English by LAYAMON, a priest of Arley

Regis in Worcestershire. Layamon's *Brut* was written about 1205 and was a long poem in alliterative verse (32,241 lines). It has come down to us in an almost contemporary manuscript, which has been edited by Sir Frederic Madden and is of considerable importance in illustrating the language and learning of that period. As an example a short passage may be quoted narrating the last fight of King Arthur, in which the knights of the Round Table were all slain and Arthur himself wounded to the death:

> And Arður forwunded/mid wal-spere brade.
> Fiftene he hafde/feondliche wunden.
> Mon mihte i þare lasten/twa glouen iþraste.
> Ða nas þer na mare/i þan fehte to laue
> Of twa hundred þasend monnen/þa þér leien to-hauwē,
> Buten Arður þe king ane/& of his cnihtes tweien.
> Arður wes for-wunded/wonder ane swiðe.

The passage beginning with the lines quoted above may be put into modern English as follows:

> And Arthur sore wounded/with a great battle-spear,
> Fifteen he had/fearful wounds.
> One could in the least of them/thrust two gloved hands.
> Then was there no more/left in the fight
> Of two hundred thousand/there hewn to pieces
> But King Arthur alone/and two of his knights.
> Arthur was wounded/wondrously sore.
> There came to him a young knight/that was of his kin.
> He was Cador's son,/the Earl of Cornwall.
> Constantine was his name/to the king dear.
> Arthur looked on him/where he lay afield
> And this word said to him/with sorrowful heart:
> "Constantine, thou art welcome,/thou wert Cador's son.
> I bequeath thee/my kingdom,
> And defend thou my Britons/all through thy life,
> And keep for them all the laws/that have stood in my days
> And all the good laws/that in Uther's days stood,
> And I will go to Avalon/to the fairest of all maidens,
> To Argante the Queen,/the brightest of elves.

And she shall my wounds/make all again whole,
And make me hale again/with hallowed drafts.
And soon I will come/again to my kingdom,
And dwell with the Britons/with greater delight."
Even with these words/there came from the sea
A little boat sliding,/driven by the waves,
And two women therein/wondrously dight,
And they took Arthur anon,/and bore him quickly,
And laid him down softly/and slided away.
Then was fulfilled/what Merlin foretold,
Unmeasured woe to come/of Arthur's forth-faring.
Britons believe yet/that he is alive,
And dwells in Avalon/with fairest of all elves.
Looks every Briton yet/for Arthur's home-coming.
Never was man born/or wedded of woman
That can of a truth/of Arthur tell more.
But there was a wizard,/Merlin by name,
Who bore this witness/and his words were true,
That an Arthur should yet come/to help the English.
In the land Constantine ruled/and Britons loved him;
Very dear to them he was.

In spite of his thirty-two thousand lines of antiquated diction, Layamon is an author of considerable interest to the student, but we must pass on to writers who present things worth remembering in more concentrated form. About 1240 we have this charming song set to music as a round for four voices, with the words of a Latin hymn interpolated for the benefit of the more serious-minded, and instructions for the singers, also in Latin. It was sung, as is more fully explained in the *Notes on the Illustrations,* as a part-song with a refrain or burden (technically called the *Pes,* or foot), which echoes the song of the cuckoo, or invites him to sing *now.* A version, slightly modernized, follows:

> Summer is icumen in
>   Loud sing, Cuckoo!
> Groweth seed and bloweth mead,
>   And springeth the wood now.
>   Sing, Cuckoo!

Ewe bleateth after lamb,
Loweth after calf, cow;
Bullock sterteth, buck verteth,
Merry sing, Cuckoo!

Cuckoo, Cuckoo!
Well singest thou, cuckoo!
Cease thou never now!
Sing, Cuckoo! Sing, Cuckoo!
Sing, Cuckoo, now!

A love-song of a somewhat later date (about 1310) may also be quoted in a slightly modernized form:

Between March and April
When spray begins to spring,
The little bird has her will
Her own note to sing.
I live in love-longing
For seemliest of all thing,
She may me bliss bring,
    I am in her baundoun [power].
A lucky lot is to me lent
    I wot from heaven it is me sent,
From all women my love is bent,
    And lit on Alysoun.

A longer and more elaborate poem employing both rime and alliteration in twelve-line stanzas is *Pearl*, which tells of a father's grief for his little daughter and a dream he had while sleeping on her grave; he sees her in eternal bliss and is reconciled to God's will:

Then woke I in that garden fair,
My head upon that mound was laid,
There where my Pearl had strayed below.
I roused me and felt great dismay,
And sighing to myself I said:
"Now all be to that Prince's pleasure."

(Modernized version by Sir Israel Gollancz.)

Found in the same manuscript and assigned to the same unknown author is the romance of *Sir Gawain and the Green Knight,* of which there is an excellent prose rendering by Miss Jessie Weston; the verse of the original is again a combination of rime and alliteration.

The last great poem to employ the old alliterative measure of four accents was *The Vision of William concerning Piers the Plowman,* ascribed to WILLIAM LANGLAND, of Cleobury Mortimer, who was educated at a Benedictine monastery in the Malvern Hills. The opening lines may be modernized thus:

> In a summer season/when soft was the sun
> I shaped me a shroud/as I were a shepherd.
> In habit of a hermit,/unholy of works,
> Went I forth in the world/wonders to hear.
> But in a May morning/on Malvern hills
> I fell asleep/for weariness of walking.
> In a glade as I lay/I leaned down and slept.
> Marvellously I dreamed,/as I shall you tell,
> Of all the wealth of the world/and the woe also.

An elaborate allegory follows as to the ways of the world and the one way of salvation offered by the Saviour, figured as Piers Plowman.

Contemporary with Langland, and also harking back to a poetic past which was disappearing before the genius of Geoffrey Chaucer, was JOHN GOWER (d. 1408), the author of three books upon which the head of his effigy rests in St. Saviour's Church (now Southwark Cathedral), on the South side of London Bridge—*Speculum Meditantis* or *Mirour de l'Omme,* a poem of nearly 30,000 lines, in French; *Vox Clamantis*—the voice of one crying in the wilderness—in Latin; *Confessio Amantis,* which contains 33,000 four-accent lines in English. The "moral Gower," as Chaucer calls him, adorns his themes with abundant allegory and many stories which his wide erudition has found in many authors, ranging in diversity from Ovid to the Bible.

Joannes Gower.
Armiger

Anglorum Poeta Celeberrimus

Chaucere Poeta
Contemporar

G. Vertue Sculp. 1727.

Gower was a considerable artist compared with the writers of riming romances, who went lumbering on and on for another century or two; but he has nothing of the liveliness of spirit of his friend GEOFFREY CHAUCER (1340-1400) whose tender sympathy, gay humor, and quick wit have for more than five hundred years delighted the hearts of all true lovers of English poetry. If Chaucer had written two hundred years later, after printing had to some extent normalized English spelling and arrested changes in pronunciation, he would still be a popular author; and even yet those who will make an effort to overcome the first impression of strangeness in the look of his words will find themselves more than amply rewarded.

Learned he was according to the opportunities of his time; like his own Clerk of Oxford,

> To him 'twas dearer have at his bed's head
> Twenty bookès clothèd in black and red,
> Of Aristotle and of his philosophíĕ
> Than robès riche, or fiddle, or gay psaltríĕ.
> (í=ee, and the final ĕ is pronounced.)

But, unlike some Oxford scholars, Chaucer did not often allow his learning to oppress him or run away with him. In *Sir Thopas* he scoffed at the prolixity of the riming romancers, and though his was an age of greater leisure than ours, it is seldom that he tires us with too much detail or bores us with extended general reflections after the manner of his time. A soldier, a diplomat, and a member of Parliament, Chaucer was in his youth a prisoner in France, and in his manhood went on missions to Italy and Flanders in the king's service; he knew French and Italian well, and his indebtedness to both literatures has been diligently investigated, only to establish his claim to substantial originality. He was a student, but he was also a man of affairs, in touch with many sides of active life, as the Prologue to the Canterbury Tales abundantly shows. The Knight with his modest dignity; the curly-headed Squire, singing and jesting along the road, "as fresh as is the month of May," the

CHAUCER

nut-headed yeoman, with his brown face and well-appointed arms; the smiling Prioress, with her French "of Stratford at the Bowe"; the Monk, with his taste for hunting, fine clothes, and a good table; the Friar, "an easy man to give penance"; the merchant, who talked always of his profits; the Clerk of Oxford, eager to learn, and eager to teach; the Lawyer, nowhere so busy a man as he, "And yet he seemèd busier than he was"; the Doctor of Physic, who loved gold in especial, "For gold in physic is a cordial"; the Wife of Bath, with her expert knowledge of the art of love; the poor Parson, summed up in the couplet:

> But Christ his lore and his apostles twelve
> He taught, and first he followed it himself;

the Miller, with a wart on his nose and harlotries on his tongue; the Summoner, with his fire-red face, carrying a cake as a shield; the Pardoner, with his wallet, "Brimfull of pardons, come from Rome all hot"—these (and they are by no means all the characters Chaucer created) come not from books but from life.

Student as he was, Chaucer was also a lover of the haunts of men and of the open air. When he heard the birds sing on a May morning, then—"Farewell my book and my devotion!"

All these qualities made Chaucer easily the greatest teller of tales in verse; and the best of modern narrative poets in English—down to John Masefield in our own time—have turned to him for inspiration, without surpassing him. W. P. Ker remarks that the English medieval romancers failed to establish a pattern of narrative that might be compared with the modern novel. In *Troilus and Criseyde* Chaucer certainly came very near it. His story has "what, as a rule, medieval romance conspicuously lacked—interest of character as well as of incident, and interest of drama as well as of narrative."

CHAPTER III

THE INVENTION OF PRINTING

The fifteenth century in England was a century of wars, first with France, then between the contending houses of York and Lancaster, and it was not till the house of Tudor was firmly seated on the throne (Henry VII, 1485-1509) that English writers were in a position to take full advantage of the Continental movement known as the Revival of Learning. Under a more settled government, art, especially architecture, began to flourish as the country became prosperous. Men's minds were stirred by the new theory of Copernicus making the sun, instead of the earth, the center of the universe; by the discovery of America; and by the great intellectual movements we know as the Renaissance and the Reformation. These will be more fully discussed later; but it seems convenient here to consider the effects of the invention of printing, which brought classical learning and modern discoveries within reach of the masses, made newspapers possible, and so brought about the democratic and industrial civilization in which we live.

Naturally the new invention made its power and influence felt slowly; at first the Government feared the press rather than welcomed it, and sought to hamper its extensive use by licensing printers, presses, and printed books; the lapse, not merely of years but of centuries, was necessary before the opportunities afforded by the printing-press were realized and the primitive mechanism was sufficiently improved to make the circulation of cheap books and newspapers really effective. The establishment of authorship as a profession except for plays is of comparatively recent occurrence; well into the eighteenth century men of a certain social standing generally preferred to print their works under an assumed name or made a pretense that they were published without their consent. Even the popular novelists of the nineteenth century—Dickens, Thackeray, and George Eliot—made incomes that were small in comparison with the earnings of a successful story-writer of our own time, and the circulation of their works was small in comparison with present-day figures.

One of the earliest examples of the effect of printing is the rapid growth of Protestantism. Politically, Protestantism transferred the seat of authority in spiritual matters from the pope to the king; intellectually, it rests upon a Book and the right of private judgment. Until the Bible could be brought within reach of the ordinary man, Protestantism had little chance, and the fourteenth-century movement under Wyclif died away. The Reformers, with Martin Luther at their head, set diligently to work to translate the Scriptures into the vernacular. Tyndale, the translator of the earliest printed version of any part of the Bible in English, in a heated discussion with an ignorant friar, said angrily, "I will cause a boy, that driveth the plough, shall know more of the Scripture than thou dost."

It must not, however, be hastily assumed that those of our early ancestors who could read had no opportunity of becoming acquainted with the Bible. Apart from what they heard or saw in church, learned men—and any man who could read was a clerk, or scholar—had access to monastic or private libraries in which translations of the Bible or parts of it were to be found. Some of the most beautiful illuminated manuscripts that have come down to us are Latin or English translations of the Bible, as will be seen from the next illustration. And one of the most touching stories of the early Church is the account of the death of BEDE while engaged on a translation of the Gospel of St. John, which he persisted in completing though exhausted by mortal sickness, "for I would not," he said, "have my boys read a lie, nor labor herein without profit after my death." The following account of Bede's last hours is taken from a letter written by Cuthbert, one of Bede's pupils, to his fellow-student Cuthwin:

"When the Tuesday before the Ascension of our Lord came, he began to suffer still more in his breathing, and there was some swelling in his feet. But he went on teaching all that day and dictating cheerfully, and now and then said among other things, 'Learn quickly; I know not how long I shall endure, and whether my Maker will not soon take me away.' But to us it seemed that haply he knew well the time of his departure; and so he spent the night awake, in giving thanks. And when the morning dawned, that is, on the Wednesday, he bade us write with all speed what we had begun. And this we did until the third hour. And from the third hour we walked in procession with the relics of the saints, according to the customs of that day (Rogation Wednesday). And there was one of us with him who said to him, 'There is still one chapter wanting of the book which thou hast been dictating, but I deem it burdensome for thee to be questioned further.' He answered, 'Nay, it is light, take thy pen and make ready, and write quickly.' And this was done. But at the ninth hour he said to me, 'I have certain treasures in my coffer, some spices, napkins and incense; run quickly and bring the priests of our monastery to me that I may distribute among them the gifts which God has bestowed on me.' And this I did trembling, and when they were come, he spoke to every one of them, admonishing and entreating them that they should diligently offer masses and prayers for him, and they promised readily. But they all mourned and wept, sorrowing most of all for the words which he spake, because they thought they should see his face no long time in this world. But they rejoiced for that he said, 'It is time for me, if it be my Maker's will, to be set free from the flesh, and come to him who, when as yet I was not, formed me out of nothing. I have lived long; and well has my pitiful judge disposed my life for me; the time for my release is at hand; for my soul longs to see Christ my King in his beauty.'

"Having said this and much more for our profit and edification, he passed his last day in gladness till the evening; and the aforesaid boy, whose name was Wilbert, still said, 'Dear Master,

LINDISFARNE GOSPEL   RICHARD II'S BIBLE

WYCLIFFITE BIBLE

there is yet one sentence not written.' He answered, 'It is well, write it.' Soon after, the boy said, 'Now it is written.' And he said, 'It is well, thou hast said truly, it is finished. Take my head in thy hands, for I rejoice greatly to sit facing my holy place where I was wont to pray, that I too, sitting there, may call upon my Father.' And thus on the pavement of his cell, chanting 'Glory be to the Father, and to the Son, and to the Holy Ghost,' and the rest, he breathed his last."

Bede's translation has not come down to us. The first manuscript reproduced on the preceding page is from the Latin version of the Gospels, made during Bede's lifetime (about 700) by Eadfrith, Bishop of Lindisfarne; the interlined Old English translation is attributed to the beginning of the tenth century. It is said that King Alfred at the end of his life began a translation of the Psalms, but he was unable to complete it. The Wessex version, which our second example reproduces (from a twelfth century MS.), was made about the end of the tenth century—a century after Alfred's death. The curiously illustrated Latin version said to have been done for Richard II (1377-99) is from a manuscript of that period. About the same time was written the fourth manuscript reproduced from the first complete translation of the Bible into English, ascribed to the early reformer Wyclif, but more probably made by his followers at his prompting. Of a translation made by John Trevisa (1326-1412), nothing has come down to us beyond a passing mention by Caxton.

When WILLIAM CAXTON introduced printing into England toward the end of the fifteenth century, the translation of the Bible into the vernacular was already opposed by the ecclesiastical authorities, and our first printer naturally turned his attention to books that were likely to be popular—and not likely to get him into trouble. His first publication was the *Recuyell of the Histories of Troy,* a translated compilation from French romances, which was printed at Bruges about 1475; and the following year Caxton set up his press at Westminster. The first book with a date printed in England was his *Dictes and Sayings*

The first Chapter.

IN ye begyn
nynge God
created hea
ven z earth:
and y earth
was voyde
and emptie,
and darck-
nes was v-
pon the de-
pe, z y spre-
te of God
moued vpō
the water.

FIRST PRINTED ENGLISH BIBLE

❡ The fyrst Chapter.

❡ How heauen z erth: the light: the firmament: the son-
ne: the mone: the sterres: and all beastes: foules z fisshes
in the see were made by the worde of God. And how man
also was created.
✠

IN the beginnyng ✶
God created heauen
z erth. The erth was
voyd z emptie, and
darknesse was ✦ vpō
the face of the depe,
z the spreite of God
moued ✦ vpō the fa-
ce of the waters.

And God sayd: let there be made light,
and there was light made. And God sawe
the light that it was good. And God made
a diuisiō betwene the lyght and darknesse.
And God called the light, daye: z the dark
nesse called he, night. And the euenyng z
the mornynge was made one daye.

FIRST "GREAT BIBLE"

Here endeth the book named the dictes or sayengis
of the philosophhres enprynted / by me William
Caxton at Westmestre the yere of our lord ⋅M⋅
CCCC⋅Lyxvij⋅ Whiche book is late translated out of
Frensshe into englyssh ⋅ by the Noble and puissant lord
Lord Antone Erle of Ryuyers lord of Scales z of the
Ile of Wyght / Defendour and directour of the siege apos-
tollique / for our holy Fader the Pope in this Royame of
Englond and Gouernour of my lord Prynce of Wales
And It is so that at suche tyme as he had accomplysshid
this sayd Werke / it liked him to sende it to me in certayn
quayers to ouersee / Whiche forthwith I sawe z fonde therin

AN EARLY CAXTON

of the Philosophers (1477), but before this he had issued *Chaucer's Canterbury Tales* and other books of poetry, romance, and popular edification. The book for which we are most grateful to him is Sir Thomas Malory's *Morte d'Arthur* (1485).

WILLIAM TYNDALE, a pupil of Erasmus, who in Protestant ardor went far beyond his master, sought help for the printing of a new translation of the Bible, from the Bishop of London, and finding no encouragement in that quarter, shifted his basis of operations to the Continent. In Cologne he had ten sheets of his English New Testament printed, and then was forced to flee with them to Worms. There he got the book out in 1525, and smuggled it into England, to the great perturbation of the bishops, who seized and burnt all the copies they could lay their hands on, in spite of Cardinal Wolsey's plea for a more tolerant policy. The personal friend of Luther and other reformers, Tyndale was regarded as an arch heretic by the more conservative English prelates and statesmen, and was engaged in a long controversy, appealing to Scripture and the right of private judgment against Sir Thomas More, who maintained the paramount authority of the Church. Both were ultimately executed for their opinions, Tyndale in Flanders, in 1536, because he went too far for the Emperor Charles V, and More in England, in 1535, because he did not go far enough for Henry VIII in upholding the royal supremacy.

Tyndale did not succeed in completing his enterprise of translating the whole Bible, but he gave it sufficient impetus to carry the undertaking through; before his death his work was taken up by Miles Coverdale, a man of less learning and reforming zeal but of greater prudence and tact. In his earlier years the friend of Sir Thomas More and Thomas Cromwell, Coverdale later became Tyndale's assistant, and brought out the whole Bible in English in 1535; the New Testament is substantially that of Tyndale; for the Old Testament, Coverdale relied mainly on Latin and German versions; the translation was prepared at Antwerp and printed at Zurich. The second edition (1537) was licensed by Henry VIII; it was the first complete

HENRY VIII

CARDINAL WOLSEY

SIR THOMAS MORE

THOMAS CROMWELL

Bible in English printed in England. Coverdale became Bishop of Exeter in 1551, was deprived of his see under the Catholic reaction of Mary's reign (1553-58), was restored to favor under Elizabeth, and died at the ripe old age of eighty-one, much respected by the Puritan party of the Church, of which he was a recognized leader.

The first Bible actually set up (and often chained) in the English churches was the Great Bible (1539); to the second edition Cranmer prefixed a preface, and it became known as Cranmer's Bible (1540).

In 1557 the English Puritans at Geneva, for whom the foregoing versions were not radical enough, brought out the New Testament translated by William Whittingham, the English pastor at Geneva, who had married Calvin's sister; the Geneva Bible appeared in 1560 with a dedication to Queen Elizabeth and was (like the Testament) popular because of (1) its doctrinal bias; (2) its Roman type; and (3) the division into verses, which was maintained in the Bishops' Bible of 1568 and the Authorized Version of 1611.

Meanwhile the Catholics published English versions prepared by their own scholars—the New Testament at Rheims in 1582 and the whole Bible at Douai in 1609.

There have been many testimonies from skeptics as well as from divines, regarding the beauty and literary influence of the English Bible. (See Introduction to Century Readings in the Bible.) It will be enough to quote here two of them—the first from William Hazlitt concerning the effect upon the popular mind of access to the Scriptures, given in his celebrated course of lectures upon *The Age of Elizabeth:*

"It threw open, by a secret spring, the rich treasures of religion and morality, which had been there locked up as in a shrine. It revealed the visions of the prophets, and conveyed the lessons of inspired teachers (such they were thought) to the meanest of the people. It gave them a common interest in the common cause. Their hearts burnt within them as they read. It gave a *mind* to the people, by giving them common subjects of thought and feeling. It cemented their union of character and sentiment; it created endless diversity and collision of opinion."

The second testimony, from Professor T. H. Huxley, stresses the influence of the Authorized Version on later generations:

"Consider this great historical fact, that, for three centuries, this book has been woven into all that is noblest and best in English history; consider that it has become the national epic of Great Britain, and that it is as familiar to noble and simple, from John O'Groat's to Land's End, as Tasso and Dante once were to the Italians; consider that it is written in the noblest and purest English, and that it abounds in exquisite beauties of literary form; and, finally, consider that it forbids the veriest hind, who never left his native village, to be ignorant of the existence of other countries and other civilizations, and of a great past stretching back to the furthest limits of the oldest nations in the world."

TYNDALE   AN EARLY PRINTING-OFFICE

CHAPTER IV

THE ELIZABETHANS

The translation of the Bible into English was only one example of the prevailing passion for access to the literary treasures of other nations, especially the Greek and Latin classics, among which the Greek version of the Old Testament (the Septuagint) and the Latin version of the New Testament (the Vulgate) might well be counted. The Revival of Learning had already given to Italian literature the great names of Dante, Petrarch, and Boccaccio, Ariosto and Machiavelli; in France it had produced Rabelais and Montaigne, and in the Low Countries, Erasmus; it came late to England, and by the time it arrived there it had gathered in its train elements which involved the break-up of the medieval system and the triumph of modern democracy and industrialism. As Professor Hayes points out in his *Modern History:* "It seemed to our ancestors in the Middle Ages as well as in ancient times that it was vitally necessary to civilization to preserve a common faith and a common moral code and to compel the individual to subordinate his private judgment and personal wishes to the demands of a common religion." But in Athens, although Socrates was sacrificed to the desire of his fellow-citizens for conformity with ancestral beliefs, free speculation about religious and philosophical opinions prevailed to an extent that was not again tolerated for over two thousand years. It took centuries of persecution for religious belief and political opinion before England arrived at the principles of liberty of thought and speech embodied in the American Constitution.

The first effect of the freeing of men's minds from subjection to authority in matters of State and Church was the outflow of an immense volume of intellectual energy to which permanent

GASCOIGNE PRESENTING HIS WORK TO ELIZABETH

expression was given by means of the newly invented printing-press. And even in lines of literary activity long established and not apparently dependent upon printed publication, such as poetry and the drama, there was an added stimulus in the new ideas abroad, the foreign models accessible, and the sweep given to the imagination by the opportunities afforded for trade and adventure through the discovery of the Americas and the West Indies. Wyatt and Surrey, who introduced the Italian sonnet form into England, were noblemen whose poems found their way into print through a popular collection known as *Tottel's Miscellany* (1557); and George Gascoigne (1525?-77), another of the early Elizabethan poets, made the pretense that his first volume of poems was done by various hands, "a posie presented out of sundry gardens" (1573). In the edition of 1575 he called the "posie" his own, but he was still as eager as a modern athlete to preserve his amateur standing; he protests that he received no money. A member of Parliament, a courtier, and a royal messenger, he was busy with his pen in various kinds of litera-ture, in prose and verse, tragedy and comedy, satire and sermon, pamphlet and short story, original work and translations; his motto, "Tam Marti quam Mercurio," expresses equal devotion to the God of War (he served with the English forces in the Low Countries) and to the God of Letters; and a drawing in the manuscript of his tale *Hemetes the Hermit* represents him as appealing, with pen in ear and sword in hand, to the bounty of Queen Elizabeth, to whom the little work was dedicated.

Remarkable rather for promise than for actual achievement, Gascoigne was the precursor of that brilliant period in drama and poetry known as the Elizabethan Age, which remained un-equaled for centuries in the history of English literature, and has in some ways never been surpassed. The period is justly asso-ciated with the name of Elizabeth, to whose court many of the poets were attached, but its glories did not as a matter of fact make a real beginning until twenty years or so after the queen's accession to the throne in 1558, and some of the greatest master-pieces known as "Elizabethan" were produced after her death

SPENSER

in 1603. Shakspere, as Ben Jonson's lines to his memory remind us, delighted both "Eliza and our James," and it was after the latter's accession that he became one of the King's Players.

The work of EDMUND SPENSER, however, fell entirely within the reign of Elizabeth, to whom he dedicated his great epic *The Faerie Queene*. Born in London in 1552, Spenser received a good classical education at the Merchant Taylor's School and at Cambridge University. Attaching himself to the Puritan party, he took service with Sir Henry Sidney and the Earl of Leicester, the first the father and the second the uncle of Sir Philip Sidney, himself a courtier poet and Spenser's personal friend. Spenser's *Shepherd's Calendar* (1579) marks the definite arrival of a new spirit and a new grace in English poetry. Modeled upon the *Eclogues* of Virgil and Virgil's imitators on the Continent, Spenser's pastorals nevertheless kept in the true line of English poetry by harking back to Chaucer, and showed personal independence by an astonishing degree of metrical variety and versatility, and courageous allusions to current issues in Church and State. Young as he was, the poet was already meditating a more ambitious and independent effort, in celebration of the heroic virtues of his patron Leicester or of the glory of Queen Elizabeth. But before he could begin to carry out this great design, Spenser had to make his way as a servant of the Crown, and so became the owner of Kilcolman Castle in Ireland. Here he had as a not too remote neighbor a fellow-poet and adventurer, Sir Walter Raleigh. To Raleigh, Spenser showed in 1589 the first three books of *The Faerie Queene;* Raleigh's enthusiastic admiration was such as to persuade Spenser to accompany the more successful courtier to London to lay his work at the queen's feet. Spenser's hopes of preferment were bitterly disappointed, and he returned to Kilcolman Castle to complete three more books of *The Faerie Queene,* paying court meanwhile to the beautiful Elizabeth Boyle, a merchant's daughter of the neighboring town of Cork, where he was married to her on June 11, 1594. His courtship and marriage were the occasion of a charming series of sonnets and of the most magnif-

THE FAERIE
QVEENE.

Difpofed into twelue books,
Fashioning
XII. Morall vertues.

LONDON
Printed for William Ponfonbie.
1 5 9 0.

TO
THE MOST HIGH,
MIGHTIE
And
MAGNIFICENT
EMPRESSE RENOVV-
MED FOR PIETIE, VER-
TVE, AND ALL GRATIOVS
GOVERNMENT ELIZABETH BY
THE GRACE OF GOD QVEENE
OF ENGLAND FRAVNCE AND
IRELAND AND OF VIRGI-
NIA, DEFENDOVR OF THE
FAITH, &c. H·ER MOST
HVMBLE SERVAVNT
EDMVND SPENSER
DOTH IN ALL HV-
MILITIE DEDI-
CATE, PRE-
SENT
AND CONSECRATE THESE
HIS LABOVRS TO LIVE
VVITH THE ETERNI-
TIE OF HER
FAME.

SIR PHILIP SIDNEY

SIR WALTER RALEIGH

icent wedding song in the English language, the *Epithalamium*. In 1596 he visited London to publish Books IV-VI of *The Faerie Queene* and to push once more his claims to advancement —only to be again disappointed. Once more he returned to Ireland, which he regarded as a land of exile among savages. The natives returned with bitter hatred the contempt of the English colonists, and in 1598 burnt Kilcolman Castle to the ground. Spenser fled with his family to Cork and then to London, where he died early the following year and was buried in Westminster Abbey.

So *The Faerie Queene* remained a fragment covering little more than a quarter of the author's original scheme of composition; but it is still long enough to make the perusal of the whole of it a considerable achievement. Lacking the careless gaiety and power of burlesque of Ariosto, whose rimed romance, *Orlando Furioso,* he took as his model, Spenser substituted for the light-hearted and rippling Italian octave verse a more complicated and dignified stanza of his own invention—the Spenserian stanza, which many subsequent English poets have practised, though none of them with quite the same majestic ease and continuous yet varied melody. With Puritan seriousness, Spenser gave also to his romantic story deeper meanings of moral philosophy, religion, and statecraft. In the first twelve books of his romantic epic he intended to set forth the twelve private moral virtues enumerated by Aristotle; and side by side with this moral allegory, or at one with it, he endeavored to celebrate or criticize certain contemporary persons and relate certain historical events, considered from his own point of view as an Englishman and a Protestant of his time. This complicated scheme inevitably causes confusion in the mind of the modern reader, if he pays any close attention to it; but by most the story is accepted as a romantic narrative, and its moral, historical, and personal implications are discerned only when they are obvious; or are disregarded altogether. The spiritual elevation of Spenser's thought does, indeed, count for something, but what mainly holds one's interest is the luxuriance of the poet's imagery, the splendor—

even gorgeousness—of his descriptive passages, the spirited narration of certain romantic episodes, and the music of the verse, which flows on with the effortless power and beauty of a great river.

Spenser's genius was essentially undramatic and he shows no interest in the theater, save for a brief reference, in an early minor poem, to the degradation of the contemporary stage. His friend Sir Philip Sidney ridicules the extravagances of the popular drama and deplores its lack of classical decorum. SIR WALTER RALEIGH was indeed associated with the dramatist Marlowe as a member of a skeptical group, suspected of the crime of atheism and spied upon by agents of the Government. But Spenser, Sidney, and Raleigh were all court poets, looking to the queen for advancement and scorning the favor of the populace, upon which the theater was dependent for support. It was the theater that first freed the English author from reliance upon the patronage of the sovereign or some great noble.

The English drama had already had a long history as a popular institution. There is no need here to go back to the early mysteries and miracle plays, or to the later moralities and interludes, which flourished for generations before the building of the first public theater in London in 1576; but it is well to remember that they contributed materially to the traditions with which the Elizabethan drama began. The newly introduced classical influence imposed blank verse as the recognized medium for tragedy, and suggested certain formal restrictions and restraints which the writers for the public stage were in general slow to acknowledge; but the robust demands of the popular taste continued to exercise a dominant power. The Latin tragedies of Seneca and the comedies of Plautus were accepted as models of classical correctness, but they were worshiped afar off except in the learned circles of the universities, the inns of court, and the leading grammar-schools. Seneca's favorite themes of lust and crime fell in with the popular desire for blood and bawdry, and the melodramatic tragedy of horrors was one of the first types to establish itself as a stage fashion. We have a good example of this kind of play (first brought into favor by Kyd's *Spanish Tragedy*) in Shakspere's *Titus Andronicus,* and it left its mark upon *Hamlet,* of which Kyd probably wrote an earlier version. Rhetorical extravagance also was a characteristic feature of Senecan tragedy very welcome to the Elizabethan public; and the Elizabethan stage, which thrust the actor forward on an open platform with his audience all around him, gave ample opportunity for the display of his histrionic powers. Thus a young Cambridge scholar, CHRISTOPHER MARLOWE, in 1587-88 took the town by storm with the two parts of *Tamburlaine,* bringing the glow of poetry to the inordinate ambitions and bombastic ravings of the Asiatic adventurer who in the fourteenth century conquered a large part of the Oriental world. Drawn in his chariot by kings whom he lashes with a whip, he exclaims:

> Holla, ye pampered jades of Asia!
> What! can ye draw but twenty miles a day?—

a scene that long remained famous on the Elizabethan boards. The same potent rhetoric and the same poetic passion are applied to the story of the famous medieval magician in *The Tragical History of Dr. Faustus;* when Helen of Troy is brought back to life by Mephistopheles, Faust exclaims:

> Was this the face that launched a thousand ships
> And burnt the topless towers of Ilium?
> Sweet Helen, make me immortal with a kiss.
> Her lips suck forth my soul; see where it flies! . . .
> Oh, thou art fairer than the evening air
> Clad in the beauty of a thousand stars.

Marlowe's *Jew of Malta* (1589) gave hints for the more famous Jew of *The Merchant of Venice,* and his *Edward II* (1592) was the first historical tragedy on the English stage worthy the name of art. In 1593, Marlowe was killed in a miserable tavern quarrel on the outskirts of London, before he was thirty years of age. What he might have accomplished if he had come to greater maturity can only be imagined; as it is, his short career marks the advent of genius to the popular drama.

Less brilliant but still greatly gifted was Marlowe's contemporary and comrade, ROBERT GREENE, who died in 1592 under circumstances of peculiarly repulsive Bohemian squalor from a surfeit of Rhenish wine and red herrings. Popular both as novelist and dramatist, Greene, in spite of his disgusting debauches and his even more disgusting fits of repentance, was able to capture and convey the charm of the English countryside and of English maidenhood, investing both with a romantic glamour that is still fresh and natural among many absurdities and extravagances.

Another predecessor to whom Shakspere was considerably indebted was JOHN LYLY (1554-1606), an Oxford scholar and court poet who first won fame by the two parts of his novel *Euphues* (1578-80), which gave a permanent name to their peculiarly mannered style. These affectations are less marked in the plays which he subsequently wrote for the delectation of Elizabeth, combining extravagant flattery of the queen, under various classical disguises, with daring allusions to contemporary political intrigues and international rivalries. He has often a lively wit and pretty fancies, interspersed with charming songs, a combination awaiting only the touch of genius to produce *A Midsummer Night's Dream,* to which some of Lyly's plays have obvious resemblances.

Such was the situation of the English drama when Shakspere came to it. There were theaters, built around an inclosed space, open at the top, after the fashion of the inn yards in which the earlier plays were performed. The open space was occupied by the lowest order of spectators, standing about the projecting platform which constituted the front part of the stage. Around the yard on three sides were galleries for the wealthier spectators, with rising tiers of seats. The fourth side was occupied by the back stage, with a curtain drawn in front of a room with a balcony above it: in this, interior scenes could be set while the

SWAN THEATER ABOUT 1596

action proceeded on the main open stage, upon which a few gallants were allowed to sit on stools placed out of the way of the actors. The shape of the Elizabethan stage affected the construction of the Shaksperian plays.

The actors were organized in companies under the patronage of a leading nobleman, who was nominally responsible for their good conduct; legally, they were his "servants," but the relation was often little more than a subterfuge to meet the necessities of the law which punished unattached players as "rogues and vagabonds." Then, as now, successful actors were popular favorites, both with foolish women and fashionable society, and the leading members of the profession, such as Richard Burbage and Edward Allen, were men of substance, making considerable sums out of their share of the takings at each performance. Lower in professional rank were the journeymen actors, hired by the sharers at fixed wages, and below these again the apprentices or boys, who played the women's parts, the whole company being organized like a medieval gild. A successful actor earned more than a successful dramatist, the usual fee for the composition of a play being between five and ten pounds—representing from two hundred and fifty to five hundred dollars of our money. The play became the absolute property of the company and was cut down, amplified, revised, or remade at their discretion. Unless they were in great straits, companies did not sell their plays for publication by the booksellers, as this was thought likely to lessen the profits of performance; but pirated versions were not uncommon, printed from copies obtained from the actors or from shorthand reports made in the theater.

About WILLIAM SHAKSPERE'S first connection with the stage we know very little. The baptismal register of the parish church of Stratford-on-Avon shows that he was the son of John Shakspere, a local dealer in agricultural produce and a man of some note in the town, whose wife was Mary Arden; the date is April 26, 1564, and as in those days baptism speedily followed birth, the accepted date of his birthday is April 23, which is also St. George's Day and the date of the poet's death in 1616. Church

SHAKSPERE'S BIRTHPLACE

THE BIRTHPLACE RESTORED

records also tell us that when he was eighteen (in the autumn of 1582) he was hurriedly married to Ann Hathaway, who was some years older than the youthful bridegroom; that a daughter was born to them on May 26, 1583, and twins on February 2, 1585. How he was earning a living at this time is not known. There is an early tradition that he was employed in his father's not too flourishing business; and from rather slight internal evidence afforded by his plays it has been suggested that he taught school for a while or worked in a lawyer's office. But such knowledge of the Latin classics as he displays might very well have been gained at the grammar-school in Stratford and by subsequent study, and his acquaintance with the law is not beyond the powers of a writer shrewdly observant of men and things and a keen man of business, as Shakspere turned out to be after he had made his way in London. He may have held horses for the gallants coming to the theater (as one story has it) and it seems probable that he was an actor before he was a playwright; but the first definite piece of biographical evidence we have about his dramatic career is a passage in an autobiographical pamphlet by the Robert Greene mentioned above, *A Groatsworth of Wit Bought with a Million of Repentance,* published in 1592. Greene in the last of his repentant moods (he died soon after) had undertaken the congenial task of warning his quandam associates against "spending their wits in making plays," for, he says, "there is an upstart crow beautified with our feathers, that with his *Tiger's heart wrapped in a player's hide,* supposes he is as well able to bombast out a blank verse as the best of you; and being an absolute *Johannes factotum,* is in his own conceit the only Shake-scene in a country." The pun upon Shakspere's name makes the reference to him unmistakable, and the line parodied, "Oh, tiger's heart wrapped in a woman's hide," occurs in the third part of Shakspere's *Henry VI.* Chettle, who published the tract, lost no time in issuing an apology to Shakspere for Greene's strictures upon him, "because myself have seen his demeanor no less civil than he excellent in the quality he professes [i.e. as an actor]; besides, divers

STRATFORD CHURCH

ANNE HATHAWAY'S COTTAGE

of worship have reported his uprightness of dealing, which argues his honesty, and his facetious grace in writing that approves his art."

Greene's outbreak of spleen therefore gives us three noteworthy items of information about Shakspere in 1592: (1) His success as a dramatist had become remarkable enough to arouse the jealousy of one of his most successful competitors; (2) he was also an excellent actor; (3) his honorable character had won for him friends in high places. The publication of *Venus and Adonis* in 1593 and *The Rape of Lucrece* in 1594, luscious love-poems after the fashion of the day, enhanced his reputation for "grace in writing"; and their dedication to a distinguished patron, the young and brilliant Earl of Southampton, confirmed the impression that he had powerful friends. A little later we find his name mentioned along with those of the famous actors Kemp and Burbage, "servants to the Lord Chamberlain," as in receipt of the royal bounty for acting two plays before her Majesty at Christmas-time in 1594. Shakspere was now only thirty years of age, and it is evident that his progress since his arrival in London had been remarkable.

In 1598 appeared a small literary handbook entitled *Wit's Commonwealth* by Francis Meres, who states forthright that in both tragedy and comedy Shakspere is the most excellent among the English, "for comedy witness his *Gentlemen of Verona*, his *Errors*, his *Love's Labor's Lost*, his *Love's Labor's Won*, his *Midsummer Night's Dream*, and his *Merchant of Venice;* for tragedy his *Richard II*, *Richard III*, *Henry IV*, *King John*, *Titus Andronicus*, and his *Romeo and Juliet*." The dozen titles here listed are easily identified with plays in the Shakspere folio edition if we accept *Love's Labor's Won* as an earlier name for *All's Well that Ends Well*. *Errors* is evidently *The Comedy of Errors*, a bustling farce founded upon the popular *Menæchmi* of Plautus, which depends upon the mistakes made owing to the close resemblances of twin brothers. *Love's Labor's Lost* is a mannered comedy dealing with contemporary styles and affectations (including some personal allusions), after the example of

Lyly. There are traces of Lyly, also, in *A Midsummer Night's Dream,* combined with far greater mastery of character and construction than in the earlier comedy, a lovelier play of fancy, a richer humor, a deeper insight. There is a lyrical exuberance about *A Midsummer Night's Dream* which marks it as the work of a poet still young, but a poet who has already gained full control of his material. There is the same gush of conscious power in *Romeo and Juliet* and the same exuberance of lyric emotion, fancy, and humor; it is only when the passion of the two youthful lovers darkens under the shadow of the tomb that we get the tone of tragedy, and even then it is the pathos of "bright things come to confusion" that moves us, rather than the sense of any profound clash between Man and Fate, for the intensity of this youthful passion triumphs over death. Shakspere's true tragic period was not yet. His romantic comedy, progressing from the rather clumsy construction of *Two Gentlemen of Verona* to the skilled combination of *The Merchant of Venice,* has already come very near perfection.

Shakspere's progress in the composition of historical plays (which Meres includes under the head of tragedy) is equally remarkable. How much of the three parts of *Henry VI* is Shakspere's (though they are included by the editors of the folio) has been much contested, but there is general agreement that they are not wholly his—more probably a revision of others' work. It may be for this reason that Meres makes no mention of them, though they undoubtedly belong to an early stage of Shaksperean authorship—perhaps the very first to which he set his "prentice hand." *Richard III,* though still built on Marlowe's extravagant lines, is more coherent in its construction and more artistic in its workmanship. A much more original conception is that of the weak and wilful hero of *Richard II,* so outrageous in his youthful imperiousness and disregard of right and justice, and so pathetic in his lyrical self-pity after his fall. His character is well contrasted with the self-contained, ambitious Bolingbroke, who can bide his time and take, one by one, the necessary steps to the attainment of his desires. *Henry IV* con-

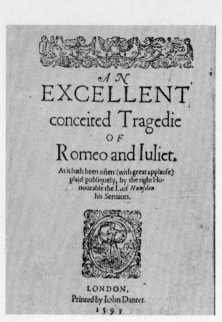

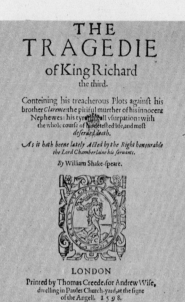

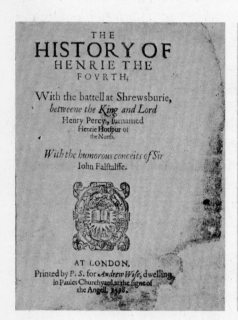

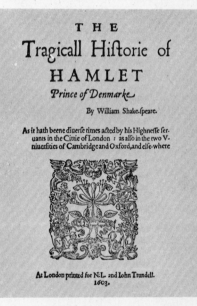

EARLY SHAKSPERE QUARTOS

tinues the story of Bolingbroke as king, though the center of interest shifts to his son, Prince Hal, and his companions, especially Falstaff, the most triumphant creation of Shakspere's comic genius. The madcap Prince of Wales becomes a serious and heroic king in *Henry V,* in which Falstaff dies heartbroken, owing to the loss of the new king's favor. The three parts of *Henry VI* and *Richard III,* which Shakspere had already written, complete his dramatic studies of English history from the latter part of the fourteenth century to the accession of the house of Tudor at the end of the fifteenth.

In *Henry V* Shakspere compared the return of that victorious monarch from France to the expected return of the Earl of Essex from his campaign against the rebels in Ireland, then proceeding (1599). The campaign, however, ended disastrously, and the imprudent return of Essex to London resulted in his death on the scaffold and the imprisonment of his second in command, the Earl of Southampton, Shakspere's patron and personal friend. Shakspere seems to have kept himself clear from the insurrectionary movement in which Essex and Southampton were involved, and he continued to prosper, enjoying an enlarged share of the profits of the new Globe Theatre, owning the largest house and other property in Stratford, playing before the queen just before her death in 1603, and almost immediately after the accession of James licensed by him as one of the King's Servants along with Burbage and other members of the company. They acted some of Shakspere's plays before the king in 1603-1604, and walked in the royal procession at the formal entry into London, each receiving four and a half yards of scarlet cloth as a mark of the royal favor.

About the turn of the century Shakspere was at the height of his power of creation in comedy, producing in rapid succession *Much Ado About Nothing, As You Like It,* and *Twelfth Night,* all apparently in 1599-1601. But before the new century was a year old Shakspere was already turning his mind to tragedy. Notice to secure copyright for the publication of *Hamlet* was given in 1602, and in 1603 an imperfect edition

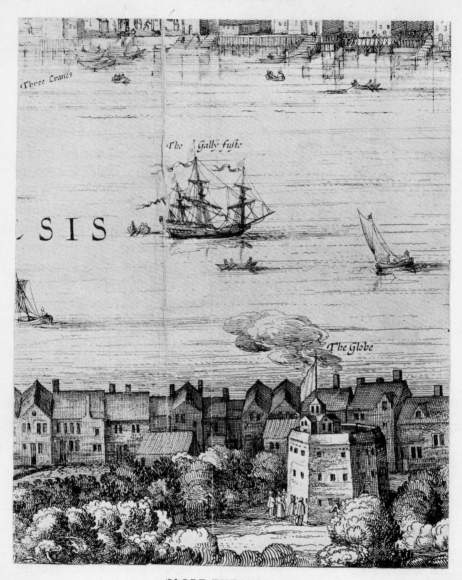

Three Cranes

The Gally fuste

SIS

The Globe

GLOBE THEATER 1616

appeared, possibly representing Shakspere's first revision of an old play on the subject, belonging to his company. A second edition "enlarged to almost as much again as it was, according to the true and perfect copy," was published in 1604. *Othello, King Lear,* and *Macbeth* complete Shakspere's great tragic period, which covered probably the first half-dozen years of the seventeenth century. These four masterpieces reach the highest mark in tragedy since the time of Sophocles and probably the highest in human history. The masterpieces of Greek tragedy are more nearly perfect, but they are on a smaller scale; Shakspere attains the supreme heights of thought and passion at the same time that he satisfies the popular demand for an exciting plot. He is the most human of all tragic writers, and the most modern—or perhaps it would be more correct to say timeless. He is singularly free from the religious prejudices common in his day, and his sympathies are well-nigh universal.

About the time that Shakspere was producing his tragic masterpieces, or perhaps a little later, he was at work on a series of plays derived from Roman history, hence called the Roman tragedies: *Julius Cæsar, Antony and Cleopatra,* and *Coriolanus.* He found excellent material for these plays in Plutarch's *Lives of Distinguished Greeks and Romans,* translated by Amyot from Greek into French, and by Sir Thomas North from French into English. North's translation was a very popular book and had already passed through two or three editions. Shakspere took from it not only incidents and characters, but a good deal of dialogue, often contenting himself with putting North's prose into blank verse. But he re-fused the old material in the fire of his genius and made it his own. The tragic fall and death of the famous lovers Antony and Cleopatra, has been the subject of more than a score of tragedies, but only Shakspere's play now holds the attention of any but the literary historian. Cleopatra is magnificently conceived as the woman of long experience in the art of love, who in spite of her many faults of temper and character commands respect by the keenness of her wit and the courage and dignity with which she faces the last extremity.

About 1608, Beaumont and Fletcher's *Philaster* brought into fashion a new type of romantic play, resembling the romantic comedy of Shakspere's earlier career, with more pathos and less gaiety. Shakspere accordingly returned to the adventures and disguises of *Two Gentlemen of Verona, Twelfth Night,* and *As You Like It.* Both *Cymbeline* and *The Winter's Tale* have extravagant plots quite regardless of history and probability, but Imogen and Perdita are among the most charming of Shakspere's heroines, yielding nothing to Rosalind and Viola. The third play belonging to this group, *The Tempest,* was probably the last of his entire construction, though he may have assisted in others. It is very closely built, coming nearer to an observance of the famous unities of time and place than is Shakspere's usual practice; and its plot seems to be his own invention. Some slight hints were doubtless given by a pamphlet, published in 1610, describing the wreck of part of the expedition of Sir George Somers at the Bermudas on their way to Virginia. The pamphlet describes the islands as "never inhabited by any Christian or heathen people" but "reported a most prodigious and enchanted place." So Caliban reports Shakspere's enchanted island to be "full of noises, Sounds and sweet airs that give delight and hurt not." "The still-vexed Bermoothes" are mentioned in the play, which in many ways reflects the interest taken at the time in the inhabitants of the New World. "Caliban" is merely the word "cannibal" rearranged, and Gonzalo's description of the ideal commonwealth is taken from Florio's translation of a passage in Montaigne's essay "on the cannibals" (as the natives of America were then called). The wonder-working Prospero has been identified with Shakspere himself, and his speeches at the end of the play have been interpreted as Shakspere's farewell to the stage. This theory may be fanciful, though one is tempted to read a personal reference into the following lines:

> Our revels now are ended: these our actors
> (As I foretold you) were all spirits, and

Are melted into air, into thin air.
And like the baseless fabric of this vision,
The cloud-capped towers, the gorgeous palaces,
The solemn temples, the great globe itself,
Yea, all which it inherit shall dissolve,
And like this insubstantial pageant faded
Leave not a rack behind: we are such stuff
As dreams are made on, and our little life
Is rounded with a sleep.

The last sleep came to Shakspere in April, 1616, and he was buried, as befitted the leading man of the town, in the chancel of Stratford Church, with a suitable monument. Few of his townsmen could have realized at the time that this tomb was to become the most honored shrine of the English-speaking world, nor was this realization more common anywhere else. When the collected edition of Shakspere's plays known as the first folio was published in 1623, Ben Jonson in some commendatory verses, prefixed to the text, published the prophetical line "He was not of an age, but for all time," but the boast must have been regarded as the hyperbolical praise called for by the occasion rather than as a sober statement of fact. It took centuries of criticism and popular appreciation to establish Shakspere's supremacy as a dramatic artist.

BEN JONSON himself was thought by many of his contemporaries to be the better man—better equipped with classical learning (as he himself suggests in his commendatory poem) and better versed in the theory and practice of dramatic composition. Self-assertive to the point of arrogance and little inclined to yield to the taste of the day, Jonson imposed his personal authority upon some of his contemporaries and quarreled violently with others. For Shakspere he had a genuine admiration and a personal liking, and their wit-combats at the Mermaid Tavern became famous. Shakspere acted in Jonson's first notable comedy, *Every Man in his Humour,* in which Jonson developed his characteristic attitude and method. He takes "humor" in the sense of some extravagant failing or vice, some

SHAKSPERE'S BUST

Mr. WILLIAM

SHAKESPEARES

COMEDIES,
HISTORIES, &
TRAGEDIES.

Published according to the True Originall Copies.

LONDON
Printed by Isaac Iaggard, and Ed. Blount. 1623.

FIRST FOLIO TITLE-PAGE

outstanding peculiarity, which renders its victim absurd or contemptible. Jonson sometimes made these "humors" merely ridiculous, but more often his strong tendency to satire used them as a vehicle for moral indignation. As an example of the former we may take *The Silent Woman,* in which a miserly old man, Morose, marries in order to disinherit his nephew, who has annoyed him by extravagance. As Morose objects most strongly to noise or even ordinary conversation, he has sought out a bride recommended for her peculiar taciturnity. He is driven to distraction by her clamor and incessant chatter, and the long-winded speeches of the lawyers he has called in to enable him to get a divorce reduce him to despair. His nephew (who has really provided the bride) offers to get him out of the hobble, and reveals the fact that the supposed "silent woman" is really a boy.

The best example of Jonson's satiric vein is *Volpone,* which in a modified form has been revived on the modern stage. *Volpone* is a rich scoundrel who enjoys the exercise of his craftiness as much as the wealth he gains by it, and, with the help of his astute serving-man Mosca, he brings the creatures who fawn on him to sacrifice everything in their desire to win succession to his estate. The plot is deftly constructed and brings out a depressing exposure of human folly, weakness, and vice with the biter bit as the culmination. Violent attacks upon the Puritans in *The Alchemist* and *Bartholomew Fair,* and upon his stage rivals in *The Poetaster* are more relieved by humor, but the satire is still too strident for modern taste. Jonson's Roman tragedies *Sejanus* and *Catiline* are solidly built plays and accurate historical studies, but lack the breath of life.

From 1592-93, when Greene and Marlowe died, to 1598, when Jonson's *Every Man in his Humour* was acted, Shakspere reigned without a rival on the popular stage; from about 1608 on, the most serious competition came from the collaboration of BEAUMONT AND FLETCHER. They had humor (best seen in *The Knight of the Burning Pestle*) and sentiment (as in *Philaster*), a much easier and more lucid style than Shakspere commonly

BEN JONSON   CHAPMAN

employed in his later work, and great skill in plot-construction and the presentation of characters somewhat conventionally conceived.

It is our habit to regard the multifarious dramatic activity of the Elizabethan period as centering in Shakspere, and to classify other dramatists as his contemporaries, predecessors, or successors; and this habit has been sanctified by time. But the dramatists did not regard themselves in that light, nor were they so regarded by one another or by the public of that day. Jonson's admiration for Shakspere was sincere and whole-hearted, but there can be no doubt that he regarded himself as in many ways Shakspere's superior. Beaumont and Fletcher were for a time more popular than either Shakspere or Jonson. And there were others who won the suffrages not only of their own day but of posterity—Chapman and Marston, who collaborated with Jonson in the amusing play of city life *Eastward Ho,* in which satire of the ambitious Scotchmen who were pushing their way in London after the accession of James I brought about the imprisonment of the three authors; Dekker for his joyous *Shoemaker's Holiday,* which treats also of the life of the London merchant and apprentice, but with romantic sentiment and good humor instead of satire; Thomas Heywood for his domestic tragedy *A Woman Killed with Kindness;* John Webster for his tragedies of horror *The White Devil* and *The Duchess of Malfi;* Ford for his sensational and pathetic tragedy *The Broken Heart.* These—and they are but a few titles among hundreds of others—are enough to show the astonishing fertility and variety of dramatic production in the seventeenth century until it was brought to an end by the Puritan triumph over Charles I and the suppression of the theaters (1642).

The prose of many of these comedies is vigorous, lively, and clear, but for ordinary narrative and expository communication the standards of an ordered lucidity had yet to be established. HAKLUYT'S *Voyages* show a remarkable variety of styles, from that of the log-book of the uneducated mariner, who wishes simply to jot down the facts, to the courtly dignity of Sir Walter

Raleigh's report of the last fight of the *Revenge* at sea; but in general the prose of the period hesitates between a disorderly plainness and a gorgeously elaborate maze of complicated clauses, which are rendered even more tedious by the affectations of Lyly, Sir Philip Sidney, and other writers of romance. The most enduring prose achievement of the period is the translation of the Bible published in 1611 and now known as the Authorized Version.

An admirable example of the epigrammatic style is afforded in the *Essays* of FRANCIS BACON (1561-1626), whose work demands more extended survey. His father held a distinguished position at Elizabeth's court as Lord Keeper of the Great Seal, and the boy's grave and studious demeanor led the queen to style him the "young Lord Keeper." Sent to Trinity College, Cambridge, at the age of twelve, when he was about sixteen he fell into dislike of the medieval Aristotelianism still in vogue there, as "only strong for disputations and contentions, but barren of the production of works for the benefit of the life of man (in which mind he continued to his dying day)." He set himself to find out a better way, believing that he was specially fitted for this ambitious design, having, as he thought, "a mind nimble and versatile enough to catch the resemblances of things (which is the greatest point), and at the same time steady enough to fix and distinguish their subtler differences; as being gifted by nature with desire to seek, patience to doubt, fondness to meditate, slowness to assert, readiness to think again, carefulness to dispose and set in order; and as being a man that neither affects the new, nor admires the old, and hates every kind of imposture. So that I thought my nature had a kind of familiarity and relationship with truth."

On leaving the university he entered the diplomatic service and was called home from Paris by the sudden death of his father. As a younger son he was left ill-provided, and diplomacy had to be abandoned for law and politics. At twenty-three he became a member of the House of Commons and displayed conspicuous ability; but he found the path of promotion slow and

BACON

difficult. Although Burghley was his uncle, he attached himself to the shiftier fortunes of Essex, and when Essex fell at the turn of the century, Bacon, who had as yet received no substantial advancement, took part in the government prosecution which brought his former patron to the scaffold. At the end of Elizabeth's reign, Bacon, now forty years of age, was free from debt, had a little money in hand, an income of three hundred pounds a year from land, "a fair house and the ground well timbered." He had found "to his liking" an alderman's daughter, a "handsome maiden" of moderate fortune, and he asked to be knighted in order to marry her. He was knighted, married, rewarded with a small pension, and in 1607 received his first important government office, that of Solicitor-General.

During all this long period of waiting and working at uncongenial tasks, Bacon had not relinquished his intellectual ambitions. When he was twenty-one, he made a first sketch of his new method and at the age of thirty he wrote to Burghley, "I have as vast contemplative ends as I have moderate civil [i. e., political] ends: for I have taken all knowledge to be my province." The first edition of the *Essays* was published in 1597, and in 1605 *The Advancement of Learning* appeared. In this he set forth the weaknesses of the existing system of education, as he saw them: its insistence upon authority, especially that of Aristotle, its subjection to tradition, its fondness for abstract reasoning and neglect of the study of nature, the lack of laboratories and of money for experiments, the low salaries of the professors, the absence of teaching in history, modern languages, and politics to train men for the service of the State, and above all the failure to realize the true end of knowledge.

"For men have entered into a desire of learning and knowledge, sometimes upon a natural curiosity and inquisitive appetite; sometimes to entertain their minds with variety and delight; sometimes for ornament and reputation; and sometimes to enable them to victory of wit and contradiction; and most times for lucre and profession; and seldom sincerely to give a true account of their gift of reason, to the benefit and use of men."

In this and other passages Bacon gave hints of his new method, but he still hesitated to publish it. Two years later he submitted it in outline to Sir Thomas Bodley (the great benefactor of the Oxford University Library), who wrote him in reply: "I must tell you, to be plain, that you have very much wronged yourself and the world, to smother such a treasure so long in your coffer." About this time Bacon set to work preparing a statement of the new method for publication, but he revised it annually for a dozen years before printing it in 1620 under the title *Novum Organum*. Even so, he regarded it as merely one part of a greater work, the *Instauratio,* which at his death he left uncompleted.

The *Novum Organum* was published in Latin, probably not from any desire to restrict its circulation, but because Bacon thought (as Sir Thomas More did in publishing his *Utopia*) that the Latin language was more likely to endure. The terseness of style which the Latin language makes possible and which Bacon strove after in his English essays, is in the *Novum Organum* reduced to extreme conciseness by repeated condensation. The text is divided into aphorisms, of which the first may serve as an example:

"Man, being the servant and interpreter of Nature, can do and understand so much and only so much as he has observed, in fact or in thought, of the course of nature: beyond this he neither knows anything nor can do anything."

The subtlety of nature, he continues, is very much greater than the subtlety of the senses and understanding, for the human mind is beset by inherent deficiencies and external obstacles. A famous passage of the *Novum Organum* divides these into four *idola* or illusions: (1) *idola tribus,* of the tribe or race, deficiencies innate in human nature; (2) *idola specus,* of the cave, inherent in the individual or produced by his education; (3) *idola fori,* of the market-place, prejudices resulting from his intercourse with his fellows or his occupation; (4) *idola theatri,* superstitions which have no foundation in fact, but by tradition, credulity, and negligence, have come to be received; "in this vanity some of the moderns have with extreme levity indulged so far as to attempt to found a system of natural philosophy on the first chapter of Genesis."

How are these illusions of the human mind, these self-deceptions, to be overcome? Only, as Bacon thinks, by the organized and systematic study of nature by means of a series of carefully planned and controlled experiments, upon which general principles (or axioms, as he calls them) should be founded. Accounts of the experiments as well as the results should be published, and every step tested by many minds:

"Men have hitherto made short stay with experience, but passing her lightly by, have wasted an infinity of time on meditations and glosses of the wit. But if some one were at hand able to answer our questions and tell us in each case what the fact in nature is, the discovery of all causes and sciences would be but the work of a few years.

"My way of discovering sciences goes far to level men's wits, and leaves but little to individual excellence; because it performs everything by the surest rules and demonstrations."

Evidently Bacon underestimates the difficulty of the operations he projected and the length of time it would take to carry them out. An organized beginning of scientific investigation of the kind he desired was made by the foundation in London in 1662 of the Royal Society for the Advancement of Science, of which ISAAC NEWTON became a fellow in 1672 (he was already a fellow of Trinity College, Cambridge) and in the same year submitted a paper describing his invention of the reflecting telescope. Soon afterward he demonstrated to the society his discovery of the spectrum, and ten years later showed that the force of gravitation which makes an apple fall to the earth controls the movements of the stars in their orbits. The latter discovery was confirmed by a more accurate measurement of the size of the earth by the French astronomer Picard. Newton believed no less firmly than Dante in the Divine Love "which moves the sun and the other stars," but this new astronomical conception, following upon the Copernican theory deposing the earth from her traditional position as the center of all things to that of a

FRANCISCI
DE VERULAMIO,
Summi Angliæ
CANCELARIJ,
Instauratio
magna.

Multi pertransibunt & augebitur scientia.

Anno

LONDINI
Apud Joannem Billium
Typographum
Regium.

1620

subordinate solar planet, greatly affected men's ideas about their relation to the universe. All this was in accordance with Bacon's method, for though he insisted upon experience and utility, he held that "the contemplation of truth is a thing worthier and loftier than all utility and magnitude of works." Man must be the interpreter as well as the servant of Nature, and must strive for knowledge of her secrets as well as use of her powers. He strongly recommends experiments which are of no use except for the discovery of causes, what he calls *experimenta lucifera* —"experiments of light"—to distinguish them from *experimenta fructifera,* experiments fruitful for practical use. Of the light-giving experiments he says:

"Now experiments of this kind have one admirable property and condition; they never miss or fail. For since they are applied, not for the purpose of producing any particular effect, but only of discovering the natural cause of some effect, they answer the end equally well whichever way they turn out; for they settle the question."

Both kinds of experiments are founded upon the investigation of nature, and Bacon accordingly identified utility with truth. Even the practical applications of knowledge "are of greater value as pledges of truth than as contributing to the comforts of life."

To the matter-of-fact English temper Bacon's insistence upon experience and practical utility naturally commended itself, and a great stimulus was given to scientific investigation by the successful application of science to English industry in the eighteenth and nineteenth centuries. But even with the establishment of laboratories at the universities and in connection with great industrial concerns, backed up by the organization of societies international in scope, Bacon's scheme of an ascending series of scientific experiments and general principles founded upon them has not yet been realized. Since his time the bounds of scientific knowledge have been expanded to such an extent that to bring all science under one control would be a herculean, even an impossible task. But in a more limited way the plan of organized research he advocated has been adopted and has proved exceedingly fruitful. It lies at the basis of modern life.

Bacon had no hope that his plans would be carried out in his own lifetime; and he was, indeed, too deeply immersed in public affairs and private aggrandizement to be well informed concerning the scientific discoveries of his own time. Within two years of the publication of *The Advancement of Learning* he became Solicitor-General and was successively appointed Attorney-General, Privy Councillor, Lord Keeper, Lord Chancellor, and Viscount St. Albans. The last honor fell upon him in January, 1621, soon after he had presented the *Novum Organum* to the king. The next month his political enemies began proceedings against him which resulted in his being stripped of his offices and banished from court. He was in very poor health and died five years later from a cold caught through experimenting with snow as a preservative of meat.

The achievements of two men of such very different genius as Shakspere and Bacon are impressive as examples of the extraordinary variety of the activities of the Elizabethan age. Taken as a whole (in the wider sense suggested above), the period shows a most astonishing record for a population of five millions or thereabouts. A virile people, hammered into unity by geographic isolation and bitter experience of internal broils, had been brought to power and prosperity by the administrative ability of the Tudor sovereigns and statesmen just at the moment for expansion and achievement. The discovery of the New World placed England at the gateway of the ocean route between Europe and America, and gave her a unique opportunity for exploration, adventure, trade, and colonial enterprise. The intellectual movement heralded by the Continental Renaissance opened men's minds to higher issues and gave a stimulus to art, literature, and science. The reformation of the Church made a natural appeal to the Englishman's love of personal and national independence, and his dislike of external control. The outcome of the whole situation was an exaltation of the national spirit and a consciousness of power which found supreme expression

QUEEN ELIZABETH

in literature and more especially in drama. This exceptional combination of circumstances was inevitably transient, and the creative power evoked by a passing mood of exultation fell away again; but it bequeathed to Englishmen a sense of confidence in themselves and their national destiny which they have never lost. There have been periods of depression and stagnation in literary and especially in dramatic production, but the nation never again returned to the aimless and ineffective drifting of the period separating the age of Chaucer from the age of Shakspere. By its actual achievements the Elizabethan age established standards which subsequent English writers might fail to attain, but which they could never quite forget.

CHAPTER V

THE FIGHT FOR FREEDOM

The Elizabethan compromise in religion embodied in the thirty-nine Articles of 1562-71 was bound to leave unsatisfied the Catholics (who wished to cleave to the old ways) and the Puritans (who thought the reformation of the Church had not gone far enough). Elizabeth herself, unlike her sister Mary, cared little for religion, and would probably have been willing to accept any settlement that made her throne secure; but her formal deposition by the Pope, absolving her subjects from their allegiance to her, inevitably threw her into the arms of the Protestant party. She was keenly conscious of her prerogative as head of the English Church. To the Bishop of Ely, who demurred to one of her requests, she sent the arrogant message, "Proud prelate, you know what you were before I made you what you are. If you do not immediately comply with my request, by God I will unfrock you." But she clung to the Catholic rule of the celibacy of the clergy; acknowledging her entertainment by the primate's wife at Lambeth Palace, she said, "Madam I may not call you, and Mistress I am loth to call you; however, I thank you for your good cheer." Elizabeth and her councilors treated with equal severity those who plotted for the return to the ancient national faith and those who advocated extreme measures of religious reform. Penry, who with other assailants of episcopacy in the famous Marprelate controversy was executed in 1593, almost with his dying breath assured the queen of his loyalty, and said that if his death could procure quietness for the Church of God, and for his prince and kingdom, he was satisfied to die. Another Puritan, when his right hand was cut off at the pillory, seized his hat with the left hand to wave it and cry, "God save the queen!" At the end of her reign Elizabeth was the leader of a united nation and could assure her faithful Commons of her continued confidence in their affection. "Though God hath raised me high, yet this I account the glory of my crown, that I have reigned with your loves."

When James came to the throne, the Puritan opponents of episcopacy had hopes of a further reform of Church government, but the new monarch was shrewd enough to see that religious democracy might be dangerous: "No bishop, no king." The royal and the episcopal prerogatives did, indeed, in the end fall together, but the critical conflict between Crown and Church on the one hand and the new forces of reform on the other was deferred until the reign of James's son and successor, Charles I, who paid with his life for his obstinate insistence on his rights.

Our opinion of the early Puritans is often unduly affected by the caricatures of the contemporary dramatists, who were naturally antagonistic toward them, as the Puritans had from the beginning been opposed to the theater and had done all they could to hamper its progress: one of their first measures on attaining power was to interdict the performance of stage plays altogether. Some of them were no doubt fanatical to the point of absurdity, but their power as a party in the State consisted in the strength of character and practical common sense of many of its adherents, whose honest diligence and business ability gave them increasing wealth and influence. The authorities of the City of London always had Puritan leanings, and the fact that the party came to be known in the Civil War as the Parliamentarians may serve to remind us that most members of the House of Commons and some members of the House of Lords were opposed to the king, though the majority of the latter House were naturally Royalists. It is a mistake to suppose that Puritanism necessarily meant sniveling hypocrisy or even a strait-laced bigotry which excluded from life every inclination to cheerfulness and joy and beauty. As an example of the type of liberal and educated Puritan we may take the leading exponent of the creed and valiant defender of the policy of the Parliamentary party after it came to power—JOHN MILTON (1608-74).

Milton's father was a London business man in comfortable circumstances who had been a student at Christ Church, Oxford, and was a lover of music and literature; his mother was well-known in the neighborhood as a woman of high character and generous disposition. From early childhood Milton was "destined for the study of humane letters," and his parents, who both still counted themselves members of the Church of England, encouraged their son's youthful desire to be a clergyman. He had a Puritan tutor until he was ten years old, when he went to the famous London school of St. Paul's, from which he proceeded to the University of Cambridge, already notable for its Puritan tendencies. On account of his girlish beauty he was known at Cambridge as "our fair lady of Christ's," the last an allusion to Christ's College, of which he was a member, but no doubt with a covert reference to the staidness of his demeanor as well as the delicacy of his features. He was little given to the rough and boisterous games which have characterized Anglo-Saxon youth in all periods, and probably it was a self-portrait he drew when in *Paradise Regained* he described the youth of John the Baptist in the following lines:

> When I was yet a child, no childish play
> To me was pleasing; all my mind was set
> Serious to learn and know, and thence to do
> What might be public good; myself I thought
> Born to that end, born to promote all truth,
> All righteous things.

He was a diligent student, not only of the mathematics, Latin, and Greek which constituted the ordinary curriculum, but of theology, of Hebrew and Syriac, of Italian and Spanish; and all through his life he was a lover of music. The seriousness of mind which inspired in him the desire to become a clergyman of the Church of England made him unable to carry out that

MILTON AGED TEN

purpose when he realized that to take holy orders he must become a slave to what he regarded as ecclesiastical tyranny and take an oath which he regarded as perjury; rather than buy the sacred office of the ministry with servitude and forswearing, he preferred "a blameless silence."

After seven years' study at Cambridge, he retired for further reading and meditation to his father's house at Horton, a little village in Buckinghamshire, and there followed his chosen vocation as a poet. When he was twenty-one and still a student at Cambridge, he had given earnest of his powers in an *Ode on the Morning of Christ's Nativity,* but finding the subject beyond his years, he left it a magnificent fragment—enough, however, to show a very remarkable mastery of the sonorities of English verse. During his residence at Horton (1632-37), he wrote *L'Allegro* and *Il Penseroso,* two charming companion poems celebrating the joys of Mirth and Melancholy. The cheerful pleasures are those of the quiet country life with which he was surrounded—rustic jests and dances, stories by the fireside spiced with nut-brown ale—and the music and stage plays of the city:

> If Jonson's learnèd sock be on,
> Or sweetest Shakspere, Fancy's child,
> Warble his native wood-notes wild.

Milton had previously written a eulogium of Shakspere for the folio edition of the plays published in 1632, so that he evidently did not share the Puritan prejudice against the theater. Among the delights of Melancholy he counts classical or modern tragedy or an old tale by Chaucer, expressing his final preference for "the studious cloister's pale."

To this Horton period belong also two dramatic exercises, *Arcades* and *Comus,* which he wrote in compliment to the Countess of Derby, who had, a generation earlier, received the poetic adoration of Spenser; but the most finished achievement of this early group of poems was his pastoral elegy *Lycidas.* This is an elegy, following the established conventions of pastoral poetry, for Edward King, a college friend of Milton's,

POEMS

OF
Mr. *John* *Milton* ,

BOTH
ENGLISH and LATIN,
Compos'd at several times.

Printed by his true Copies.

The S O N G S were set in Musick by
Mr. H E N R Y L A W E S Gentleman of
the K I N G S Chappel, and one
of His M A I E S T I E S
Private Musick.

————*Baccare frontem*
Cingite, ne vati noceat mala lingua futuro,
Virgil, Eclog. 7.

Printed and publish'd according to
ORDER.

LONDON,
Printed by *Ruth Raworth* for *Humphrey Moseley,*
and are to be sold at the signe of the Princes
Arms in *Pauls* Church-yard. 1645.

himself a poet, who was drowned in crossing from Ireland in 1637. Presumably the friendship with King was not very close, for the poem shows little personal feeling—nothing like the passionate grief for Keats expressed by Shelley in *Adonais* or that for Lincoln in Whitman's *When Lilacs Last in the Dooryard Bloomed;* but its control of ancient traditions and of new cadences added fresh music and dignity to English verse, and in one passage, denouncing the idle and selfish shepherds of the English Church, Milton rises to a height of genuine indignation, ending with a threat which seems prophetic of the doom soon to overtake the party in power:

> But that two-handed engine at the door
> Stands ready to smite once, and smite no more.

The head of Archbishop Laud, the leader of the party for the suppression of Puritanism in the English Church, fell on the scaffold in 1645 and that of his royal master in 1649.

In 1637, when Milton wrote *Lycidas,* the political and ecclesiastical situation, though threatening, had not yet reached its final crisis, and the poet felt free in the following year to start on a prolonged tour of the European Continent. Handsome and highly educated, knowing both modern and ancient languages well, he made his way easily, by his dignified manners and scholarly seriousness, among the leaders of European thought. He met Grotius, the learned Dutch jurist who founded international law, and Galileo, who founded modern physical science; he wrote five sonnets in Italian to an Italian lady, with whom he was for a while in love, and a Latin poem to a famous Italian singer; but amid the intoxicating delights and manifold temptations of Italian society he never lost his self-control. Later, when he was engaged in political controversy, and his personal character was attacked, he called God to witness that "in all those places in which vice meets with so little discouragement, and is practised with so little shame, I never once deviated from the paths of integrity and virtue, and perpetually reflected

IOANNES MILTON.
Ætatis LXII 1670.

Τὸν περὶ Μꝯ' ἐφίλησε,
δίδυ δ' ἀγαθόῃε κακόῃε·
Οφθαλμῶν μὲν ἄμεϱσε,
δίδυ δ' ἡδεῖαν ἀοιδήν.

that, though my conduct might escape the notice of men, it could not elude the inspection of God."

Milton scorned the idea of inchastity as unworthy of any "free and gentle spirit" and degrading to the poetic vocation to which he had devoted himself. He wrote: "I was confirmed in this opinion, that he who would not be frustrate of his hope to write well hereafter in laudable things, ought himself to be a true poem; that is, a composition and pattern of the best and honorablest things; not presuming to sing high praises of heroic men, or famous cities, unless he have in himself the experience and the practice of all that which is praiseworthy."

As to his religious opinions he kept silence unless they were attacked; but when challenged, he defended himself fearlessly, even in Rome. When the revolution broke out in England, he came back at once, for "I thought it base to be traveling for amusement abroad while my fellow citizens were fighting for liberty at home."

With his scholarly attainments, it was evident that he could do more service with the pen than with the sword. There were three kinds of liberty which he regarded as essential to the happiness of society—religious, domestic, and political. It was the first that attracted his immediate attention, for a violent controversy was raging between the Puritans and the bishops led by Archbishop Laud. Milton plunged into the fray in 1641 with a tract *Of Reformation in England and the Causes that hitherto have hindered it*. He recognized that as a poet he was fighting left-handed, but his zeal, his ample erudition, his command over language, and his deep sense of conviction made him a formidable pamphleteer. The violent arguments about episcopacy, pro and con, have lost their interest beyond revival, but any one who will plow his way through confutations, refutations, and refutations again confuted, will find in Milton's tracts an occasional passage of sustained eloquence or biographical interest which almost repays the tedium and bewilderment that such issues should ever have excited the minds of men.

In 1643 an unhappy personal experience diverted Milton's

attention to the issue of domestic liberty. Sensitive to feminine beauty, he had been attracted to Mary Powell, a girl about half his age and a Royalist, and he had married her; she found life with the Puritan pamphleteer "very solitary" and too "philosophical" for her tastes, and after a month's experience of it she went home to her father. Milton, outraged and indignant, made the matter a public issue, and submitted to Parliament a series of hurried pleas in favor of divorce. Since the controversy about the first marriage of Henry VIII, jurisdiction in annulling marriage in England had passed from the pope to the English ecclesiastical courts, and the Puritan authorities were divided on the divorce issue. Parliament was in no hurry to give Milton relief, and he was in a mood to take matters into his own hands; he appears even to have chosen as Mary Powell's successor a "virgin wise and pure" to whom he addressed one of his best sonnets, a Miss Davis; but when this came to his wife's ears, she implored forgiveness and Milton took her again to his bosom. So the repentant Eve in *Paradise Lost* is reconciled to her offended spouse:

> She ended, weeping; and her lowly plight,
> Immoveable till peace obtained from fault
> Acknowledged and deplored, in Adam wrought
> Commiseration. Soon his heart relented
> Towards her, his life so late and sole delight,
> Now at his feet submissive in distress,—
> Creature so fair his reconcilement seeking
> His counsel whom she had displeased, his aid;
> As one disarmed, his anger all he lost.

Milton seems to have held the somewhat Oriental view that woman was subject to man as man was subject to God. He was thrice married, so that his first unfortunate experience did not deter him from repeated trials; but his family life, even with his own daughters, seems to have been difficult. He thought them undutiful and unkind because they rebelled against the task of reading to him in languages they did not understand. Apparently he thought that one tongue was enough for any woman.

AREOPAGITICA;

A

SPEECH

OF

Mr. JOHN MILTON

For the Liberty of VNLICENC'D
PRINTING,

To the PARLAMENT of ENGLAND.

Τὐλдίθεϱον δ' ἐκεῖνο, εἴ τις θέλε πόλε
Χρηςόν τι βόλδμ' εἰς μέσον φέρειν, ἔχɤ.
Καὶ ταῦθ' ὁ χϱήζων, λαμπϱός ἐσθ, ὁ μὴ θέλων,
Σιγᾷ, τί τέτων ἐστὶν ἰσαίτεϱον πόλε;

Euripid. Hicetid.

This is true Liberty when free born men
Having to advise the public may speak free,
Which he who can, and will, deserv's high praise,
Who neither can nor will, may hold his peace;
What can be juster in a State then this?

Euripid. Hicetid.

LONDON,
Printed in the Yeare, 1644.

The following year (1644) Milton's mind was engaged with an issue more worthy of his pen—that of the liberty of the press. This was another issue that the Reformation had left undecided. The notions of freedom of opinion and freedom of publication are hard for the human mind to come by and harder to stick to. The plea for toleration is nearly always made by the party which wishes to be tolerated by the majority; it does not follow that when the minority becomes the majority it will tolerate its opponents. Jeremy Taylor, at this time a representative of the defeated episcopal party, pleaded in 1647 for *The Liberty of Prophesying,* which was indeed a reasonable attitude for the Church of England with its policy of compromise. But before the Commonwealth and after it, the episcopal party in the Church claimed and exercised the right to control the opinions and publications of its opponents. In 1644, when the Presbyterians were in power, they were not inclined to grant to their opponents the freedom they had demanded for themselves when they were in opposition to the governing episcopacy. They had, moreover, given an unsympathetic reception to Milton's divorce pamphlets, and he was being driven to the conclusion that "New Presbyter is but old Priest writ large"—a conclusion always justified by etymology and perhaps now by experience. When the Presbyterian Parliament claimed for itself the power of restricting the privilege of publication to such books and pamphlets as it chose to license, Milton protested in a plea "for the liberty of unlicensed printing," addressed to the Parliament of England and entitled *Areopagitica* in allusion to the high court of the Areopagus which had authority in classical Athens. His theme cannot be better stated than in his own words: "Though all the winds of doctrine were let loose to play upon the earth, so Truth be in the field, we do injuriously by licensing and prohibiting to misdoubt her strength. Let her and Falsehood grapple; who ever knew Truth put to the worse, in a free and open encounter?"

This position he supports with all the eloquence and all the wealth of classical allusion of which he is capable, and it is one of his noblest efforts in behalf of liberty. Unfortunately, neither the Puritans nor the Royalists saw the wisdom of giving their opponents freedom to express their opinions, and the battle had to be fought over again at the Revolution of 1688—and has often been fought since.

When the Independents under the leadership of Cromwell displaced the Presbyterians, Milton took office as Latin secretary and defended the action of the Government in the trial and execution of Charles I. Regicide was naturally regarded by the European monarchs as an unpardonable offense and in a campaign which became international in scope the Puritan leaders were denounced as desperate criminals. Milton's command of vituperative Latin, his learning, and his gift for controversy became an important asset on the side of the English Commonwealth. The battle was at its height when he was threatened with blindness, but he went on with his work regardless of the personal danger and paid the inevitable penalty for his devotion to the cause. Three years after he lost the use of his eyes he addressed to a personal friend one of his best sonnets, expressing the pride and courage which sustained him in his affliction:

> I argue not
> Against Heaven's hand or will, nor bate a jot
> Of heart or hope, but still bear up and steer
> Right onward. What supports me, dost thou ask?
> The conscience, friend, to have lost them overplied
> In liberty's defense, my noble task,
> Of which all Europe rings from side to side.

So long as the Commonwealth stood, Milton's brains and pen were actively engaged in its service. But the courage that sustained him under the calamity of total blindness was not gained without a severe inward struggle. The stern Puritan who was later to undertake to "justify the ways of God to men" had first of all to justify the ways of God to himself. He was not unaware of the natural gifts with which he had been endowed, and he had devoted half the ordinary span of human life to the development of those gifts. Arriving at the height of his powers at a great national crisis, he had devoted those powers to the service of a cause which he believed was not only the cause of liberty but the cause of God. To be stricken with blindness before that cause was won was to him not merely a personal affliction but a torturing mystery, for it was a misfortune to the cause and to the nation as well as a bitter disappointment to him. He tried to console himself with the thought:

> God doth not need
> Either man's work or his own gifts. Who best
> Bear his mild yoke, they serve him best. His state
> Is kingly: thousands at his bidding speed,
> And post o'er land and ocean without rest;
> They also serve who only stand and wait.

But to "stand and wait" was for a man of Milton's temperament impossible. He felt in himself a "talent which is death to hide" and he could not resign his task to smaller men. Years afterward the death of Cromwell brought the whole structure of the Commonwealth tumbling about Milton's ears. Lost in books and metaphysical arguments, he had little conception of the motives and concerns of ordinary men; he did not realize that the average Englishman was tired of Puritan strictness and Puritan bigotry, for in periods of intense feeling the extremists easily push themselves to the front, gain power, and misuse it. Probably the Puritans had always been a minority, although a ruling minority, because it was determined, well organized, and efficient so long as it had capable leadership. When the army led by General Monk brought Charles II back to the vacant throne, Milton was engaged in drawing up a scheme for the government of England as an ideal republic, looking back to the classical democracy of Athens and forward to the Constitution of the United States.

As in his divorce tracts and his plea for freedom of public discussion, Milton was far in advance of his time. While he was reasoning, more practical men were acting. He who had felt unable to withdraw from the great national struggle found himself thrust aside from it and contemptuously forgotten. His republican and heretical pamphlets were burnt by the hangman and he himself imprisoned, but he was speedily released; poor, blind, helpless, he was allowed to retire into obscurity.

The cause for which Milton had made such great sacrifices seemed definitely lost. The Puritan clergy in the national Church were driven from their livings, forbidden to preach, forbidden to teach on pain of imprisonment; excluded from the universities, those who did not conform to the established religion were excluded also from public office. Charles II, a skeptic when he was in health, and on his sick-bed a Catholic, a debauchee and a trifler, a pensioner of the French king who had given him refuge in his exile, cared nothing for religion or for liberty; but the Royalists, returned to power, were determined to harry their fallen adversaries. A few of the leaders were executed; the bodies of those who were dead were hung in chains as a public spectacle. The court and the capital sank to scenes of public profligacy hitherto unknown in English history.

Milton returned to his books. Sightless and poverty-stricken, he was still a scholar and a poet. He busied himself with various educational works, and took up again the design he had formed twenty years before of enriching English literature with a great epic poem on a subject of appropriate dignity. He had drawn up, before he took the plunge into politics, a list of about a hundred possible themes, and from these he chose *Paradise Lost*.

It may be questioned whether the choice was altogether fortunate. Milton was a sincere but not an orthodox Christian; in religion as in politics, he was in advance of his time, and he was too widely read to accept the Bible stories with the simple faith of an unlettered, devout Englishman of his day. Yet he chose as the foundation of his poem one of the most naïve of these stories:

> Of man's first disobedience, and the fruit
> Of that forbidden tree, whose mortal taste
> Brought death into the world, and all our woe,
> With loss of Eden.

Paradife loft.

A
POEM
Written in
TEN BOOKS
By *JOHN MILTON*.

Licenfed and Entred according
to Order.

LONDON
Printed, and are to be fold by *Peter Parker*
under *Creed* Church neer *Aldgate*; And by
Robert Boulter at the *Turks Head* in *Bifhopfgate-ftreet*;
And *Matthias Walker*, under St. *Dunftons* Church
in *Fleet-ftreet*, 1667.

On this basis he undertook to:

> Assert eternal Providence
> And justify the ways of God to men.

It was a very difficult undertaking. The serpent in Genesis has the impressiveness of the hero-villain of an ancient folk-tale; but when he is transformed into the Prince of Darkness and elected president of an infernal republic organized at a kind of constitutional convention, he is too difficult for even the popular mind to accept, and the more sophisticated are tempted to derision. It is a remarkable achievement that the Miltonic scheme, reduced or enlarged to the machinery of a parliamentary party with elections and debates, has taken such a hold of the national imagination that, ever since, many Englishmen who have been brought up on Milton and the Bible have been at a loss to decide how much of their conception of Satan they owe to the Bible and how much to *Paradise Lost*.

There was the further difficulty that Milton could hardly help sympathizing with the defeated adversary. Milton's Jehovah is an absolute monarch, who rules by divine right, crushes a rebellion, and of his own motion establishes his son as next in authority to himself; Satan owes his position to the free choice and full consent of his peers "with what besides, in council or in fight, hath been achieved of merit"—a sort of cosmic Cromwell, not unlike the Oliver to whom, in happier times, Milton had addressed encouraging and congratulatory sonnets. Defeated and driven into obscurity by an absolute monarch he despised, how could Milton avoid putting some of his personal feeling into the mouth of Satan:

> What though the field be lost?
> All is not lost; the unconquerable will,
> And study of revenge, immortal hate,
> And courage never to submit or yield,
> And what is else not to be overcome;
> That glory never shall his wrath or might
> Extort from me.

Milton too possessed "a mind not to be changed by place or time":

> What matter where, if I be still the same
> And what I should be.

So in spite of theology, Milton makes Satan the hero of the poem, and many readers have shared the feelings of the English judge who after reading the first two books of *Paradise Lost* ejaculated: "This is a fine fellow. I hope he'll win."

With the loyalist angels and with Adam and Eve, Milton is less successful. Continental critics scoff at an archangel who not only eats a hearty meal "with keen dispatch of real hunger" but speedily digests it with "concoctive heat"; and in their view Adam is too much the grave Puritan husband, Eve the submissive spouse skilled in household arts, whom the Puritan husband accepted, directed, counseled and consoled when feminine weakness led her into error.

Milton had no saving sense of humor to prevent the eloquence of his characters—always excepting the arch-rebel—from becoming a bore; and with the lapse of centuries his celestial and diabolical machinery becomes increasingly difficult for even momentary illusion. But he is the master of the grand style in English poetry, and the astonishing power and variety of his verse have never ceased to obtain recognition. Dryden acknowledged Milton as his master, as (according to Dryden) Milton regarded Spenser as his "original." It was to Dryden, who began his poetic career with an appreciation of Cromwell, and was a submissive Anglican under Charles and a Catholic under James, that Milton said when Dryden wished to use *Paradise Lost* for the libretto of an opera, "Aye, you may tag my verses if you will." And assuredly, after Milton, the grand manner suffered a relapse from which it has never recovered. Milton gave to the Renaissance exuberance of Spenser something of classical reserve and dignity; something too, perhaps, of Puritan sternness. But he had as high a standard for himself as for others, and if he reveals traits of character for which many moderns have small liking, as a man and a poet he never fails to command our respect. No nobler tribute has been paid by one poet to another than Wordsworth's sonnet beginning, "Milton! thou shouldst be living at this hour":

> Thy soul was like a Star, and dwelt apart;
> Thou hadst a voice whose sound was like the sea;
> Pure as the naked heavens, majestic, free,
> So didst thou travel on life's common way,
> In cheerful godliness; and yet thy heart
> The lowliest duties on herself did lay.

It may seem curious that what Milton, in spite of all his learning (or perhaps because of it), failed to accomplish, was achieved by his contemporary JOHN BUNYAN (1628-88), who knew his English Bible exceedingly well but knew very little else. It is perhaps still more strange that he succeeded in presenting the Protestant view of the scheme of redemption by way of an allegory and that of the homeliest kind. *The Pilgrim's Progress* is a dream of the believer's earthly pilgrimage on the way to heaven, and it is noteworthy that while English-speaking Protestants owe (or used to owe) much of their conception of hell and the fall of man to Milton, their notions of heaven and the way of salvation are largely due to Bunyan, who was in his turn greatly indebted to passages in the Bible with which few people, even in his own time, were familiar. To modern readers few forms of literature are so fantastic as the Oriental allegory, and the elaborate medieval allegories are insufferably tedious. Bunyan's use of the Oriental allegories found in the Bible is constant and tireless; and the reader's mind is so seldom released from the unmistakable religious meaning that he can rarely interest himself in the story for its own sake, as one can very easily in Spenser's *Faerie Queene*. It is Bunyan's quiet, homely narrative, his obvious sincerity, and the easy simplicity of his style that lead the reader onward and somehow rob so much good counsel of its usual tedium. He has no need to moralize, for the story carries its own moral beyond escape or misunderstanding. Christian flees from the City of Destruction, leaving

we pray you in the bowels of Christ.

Jo: Bunyan 1682

behind the wife and children who refuse to accompany him, and, directed by Evangelist, struggles through the Slough of Despond, and, entering in by the Strait Gate, makes his way to the foot of the Cross, where his burden of Sin rolls off his back and disappears forever in the Sepulcher. After climbing the Hill Difficulty, he arrives at the House Beautiful, to which he is admitted by a grave and beautiful damsel named Discretion, and has discourse with Piety, Prudence, and Charity. They show him Moses's rod, the hammer and nail with which Jael slew Sisera, the jawbone with which Samson did such mighty feats, the sling and stone with which David slew Goliath of Gath, and the sword also with which the Lord will kill the Man of Sin in that day that he shall rise up to the prey. Christian himself is armed by them with the Sword of the Spirit (which is the Word of God) and another weapon called All-Prayer. With these, after a terrific fight, he defeats the monster Apollyon, and escapes from the two giants, Pagan and Pope. Next he meets Faithful, who has narrowly escaped from the flattering tongue of Wanton (the same who tempted Joseph), who promised him all fleshly and carnal content. Together, with much edifying conversation, the two pilgrims pass through Vanity Fair, where they are accused of making a hubbub by their odd dress and speech, and are condemned by Judge Hate-good on the evidence of Envy, Superstition, and Pickthank, the jury being composed of Mr. Blindman (foreman), Mr. No-Good, Mr. Malice, Mr. Love-lust, Mr. Live-loose, Mr. Heady, Mr. High-mind, Mr. Enmity, Mr. Liar, Mr. Cruelty, Mr. Hate-light, and Mr. Implacable. Faithful, after being scourged, beaten, stoned, and otherwise maltreated, is burnt at the stake and goes to heaven in a chariot of fire; Christian (like Bunyan himself) gets off with imprisonment, and on his release is thrust by Giant Despair into Doubting Castle. But he and his new comrade, Hopeful, persevere to the Delectable Mountains of Immanuel's land, where the shepherds Knowledge, Experience, Watchful, and Sincere show them great wonders, and they arrive finally at the Gate of Heaven.

"Now I saw in my dream that these two men went in at the Gate; and lo! as they entered, they were transfigured, and they had raiment put on that shone like gold. There were also that met them with harps and crowns, and gave them to them; the harps to praise withal, and the crowns in token of honor. Then I heard in my dream that all the bells in the City rang again for joy; and that it was said unto them, 'Enter ye into the joy of our Lord.'

"I also heard the men themselves sing with a loud voice, saying, 'Blessing, and honor, and glory, and power be unto him that sitteth upon the throne, and unto the Lamb, for ever and ever.'

"Now, just as the gates were opened to let in the men, I looked in after them, and behold the City shone like the sun; the streets also were paved with gold, and in them walked many men with crowns upon their heads, palms in their hands, and golden harps to sing praises withal."

The imagery of this passage is taken from the Book of Revelation, but it is probably through the homelier medium of Bunyan that its details have taken possession of the popular imagination. Beside what he borrowed from Scripture, Bunyan has many striking comparisons of his own, as when he makes Faithful say of Talkative: "Some cry out against sin even as a mother cries out against her child in her lap, when she calleth it slut and naughty girl, and then falls to hugging and kissing it."

On the giant Pope, who, as Christian goes by, says to him, "You will never mend till more of you be burnt!" Bunyan makes the comment: "Though he be yet alive, he is, by reason of age and also of the many shrewd brushes that he met with in his younger days grown so crazy and stiff in his joints, that he can now do little more than sit in his Cave's mouth, grinning at Pilgrims as they go by, and biting his nails because he cannot come at them."

But Bunyan's bitterest satire is naturally reserved for the political and ecclesiastical opponents of his own day. The con-

THE
Pilgrim's Progress
FROM
THIS WORLD,
TO
That which is to come:

Delivered under the Similitude of a

DREAM

Wherein is Discovered,
The manner of his setting out,
His Dangerous Journey; And safe
Arrival at the Desired Countrey.

I have used Similitudes, Hos. 12. 10.

By *John Bunyan.*

Licensed and Entred according to Order.

LONDON,
Printed for *Nath.* Ponder at the *Peacock*
in the *Poultrey* near *Cornhil*, 1678.

sultation of the jury which tries Faithful in Vanity Fair is Bunyan's own, and presents Puritan feeling toward their accusers rather than any Christian doctrine.

"And first, among themselves, Mr. Blindman, the foreman, said, 'I see clearly that this man is a heretic.' Then said Mr. No-Good, 'Away with such a fellow from the earth.' 'Ay,' said Mr. Malice, 'for I hate the very looks of him.' Then said Mr. Love-lust, 'I could never endure him.' 'Nor I,' said Mr. Live-loose, 'for he would always be condemning my way.' 'Hang him, hang him!' said Mr. Heady. 'A sorry scrub,' said Mr. High-mind. 'My heart riseth against him,' said Mr. Enmity. 'He is a rogue,' said Mr. Liar. 'Hanging is too good for him,' said Mr. Cruelty. 'Let us despatch him out of the way,' said Mr. Hate-light. Then said Mr. Implacable, 'Might I have all the world given me, I could not be reconciled to him; therefore let us forthwith bring him in guilty of death.' And so they did."

The success of *The Pilgrim's Progress* was so marked that Bunyan followed it six years later with a second part, recounting the adventures of Christian's wife and children on their way to the Promised Land after Christiana heard that her husband had gone over the River. Many of the old characters and features are introduced and there are some new ones, such as Madam Bubble, a tall comely dame, with something of a swarthy complexion, whose temptation of the worthy Stand-fast is thus recounted by himself:

"As I was thus musing, as I said, there was one in very pleasant attire, but old, who presented herself to me, and offered me three things, to wit, her body, her purse, and her bed. Now, the truth is, I was both aweary and sleepy: I am also as poor as a howlet, and that perhaps the Witch knew. Well, I repulsed her once and again; but she put by my repulses, and smiled. Then I began to be angry; but she mattered that nothing at all. Then she made offers again, and said, if I would be ruled by her, she would make me great and happy; for, said she, 'I am the Mistress of the World, and men are made happy by me.' Then I asked her name, and she told me it was Madam Bubble.

This set me farther from her; but she still followed me with enticements. Then I betook me, as you saw, to my knees; and with hands lifted up, and cries, I prayed to him that had said he would help. So, just as you came up, the gentlewoman went her way. Then I continued to give thanks for this my great deliverance; for I verily believe she intended no good, but rather sought to make stop of me in my journey."

Christiana and Stand-fast cross the River and arrive at the Celestial City, "welcomed with trumpeters and pipers, with singers and players upon stringed instruments." But, on the whole, like most sequels, Part II of *The Pilgrim's Progress* is inferior to the work as originally projected by Bunyan's creative imagination.

Bunyan wrote other religious books, but none of so general an appeal as *The Pilgrim's Progress*. Of his other works the most interesting is the spiritual autobiography to which he gave the characteristic title, *Grace Abounding to the Chief of Sinners*. Like most converts, he seems anxious to make the sins of his youth as lurid as possible, but does not find a great deal to confess. A tinker and the son of a tinker, he had little education, but he was from childhood "greatly troubled with the thoughts of the fearful torments of hell-fire." In the deep spiritual depression into which he sank in his youth he was helped by his young Puritan wife, who brought about his conversion to her own faith. But he found it hard to break away from his habit of constant swearing—"I knew not how to speak unless I put an oath before and another behind to make my words have authority"—and still harder to give up the delights of "tip-cat." Tip-cat is "a game in which a small piece of wood called a *cat,* is tipped, or struck with a club or bat," and Bunyan was in the middle of a game, standing with club in hand, when he heard a voice from heaven saying, "Wilt thou leave thy sins and go to heaven, or have thy sins and go to hell?"

"At this I was put to an exceeding maze; wherefore, leaving my cat upon the ground, I looked up to heaven, and was as if I had, with the eyes of my understanding, seen the Lord Jesus

ELSTOW CHURCH AND BELFRY

BUNYAN'S BIRTHPLACE

look down upon me, as being very hotly displeased with me, and as if He did severely threaten me with some grievous punishment for these and other ungodly practices."

The ungodly practice which Bunyan found it hardest to give up was that of ringing the bells in the parish church of the neighborhood in which he followed his craft of a wandering tinker, that of Elstow in Bedfordshire. Even when he gave up pulling a bell rope himself, he could not keep away from the belfry, but hung about, watching the ringers:

"But quickly after, I began to think, 'How if one of the bells should fall?' Then I chose to stand under a main beam, that lay overthwart the steeple, from side to side, thinking here I might stand sure: but then I thought again, should the bell fall with a swing, it might first hit the wall, and then, rebounding upon me, might kill me for all this beam. This made me stand in the steeple-door; and now, thought I, I am safe enough, for if a bell should then fall, I can slip out behind these thick walls, and so be preserved notwithstanding. So after this I would yet go to see them ring, but would not go any farther than the steeple-door; but then it came into my head, 'How if the steeple itself should fall?' "

He fought in the civil war on the Parliamentary side, became a member and then minister of the local Baptist community, and, on the Royalists' coming into power again at the Restoration, was put in prison for twelve years under the Act of Conformity in matters of religion. During his first imprisonment he wrote *Grace Abounding*. It was during the enforced leisure of a second imprisonment imposed upon him by an unsympathetic Government that he wrote the first part of *The Pilgrim's Progress,* which was published in 1678.

It is obvious that Milton and Bunyan did not represent the prevailing tendencies of the Restoration period; they represented the spirit of revolt and protest. The spirit of the time was much better represented by JOHN DRYDEN (1631-1700), who wrote excellent prose and verse of a kind now interesting only to the student. He began his poetical career with a eulogy of

Sr. G: Kneller. Pinxit.

M V. Gucht Sculp.

Mr IOHN DRYDEN.

Anno. 1693. Ætat: 62.

Cromwell, became poet laureate under Charles II, and wrote a poem in defense of the Established Church; after the accession of James, who was a Catholic, he wrote another long poem in defense of Catholicism. It is to Dryden's credit that he refused to change his faith again in the Revolution of 1688 and spent his declining years, as he puts it, "struggling with wants, oppressed with sickness, curbed in my genius, liable to be misconstrued in all I write." Dryden was an admirable critic and his essays on drama did much to establish the supremacy of Shakspere; but his versions of Shakspere's plays began the depravation of the text upon the stage which continued down to modern times. His original plays went off into the absurdities of the so-called heroic drama or contributed to the degradation which reflected alike the indecency of manners and the lack of moral sense then prevailing.

A poet better worth the consideration of the reader of to-day is JOHN DONNE (1572-1631), who belongs, indeed, to an earlier time, but is in both form and matter more in accord with modern tastes. His precocious satirical genius flowered before the end of the sixteenth century, and he might therefore be strictly considered an Elizabethan, but most of his poems were not published till 1633. After a somewhat tempestuous youth he was ordained in 1615 and later became Dean of St. Paul's Cathedral. In the latter part of his lifetime he was a popular preacher; but it was the keenly satirical poems of his youth that won him posthumous fame and enduring influence. Milton, with all his weight of learning and the vein of sternness that was in his character as well as in his creed, said poetry should be simple, sensuous, passionate. Donne's poetry is subtle to the point of obscurity; it endeavors to pack into words more than their ordinary meaning and to present abstruse thoughts in a form that is striking rather than musical; it appeals above all to the intelligence, and therefore to the intelligent. Browning, it has often been noted, has much in common with Donne, but Donne's point of view is more in accord with the modern temper than that of Browning, who is essentially romantic. "The Donne Tradition" was recently

DONNE

made the subject of an elaborate investigation by a Harvard scholar, and the London "Times," in reviewing it (July 31, 1930), suggested that, with the exception of Shakspere, Donne "is more widely read to-day than any other of the early poets." "Since the War the younger generation has made a particular study of him, appropriating him, as it were, for its own, and using his poetry—for his prose is still for the most part neglected —as a kind of foundation for its own exercises in verse, and his intellectual conception of the passions as a model for its own." An English poet, Sacheverell Sitwell, published in 1930 an elaborate poem, said to have occupied his attention for the last ten years, founded on a single couplet by Donne, and entitled, *Dr. Donne and Gargantua*. An American poet, Genevieve Taggard, published in the same year a volume called *Circumference,* giving examples of "varieties of metaphysical verse" during the last four centuries. The term "metaphysical," as applied to Donne's poetry, was suggested by Dryden and adopted by Pope and Johnson; but none of them arrived at a precise definition. Nor are modern critics in complete agreement: it may mean (1) a poet "inspired by a philosophical conception of the universe" or (2) "one who relies on inverted thoughts and phrases, curiosity of images, violences and vagaries of expression." One may seek for an explanation of the term and a clearer definition in the origin of the school, which arose in the heyday of romantic exuberance in the last decade of the sixteenth century, when the Elizabethan sonnet was at the height of fashion. Three young scholars protested against the prevailing extravagance of amorous fantasy—Joseph Hall, who afterward became a bishop; John Marston the dramatist; and Donne. All three were satirists and professed a moral intention; and all three became clergymen. The publication of Donne's poems, after his death, brought into vogue this kind of poetry, sometimes metaphysical or religious in spirit, but not always; sometimes it dealt with amorous passion, mainly from the physical or intellectual side, with no obvious spiritual intent; in either case its mode of expression was keenly subtle, aiming at a precise epigrammatic terseness rather than the florid and sometimes careless exuberance of the Elizabethans, which produced so many lovely songs and sonnets. Donne's rhetorical extravagances are carefully calculated so as to make his point. Take, for instance, the well-known couplet selected by Sacheverell Sitwell as the text for his six cantos:

> Go and catch a falling star,
>   Get with child a mandrake root . . .

these and other hyperboles serve to emphasize the theme of the poem, that "No where lives a woman true and fair." Even if one such should be found—

> Though she were true when you met her,
> And last till you write your letter,
>   Yet she
>   Will be
> False, ere I come, to two or three.

Donne has no more faith in male fidelity than in female constancy: the "indifferent" hero of a companion poem begins, "I can love both fair and brown," and ends the stanza:

> I can love her, and her, and you, and you;
> I can love any, so she be not true.

It seems as if it could be hardly the same poet who wrote on sin in the poem entitled "Forget" or on "Death," or addressed to God the Father a hymn on divine forgiveness; but the style, the workmanship is the same.

The differences in tone (as well as in subject) are accounted for by the more serious temper and pursuits of Donne's later life. Born into a Catholic family, he spent his childhood and youth "with men of a suppressed and afflicted religion, accustomed to the despite of death, and hungry of an imagined martyrdom." But he reconciled himself to the Established Church, became a law student in Lincoln's Inn and private secretary to Sir Thomas Egerton, Lord Keeper of the Great Seal, whose niece he "secretly and hastily" married in December, 1602. This escapade landed him for a time in prison and lost him his secretaryship; for some years he suffered poverty and the humiliations which poverty and a growing family bring; they were commemorated in his epigram "John Donne—Anne Donne—Undone," which incidentally tells us how he pronounced his name. He apparently began to write about 1593, and some of his youthful satires, elegies, songs, sonnets, and rimed letters to friends were circulated in manuscript in a select circle; they attracted attention by their concentrated, abrupt style, intellectual content, and frank sensuality. Perhaps the limit for this kind of composition may be set at 1613, the date of the wedding-song to Princess Elizabeth. Two years later he was ordained and his life took on a different color; it was the period of his "divine poems." In 1623 he had a serious illness, and wrote the hymn "To God My God, in my Sickness," which was set to music, and, to his delight, often sung by the choristers of St. Paul's. "He did much contemplate," says his first biographer, Izaak Walton, "the mercies of God, the immortality of the soul, and the joys of heaven; and would often say in a kind of ecstasy, 'Blessed be God that he is God, only and divinely like Himself.'"

ROBERT HERRICK (1591-1674), like Donne, became a clergyman after a rather gay youth in London, and continued to write poetry in a retired Devonshire parsonage. The gayer side of his nature is represented in his famous lyric "Corinna Going A-Maying":

> Many a green gown has been given;
> Many a kiss, both odd and even:
> Many a glance too has been sent
> From out the eye, love's firmament;
> Many a jest told of the keys betraying
> This night, and locks picked, yet we're not a-Maying.
> Come, let us go while we are in our prime;
> And take the harmless folly of the time.

His more serious side is expressed in his final "Prayer for Absolution":

HERRICK

MARVELL

For those my unbaptizèd rimes,
Writ in my wild unhallowed times,
For every sentence, clause, and word,
That's not inlaid with thee, my Lord,
Forgive me, God, and blot each line
Out of my book that is not thine.

THOMAS CAREW, also born in the sixteenth century, was court poet under Charles I, and acknowledged the mastership of Donne, in an elegy dedicated to his memory. His best poem, *The Rapture,* recalls Donne's insistence on the physical side of love, but he shows otherwise little trace of Donne's influence.

ANDREW MARVELL (1621-78) should perhaps be counted a Puritan poet, for he was a friend of Milton's and shared with him the Latin secretaryship to the Council under the Commonwealth. He wrote the best of the elegies on Cromwell and in the course of it the lines which best keep in mind the dignity with which Charles I conducted himself at his execution:

He nothing common did, or mean,
Upon that memorable scene,
But as upon a bed
Laid down his kingly head.

A certain manly dignity and uprightness sustained Marvell under the extravagances of the Restoration period and gave weight to his satires on the degradation of the times; but he has only an occasional touch of Donne's concentrated bitterness and epigrammatic force.

His Royalist contemporaries SIR JOHN SUCKLING (1609-42) and RICHARD LOVELACE (1618-58) are more in the spirit of the new era. The former is remembered for his ironical poem "The Constant Lover":

Out upon it, I have loved
    Three whole days together!
And am like to love three more,
    If it prove fair weather,

and for the verses beginning, "Why so pale and wan, fond lover?" and ending

> Quit, quit for shame! This will not move;
> This cannot take her
> If of herself she will not love,
> Nothing can make her:
> The devil take her!

Lovelace's "I could not love thee, dear, so much, Loved I not honour more," and his "Stone walls do not a prison make, Nor iron bars a cage," still dwell in the minds of many who remain oblivious of the fact that Lovelace spent the last years of his life in extreme and undignified misery. To avoid a similar fate, Suckling, who had spent £12,000 in the King's service during the Civil War, committed suicide in Paris.

The last echo of Donne's satiric treatment of love is in the charming bit of frivolity written by CHARLES SACKVILLE, Earl of Dorset (1638-1706), while on service with the British Navy against the Dutch, "To all you ladies now at land," with its merry burden of "fal, la, la" and its final injunction:

> Let's hear of no inconstancy—
> We have too much of that at sea.

Donne's influence on religious poetry may be traced in the work of GEORGE HERBERT (1593-1633), Richard Crashaw (d.1649), and HENRY VAUGHAN (1622-95). The last-named was the author of the lines, often quoted as an example of "metaphysical" poetry:

> I saw Eternity the other night,
> Like a great Ring of pure and endless light,
> All calm, as it was bright.

His poem "The Retreat"—

> Happy those early days, when I
> Shined in my angel-infancy—

LOVELACE

SUCKLING

DORSET

after the lapse of more than a century, suggested Wordsworth's great "Ode on Intimations of Immortality from Recollections of Early Childhood," which in the opinion of competent critics marked the highest tide of poetic inspiration since the days of Milton.

The intervening period was, indeed, an age of great prose rather than of great poetry. The nation which had joyfully called the Stuarts back to the throne in 1660 was convinced after less than thirty years' experience that they were impossible, and the Revolution of 1688 opened an era of liberty, of government by public opinion, of toleration for differences in religious belief, the age of reason and of law, of Newton and Locke. The plea which Milton had made to Parliament in 1644 for the liberty of unlicensed printing went quietly into effect in 1695, and the new century saw the rapid development of the periodical press, the novel, and the newspaper.

CHAPTER VI

COFFEE-HOUSES, CLUBS, AND PERIODICALS

Thomas Jefferson said that if he had to choose between democracy without newspapers and newspapers without democracy as an instrument of popular government, he would choose newspapers. In England the press, public opinion, and representative government developed side by side. It was fortunate that William of Orange, though he had English princesses for mother and wife, was brought up in Holland, where the principles of freedom of religious belief and freedom of the press were already accepted. He succeeded in persuading Parliament to pass a Toleration Act giving Dissenters freedom of worship, though leaving them still subjected to certain civil disabilities and excluded from the universities; the statute restricting the liberty of the press was allowed to lapse in 1695. Moreover, William's accession, established by a convention of national representatives, was in itself an emphatic recognition of the fact that he ruled by consent of the people and not by divine right. But, being a European statesman of clear views and unusual ability, William still ruled, though he left details of government to his ministers. It was not till George I, who hardly knew English, ceased to attend the meetings of the privy council that the direction of the national policies passed to ministers responsible nominally to the king but actually to Parliament and the public opinion upon which the authority of Parliament was supposed to rest.

The invitation on which William of Orange left Holland for England assured him that if he landed in England he would have the support of nineteen-twentieths of the nation. And this proved to be the case: the army, the navy, the nobility, the House of Commons, the people—all declared against James, who was

107

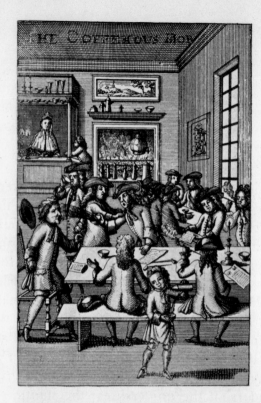

A LONDON
COFFEE-HOUSE

AUCTION MART COFFEE-ROOM

expelled from the kingdom by the force of public opinion. Naturally, the great head and fount of public opinion was London, which was not only the political capital, but the center of domestic trade and foreign commerce. But even in London public opinion was not formed by the printing in the newspapers of speeches in Parliament or on the public platform: facilities for such publicity did not yet exist; news still spread mainly by word of mouth, and the chief centers for the dissemination of news were the coffee-houses. Coffee was introduced into England during the Commonwealth, and by the beginning of the next century there were five hundred coffee-houses in London. To some extent the new beverage supplanted beer, which had been the ordinary drink of Englishmen, even for breakfast; wine, which was imported for the well-to-do; and spirits, including gin, which had recently been introduced from Holland and by its cheapness worked havoc among the lower classes. The coffee-house was a sort of democratic club, where ministers and noblemen could be seen sitting familiarly with private gentlemen "as if they had left their quality and degrees of distance at home." G. M. Trevelyan, professor of history at Oxford, in his recent book *England under Queen Anne* describes the coffee-house as the center of social life:

"The *beau monde* assembled at White's Chocolate House in St. James's Street, where, as Harley bitterly complained to Swift, young noblemen were fleeced and corrupted by fashionable gamblers and profligates. Tories went to the Cocoa Tree Chocolate House, Whigs to St. James's Coffee House. Will's, near Covent Garden, was the resort of poets, critics and their patrons; Truby's served the clergy, and the Grecian the world of scholarship; nor were there lacking houses for Dissenters, for Quakers, for Papists, and for Jacobites. The 'universal liberty of speech of the English nation,' uttered amid clouds of tobacco smoke, with equal vehemence whether against the Government and the Church, or against their enemies, had long been the wonder of foreigners; it was the quintessence of coffee house life."

The Oxford Gazette.

Published by Authority.

Oxon, Nov. 7.

THis day the Reverend Dr. *Walter Blandford*, Warden of *Wadham Colledge* in this University, was Elected Lord Bishop of this See, vacant by the death of Dr. *Paul*, late Bishop here.

Oxon, Nov. 12. This day His Majesty in Council, according to the usual custom, having the Roll of Sheriffs presented to him, pricked these persons following, to be Sheriffs for the succeeding year, in their respective Counties of *England* and *Wales*.

Berks.   Basil Brent, *Esquire*.

sieur *de Cannillat* having been put to death by the Commissioners of the *Grands Jours* : It seems they have laid some new Taxes or Impositions on those parts, There are Troups marching against them, and it is thought they will soon be reduced. my Lord *Aubigny* Lord Almoner to her Majesty, having lain sick some time here of an Hydropsie attended with a Flux, is this week dead.

Paris, Nov. 18. The Mareschal *de Turenne* arrived here on Sunday last from the Frontiers, whence he brings account that the Succors intended against the Prince of *Munster* had passed in small parties, and that they had been received at *Maestricht* by Monsieur *Beverning* in the name of the States General.

A

Weekly Review,

OF THE

Affairs of FRANCE.

Purg'd from the Errors and Partiality of *News-Writers* and *Petty-Statesmen*, of all Sides.

Saturday, Feb. 19. 1704.

The coffee-house was a place not merely for relaxation but for serious business. The London shopkeeper would leave word with his apprentice that he had gone "to the Coffee House":

> Then at Lloyd's Coffee House he never fails
> To read the letters and attend the sales.

Edward Lloyd, the founder of the greatest maritime insurance office in the world, kept a coffee-house in Lombard Street, set up a pulpit for auctions and reading out the "news letters," which the visitor could also peruse for himself. These "news letters" were the forerunners of the modern newspapers, and came as yet chiefly from the Continent. The Windsor Coffee House in Charing Cross promised in its advertisement the "best chocolate at twelve pence the quart and the translation of the *Harlem Courant* soon after the post is come in."

In England, as on the Continent, the irregularly published news letter gradually gave way to the newspaper, appearing at stated intervals. The first English newspaper which has continued to be published down to the present day was the "London Gazette," a government organ founded in the reign of Charles II by Sir Roger L'Estrange, who was at that time censor under the Licensing Act. A much more interesting figure in the early history of journalism is DANIEL DEFOE (1661-1731).

The son of a nonconformist butcher, Defoe would have found the gates of the universities closed to him if he had turned his steps in that direction; but he apparently received a good education, more liberal than was usual at the time, at the hands of a dissenting divine named Morton, who afterward became vice-president of Harvard College. On the death of Charles II, in 1685, Defoe showed the sincerity of his anti-Catholic convictions by taking part in Monmouth's rebellion, and very naturally welcomed the abdication of James and the accession of William of Orange in 1688. When Dutch William was attacked as a foreigner, Defoe came to his defense with a boldly satirical poem, *The True-Born Englishman,* which was exceedingly popular. He was less successful with an ironical pamphlet, *The*

DEFOE

Shortest Way with the Dissenters, published in the beginning
of the new century when the High-church party was complain-
ing of the privileges granted to Dissenters under the Toleration
Act. Taking up (anonymously, of course) the position of an
extreme High Anglican, Defoe asked why the nonconformists
should be treated with less severity than the Catholics:

"Both are enemies of our Church, and of our peace; and why
should it not be as criminal to admit an enthusiast as a Jesuit?
Why should the Papist with his seven sacraments be worse than
the Quaker with no sacraments at all? Why should religious
houses be more intolerable than meeting houses?

"Alas, the Church of England! What with popery on one
hand, and schismatics on the other, how has she been crucified
between two thieves. Now, let us crucify the thieves!"

The first effect of the pamphlet was to please the extreme
High-church party and to annoy the Dissenters; and when Defoe
revealed the hoax, the High-church people were annoyed more
than the Dissenters were pleased. The upshot was that Defoe
found himself subjected to fine, imprisonment, and exposure in
the pillory. Defoe took his humiliation gallantly, distributed his
Hymn to the Pillory, in which he defied and derided his an-
tagonists, and was cheered by the mob which was expected to
put him to scorn.

While in prison Defoe conceived the design of "A Review of
the Affairs of France and of all Europe, as influenced by that
Nation," which began publication in 1704 and continued, first
once a week, then twice a week, for nine years. It was the period
of Marlborough's great victories over Louis XIV, who, after
keeping Charles and James as his pensioners, had found in
William the leader of Europe against him. Queen Anne, who
succeeded, was bound to continue William's policy, because
Louis had recognized her younger half-brother as the rightful
occupant of the English throne. Defoe's business in the "Review" was to explain and justify this policy; incidentally he
established the institution of the editorial article. Professor
Trevelyan says of the London newspapers at Anne's accession:

ROBINSON CRUSOE
Original Frontispiece

"The newspaper usually consisted of a single sheet of two printed sides, sometimes folded into four pages; it appeared two or three times in the week, and contained the main items of home and foreign intelligence, set down without comment. The last half page was devoted to advertisements of such items as patent medicines, sales of houses, meetings for 'the noble and heroic sport of cockfighting,' or the vent of Portugal wine by Messrs. Brook and Hellier. Some papers gave a Tory twist to their news, like the *Postboy,* or a Whig twist like the *Postman.* But the news was much the same in all, and there was no leading article."

Defoe not only was the first editorial writer; he invented also the personal interview, answers to correspondents, gossipy paragraphs, and many less creditable devices of the modern newspaper, such as writing the last dying speech of a condemned criminal to be handed to Defoe by the criminal on the scaffold. It is impossible here even to outline the devious ways pursued by Defoe in the journalism of his time. After the death of Anne he was for a time engaged in editing a Tory paper under secret instructions from the Whig Government; he had to keep the paper Tory enough to please his Tory employers and harmless enough to satisfy the Whig Government of which he was the secret agent. It was a difficult position, and Defoe just escaped death, from the sword of the owner of the paper, when his perfidy was discovered.

In other departments of literature, for the guidance and edification of the public, Defoe's activities were less equivocal. In volumes like *Religious Courtship, The Complete English Tradesman, The Complete English Gentleman,* he ministered to the wants of the English middle class to which he belonged. In *A Journal of the Plague Year, A True Relation of the Apparition of one Mrs. Veal* and *Moll Flanders* (the professed autobiography of a notorious prostitute) he catered to the public appetite for horror and scandal after a fashion not unknown to modern journalism of a certain sort. His gifts for presenting fiction in the guise of fact, or mingled with fact so that it is

impossible to distinguish between fact and fiction, remain un-
surpassed. It is no wonder that some of his inventions were
regarded as facts, and some of his facts regarded as fictitious.
Even his greatest fiction, *The Life and Adventures of Robinson
Crusoe,* was put forth by him as an authentic autobiography:
"The editor believes the thing to be a just history of facts;
neither is there any appearance of fiction in it."

Defoe probably was in earnest in the accompanying protesta-
tion that the story was told for "the instruction of others by this
example, and to justify and honor the wisdom of Providence."
Crusoe certainly is a wonderful example, not only of untiring
piety, but of the courage, resource, and determination with
which English colonists were subduing the desolate shores of
the North Atlantic. The central fact of Alexander Selkirk's
marooning on a desert island is of course a matter of history and
was known to Defoe through a contemporary pamphlet, but the
wealth of detail which made the story of *Robinson Crusoe* con-
vincing is Defoe's own.

It is astonishing that a man of Defoe's genius, energy, and
multifarious activity should have died in want, but the rewards
of authorship, even of popular works, were still very miserable.
The publisher's payment to Milton of ten pounds for *Paradise
Lost* is a byword, but the distressful closing years of Dryden's
life were equally significant; deprived, by the revolution, of the
government posts of poet laureate and historiographer royal, he
was bullied by his publisher, harassed by debts, crippled by disease. Even such successful purveyors of fashionable literature
as Addison and Steele lived by political patronage, not by their
pens. Swift published his masterpieces anonymously and was
rewarded with ecclesiastical preferment. Pope made money by
the translation of Homer, and Dr. Johnson by his dictionary;
both performed what Johnson described as the dull but necessary task of editing Shakspere. When Goldsmith died two thousand pounds in debt, Johnson was overcome with astonished
admiration and ejaculated, "Was there ever poet more trusted!"
Probably not. If this was the fate of the leading man of letters

of the eighteenth century, one may imagine what happened to the small fry. The "authentic unhappy voice of Grub Street," as Professor Trevelyan puts it, speaks in the plea addressed by one Joseph Harris to Thomas Coke M.P.:

"Some time since I presented to your honor a book which I writ on my Lord Duke of Marlborough; and last summer I presented another book to you, called Luzzara, being an encomium on Prince Eugene of Savoy. As yet I have never had any return for either of those presents to your honor, wherefore now, by reason I am very ill and lame of rheumatism, I humbly make bold to address myself to your honor either for small charity, or for return of the books that I may present them to some other person of quality. I have nothing but what I get by translating out of Latin, Greek, and Spanish to maintain my wife and four children."

One improvement in the situation was that professional men of letters no longer felt called upon to echo the licentiousness and frivolity of the court during the Restoration period, mirrored for us by the diarists John Evelyn and Samuel Pepys, and reaching its culmination in the calculated obscenity of the Earl of Rochester, the author of the famous epitaph on Charles II:

> Here lies our Sovereign Lord the King,
>   Whose word no man relies on,
> Who never said a foolish thing,
>   Nor ever did a wise one.

William of Orange was a man of high character and exceptional ability, a devoted (if not absolutely faithful) husband; Mary's wifely devotion, her piety, her puritanical strictness had considerable effect on the court and society, though the debauchery made fashionable during the reign of Charles could not, of course, be ended in a day. The degradation of the drama was attacked in 1698 by a clergyman, Jeremy Collier, in *A Short View of the Profaneness and Immorality of the English Stage,* which caused a lively discussion and made a considerable impression on public opinion.

STEELE

ADDISON

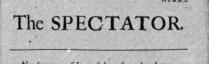

The time was ripe for a combination of the superficial polish which distinguished Restoration literature with the solider virtue esteemed by the English middle class, which was steadily growing in power and influence. This important task was successfully undertaken by RICHARD STEELE and JOSEPH ADDISON, both born in 1672, educated at the famous Charterhouse School, and passing thence to Oxford. Steele, the more volatile character, soon left the university, to enter the army; at the beginning of the eighteenth century he was a captain in the Guards and a lively figure at the London coffee-houses, clubs, and theaters. Responding to the call to reform the stage, Steele wrote two or three sentimental comedies, which were well received by the public, and the Government appointed him editor of the official "Gazette," which he successfully conducted by "keeping that paper very innocent and very insipid." But feeling himself trammeled by official bonds, he started in 1709 a more popular sheet, "The Tatler," which marked a new era in periodical literature. The title was intended to encourage the fair sex to look for light entertainment in its columns, and the editor promised to "report and consider all matters of what kind soever that shall occur to me":

"All accounts of gallantry, pleasure, and entertainment shall be under the article of White's chocolate house; poetry, under that of Will's Coffee house; learning, under the title of Grecian; foreign and domestic news, you will have from Saint James's coffee house; and what else I have to offer on any other subject shall be dated from my own apartment."

The talent of Addison, whom Steele soon called to his aid, was of a somewhat different order—more weighted with learning, more polished and urbane. Even in his youth Addison gave promise of literary distinction, and after taking his degree at Oxford he stayed on as a fellow of Magdalen College, where one of the most delightful walks in the college grounds still bears his name. When he was twenty-one, Dryden, the dictator of London literary circles, bade him welcome, and at the turn of the century the Whig Government diverted him from his purpose of becoming a clergyman, offering him a pension to travel abroad. He accepted the pension, but remained, according to one of his critics "a parson in a tye-wig," while another declared "one day or other you'll see that man a bishop." Returning to London, after his four years' Continental travel, he found the town agog with Marlborough's recent victory over the French at Blenheim, and celebrated the event in a conventionally ornate poem entitled *The Campaign*. Patriotic verse was at this time the sure path to preferment and Addison soon found himself a member of Parliament with one secretaryship after another falling into his lap. His somewhat limited coöperation with Steele in "The Tatler" was enlarged when in 1711 they jointly undertook the more famous and successful "Spectator." Its aim was "to banish vice and ignorance out of the territories of Great Britain," but its method was gentle, light, and easy. Dr. Johnson considered Addison's prose the model English style, "familiar but not coarse, and elegant but not ostentatious." More recent critics have thought that Steele had a larger part in the undertaking than he obtained credit for. The partnership was so successful that "The Spectator" was able to survive the attempt to crush the periodical press made by the Tory minister Harley through the imposition of the stamp tax; but Steele and Addison parted company when Steele in 1713 started "The Guardian," with a more active support of Whig policy than Addison cared for. Steele went on to become supervisor of Drury Lane Theatre and was knighted by George I for his stalwart support of the Hanoverian succession. With the return of the Whigs to power, on the death of Anne, Addison received further political promotion; he became Chief Secretary for Ireland and then Secretary of State, carrying on for a while a periodical in the Whig interest called "The Freeholder." But his health was broken and he retired, only to die at forty-seven. He was buried in Westminster Abbey.

The defeat of Tory maneuvers by the accession of George I in 1714, which brought promotion to Steele and Addison, caused bitter disappointment to the greatest of contemporary prose writers, JONATHAN SWIFT (1667-1745), who had enlisted his unequaled powers as a satirist and pamphleteer on the Tory side. His editorship of "The Examiner" (1710-11) is almost the high-water mark of ferocity in political journalism. But his political activities, except in so far as they affect his literary career and personal character, need not detain us. Born in Dublin of Protestant parents, he went to Trinity College and received his B.A. degree there in 1685 "by special favor" after it had once been refused because he would not learn the old-fashioned logic taught in the Irish capital; he thought he could reason well enough without it, and he was undoubtedly right, but such arrogance shocked the tutors. Supported at the university by the charity of one relative, he passed into the service of another, Sir William Temple, a statesman and writer of some note in his own day; in Temple's household he met another dependent, younger than himself, Esther Johnson, whom he befriended and perhaps ultimately married, though this is not certain. Flinging himself out of Temple's service, in a fit of temper, he returned to Ireland, became a Protestant clergyman, and obtained a small living at Laracor near Dublin. But, being fiercely ambitious, he spent most of his time in London. An eighteenth-century *Life of Swift* tells an odd story of his first appearance at the St. James's coffee-house. One day Addison and his friends saw there a clergyman who came in and put his hat on the table, walked back and forth for half an hour, settled his bill, and went out again without saying a word or paying any other attention to anybody. He did this several days, and the habitués called him "the mad parson." But at last, seeing a gentleman just come from the country, the strange clergyman walked straight up to him and said abruptly, "Pray, sir, do you know any good weather in the world?" A little startled, the gentleman answered, "Yes, sir, I thank God, I remember a great deal of good weather in my time." "That is more," Swift retorted, "than I can say. I never remember any weather that was not too hot or too cold, too wet or too dry; but, however God Almighty contrives it, at the end of the year 'tis all very well."

SWIFT

As Swift made himself better known in London society, the unceremonious arrogance of his manners became proverbial. When Harley, the Tory leader, sent him a bank-note in return for his first articles, Swift returned the money and demanded an apology. When St. John, Secretary of State, received him with some indifference, Swift exclaimed that he would not be treated like a school-boy, and the great minister excused himself on the ground that he had been up several nights at business "and one night at drinking." With great ladies he was equally insistent on receiving not merely courtesy but deference.

There can be no question of the force of Swift's intelligence or his power of seeing things in a way quite detached from the usual prepossessions and prejudices. But his very power of working out the logical consequences of a point of view often assumed ironically for the sake of confounding an adversary leads him into extravagances which are offensive to the cause he set out to plead. He was still in the service of Sir William Temple when he wrote his first great satire, *A Tale of a Tub* (1704), evidently intended to justify the moderate position of the Church of England as against the Catholics on the one hand and the Dissenters on the other. The Catholic doctrine of transubstantiation is set forth under the similitude of a demand made by Lord Peter (who represents the Church of Rome) upon his brothers (representing the Church of England and the Dissenters) to believe that a slice of bread is a cut of roast mutton. When they expostulate with him, Peter cries in a rage:

" 'Look ye, gentlemen, to convince you what a couple of blind, positive, ignorant, wilful puppies you are, I will use but this plain argument: by G——, it is true, good natural mutton as any in Leadenhall-market; and G—— confound you both eternally if you offer to believe otherwise.' "

Swift does not seem to see that this offhand manner of dealing with sacred things will carry a long way and be offensive not only to Catholics but to all Christians.

So, at a later date, when he wished to score a point against the tolerant policy of the Whigs in matters of religion, he offered

TRAVELS

INTO SEVERAL

Remote NATIONS

OF THE

WORLD.

In FOUR PARTS.

By *LEMUEL GULLIVER*,
First a SURGEON, and then a CAP-
TAIN of several SHIPS.

VOL. I.

LONDON:

Printed for BENJ. MOTTE, *at the*
Middle Temple-Gate *in* Fleet-ſtreet.
MDCCXXVI.

an ironical *Argument to prove that the Abolishing of Christianity in England may, as Things now stand, be attended with some inconveniences* (1708). No one had proposed to abolish Christianity or even to disestablish the Church of England, but for controversial purposes Swift puts himself into the position of one who believes that all parties are set upon this aim. He professes to be a defender of nominal, not of real Christianity, which has been for some time "wholly laid aside by general consent, as utterly inconsistent with our present schemes of wealth and power." To offer to restore primitive Christianity would indeed be "a wild project; it would be to dig up foundations; to destroy at one blow all the wit and half the learning of the kingdom."

"I do very much apprehend, that in six months time after the act is passed for the extirpation of the Gospel, the Bank and East India stock may fall at least one per cent. And since that is fifty times more than ever the wisdom of our age thought fit to venture for the preservation of Christianity, there is no reason we should be at so great a loss, merely for the sake of destroying it."

The irony is manifest enough, but it cut too deep to be easily understood by people of mediocre intelligence (including Queen Anne), and Swift never obtained the bishopric which he no doubt expected as a reward for his party zeal. He had to content himself with the deanery of St. Patrick's Cathedral, Dublin, to which he retired when the death of Queen Anne and the establishment of Whig supremacy under the first two Georges deprived him of all chance of further preferment.

Swift hated Ireland. He writes of his induction into his deanery in 1713: "I thought I should have died with discontent and was horribly melancholy while they were installing me." His return to Dublin put an end to his *Journal,* the daily record of his doings in London which he sent to Esther Johnson, who, with her companion, Mrs. Dingley, had established herself in his little parish of Laracor. He was said to have married her secretly, but he never saw her alone. During his visits to London,

STELLA HESTER VANHOMRIGH

JOURNAL TO STELLA

another young girl, Hester Vanhomrigh, rich and beautiful, fell in love with him and followed him to Ireland. He corresponded with her and sent her a long complimentary poem, *Cadenus and Vanessa,* in which she is the heroine and he is Cadenus, or Decanus, the dean. Becoming suspicious about his relations with Esther Johnson, Vanessa wrote to Stella and asked if she were married to the dean. Stella gave the letter to Swift, who rode over to see Vanessa, threw her letter on the table, and rode off again without saying a word. Within a year Hester Vanhomrigh died (1723). Swift's position with respect to Stella remained unchanged up to her death in 1728. Why did he not marry her or, having married her, acknowledge the marriage? It has been conjectured that he had some physical defect or lived perhaps in dread of the insanity which afflicted his later years. Biographers and critics have searched and studied without being able to pluck out the heart of Swift's mystery. Delany, his first biographer, relates that once when he went to see Archbishop King, he met Dean Swift coming out with a countenance distracted with grief. The archbishop, who was still in tears when Delany went in, said to him, "Sir, you have just met the most unhappy man upon earth; but on the subject of his wretchedness you must never ask a question."

The *Journal to Stella* (written 1710-13), with its playfulness, endearments, and gentle humor, shows quite another side of Swift's character from his published works. So does the significant inscription on an envelope marked "Only a woman's hair" found among Swift's private papers after his death. He had kept the tress for twenty years.

In Ireland, Swift led the life of a disappointed and embittered man. He wrote to his friends in London and occasionally visited them, but his ecclesiastical duties, which he performed punctiliously if not devotedly, kept him among an ignorant and poverty-stricken people whom he despised. He could not, however, be blind to their misery, and to the neglect, not only of their interests, but of their necessities by the English Government. The fact that it was a Whig Government no doubt made

Swift all the more willing to strike at it, and an opportunity for attack was offered by the grant, in 1724, to one William Wood to coin copper money to the amount of half a million dollars for circulation in Ireland. The transaction, politically and commercially, was a legitimate one, according to the standards of the time, and Sir Isaac Newton, as Master of the Mint, was a member of a commission which certified that the coins issued were in accordance with the contract. But Swift, writing anonymously under the guise of an ordinary dry-goods storekeeper, or "draper," solemnly warned the Irish public against a depreciation of the currency which would advance the price of "bread and clothing and every common necessary of life." The Government offered a reward for information regarding the identity of the author of the pamphlet, and Swift avowed the responsibility by walking up to the Lord Lieutenant at a public reception and exclaiming in a loud voice, "So, my lord, this is a glorious exploit that you performed yesterday, in suffering a proclamation against a poor shopkeeper, whose only crime is an honest endeavor to save his country from ruin." Openly defied, the Government had not the courage to arrest Swift, or even to prosecute him, and the contract with Wood was canceled. Swift became the idol of the Irish people.

His contempt, however, was not merely for the English Government or their Irish victims, but for all humanity. It was, indeed, a time of cynical corruption under the premiership of Sir Robert Walpole, who controlled Parliament on the basis that every man had his price, and of brutal vice and degradation among the poor, not yet mitigated by the Methodist revival of religion or the modern humanitarian movement. In the highest and in the lowest sections of the society with which Swift was acquainted, humanity presented a sorry spectacle, and he gave vent to his loathing for mankind in an elaborately devastating fashion in *Gulliver's Travels* (1726). Under the thin disguise of a romantic traveler's tale of adventures in the unexplored parts of the earth, Swift lashes with his satire the folly of princes, the corruption of politicians, the vagaries of philosophers, the pre-

tensions of scientists, and the disgusting and vicious habits of
ordinary men. Nothing is stranger in the annals of literature
than the conversion of this bitterly satirical arraignment of the
human race into an amusing pastime for ingenuous youth.
Swift's powerful imagination, the vigorous lucidity of his style,
and his humorous presentation of human littleness and absurdity have kept their charm for the young reader, who is fortunately spared, by judicious editing, from Swift's exhibition of
human vileness and indecency.

The accession of George II renewed Swift's hopes of political influence and ecclesiastical preferment, and in 1727 he paid
what proved to be his last visit to London. Returning to Ireland
again disappointed, he poured forth his indignation at human
misery as he saw it around him in a pamphlet entitled *A Modest
Proposal for preventing the Children of poor People in Ireland
from becoming a Burden to their Parents or Country and for
making them beneficial to the Public* (1729). The proposal is
that poor children, whose parents cannot afford to maintain
them, should be sold for food. "I have been assured by a very
knowing American of my acquaintance in London, that a young
healthy child, well nursed, is, at a year old, a most delicious,
nourishing, and wholesome food, whether stewed, roasted,
baked, or boiled; and I make no doubt that it will equally serve
in a fricassee or a ragout." The first recommendation for this
policy, which is elaborately developed to its logical conclusions,
is that "it would greatly lessen the number of Papists, with
whom we are yearly overrun, being the principal breeders of
the nation, as well as our most dangerous enemies"; the last
recommendation is that "it would be a great inducement to
marriage." Finally, in a few bitter words, the writer sets forth
the miserable state of Ireland—the old "every day dying and
rotting, by cold and famine and filth and vermin," the young
unable to get work and for lack of nourishment losing the
strength to perform casual labor if they should get the opportunity.

About this time Swift's health, never very robust, suffered a serious breakdown. In 1728, the year of Stella's death, he expressed his desire to "have done with the world" and "not die here in a rage, like a poisoned rat in a hole." He became deaf, partially blind, unable to read, unable to think; in his last years his mind gave way altogether, and he left a large legacy for those similarly afflicted. He was buried in his own cathedral, and his tomb bears an epitaph he had himself devised—*Ubi sæva indignatio ulterius cor lacerare nequit,* "where fierce indignation can no longer rend the heart." There are bitter and morbid elements in Swift's genius which alienate the gentle soul, but the genius is unmistakable. No one has looked more unflinchingly into the dark places of human nature, or expressed his sense of human depravity with more terrible and searching power. The foremost man of letters of his time, he despised literature as a profession and resented any suggestion of payment for his literary work, except in the case of *Gulliver's Travels,* for which Pope persuaded him to accept two hundred pounds from the publisher, on condition that the authorship remained unacknowledged, like everything else that Swift had printed or had been circulated in MS. copies. He confessed to Pope: "All my endeavors from a boy to distinguish myself were only for want of a great title and fortune, that I might be used like a lord by those who have an opinion of my parts: whether right or wrong, it is no great matter; and so the reputation of wit or great learning does the office of a blue ribbon or of a coach and six horses." After his retirement to Ireland he said: "I write pamphlets and follies merely for amusement, and when they are finished or I grow weary in the middle, I cast them into the fire, partly out of dislike, and chiefly because I know they will signify nothing." Yet he was fully conscious of his superiority to other men; he wrote, while yet a young man, to his first patron, Temple:

> To thee I owe that fatal bent of mind
> Still to unhappy, restless thoughts inclined;
> To thee, what oft I vainly strive to hide,
> That scorn of fools, by fools mistook for pride.

His last verses were, characteristically enough, on the reception of the news of his own death. Of his best friends he expected grief only for a month—or a week—or a day:

> My female friends, whose tender hearts
> Have better learned to act their parts,
> Receive the news in doleful dumps:
> "The Dean is dead—(pray what is trumps?)"

No writer ever strove more desperately to tell the truth about himself, as about other men; and no writer has remained more completely an enigma.

Though Swift hated and despised mankind in general, he made close personal friendships, most of which found their social and literary center in the Scriblerus Club, founded by Arbuthnot in 1713. Among this group of satirists DR. JOHN ARBUTHNOT (1667-1735) seems to have been closest to Swift in personal affection as well as nearest to him in the character of his genius. A Scotch physician who sought fortune in London, Arbuthnot became by a lucky chance medical adviser to Queen Anne and was in close personal relations with her up to the time of her death. His *History of John Bull* (1712) has much in common with Swift's *Tale of a Tub,* published eight years earlier; on the other hand, Arbuthnot seems to have originated and to some extent worked out the idea which was later developed by Swift into *Gulliver's Travels.* Both Swift and Arbuthnot contributed to the elaboration of the memoirs of *Martinus Scriblerus,* published among the works of Pope in 1741, and they have also been credited with a share in the plan of *The Dunciad.*

Among the members of the Scriblerus Club ALEXANDER POPE (1688-1744) is probably the most famous and the least sympathetic. This lack of sympathy on the part of the modern reader is as much due to Pope's personal character as to the character of his literary work. A modern poet, Edith Sitwell, in a recent biography (1930) has made a valiant attempt to rehabilitate Pope's reputation, both as a man of letters and as

POPE

a man, but she has to admit that he suffered from "fatal vanity," "a habit of mystification," and "a constitutional inhibition against speaking the truth." To these failings other students of the confused circumstances of Pope's literary and personal quarrels have added petty malice, vindictiveness, and a willingness to sacrifice his friends and associates if their interests clashed with his self-esteem or personal advantage.

It would be unjust to omit from the account of Pope's moral defects a consideration of the physical disabilities in which, at any rate in part, they originated. A delicate child, he grew up a humpbacked dwarf, unable to get up or go to bed without assistance. "He was so weak as to be extremely sensitive of cold, so that he wore a kind of fur doublet, under a shirt of very coarse warm linen with fine sleeves. When he rose, he was invested in a bodice made of stiff canvas, being scarce able to hold himself erect till it was laced, and he then put on a flannel waistcoat. One side was contracted. His legs were so slender that he enlarged their bulk with three pairs of stockings, which were drawn on and off by the maid." At meals he had to be accommodated, like a child, with a special chair, and when he dined with his intimates he wore a velvet cap, for "his hair had fallen almost all away."

It is doubtful whether Pope's physical weakness arose from an inherited defect (his father suffered from a slight curvature of the spine), or from being trampled upon at the age of three by an enraged cow, or from excessive study in his childhood. The son of a Catholic of the middle class, he was denied the usual opportunities for education, and spent a solitary and studious boyhood at small Catholic schools or under Catholic tutors. His enforced lack of the ordinary boyish pleasures and activities encouraged in him a natural bent for study and literary work; at the age of twelve he had made many translations, had written a tragedy (out of the *Iliad*) and an *Ode to Solitude,* and had already embarked on an epic entitled *Alexander, Prince of Rhodes.* About this time, too, he persuaded a friend to take him to the coffee-house frequented by Dryden, whom he looked upon with veneration and observed very particularly: he was "plump, of a fresh color, with a down look, and not very conversable," so the little boy did not converse with him, and Dryden died soon after.

Pope no doubt yielded to the temptation to exaggerate the literary achievements of his childhood, but he was undoubtedly precocious, and in the main the lines he penned (*Prologue to the Satires*, 1735) on his early devotion to literature are true:

> Why did I write? What sin to me unknown
> Dipped me in ink? My parents, or my own?
> As yet a child, nor yet a fool to fame,
> I lisped in numbers, for the numbers came.
> I left no calling for this idle trade,
> No duty broke, no father disobeyed.
> The Muse but served to ease some friend, not wife,
> To help me through this long disease, my life.

At seventeen Pope made the acquaintance of William Wycherley, a famous writer of Restoration comedy, now in his dotage so far as literature was concerned, but able when over seventy to trick his nephew out of an inheritance by marrying a young wife just before his death, and loading the estate with a jointure of four hundred pounds a year. Wycherley received from the youthful bride a hundred pounds cash, and made to her this last request: "My dear, it is only this, that you will never marry an old man again." Pope records this dying bon mot of the old rake who had begun his career as the lover of a royal mistress (the Duchess of Cleveland) and adds: "I cannot help remarking that sickness, which often destroys both wit and wisdom, yet seldom has power to remove that talent which we call humor. Mr. Wycherley showed this, even in this last compliment, though I think his request a little hard, for why should he bar her from doubling the jointure on the same easy terms?"

Wycherley introduced Pope to William Walsh, a famous critic of that day, who advised the young aspirant to be a *correct* poet, as that was the only way of excellency left: "We have had several great poets, but we never had one that was correct." More advantageous to the young poet than the advice was Walsh's recommendation of Pope's *Pastorals,* written in imitation of Virgil's *Eclogues,* to the leading publisher of the time, Jacob Tonson, who printed them in his *Miscellany* of 1709, together with a translation from the *Iliad* and a version from Chaucer by the same youthful hand.

It is noteworthy that this first publication involved Pope in his first literary quarrel. He had already written a treatise in verse on the art of poetry, after the manner of Horace, and this was published in 1711 under the title *An Essay on Criticism.* In this Pope made a slighting reference to John Dennis, a poverty-stricken and irascible critic who had spoken slightingly of the *Pastorals.* Dennis replied in a violent article in which he referred to Pope's physical deformity and wound up with the assertion that it was "impossible that his outward form, though it be that of downright monkey, should differ so much from human shape as his unthinking immaterial part does from human understanding."

The *Essay on Criticism* won for Pope the approval of Addison and Steele, but the political references in *Windsor Forest* (1713) alienated his Whig friends and threw him into the opposite camp, among the Tory wits of the Scriblerus Club. Thus began the friendship with Swift which lasted till Swift's mental incapacity put an end to their correspondence. Pope also blamed Addison for advising him not to attempt to improve the first version of *The Rape of the Lock* (1712); Pope was urged to write this poem in order to reconcile two Catholic families of his acquaintance; a fashionable beauty, Arabella Fermor, was offended because Lord Petre had, without her permission, cut off a lock of her hair. The poem made the lady angrier than before and some of the compliments to her are of a rather satirical turn, but in its more highly finished form it remains the best example of Pope's poetical genius. It is an elaborately elegant trifle in the mock heroic style, but its airy grace has won for it the attention of readers who have no interest in his more

MARTHA BLOUNT   LADY MARY WORTLEY MONTAGU

POPE'S VILLA AT TWICKENHAM

serious philosophical works or his embittered criticisms of the forgotten poetasters of his own time.

It was in 1713 that Pope put out his proposals for a translation by subscription of Homer's *Iliad*. This undertaking, which was zealously supported by his friends, absorbed his energies for the next half-dozen years; it consolidated alike his literary fame and financial position, enabling him to make a profit of over five thousand pounds—an enormous sum for literary work at that time—and to move into a house of his own at Twickenham on the bank of the upper Thames. Here he lived for the remainder of his life, cultivated his garden (in which he built his famous grotto), received the fashionable and aristocratic world, entertained his friends and his women worshipers, Lady Mary Wortley Montagu (with whom he had a terrific quarrel) and Martha Blount, who was his faithful adorer from the beginning to the end of his literary career. Lady Wortley Montagu as the precocious little daughter of the Duke of Kingston had been the "toast" of the Kit-Cat Club, and early won a reputation as a fashionable wit and beauty; Pope paid her ardent court (by correspondence) when her husband's appointment as ambassador took her to Constantinople, and sent her there a copy of his collected works, issued in 1717. He drew her special attention to *The Epistle of Eloisa* to Abelard, the principal novelty in the new issue, and most especially to one allusive passage in it, doubtless the concluding lines:

> And since if fate some future bard should join
> In sad similitude of griefs to mine,
> Condemned whole years in absence to deplore,
> And image charms he must behold no more;
> Such if there be, who loves so long, so well,
> Let him our sad, our tender story tell;
> The well-sung woes will soothe my pensive ghost;
> He best can paint them who shall feel them most.

Pope (alas! for the duplicity of men and poets) had previously copied out these lines for Martha Blount with the implication that she was the object of his undying attachment; but this was not the cause of his quarrel with Lady Mary. It may have sprung from a deep-seated difference of opinion on literary matters; or there may be some truth in the story that after her return from Constantinople he made her a declaration of passion and she laughed in his face.

Pope's explanation of his break with Lady Mary was that "she had too much wit." Their friendship lasted some half-dozen years and Pope obtained for her a house at Twickenham belonging to Sir Godfrey Kneller, the famous painter, whom he persuaded to do her portrait. The quarrel lasted much longer, and on either side bitter and even coarse things were said which are better forgotten.

Other quarrels and other literary activities occupied Pope at Twickenham. When he had finished Homer's *Iliad* he translated the *Odyssey* (1725-26) with the aid of Broome and Fenton, who did most of the work and received a small part of the pay, so that the collaborators parted company with mutual dissatisfaction. Pope's edition of Shakspere, which preceded the *Odyssey,* brought the poet little financial return and even less reputation. Lewis Theobald, of greater learning than Pope but with less skill in controversy, pointed out some errors in the edition, and was punished for his audacity by being made the hero of the first issue of *The Dunciad* (1728). In later editions he was displaced as king of the realm of dullness by Colley Cibber, for whom Pope had conceived an even greater antipathy on account of various grievances, including a derisive reference to a mummy and a crocodile figuring as personages in an unsuccessful play to which Pope had contributed. Finally the poet rolled up the enmities of a lifetime in an enlarged edition of the *Dunciad* (1742) which proved to be the last, for its issue was followed not long after by Pope's death.

It would be tedious to go farther into these literary animosities and recriminations, which occupied a large share of Pope's attention in the closing years of his life. At the suggestion of the fallen Tory leader, Henry St. John, Lord Bolingbroke,

Pope wrote a versified philosophical treatise, *The Essay on Man* (1733), followed by four *Moral Essays* in verse, intended to be parts of a philosophical system. Neither Pope's vague Catholicism nor Bolingbroke's equally vague deism offered any basis for original thought, but some of Pope's well-turned commonplaces are still cherished in the popular memory as embodiments of traditional wisdom.

Pope brought to perfection a school of poetry which began to fall into decay almost immediately after his death, but was a long time in dying; he was still held in high honor by Byron at the beginning of the nineteenth century. It is impossible now to put him back on the throne, though the attempt has been made. But he should have credit for being the first to earn money and renown as a man of letters and nothing else. While Defoe was making a scanty living as a struggling journalist, Steele and Addison were gaining political promotion, and Swift was seeking ecclesiastical preferment, Pope was winning an independent income and a prominent place in society as a poet. It is a phenomenon to be noted, for it has not often happened in English history.

Voltaire visited Pope at Twickenham and had a cordial reception, though his naughty stories drove Pope's old mother from the room. But the French philosopher and wit met with a very different experience when he made a call upon Pope's friend and fellow-member of the Scriblerus Club, WILLIAM CONGREVE (1670-1729), whose *Way of the World* had continued and outshone the brilliant (and shameless) Restoration comedy of Wycherley. Voltaire's compliments upon Congreve's dramatic and literary work were ill received, for Congreve had forsworn the stage, to become commissioner of hackney coaches, wine licenses, etc. "I hope sir, you are calling upon me in my quality as a gentleman and not as a writer," said the offended official. "If you were merely a gentleman," retorted the French man of letters, "I should not have taken the trouble to pay you a visit."

The incident may be taken as merely an illustration of

ARBUTHNOT

BOLINGBROKE

CONGREVE

GAY

English snobbishness or indicative of the relative social position of the professional writer in England and France at the time. Another member of the Scriblerus Club, JOHN GAY (1685-1732), finding a multifarious activity as journalist, dramatist, and poet insufficient for a respectable maintenance, had recourse to the ancient system of patronage, and found refuge first in the household of the Duchess of Monmouth and then in that of the Duke of Queensbury. His greatest success, *The Beggar's Opera* (1728), was suggested by Swift, who thought a pastoral of Newgate prison, with drabs and thieves as its principal characters, might make "an odd pretty sort of thing." Gay elaborated the idea and, substituting ballad tunes for the arias of the Italian opera then in fashion, carried the town by storm. It was successfully revived in London and in the United States a few years ago, and in July, 1931, was acted in Moscow when Bernard Shaw was the guest of the Soviet Government, being the only English opera on the official repertoire.

RICHARDSON

CHAPTER VII

THE RISE OF THE MODERN NOVEL

The great achievement of the eighteenth century was the creation of the modern novel. We may recognize its ancestors in rimed or prose romance or in the Elizabethan novel (which was really a diffuse short story). We may acknowledge immediate predecessors in the realistic narrative of Defoe, the satirical inventiveness of Swift, the polished character sketches of Steele and Addison; but when all this has been taken into account, it must be admitted that the actual creator of the modern novel was SAMUEL RICHARDSON (1689-1761). We have two portraits of him—one drawn by a contemporary painter and reproduced on the opposite page, the other from his own pen: "Short; rather plump than emaciated, notwithstanding his complaints: about five foot five inches: fair wig, lightish cloth coat, all black besides; one hand generally in his bosom, the other, a cane in it, which he leans upon, under the skirts of his coat usually, that it may imperceptibly serve him as a support, when attacked by sudden tremors or startings, and dizziness, which too frequently attack him, but, thank God, not so often as formerly; looking directly foreright, as passers-by would imagine, but observing all that stirs on either hand of him without moving his short neck, hardly ever turning back; of a light brown complexion; teeth not yet failing him; smoothish faced, and ruddy cheeked; at some times looking to be about sixty-five, at other times much younger; a regular, even pace, stealing away ground rather than seeming to rid it; a gray eye, too often overclouded by mistiness from the head; by chance lively—very lively it will be if he have hope of seeing a lady he loves and honors, his eye always on the ladies: if they have very large hoops he looks down and supercilious, and as if he would be thought wise, but perhaps the sillier for that; as he approaches a lady his eye is never fixed first upon her face but upon her feet, and then he raises it up, pretty quickly for a dull eye; and one would think (if we thought him at all worthy of observation) that from her air and (the last beheld) her face, he sets her down in his mind as *so* or *so,* and then passes on to the next object he meets; only then looking back if he greatly likes or dislikes, as if he would see if the lady appear to be all of a piece, in the one light or in the other."

Before the publication of *Pamela* in November, 1740, there was nothing to indicate to the outside world that this "perfectly respectable and rather priggish tradesman, owning a suburban villa, a thriving business, two wives (one dead, of course), a family, and a fair wig," was the genius destined to start the modern novel on the way on which it was to continue for two centuries or more. The story of the composition of *Pamela* is one of the most extraordinary in the history of literature and is worth telling in some detail.

Born of humble parents in a provincial village, with few educational opportunities, Richardson at the age of thirteen had developed a talent for winning the confidence of ingenuous maidens who "revealed to him their love-secrets" in order that he might help them in the composition of their love-letters. But this did not hinder him from being apprenticed to a London printer at seventeen, setting up for himself in Fleet Street at thirty, marrying his old master's daughter a year or two later, becoming a successful business man and printer to the House of Commons, with a comfortable house at Fulham—now 111 North End Road. Except as a printer and publisher, his nearest connection with literature was membership of the Society for the Encouragement of Learning, established in 1736. Charles Rivington, the founder of the famous publishing firm of that name, also was a member of the Society, and in this way or through common business interests, Rivington and Richardson became close friends. In or before 1739, Rivington and another publisher named Osborn, to quote Richardson's own account, "entreated me to write for them a little volume of letters, in a common style, on such subjects as might be of use to those country readers, who were unable to indite for themselves." "Will it be any harm," said Richardson, "in a piece you want to be written so low, if we should instruct them how they should think and act in common cases, as well as indite?" This characteristic suggestion of moral teaching, so well calculated to attract the English middle class then coming to power, appealed instantly to the two publishers, and they were the more urgent for Richardson to begin the little volume at once. He set to work and had composed a number of letters as planned, when, as he was writing "two or three letters to instruct handsome girls who were obliged to go out to service, as we phrase it, how to avoid the snares that might be laid against their virtue," there recurred to his mind an account he had heard twenty or more years before of a beautiful and accomplished servant-girl who, by resisting the immoral pursuit of her master, had compelled him to marry her. According to Richardson's own account, he had frequently recommended this true story to professional authors as a subject for literary treatment, but without effect. "And hence sprung *Pamela*. . . . When I began to recollect what had, so many years before, been told me by my friend, I thought the story, if written in an easy and natural manner, suitable to the simplicity of it, might possibly introduce a new species of writing that might possibly turn young people into a course of reading different from the pomp and parade of romance-writing, and dismissing the improbable and marvelous, with which novels generally abound, might tend to promote the cause of religion and virtue."

When this idea occurred to him, Richardson promptly laid aside further work on the handbook of familiar letters (which was published later), and started writing *Pamela* on November 10, 1739, as he methodically noted on the manuscript at the time. On January 10, 1740, he had finished his first draft, and *Pamela* was published in two volumes in November of that year, with a few paragraphs at the end to indicate that the girl married her

CLARISSA.

OR, THE

HISTORY

OF A

YOUNG LADY:

Comprehending

The moſt Important Concerns *of* Private LIFE.

And particularly ſhewing,

The DISTRESSES that may attend the Miſconduct
Both of PARENTS and CHILDREN,

In Relation to MARRIAGE.

Publiſhed by the EDITOR *of* PAMELA.

VOL. I.

LONDON:
Printed for S. Richardſon:

And Sold by A. MILLAR, over-againſt *Catharine-ſtreet* in the *Strand*:
J. and JA. RIVINGTON, in *St. Paul's Church-yard*:
JOHN OSBORN, in *Pater-noſter Row*;
And by J. LEAKE, at *Bath*.

M.DCC.XLVIII.

foiled seducer and lived happily ever after. It is a remarkable production, setting forth by means of letters written in a simple but diffuse style, with abundant and realistic detail, the wiles and stratagems of the wicked master, and the feminine arts and contrivances by which the lovely Pamela outwits his low designs and compels him to have recourse to the honorable expedient of marriage.

The success of this "new species of writing" was immediate and enormous, and continuations of Pamela's story by other hands were announced. To defeat these imitators, Richardson speedily composed another two volumes of letters between Pamela in her exalted condition and "persons of figure and quality upon the most important and entertaining subjects in genteel life." The pretense of private correspondence is maintained and no authorship is avowed; the title-page announces that these two volumes are "printed for S. Richardson" and "sold by Rivington and Osborn." They were issued in December, 1741, and were no less popular at the time than their predecessors, though later critics have judged them of inferior interest. They show, with great skill, Pamela's wit and tact in overcoming the prejudices of her husband's relations and making herself universally respected and beloved; but the excitement of pursuit and evasion no longer sustains the reader's attention.

Even if we go back to the time of Lyly's *Euphues* (1578-80), the English novel had been written for women, and it was women who made the fortunes of *Pamela,* carrying the book publicly to places of entertainment to show that they were in the current fashion. Richardson said boldly, "My acquaintance lies chiefly among the ladies; I care not who knows it." It is not surprising, therefore, to find him surrounded by a circle of female adorers in London and a still larger circle of adoring female correspondents elsewhere. Foremost among these was the admiring lady who, when he had published four volumes of his next novel, *Clarissa* (1747-48), wrote to him under an assumed name imploring and adjuring him not to let the unfortunate heroine die of grief, but to allow her to marry her seducer. The heroine of this second story is of a higher rank than Pamela and has not her predecessor's engaging simplicity, but is a girl of excellent birth and education, who, when about to be forced by unsympathetic parents to accept an uncongenial suitor, flies for refuge to her lover, who deceives and betrays her. Richardson, in spite of his desire to please his fair correspondent and the public, was too much of an artist to allow Clarissa to escape the melancholy end he had destined for her, but he continued for over a year to exchange with his unknown correspondent long letters, which became more and more intimate in tone before she revealed herself as Lady Bradshaigh, of Haigh, in Lancashire. It was to her, still concealed under the veil of an assumed name, that Richardson wrote the description of himself quoted above, so that she might recognize him as he walked in the park, and it was not until a month or two later that she consented to an interview. A voluminous correspondence was maintained between them up to the time of his death.

It was at Lady Bradshaigh's request that Richardson attempted in his last novel, *Sir Charles Grandison* (seven volumes, 1753-54), to portray a perfect hero, in compensation to the male sex for their very faulty representatives in *Pamela* and *Clarissa;* the attempt was not altogether successful, for Grandison is too much of a prig. It was upon Lady Bradshaigh, too, that Richardson played one of his few recorded jokes. When *Sir Charles Grandison* was still in course of publication, Richardson professed to her an intention to kill off the heroine as he had done Clarissa. He had really no such intention, but he had a wicked desire to excite and alarm Lady Bradshaigh, and to enjoy her protestations. Afterward he expressed regret for his action as "a private and unexpected stab given to a beloved friend, whom I looked upon as the sweet companion of my retired hours, my guide, my instructress, my repose in weariness, my joy in trouble." The intimacy was, in fact, not so close as Richardson here suggested, for his correspondent was mindful of her dignity as a great lady and was not inclined to be on too friendly terms with the author-printer, much as she loved to discuss his creations and laud his genius by letter.

Richardson succeeded, not only in England but abroad, by his merits—his knowledge of the feminine heart, his power of psychological analysis, and his skill in telling a story in the epistolary manner—but it was by a stroke of good fortune that even his defects contributed to the development of the novel in a way that he himself entirely disapproved. It was Richardson's sentimentality and its eager acceptance by the public that spurred HENRY FIELDING (1707-54), already an established critic and dramatist, to invent a different kind of fiction—different in spirit as well as in form. The rather unctuous middle-class morality of *Pamela,* with its suggestion that, for maidens, as for merchants, honesty is the best policy, and that they should sell their chastity in the most profitable market, offended and amused Fielding, who was of aristocratic birth and connections, and on the stage and in the press had already developed his gift for satire. The son of a spendthrift general, he had failed in the attempt to retrieve the family fortunes by abducting an heiress; and as he had expensive tastes, he was driven to professional authorship because his choice was "to become either a hackney-writer or a hackney-coachman." He brought to the novel a knowledge of human nature and the ways of the world, robust humor, great physical vigor, and a frank and cheerful enjoyment of the good things of life, altogether different from Richardson's puritanical concentration on moral improvement and his somewhat morbid concern with the physical side of sex. Above all, Fielding was a professional writer; Richardson avows that when he was in course of preparing for his tradesmen friends a handbook of familiar letters, he fell by accident upon "a new species of writing," and his title-pages show that the composition of letters for moral edification and imitation continued to be a large part of his plan in fiction. Fielding aimed deliberately at the development of a new kind of writing, not hitherto attempted in the English language: he knew and used foreign models with which Richardson had little or no

acquaintance. The division of credit is very well assigned in Drinkwater's phrase: "If Richardson invented the English novel, Fielding gave it, for the first time, absolute literary distinction."

In his first irritation at the success of *Pamela,* Fielding was apparently guilty of the publication of a coarse parody entitled *Shamela.* In it Pamela is represented as the daughter of a profligate orange-woman, who trains her to practise all the wiles of her real profession. The girl writes to her mother: "I thought once of making a little fortune of my Person; I now intend to make a great one out of my Virtue." Mr. Booby, as the Mr. B— of Richardson's novel is now called, has no chance against her superior guile. Fielding seems to have been under the impression that *Pamela* was written by Colley Cibber, a personal enemy of his; he had no personal feeling against Richardson. Richardson believed Fielding was the author of *Shamela* (though the fact has never been proved) and never forgave him.

Shamela was published within six months of the first part of *Pamela:* the second part of *Pamela* appeared in December, 1741. Within three months (1742) Fielding published (first anonymously, but afterward with his name given) a more elaborate parody, under the title, *The History of the Adventures of Joseph Andrews, and of his Friend, Mr. Abraham Adams. Written in Imitation of the Manner of Cervantes, Author of Don Quixote.* The wording of the title is significant: in the first place, *Joseph Andrews* is not a series of letters, from and to imaginary persons, but a connected narrative, told by the author with such comment upon the characters and incidents as he may think appropriate. In the second place, it is a story of adventure, after the manner of *Don Quixote,* to which Fielding acknowledges his indebtedness. Most important of all, Fielding's spirit, like that of his model, is satiric and realistic. He portrays life as it is, and presents to us characters of such mixed impulses and emotions as life itself provides. *Pamela* remains the background of the satire, but only the background; she and her husband, Mr. Boothby, both appear, and her chaplain becomes Par-

THE
HISTORY
OF
TOM JONES,
A
FOUNDLING.

In SIX VOLUMES.

By HENRY FIELDING, Esq;

—— *Mores hominum multorum vidit.* ——

LONDON:

Printed for A. MILLAR, over-against
Catharine-street in the Strand.
MDCCXLIX.

son Adams, who is the Don Quixote of Fielding's adaptation
from Cervantes, but entirely his own creation. The part of
Sancho Panza, who is to play the practical accompaniment to
the Parson's reckless idealism, falls to Joseph Andrews, Pamela's
brother, a youth endowed with every physical charm, but not
overstocked with brains; he has none of the shrewdness of his
prototype, Sancho, but rather a naïve simplicity, following without question the advice and example of his sister Pamela, whom
he greatly admires. He is the handsomest and genteelest footman
in the kingdom, but when his widowed mistress, Lady Booby,
plays the part of Potiphar's wife to her Joseph, he reminds her
that he is the brother of Pamela, and would be ashamed that
the chastity of his family, which is preserved in her, should be
stained in him. His moral scruples are not altogether abstract,
but are backed up by a genuine love for his fellow-servant
Fanny. The love-sick widow, however, does not pursue her
amour with the desperate ardor shown by her brother-in-law;
when Joseph repulses her impetuous advances, she promptly
turns him out of doors. Robbed, beaten, and left naked on the
roadside, he is conveyed by a passing stage-coach to an inn,
where he falls in with Parson Adams, and they continue on their
way together. Many adventures befall them: Joseph again has
to defend his virtue; the lovely Fanny, who soon joins them, has
to be saved from abduction and worse. They return to Lady
Booby's, to find that Pamela is married to Mr. Booby, who
espouses Joseph's cause, and Pamela tries in vain to separate
Joseph from his sweetheart. Finally, it appears that Joseph is
not Pamela's brother, but that Fanny is her sister, so that the
lovers are happily united.

Fielding received £183.11 (equal to about $1,000 of our
money) for *Joseph Andrews,* and it was fairly successful,
though it never equaled *Pamela* in popularity. It grew under
the author's hands from a parody to an independent story, but
it had not a complete life of its own, apart from its predecessor.
Fielding no doubt felt that he could do better than this, and the
generosity of an admiring friend enabled him to work quietly

in the country on *Tom Jones,* which is the central work of his career and probably the greatest literary achievement of the century. He received £600 for the copyright the year before it was published, and its issue on February 28, 1749, was justly regarded as a great event in the literary world. The title runs: *The History of Tom Jones, a Foundling. In six Volumes. By Henry Fielding, Esq. Mores hominum multorum vidit.* The Latin motto, "He saw the manners of many men," probably refers to the author rather than to the hero of the novel. In 1748, Fielding had been appointed a magistrate for Westminster and for Middlesex, and no doubt felt himself a man of some public, as well as literary, importance. Richardson's *Clarissa* had completed publication only two months before *Tom Jones* appeared, so that the two great rivals might be said to be running neck and neck. *Clarissa* is generally regarded as Richardson's masterpiece, and *Tom Jones* is certainly Fielding's best novel. It carries out his conception of the novel as a description and criticism of manners on a large scale, in narrative form, in which the author's personality is subordinated to the interest of the story, with no attempt to obliterate the author altogether: frankly a work of fiction, in which plot, character, and comment each has due weight. This form, after its adoption by Jane Austen, became the standard form of the English novel.

TOBIAS SMOLLETT (1721-71) was, like Fielding, a hardworking journalist and translated *Don Quixote* and *Gil Blas,* so that he was well acquainted with his important Continental predecessors. He chose as his first model *Gil Blas,* Le Sage's episodical story of adventure, told by the hero himself—a sort of heroic vagabond. *The Adventures of Roderick Random* (1748) recounts in part the story of the author's own adventures as a surgeon's mate on the expedition to Cartagena, and gives a lively picture of the seafaring life of the period in all its crude repulsiveness, with an abundance of physical detail hard for the more delicate-minded reader to stomach. But he has a certain coarse vigor, and the wandering adventurer whom he introduced to English fiction has proved a frequent resource for

SMOLLETT
STERNE

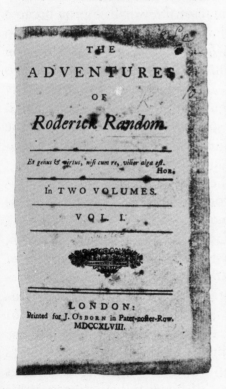

THE
ADVENTURES
OF
Roderick Random.

Et genus & virtus, nisi cum re, vilior alga est.
HOR.

In TWO VOLUMES.

VOL. I.

LONDON:
Printed for J. OSBORN in Pater-noster-Row.
MDCCXLVIII.

THE
LIFE
AND
OPINIONS
OF
TRISTRAM SHANDY,
GENTLEMAN.

Ταρασσει τὰς Ἀνθρώπες ὁ τὰ Πράγματα,
αλλα τὰ περι τῶν Πραγμάτων, Δογματα.

VOL. I.

1760.

Smollett's successors. Dickens used it with great originality and humor in *Pickwick* and *Martin Chuzzlewit,* Thackeray turned it to good account in *Barry Lyndon,* and in later times the same expedient has been freely employed by Compton Mackenzie and J. B. Priestley, whose *Good Companions* (1929) offered, at that time, the latest example of the type—but not the last.

Fielding attempted in *Tom Jones* to give the novel seriousness and greater definiteness of form by prefixing to each book a preliminary essay; he made no attempt to achieve objectivity, as it was later called, by throwing his story into the autobiographical or epistolary form; as the author-showman, he not only controls his puppets but occasionally steps forward in person to comment on their virtues or defects, their fortunes or misfortunes. This personal element was greatly extended by LAURENCE STERNE (1713-68) at the expense of the story proper. A popular clergyman, wit, and man of the world, Sterne became the darling of fashionable society by his publication in 1760 of the first two volumes of *The Life and Opinions of Tristram Shandy, Gent.* The title was, in itself, a jest, for the first two volumes left the supposed hero still unborn; but the originality of the tone of the composition, now humorous, now sentimental, and occasionally sauced with a spice of indecency, made all the more obvious by profuse apologies, won for it at the time (and have kept for it ever since) a multitude of admirers.

Sterne saw no reason why he should not produce two volumes of "Shandyism" a year for the next forty years, but his health failed, and only two more instalments appeared—the first in 1765 and the second in 1767, the year before his death, when he also published the first instalment of *A Sentimental Journey through France and Italy.* Posing always as an irresponsible trifler and fundamentally insincere, Sterne yet wins attention and even affection by the extraordinary suppleness of his style and the unexpected felicities of his turns of phrase. Although he discards the ordinary weapons of the novelist's armory, he nevertheless delights our minds and sometimes touches our hearts by the deftness of his wit, the delicacy of his sentiment, or the subtle indelicacy of some ingenious allusion. Some of his characters and situations—Uncle Toby and the Widow Wadham in *Tristram Shandy,* the *fille de chambre* and the starling in *A Sentimental Journey*—have become common-places of literary allusion. His peculiar manner has proved inimitable, though it has often been imitated. Richardson, Field-ing, Smollett, each had a line of successors, but Sterne stands alone.

Of OLIVER GOLDSMITH (1728-74) Dr. Johnson said, in a Latin epitaph and epigram which is often quoted, that he touched nothing which he did not adorn. It was a good phrase, coming rather from the head than from the heart, as most epi-taphs do; it was from the heart, however, that Johnson spoke when he ejaculated, on finding that Goldsmith had died two thousand pounds in debt, "Was there ever poet more trusted!" The irresponsible Irishman who made the tour of Europe "with a guinea in his pocket, one shirt to his back, and a flute in his hand," made his way through life in much the same fashion—except that he had not always the guinea. When he was about to be arrested for debt, he sent a note of distress to Johnson, who forwarded the necessary guinea—and Goldsmith promptly spent it on a bottle of wine; Johnson, following up the despatch of the guinea, found Goldsmith thus engaged, "put the cork in the bottle," and obtained from him the manuscript of *The Vicar of Wakefield.* This brought sixty pounds from a publisher, and that time Goldsmith escaped the debtors' prison. Similarly Dr. Percy found him engaged on *An Inquiry into the Present State of Polite Learning in Europe* in a London court inhabited mainly by washerwomen, and this was only one of the many pieces of hack writing which Goldsmith undertook and re-ceived pay for. His play *She Stoops to Conquer* alternated with Sheridan's *School for Scandal* in saving the eighteenth-century drama from oblivion for the next hundred years, and his poem *The Deserted Village* has not been altogether forgotten. But the tale of *The Vicar of Wakefield,* which saved him from prison, has done most to keep him as a living memory for posterity. Its

JOHNSON

BOSWELL

GOLDSMITH

BURKE

apparently artless simplicity and its genuine good feeling are irresistible.

In the Literary Club which Dr. Johnson and Sir Joshua Reynolds founded in 1764, Goldsmith was often the butt of other men's wit: Reynolds, it is true, said of him: "There is no man whose company is more liked," but to most of them it would have been a terrible shock to realize that of all their works, some of Goldsmith's were the most likely to endure. David Garrick, perhaps the greatest actor the English stage ever produced, said of Goldsmith that he "wrote like an angel, but talked like poor Poll"; and Johnson remarked upon his rashness in embarking upon a subject of conversation without knowing where he was to get off. The club potentate, "that great Cham of Literature, Samuel Johnson," would have been astonished if any one had dared to tell him that but for the assiduous devotion and biographical genius of his faithful BOSWELL his own vast powers of tongue and pen would have run little chance with posterity as compared with the genial fancy and ready humor of the volatile "Goldy."

Boswell's intellectual and literary powers were for a long time underestimated. Even so recently as half a century ago, an editor of the *Life of Johnson* could say in a note that certain anonymous verses quoted were "evidently Boswell's own; nobody else living would have printed anything so stupid." More recently Boswell's biographical skill has perhaps been overestimated, but it was certainly very great. The charm of the talk is principally Johnson's, but a large share of the success of the book is due to Johnson's interpreter. He was very much more than a mere recorder of other men's wit; he sets out (it was deliberate intention, as the Latin motto of the title-page shows) to bring to life again for us not merely Johnson's talk, but the whole man, with his shortcomings as well as his virtues. He shows us his hero with wig awry, his clothes unbuttoned, his stockings coming down, "and a pair of unbuckled shoes by way of slippers." He reports his contempt of clean linen and even of personal cleanliness, illustrated by his remark to a man who

THE

L I F E

OF

SAMUEL JOHNSON, LL.D.

COMPREHENDING

AN ACCOUNT OF HIS STUDIES
AND NUMEROUS WORKS,

IN CHRONOLOGICAL ORDER;

A SERIES OF HIS EPISTOLARY CORRESPONDENCE
AND CONVERSATIONS WITH MANY EMINENT PERSONS;

AND

VARIOUS ORIGINAL PIECES OF HIS COMPOSITION,
NEVER BEFORE PUBLISHED.

THE WHOLE EXHIBITING A VIEW OF LITERATURE AND LITERARY MEN
IN GREAT-BRITAIN, FOR NEAR HALF A CENTURY,
DURING WHICH HE FLOURISHED.

IN TWO VOLUMES.

By JAMES BOSWELL, Esq.

———— *Quò fit ut* OMNIS
Votiva pateat veluti deſcripta tabella
VITA SENIS.————   HORAT.

VOLUME THE FIRST.

LONDON:
PRINTED BY HENRY BALDWIN,
FOR CHARLES DILLY, IN THE POULTRY.
M DCC XCI.

showed him a cold bath, "Let well alone and be content. I hate immersion." He calls attention to Johnson's habit of "making little fishes talk like whales," as Goldsmith put it, and instances, as an example of "obscuring a thing in itself very plain," the definition, in Johnson's dictionary, of "network" as "anything reticulated or decupated at equal distances, with interstices between the intersections." Boswell was himself a great admirer of Fielding as a novelist, but he does not fail to quote Johnson's repeated and strongly expressed preference for the work of his friend Richardson, although Johnson admitted that "if you were to read Richardson for the story, your impatience would be so much fretted that you would hang yourself. You must read him for the sentiment." Boswell not only puts himself well into the background to bring forward his central figure; he gives every other speaker his place and turn, so that he succeeds in fulfilling the promise of his title page to exhibit "a view of literature and literary men in Great Britain for near half a century."

The loftiest-minded of that famous circle was EDMUND BURKE (1729-97). Although Irish by birth and education, he grasped more clearly than most Englishmen the fundamentally English conception of government as an organic process, the slow growth of centuries, not the sudden construction of any one mind or group of minds, however brilliant. He had the English distrust of mere logic, and the English faith in remedies applied to particular abuses as occasion may require; he was opposed to the abolition of ancient institutions, even if they were theoretically indefensible, so long as in practice they seemed to work for good—or, at any rate, to do no positive harm. He regarded politics as the art of doing things that were practical and expedient, rather than as a science based upon abstract principles. This explains the fervor of his defense of the American colonists on the one hand and the violence of his condemnation of the French Revolution on the other. Although Burke was easily the foremost political philosopher and orator of his time—and it was the time of Pitt, Fox, and Sheridan—he received no adequate recognition and held no government office of first-class importance. It is not to the credit of the Mother of Parliaments that his rising to speak was the signal for a general exodus, so that he became known as "the dinner bell of the House." Yet Johnson said of him that no one could shelter with him under a shed from a shower of rain without recognizing that he was in the presence of an extraordinary man. Burke united in an unusual degree two powers rare even when found alone—keen philosophic insight and the strength of feeling that lies behind all great oratory.

Other gifted members of the Literary Club besides those already mentioned were: Edward Gibbon (1737-94), the author of *The Decline and Fall of the Roman Empire;* the brothers Warton, one of whom made the first serious historical survey of English poetry; Bishop Percy, who collected English ballads and was thus an important contributor to the Romantic Revival; and ADAM SMITH, author of the first important treatise on political economy, *The Wealth of Nations* (1776).

ADAM SMITH

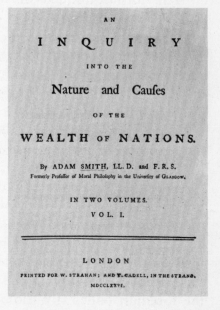

Of all these names, big with the prophecy of coming change, that of Adam Smith is perhaps the most remarkable. In its own way *The Wealth of Nations* was as important as the Declaration of Independence: it was a plea for freedom in industrial life, as the Declaration was a plea for freedom in political life. The two great movements of the eighteenth century were (1) the growth of political liberty and (2) the establishment of economics as a scientific study, offering not merely an explanation of the history of the past but guidance concerning the relations between capital and labor in the future. Its immediate effect was to help in the removal of the surviving elements of medieval practice and theory which still encumbered the industrial system; but it went much farther than the mere maxim to "buy in the cheapest market and sell in the dearest," into which its teaching was crystallized by the shrewd Manchester manufacturers of the nineteenth century. The Glasgow professor looked farther ahead and foreshadowed the economic practice not merely of the nineteenth century but of the twentieth. He says in Book I, Chapter VIII, of *The Wealth of Nations:*

"It is in the progressive state, while the society is advancing to the further acquisition, rather than when it has acquired its full complement of riches, that the condition of the laboring poor, of the great body of the people, seems to be the happiest and the most comfortable. It is hard in the stationary, and miserable in the declining state. The progressive state is in reality the cheerful and the hearty state to all the different orders of the society. The stationary is dull; the declining melancholy.

"The liberal reward of labor, as it encourages the propagation, so it increases the industry of the common people. The wages of labor are the encouragement of industry, which, like every other human quality, improves in proportion to the encouragement it receives. A plentiful subsistence increases the bodily strength of the laborer; and the comfortable hope of bettering his condition, and of ending his days perhaps in ease and plenty, animates him to exert that strength to the utmost. Where wages are high, accordingly, we shall always find the workmen more active, diligent, and expeditious, than where they are low."

But if *The Wealth of Nations* was a promise of good things to come, it was also a portent—a menace that other good things were destined to disappear. The Old England of quiet fields and peaceful villages, of country estates, churches, and cathedrals, of aristocratic institutions which had continued unchanged for more than a century—all this was to pass and in its place was coming the Modern England of mechanical industry, of noisy factories and squalid manufacturing towns, of railroads and steamboats, of automobiles and motor-buses, of telegraphs and telephones, of wireless and airplanes, of "movies" and "talkies." *Laissez faire et laissez aller*—freedom to manufacture and freedom to export—this was the simple creed that was to transform England and ultimately the entire world. Already the power-loom and the spinning-jenny had been invented, and the application of steam to purposes of manufacture and locomotion demonstrated. A revolution greater than that of 1688, more significant than the revolt of the American colonies, more terrible and more beneficent in its consequences than the political upheaval in France, threw its shadow across the horizon and stayed unheeded. Science, industrialism, democracy, the emancipation of women—these were the words of prophecy written on the sky, had there been an interpreter able to read the signs of the times. Adam Smith had begun to study these things and to him it seemed that if every man were allowed to manufacture what he would and to sell it where he would, the way would be found to national wealth, to prosperity, to happiness. He did not see that this meant the downfall of the landowning aristocracy before the manufacturing employer and the merchant, and ultimately the control of manufacturer and merchant by the men they employed, that ancient privileges would be swept away, and ancestral beliefs abandoned—a new heaven and a new earth. These things were hidden from Adam Smith as from the other members of the Literary Club over which Dr. Johnson presided.

Meanwhile life and letters went on their destined way. Living in the house at Westminster where Sir Isaac Newton had had his observatory was a lively little girl, the daughter of Dr. Burney, who attracted the attention of Garrick, and was later introduced by him to the other members of the Literary Club, Boswell, Burke, Bishop Percy, Sir Joshua Reynolds, even to the great Dr. Johnson himself. By the time she was twenty-five Frances, or as she was familiarly called, FANNY BURNEY, had written a new kind of novel, *Evelina; or The History of a Young Lady's Entrance into the World* (1778). Evelina was a young lady after the manner of Richardson, who spent so much of her time writing letters that one wonders how she did anything else; she wrote many letters and very long ones, but Dr. Johnson said he read every word of them. The revered doctor regarded Miss Burney's work with genuine and enthusiastic admiration; yet even he would have been astonished if any one had told him that before the century turned she would make as much from the sale of one novel, *Camilla* (1796), as he did from thirty years of arduous toil as a professional writer in Fleet Street. Fanny Burney became second keeper of the royal robes and Madame d'Arblay; she lived to a good old age (1840)—long enough to see her literary fame outshone by her younger contemporary Jane Austen (1775-1817).

JANE AUSTEN belonged to an old-established Hampshire family and was born in that county, at Steventon, of which her father was the handsome and accomplished rector. She herself is described by her nephew and biographer as personally attractive: "Her figure was rather tall and slender, her step light and firm, and her whole appearance expressive of health and animation. In complexion she was a clear brunette with a rich color; she had full round cheeks, with mouth and nose small and well-formed, bright hazel eyes, and brown hair forming natural curls close round her face." As he remembered her, she habitually wore a cap, and took to the garb of middle age earlier than her years or looks required, being "scarcely regardful of the fashionable or the becoming." She was devoted to her elder

FANNY BURNEY

sister Cassandra and to her two younger brothers, both of whom rose to the rank of admiral in the British Navy.

For the first twenty-five years of her life, Jane Austen lived in this quiet country parsonage of Steventon; her father held also the rectorate of the adjoining parish, but the population of the two together counted less than three hundred souls. He took pupils and was thus enabled to keep a carriage in which the family traveled about, but it is recorded that in bad weather the two Austen sisters walked the wet country roads in pattens. The society they frequented was necessarily confined to the small gentry who play so large a part in Jane Austen's novels. Her biographer finds in this circumstance the explanation of the fact that "she deals as little with very low as with very high stations in life." Certain it is that the humble poor, of whose lot Jane Austen could not be altogether ignorant, play little or no part in the scenes of contemporary life her pen has preserved for us in quiet but undying colors.

Probably owing to her father's advancing age, the family passed the first four years of the nineteenth century at Bath, and the next four (after his death) at Southampton, where she resided with her widowed mother and her sister. In 1809 they moved to another small Hampshire village, Chawton, and here she lived until her declining health and the need for medical attendance compelled her removal in 1817 to Winchester, where she died the same year and was buried in the cathedral. Her modest home, and her equally modest tomb, are often visited.

It is necessary to keep this biographical background in mind in order to realize the conditions under which Jane Austen's novel-writing was done. It was at Steventon that before she was twenty-one she began, in the epistolary style initiated by Richardson and continued by Fanny Burney, a novel which was later recast in narrative form under the title *Sense and Sensibility*. In its earlier shape it was laid aside in favor of *Pride and Prejudice,* begun in October, 1796, and completed in the following summer, also in the narrative style of Fielding. Both these were in the light and lively vein of social satire which she has done

better than any other English writer. Sir Walter Scott, after
reading *Pride and Prejudice* for the third time, wrote in his
diary (Jane Austen being then dead): "That young lady had a
talent for describing the involvements and feelings and characters of ordinary life which is to me the most wonderful I
ever met with. The Big Bow-wow strain I can do myself, like
any now going; but the exquisite touch which renders commonplace things and characters interesting from the truth of the
description and the sentiment is denied to me." The clever
heroine with her witty father and ingenuously stupid mother,
her affectionate elder sister, and her priggish or flighty juniors,
make up a family group charming in its naturalness, and need-
ing only the addition to the circle of the heir-presumptive,
the fatuous Rev. Mr. Collins, to make it a source of perpetual
delight to the discerning reader. Jane Austen's father, sensible
of the novel's merits, sent it to a London publisher with a proposal for publication at the author's risk, which was declined
by return of post. *Northanger Abbey,* a third novel which she
wrote at Steventon (completed in 1798), a satire on the romances
of horror which had lately come into vogue, had no better fate;
the manuscript was sold to a Bath publisher for ten pounds
(fifty dollars) and, remaining unpublished for many years, was
bought back from him by Jane Austen's brother for the same
sum.

These three masterpieces, all written in the eighteenth century, remained unknown until well on into the nineteenth. It was
not till after Jane Austen was settled at Chawton in 1809 that
she prepared *Sense and Sensibility* again for the press and secured £150 for its issue by a London publisher in 1811. *Pride
and Prejudice* appeared in 1813. As to its publication, a letter
from Jane Austen to a friend says: "Egerton gives £110 for it.
I would rather have had £150, but we could not both be pleased,
and I am not at all surprised that he should not choose to hazard
so much." It was, at any rate, enough to induce Jane Austen to
go on novel-writing in the family sitting-room with a piece of
embroidery at hand to protect her manuscript from the curiosity

of a friendly caller. *Mansfield Park* (1814) and *Emma* (1816) were both written at Chawton, and the latter was published with a dedication to the Prince Regent (George IV), inserted at his suggestion, for he professed to be an admirer of her work. As this is one of the few things to his credit, it seems a pity that he spoiled it by his form of acknowledgment of the presentation copy. Jane Austen wrote to her publisher (Chawton, April 1, 1816): "You will be pleased to hear that I have received the Prince's thanks for the *handsome* copy I sent him of *Emma*. Whatever he may think of my share of the work, yours seems to have been quite right."

In all, Jane Austen received less than £700 for the four novels published during her lifetime; (*Northanger Abbey* and *Persuasion* were published together the year after her death). It is interesting to note that in 1930 a sum of £1,000 was paid in a London auction room for the four-page letter about *Pride and Prejudice* from which a few lines are quoted above. Unlike most of the eighteenth- and early nineteenth-century novels, Jane Austen's work gained in reputation after her death. Sir Walter Scott's tribute has already been quoted; Macaulay and Lewes, two eminent Victorian critics, were equally enthusiastic. Rudyard Kipling, in *Debits and Credits,* consecrated a short story and three poems to her memory; in one of them he pictures Jane as welcomed into heaven by all her great predecessors (including Sir Walter Scott, who, as a matter of fact, survived her). It was Jane Austen's rejection of the epistolary manner of Richardson, and her acceptance of the Fielding model, which was adopted by Thackeray, George Eliot, Anthony Trollope, and the Victorians generally, that established what has been called the standard form of the English novel; the autobiographical method of *Robinson Crusoe* and *Gulliver's Travels* is still practised, especially for stories of adventure; but the epistolary manner of Richardson has fallen into complete disuse. In these days of rapid transportation and communication, people do not write such long letters, and it is hard to believe that they ever did.

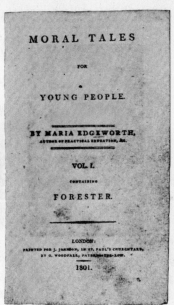

MARIA EDGEWORTH

Another predecessor of Sir Walter Scott to whom he made generous acknowledgment of his indebtedness was MARIA EDGEWORTH (1767-1849). In the General Preface to the Waverley Novels (1829) he speaks of "the extended and well merited fame of Miss Edgeworth" and adds: "Without being so presumptuous as to hope to emulate the rich humor, pathetic tenderness, and admirable tact which pervade the works of my accomplished friend, I felt that something might be attempted for my own country of the same kind with that which Miss Edgeworth so fortunately achieved for Ireland." Macaulay in his *History* went out of his way to testify to "the enjoyment which during more than forty years" he had derived from "her charming writings," and other Victorian critics greatly admired her work.

To us she is of interest mainly for her lively and amusing pictures of Irish life. Though she was born in England, her family belonged to Edgeworthstown, County Longford, and she lived there from childhood to the end of a long life. In her own time she was appreciated as the leading exponent of that moral trend which has always been a distinguishing feature of English fiction. She called one of her collections of stories "Moral Tales," and one of her contemporaries ingenuously remarked that all her work falls under this category. Her didactic purpose was partly due to the influence of her father, who "corrected" her work and sometimes collaborated in it, and partly to the influence of Thomas Day, who half a century ago was known to every English school-boy as the author of *Sandford and Merton,* now remembered only as having provided Bernard Shaw with the subject of *Androcles and the Lion.*

Her Irish novels, especially *Castle Rackrent* and *The Absentee,* have now fallen into undeserved neglect. In them the moral is not too obvious, being chiefly conveyed indirectly in humorous or pathetic pictures of the poverty of the Irish peasantry and the shiftlessness of the English gentry whom they served. Her humor, though not so extravagant as that of her successors in the representation of Irish peasant life, is more natural, and her portrayal of the failings of gentle and simple alike is founded upon a genuine love of the Irish people, as was shown by her devoted efforts to help them in her extreme old age, during the calamitous days of the famine of 1846.

CHAPTER VIII

THE ROMANTIC REVIVAL

The Romantic Revival was a movement affecting not only literature, music, and the plastic arts, but people's way of thinking and feeling with regard to things in general. It began about the middle of the eighteenth century and rose to its height before the middle of the nineteenth, when it died away before the accumulating forces of modern science, industrialism, and realism. In France it began with Rousseau, whose influence extended far beyond his own country and his own time, and came to an end with Victor Hugo. In German literature it is associated with the great names of Lessing, the Schlegels, Goethe, and Schiller.

Great intellectual and spiritual movements do not happen suddenly and definitely, for the convenience of professors and students of literature, who would like to put them into tidy pigeonholes. The Romantic Revival, like other great social changes, was a gradual transition. Looking back on it, we mark as among its first characteristics a reaction from a reasonable, orderly, even conventional literature, written by educated men for an educated class, to something more popular and spontaneous, more imaginative and sentimental, less regular and intellectual. The literary historians have discerned as one of the earliest signs of this change of mind and outlook a renewed interest in the popular ballad, which is associated with the publication of Bishop Thomas Percy's *Reliques of Ancient English Poetry* in 1765. A few years earlier a Scotch student, JAMES MACPHERSON, had published *Fragments of Ancient Poetry collected in the Highlands* and two epics which he professed to have translated from the Gaelic of a prehistoric poet named Ossian. There was an immediate outcry of forgery, and when

GRAY

Dr. Johnson was asked whether he thought any modern man could have written such poems, the great literary dictator replied, "Yes, sir; many men, many women, and many children." When Macpherson wrote an expostulatory and even threatening letter, Johnson replied: "I received your foolish and impudent letter. Any violence offered me I shall do my best to repel; and what I cannot do for myself, the law shall do for me. I hope I shall not be deterred from detecting what I think a cheat by the menaces of a ruffian." Ever since, the genuineness of the Ossianic poems has been a subject of discussion, and the received opinion now is that while Macpherson had access to some ancient material, the professed translations contained a good deal of his own. The interest taken in Ossian, both in England and on the Continent, was increased rather than diminished by the heated controversy that took place at the time, and the poems were "all the rage." A similar contest arose about the forgeries of THOMAS CHATTERTON, a Bristol youth who published in a local paper a poem which he dated some five hundred years earlier and pretended that he had found among some ancient papers in St. Mary Redcliffe Church. He was still only eighteen when he made his way to London and, in desperation at his lack of success, committed suicide. A great many people accepted as genuine the fifteenth-century poems of "Thomas Rowley," published after Chatterton's death, and his undoubted literary talent and romantic end made him a memorable figure in literary history and pictorial art.

A very different figure was that of THOMAS GRAY (1716-1771), who studied ancient "Gothic" texts in the newly established British Museum Library and wrote poems in imitation of Old Norse and Welsh literature before the publication of Percy's *Reliques*. In style he kept to the classical manner, addressing an *Ode* to his alma mater, Eton College, beginning:

> Ye distant spires, ye antique towers
> That crown the watery glade,

much as Pope, in *Windsor Forest,* had described "the watery

ETON

STOKE POGES CHURCHYARD

plains" of the upper Thames in the same neighborhood. A student at Peterhouse, Cambridge, Gray settled down there to lead the studious celibate life of a college fellow, but was driven away by a practical joke of some undergraduates, who noticed his fear of fire and a rope which hung from his study window to afford him a means of escape in case of an outbreak. They staged a night alarm for his benefit and had the pleasure of seeing him descend by the rope into a butt of water they had placed below in the court for that purpose. In high dudgeon, Gray withdrew to Pembroke College, by which his fame was more appropriately cherished. He became professor of history and modern languages in the university, refused to be made poet laureate, and drew up a plan for a history of English poetry, which was afterward carried out by Thomas Warton, an Oxford professor who became poet laureate in spite of the fact that he was a much better professor than poet.

A diligent student of the classics, Gray in his careful diction kept close to the prevailing rule and practice, often giving a felicitous turn to "what oft was thought but ne'er so well expressed." Thus, in his best-known and perhaps his best poem, *An Elegy written in a Country Churchyard,* he soliloquizes:

> The boast of heraldry, the pomp of power,
>   And all that beauty, all that wealth e'er gave,
> Await alike the inevitable hour.
>   The paths of glory lead but to the grave.

The poem became immediately popular and was recited by General Wolfe as he climbed the Heights of Abraham to the conquest of Canada just before his death, with the reflection, "I had rather be the author of that piece than take Quebec."

Gray was buried in Stoke Poges Churchyard, which was the scene of the poem and, being beautifully situated in the upper Thames valley not too far from London, is a favorite shrine for the American visitor. In spite of the smallness in volume and limited scope of his verse, Thomas Gray was a true poet, with a firm grasp of classical principles on the one hand, and on the

other an inclination to break away from the conventional forms
of poetry then in fashion. He was a charming letter-writer and
a great admirer of natural scenery, both in Switzerland and in
the British Isles; the journal of his tour in the English Lake
District is an early tribute to the beauties of lake and mountain
which the poetry of Wordsworth was afterward to make
famous.

In WILLIAM COWPER (1731-1800) the love of nature and of
simple things was combined with a deeply religious spirit. The
religious awakening of the eighteenth century was mainly due
to the evangelizing zeal and organizing genius of John Wesley,
the hymns of his brother Charles, and the emotional preaching
of George Whitefield, of whom it was said that he could move
a vast congregation to tears by the mere utterance of the word
"Mesopotamia." Most of the successes of the new evangelism
were gained among humble folk, the country laborers and town
artisans who had been too much neglected by the Established
Church, then fallen into its worst period of formalism and decay. But by degrees the spirit of evangelical enthusiasm communicated itself to some of the clergy of the Anglican Church
—to which, indeed, the Wesleys and Whitefield belonged,
though their efforts met with strong opposition and condemnation from the ecclesiastical authorities.

It was an ardent evangelical clergyman, John Newton,
whose religious influence played so large a part in Cowper's
life, perhaps not always for Cowper's good, though it must be
noted that the poet's first mental breakdown came before he had
made Newton's acquaintance. Cowper was the son of the rector
of Berkhampstead, Hertfordshire, who was a royal chaplain
and had aristocratic family connections. Most of the sorrows of
the poet's life arose from the extreme delicacy of his constitution.
As a child at his first school, owing to his weakness and timidity,
he suffered mental agonies from the bullying of a bigger and
older boy. "His savage treatment of me," wrote the poet in his
Memoirs, "impressed such a dread of his figure on my mind
that I well remember being afraid to lift my eyes upon him

COWPER

higher than his knees and that I knew him better by his shoe-buckle than by any other part of his dress." At the age of ten, Cowper was removed to happier surroundings at the famous Westminster School; here his health was bad, but he was usually in better spirits, though he was still subject to moods of deep depression. When he was eighteen, he was articled to a law firm and became a student of the Middle Temple, being called to the bar in 1754. In London he had a happy and gay life, both in the law office and in the house of his uncle Ashley Cowper, where he spent most of his spare time with his fair cousins, Harriet and Theodora Jane, "giggling and making giggle." He fell in love with Theodora and the young people wished to marry. The father objected (1) on account of Cowper's unstable health; (2) because they were cousins; and (3) because they had no money. In answer to her father's question, what she would do if she married her cousin, Theodora said with much spirit, "Wash all day and ride out on the great dog at night"; but her courage was in vain; the two lovers were permanently separated. With the elder sister, Harriet, who became Lady Hesketh, Cowper in his later life maintained a lively correspondence.

Cowper had another uncle who had a high official post in Parliament, and through him obtained a nomination to a clerkship in the House of Lords; but in order to qualify for the position the young poet (this was in 1763 and he had already written love-poems to Theodora and "several half-penny ballads") had to appear in person at the bar of the House and undergo a viva-voce examination. He was given access to the Journals of the House in order to prepare himself for this ordeal, but the nervous strain was too much for Cowper's unstable wits. He fell into terrible depression, attempted suicide, and suffered from keen remorse, resulting in an attack of religious mania which necessitated his retirement from the world under medical care. Recovering to some extent, he was put in the charge of Mr. and Mrs. Unwin, kindly people to whom he became much attached. On Unwin's death, the widow took Cowper to live with her at Olney, where he fell under the influence of the local clergyman, the Rev. John Newton, an evangelist of strong religious convictions and somewhat violent character. Newton persuaded Cowper to write hymns for the "Olney" collection and to take part as lay reader and district visitor in the parish work. Whether this extreme religious devotion was good or bad for Cowper, it is hard to determine; either this or sorrow for the death of his brother or both combined led to another mental breakdown.

From this he was saved by the affectionate care of Mrs. Unwin, who induced him to take an interest in gardening and the care of animals; he made special pets of three hares and trained them to live in the house with him. By these simple pleasures he was sufficiently restored to contemplate marriage with Mrs. Unwin, but before the time came for the ceremony, he fell again into a derangement which lasted so long that the project of marriage was abandoned. On his recovery Mrs. Unwin encouraged him to write poetry and gave him as a subject *The Progress of Error*. This and other poems, largely devotional in character, were published in 1782, but this first volume met with little favor: one critic remarked that Mr. Cowper was "certainly a good pious man, but without a spark of poetic fire."

Meanwhile Cowper had made the acquaintance of Lady Austen, a lively and intelligent widow who had come to live in the neighborhood. She amused him and took his mind off more serious subjects. One evening she told him a story of a London tradesman, unused to horseback riding, who took that way of spending a holiday with his family and friends, and was carried by his headlong steed far beyond his destination, in spite of the protesting salutations of the rest of the party. The next morning at breakfast Cowper recited to her a ballad he had composed on the subject, beginning:

> John Gilpin was a citizen
> Of credit and renown,
> A trainband captain eke was he
> Of famous London town.

COWPER'S HOUSE AT WESTON, BUCKS.

The performances of the hero were described in the same jovial spirit:

> Away went Gilpin, and away,
> Away went hat and wig.

On its publication in 1783 the ballad became immediately popular, especially among the God-fearing middle class, who were delighted to see their pious poet in a lighter mood. Lady Austen urged him to continue in this vein, and on his appealing to her for another subject she told him to write "upon a sofa"; his answer to this suggestion was *The Task* (1785), which treated of homely things in a pleasant, familiar tone, and was welcomed by the public, eager for the simplicity and sincerity of Cowper in his genial mood:

> Now stir the fire, and close the shutters fast,
> Let fall the curtains, wheel the sofa round,
> And while the bubbling and loud-hissing urn
> Throws up a steamy column, and the cups,
> That cheer but not inebriate, wait on each,
> So let us welcome peaceful evening in.

In this intimate tone of simple cheerfulness, displaying the genuine charm of a gentle soul, we have Cowper at his best. Unfortunately his two Egerias could not get on together and he had to choose between them. It was Mrs. Unwin who prevailed, but *The Task* enabled Cowper to renew the correspondence with his cousin, Lady Hesketh, which had been interrupted by what she regarded as his excessive piety, and what he regarded as her indifference to spiritual things. With her moral and material support (for Cowper and Mrs. Unwin found their combined financial resources insufficient) the poet completed his translation of Homer (1791), and undertook an edition of Milton; but Mrs. Unwin's serious illness and death cast dark shadows over his last years, which were, for the most part, spent in deep mental dejection.

Equally religious in his own strange way was that erratic

WILLIAM BLAKE

genius WILLIAM BLAKE (1757-1827). In his *Milton* he pays tribute to the two prophets and servants of God, Whitefield and Wesley:

> Can you have greater miracles than these? Men who devote
> Their life's whole comfort to entire scorn and injury and death?

But Blake's religious faith was his own, communicated to him, as he believed, by divine inspiration. He held that "the poetic genius is the true man," and that "the religions of all nations are derived from each nation's different reception of the poetic genius, which is everywhere called the Spirit of Prophecy." His own "Prophetic Poems" were written by him, he says, "from immediate dictation, twelve or thirty lines at a time, without premeditation, and even against my will."

Blake's father was a London tradesman, who early perceived the boy's artistic talent, and after sending him to drawing-school, apprenticed him for seven years (he was then fourteen) to a well-known engraver, Basire. At the end of his apprenticeship he became a student at the newly organized Royal Academy of Art, where his friends Flaxman and Fuseli later became professors, the first of sculpture, the second of painting. Blake sent his work to the annual exhibitions of the Academy for nearly thirty years, but he had already undertaken work as an engraver for publishing houses, and on his father's death in 1784, he opened a print-shop with a fellow-apprentice of Basire's, taking in his own younger brother, Robert, as a pupil. His literary ability had by this time become known to his friends through his recitation and singing of his own poems, and Flaxman helped to pay for the publication of his *Poetical Sketches* (1783); this first volume contained some charming songs, but attracted little attention. Blake made no attempt to put it into commercial circulation, beyond sending copies to his personal friends; it is probable that he already had in mind the combination of his talents as an engraver and a poet by a process of his own discovery called by him "Illuminated Printing." He later believed that it had been communicated to him in a vision by the spirit of his brother Robert, who died in 1787, but in a manuscript of 1784, Blake speaks of a process of engraving by which it would be possible to print an edition of two thousand at a hundred pounds apiece, adding "whoever will not have them will be ignorant fools and will not deserve to live." In any case, immediately after Robert's death Blake gave up his partnership and set up business for himself. At the same time he became his own printer and publisher, issuing (apparently in 1788) two little religious treatises and in 1789 *Songs of Innocence,* followed in 1794 by *Songs of Experience.* These were the first examples of "W. Blake's original stereotype." The text and the pictorial design inclosing it were drawn in reverse by Blake upon copper plates which were previously varnished and afterward washed in acid. From these plates prints were made and afterward tinted by Blake himself in water-color, so that each copy was an independent work of art. The new process was, unfortunately, not the commercial success that Blake had expected, and he was driven back on engraving and water-color work to be done on commission; in addition to being unremunerative, the new process was slow and laborious and hindered the circulation of his poems.

Although the editions Blake made with his own hand are now very highly prized, only about a score of copies of the most popular, *Songs of Innocence and Experience,* have survived; a copy which one hundred years ago cost ten dollars, in 1931 fetched eight thousand dollars; of others there are only one or two copies; and one collection seems to have entirely disappeared. At his death he left a large number of poems written in notebooks or on scraps of paper, and he produced, in his "illuminated printed," beside children's books, seven series of mystical visions, and two spiritual epics of a symbolic character. Until his health failed, he was not unhappy; he wrote:

> I have mental joy; and mental health,
> And mental friends, and mental wealth;
> I've a wife I love and that loves me;
> I've all but riches bodily.

I am in God's presence night and day,
And He never turns His face away;
The accuser of sins by my side doth stand,
And he holds my money-bag in his hand.

For my worldly things God makes him pay,
And He'd pay for more if to him I would pray;
And so you may do the worst you can do;
Be assured, Mr. Devil, I won't pray to you.

Since his death Blake has come to be appreciated as he never was during his lifetime. He is now regarded as the most significant figure in the earlier phase of the Romantic Period in which the appeal to the imagination, the "element of wonder," was afterward to play so large a part. His poems for children and his prophetic books with their religious mysticism and elaborate symbolism have had great influence not only in the nineteenth century but in the twentieth. A number of the poems left in manuscript were published by W. M. Rossetti and others by Swinburne, who wrote an enthusiastic essay on the engraver-poet. In more recent years, W. B. Yeats and Walter de la Mare have continued the Blake tradition.

Blake's life was a happy one because it was all of a piece. As a boy he frequented sales of prints and became known there as "the young connoisseur." He set up his first print-shop in Broad Street, next to his father's hosiery store. His wife was the daughter of a Battersea market-gardener, and though she was a simple soul, he educated her to help him with his work and sympathize with his ideas. For holidays, they played at being Adam and Eve in the garden, before the idea of the fig leaves occurred to our first parents—thus forestalling the modern nudity cult. The poet sang his "happy songs, Every child may joy to hear" about Lambs and Tigers, and went on, undeterred by failure, with his "illuminated printing."

The humble lot of Blake's contemporary ROBERT BURNS (1759-96) was very different, and Burns had a very different disposition. Carlyle has pictured how different the life and work of the poet would have been if his father had been a little better off; but "poverty sank his whole family below the help of even our cheap school system: Burns remained a hard-worked ploughboy." The poet says himself that up to his sixteenth year he endured "the cheerless gloom of a hermit and the unceasing toil of a galley slave." Over-exertion in his childhood (he thrashed the corn on his father's small farm at thirteen) broke the health of Burns but not his spirit; he was gay and attractive, only too fond of the society of others—especially those of the opposite sex. He was hardly out of his teens before he had begun making songs to "Mary Morison" and others. At twenty-two he went to learn to be a flax-dresser, so that he would be able to get married; but "it was an unlucky affair: as we were giving a welcome carousal to the New Year, the shop took fire and burned to ashes, and I was left, like a true poet, without a sixpence." He then tried to improve himself by learning mathematics, but "a charming *fillette* who lived next door overset my trigonometry and set me off at a tangent from the field of my studies."

At twenty-three he went back to the farm, determined to be wise, "in spite of the world, the flesh and the devil," and found his father poorer than ever; overburdened by debt, the elder Burns was "just saved from the horrors of a jail" by death from consumption. With what little could be recovered from the wreck of their father's estate (and that little got by putting in a claim for personal services) Robert and his brother Gilbert took a farm at Mossgiel, and worked hard on it for four years, but without much success. It was here that Burns fell in love with Jean Armour, daughter of a stone-mason in the neighboring town of Mauchline, and gave her a written declaration of marriage, which by the Scottish law of that time would have made their coming offspring legitimate; but the stern father preferred illegitimacy for his grandchild to Jean's marriage to a person of such unstable disposition and uncertain prospects as he deemed Robert Burns to be; so he tore up the paper and bade his daughter break off all relations with the poet.

MOSSGIEL

DUMFRIES

Angered at Jean's obedience to her father, Burns offered marriage to another sweetheart, Mary Campbell, a sailor's daughter from Argyllshire, and invited her to accompany him to the island of Jamaica, where he had obtained an engagement as bookkeeper or overseer. In order to pay their passage-money, he arranged with a Kilmarnock printer to bring out an edition of his poems. This appeared in July under the title *Poems chiefly in the Scottish Dialect,* and brought immediate fame but very little money. Mary fell ill and died in October. Her memory is enshrined in "Will ye go to the Indies, my Mary," "To Mary in Heaven," and "Highland Mary," all written when Mary Campbell lay in her grave with a child's coffin beside her.

The Kilmarnock poems made an enormous hit. They included two of Burns's most charming and popular idylls, "To a Mouse" and "To a Mountain Daisy"; a serious and sympathetic study of Scottish family life, "The Cottar's Saturday Night"; the more frolicsome "Hallowe'en"; the rollicking and uproarious picture of low life, "The Jolly Beggars"; and the bitter satirical poems, "Death and Dr. Hornbrook" and "Holy Willie's Prayer." "Old and young, high and low, grave and gay, learned and ignorant, were alike transported. Even ploughboys and maidservants would have gladly bestowed the wages they earned the most hardly, and which they wanted to purchase necessary clothing, if they might but procure the works of Burns." But the return to the author was less than a hundred dollars.

Burns had apparently actually started for Greenock to set sail for Jamaica, when he was recalled by Mary Campbell's last illness in October. But November found him in Edinburgh, where favorable reviews of his poems in the magazines won him a warm welcome in literary circles, and his convivial habits made him popular at the clubs. Sir Walter Scott, then a boy of fifteen, took an opportunity to see the new social lion and later left on record his impressions: "His person was strong and robust; his manners rustic, not clownish; a sort of dignified plainness and simplicity, which received part of its effect per-

POEMS,

CHIEFLY IN THE

SCOTTISH DIALECT,

BY

ROBERT BURNS.

THE Simple Bard, unbroke by rules of Art,
He pours the wild effusions of the heart:
And if inspir'd, 'tis Nature's pow'rs inspire;
Her's all the melting thrill, and her's the kindling fire.

ANONYMOUS.

KILMARNOCK:
PRINTED BY JOHN WILSON.

M,DCC,LXXXVI.

haps from one's knowledge of his extraordinary talents. His features are represented in Mr. Nasmyth's picture, but to me it conveys the idea that they are diminished, as if seen in perspective. I think his countenance was more massive than it looks in any of the portraits. I should have taken the poet, had I not known what he was, for a very sagacious country farmer of the old Scotch school, i.e. none of your modern agriculturists who keep laborers for their drudgery, but the *douce gudeman* who held his own plough. There was a strong expression of sense and shrewdness in all his lineaments; the eye alone, I think, indicated the poetical character and temperament. It was large, and of a dark cast, which glowed (I say literally *glowed*) when he spoke with feeling or interest. I never saw such another eye in a human head, though I have seen the most distinguished men of my time. His conversation expressed perfect self-confidence, without the slightest presumption."

With the men of the Scottish capital Burns held his own very well, whether in literary chat or at a drinking bout. "Between the men of rustic life and the polite world, I observed little difference," he says. "But a refined and accomplished woman was a being altogether new to me, and of which I had formed a very inadequate idea." Scott heard that the poet's "address to females was extremely deferential, and always with a turn either to the humorous or the pathetic, which engaged their attention particularly." Among the Edinburgh ladies by whose conversation and correspondence Burns may be said to have benefited was a Mrs. Dunlop, who had a wholesome influence over him, and "Clarinda," a Mrs. McLehose with whom (in the absence of her husband) he conducted a flirtation on terms very different from those he used with the Mauchline lassies. "He was much caressed in Edinburgh," says Sir Walter, "but (considering what literary emoluments have been since his day) the efforts made for his relief were extremely trifling." The Edinburgh edition of his poems (1787) brought him in $2,500, which included the price of the copyright. In 1788 two editions were published in the United States, but under the American

BURNS

copyright law of that time Burns was entitled to no return from them.

Burns spent part of his Edinburgh gains on wandering about in Scotland and the North of England, and with what was left settled down on a farm near Dumfries, Ellisland in Niths-dale, where he wrote "Auld Lang Syne" and "Tam O'Shanter." He "made an honest woman" of Jean Armour by marrying her, and wrote for her "O' a' the airts the wind can blaw." The farm did not succeed and he was glad to obtain the post of excise officer for the district at a yearly salary of $250. In a year or two he was promoted to a similar position for a larger district at an increase of $100, and gave up his farm to live in the neighbor-ing town of Dumfries, which was more central for his work.

Burns nearly lost his position on account of his openly ex-pressed sympathy with the French Revolution, and fell into disfavor with the local gentry. This had the disadvantage of throwing him into convivial company of a less desirable class. He continued to write, contributing to two collections of songs— the *Scots Musical Museum* and *Melodies of Scotland with Sym-phonies and Accompaniments for the Pianoforte and Violin: the Poetry by Robert Burns.* To the latter he contributed a hun-dred songs, original and adapted, and had in return twenty-five dollars in cash and a shawl for his wife. The Dumfries edition of his works was published in 1793. He was still desperately poor and in broken health. As late as 1794 he had enough spirit left in him to write the "Address to the De'il," but in the spring of 1796 he wrote to a friend: "I fear it will be some time before I tune my lyre again. By Babel's streams I have sat and wept. I have only known existence by the pressure of sickness and counted time by the repercussion of pain. I close my eyes on misery and open them without hope." His forebodings were justified. He fell asleep by the roadside after a carouse, caught rheumatic fever, and died on July 21. On July 12 he had writ-ten to a cousin to beg for a loan of fifty dollars to save him from dying in jail.

The defects of character from which Burns suffered are

obvious; he shared them with millions of men in his own time—
indeed, in any time. What distinguished him from the rest of
humanity was a unique lyric gift which his own generation
should have known enough to cherish instead of letting him
wear out body and soul in struggling with barren farms and
discharging the dreary tasks of an exciseman in order to earn
a scant subsistence. His first fame was that of the Scottish peasant poet; he had a very close relation to the Scottish songs and
ballads of the past; and no one has written poems of country
life which have so distinctly the tang of the soil; but quite
beyond and apart from these minor virtues he had the supreme
gifts of sincerity and musical charm which make the true poet.

With WILLIAM WORDSWORTH (1770-1850) the Romantic
Revival passes from the pioneer stage of struggle and promise
to that of established supremacy. He was born at Cockermouth
in Cumberland on the edge of the Lake District, which contributed by its natural beauty to the building up of poetic genius
and which his poems were afterward to make famous. His
father was a lawyer and agent to a great landowner and famous
politician of the neighborhood, Sir James Lowther, afterward
Earl of Lonsdale, who not only borrowed all his agent's fortune
($25,000), but refused to pay it back when the elder Words-
worth died in 1783. The boy was, however, well cared for by
his uncles, who kept him at Hawkshead Grammar School, in
the Esthwaite valley, between two of the principal lakes of the
district, Windermere and Coniston. He was an active and vigorous youngster, taking a keen delight in the sports and pleasures
of the country-side—boating on the neighboring lakes in summer, skating on them in winter, climbing the crags for birds'
nests, and enjoying all the "glad animal movements" of a healthy
boy. Then there came the period of more mature growth—

>   when like a roe
> I bounded o'er the mountains, by the sides
> Of the deep rivers, and the lonely streams,
> Wherever nature led . . . For nature then
> To me was all in all. I cannot paint

WORDSWORTH'S SCHOOL, HAWKSHEAD

WINDERMERE AND ESTHWAITE WATER

What then I was. The sounding cataract
Haunted me like a passion: the tall rock,
The mountain, and the deep and gloomy wood,
Their colors and their forms, were then to me
An appetite, a feeling and a love
That had no need of a remoter charm,
By thought supplied, nor any interest
Unborrowed from the eye.

From Hawkshead Wordsworth went to St. John's College, Cambridge, where he was less happy. He was not so much at home in the flat scenery of the fen country as he was among his native lakes and hills, and college life meant little to him; the intellectual current at the English universities at that time was running low. Wordsworth read largely in both classical and modern literature, but he wrote later that he was neither among the "loyal students faithful to their books," nor among the "honest dunces," but one of the "half-and-half idlers" who "read lazily in trivial books," amused themselves with sports, "and let the stars come forth, perhaps without one quiet thought." He "was not for that hour, nor for that place"; but long before this, as a school-boy of fourteen, he had devoted himself to the minute observation of nature and the interpretation of nature in a new kind of poetry; even in Cambridge, returning from a dance, he suffered revulsion from the frivolities in which he was entangled, and felt himself "a dedicated spirit." His first poems were published in 1793—two slim volumes, one entitled *An Evening Walk, An Epistle in Verse addressed to a Young Lady from the Lakes of the North of England,* and the other, *Descriptive Sketches,* founded upon a tour he took in his last college vacation along with a fellow-student.

Wordsworth took his B.A. in January, 1791; but for him, as for many a young man since, Commencement seemed more like an end than a beginning. His mother, who died when he was eight, had noticed in him "a stiff, moody, and violent temper," and feared for his future. He showed at this point unusual obstinacy: he persisted in his determination to be a poet. But

that was nonsense, thought the uncles. Was there any profession
for which he wished to qualify himself? Would he be a clergyman? He would not. Would he be a lawyer? He would not. Was
there anything sensible he wished to do? He wanted to travel;
and as it was not unusual for young men of that time to travel,
to this the uncles agreed.

Wordsworth made for France, which was in a state of
extraordinary ferment. The French Revolution had progressed,
but was still in its early stages of ardent enthusiasm for the re-
generation of mankind by the simple formula of Liberty, Equality, Fraternity. Wordsworth plunged into the movement with
all the passion of a youthful poet:

> Bliss was it in that dawn to be alive
> But to be young was very heaven.

He spent the winter at Orleans and Blois. At the latter place
he formed a close friendship with a family named Vallon, and
fell in love with the daughter, Annette. In the autumn of 1792
he went to Paris with the intention of taking a more active part
in the revolutionary movement. The uncles, in alarm, recalled
him—and stopped his allowance.

There was nothing for Wordsworth to do but to go home and
rejoin his family. At this crisis in his fortunes, the only occupation to which he was inclined was journalism, and his only
suggestion in that direction was that he might start a revolutionary paper to be called "The Philanthropist." In the England of
1792 this could not be called a practical proposal—being in
fact much more likely to land young Wordsworth in jail than
to put him in a position to earn his own living. When the French
Revolution began, the English were well inclined toward it;
had they not had a revolution of their own in 1688? But the
French Revolution of 1788 took strange courses: the National
Assembly seemed more inclined for breaking than making. It
abolished the privileges of the clergy and the nobility; it imprisoned the king; and in January, 1793, it executed him. Moreover, it was very much inclined to induce other nations to do

the same. This was going too far; public opinion in England revolted.

Wordsworth, meditating on Annette Vallon and her baby, was in despair; but he could not return to France. The feeling between the English and French governments became more and more embittered, and the French in February, 1793, declared war. Meanwhile Wordsworth was devoting himself to nursing a young friend of his, Raisley Calvert, who died early in 1795 and left him a legacy of $4,500.

De Quincey remarked years afterward, not without a pang of envy (for no Special Providence looked after *him*), that whenever Wordsworth got himself into a hole some helping hand pulled him out of it. But it must be remarked that Wordsworth helped himself. On that legacy Wordsworth lived for eight years, devoting himself to preparation for his poetic career. In 1801 there was a new Earl of Lonsdale who paid over the money due to the Wordsworth estate, with interest. In 1802, Wordsworth consolidated his financial position by a marriage with the daughter of a neighboring landowner. In 1813 he was appointed stamp-distributor for the district of Westmoreland—his own Lake District; the yearly salary was $2,500 and the duties could be discharged by a deputy; later the district was enlarged, and the salary almost doubled. Wordsworth retired with a pension in 1842, and the next year was appointed poet laureate. Truly "the Lord was mindful of his own."

But in 1795, when Wordsworth's revolutionary enthusiasm had been extinguished by the Reign of Terror in Paris, his real good fortune was not the legacy, but the sympathy of his sister Dorothy, a gifted and high-spirited girl, who believed in him, encouraged him, and agreed to share his determined effort to make the legacy go as far as possible. Wordsworth was not unaware of his indebtedness to her: he wrote

> She gave me eyes, she gave me ears,
> And humble care and delicate fears,
> A heart the fountain of sweet tears,
> And love and faith and joy.

In order to husband their small resources William and Dorothy took a little cottage at Racedown in Dorsetshire. There another piece of good fortune befell them. The poems Wordsworth had published in 1793 attracted no attention; nor, indeed, even at this day, can the ordinary reader see anything extraordinary in them. But in June, 1797, Wordsworth was visited at Racedown by an enthusiastic admirer who saw in them the promise of "original poetic genius." His name was SAMUEL TAYLOR COLERIDGE.

Of Coleridge's past history and future performances there will be more to say later; for the moment we wish to note the stimulus he gave to Wordsworth and the importance of their collaboration. Their natures were happily complementary to each other. Coleridge, two years younger than Wordsworth, was easy-going, impulsive, impractical, with long curly black hair and ardent gray eyes; Wordsworth was taller as well as older, with a reserved, self-contained manner, and a high ascetic forehead.

Wordsworth thought Coleridge the only wonderful man he had ever known; Coleridge said of Wordsworth, "I feel myself a little man by his side." Both were interested in philosophy, and both had been touched by the republican ardor of the French Revolution, though neither was at this period (June, 1797) in sympathy with France. When the Wordsworths in July moved into Somersetshire, and took Alfoxden Manor, within a mile or two of the cottage in which Coleridge was living at Nether Stowey, the conversations between the two friends were so constant and prolonged as to excite suspicion of a conspiracy against the Government. A spy was sent down from London to watch and listen, and as their favorite seat was on a bank at the seaside he had no difficulty in hiding behind it and overhearing their conversation. They were much interested at that time in the doctrines of Spinoza (then pronounced in England with a long i) and from the frequent occurrence of this name in the discussion, the spy thought at first that they were referring to himself and his red nose as Spy Nozy; but he was soon convinced that "it was the name of a man who had made a book and lived long ago," and so reported to his employers.

Next to talking, the favorite amusement of the little group was walking, and all three took part in an excursion from Alfoxden in the autumn during which *The Rime of the Ancient Mariner* was planned, as Coleridge says, "to defray the expense of the tour," their united funds being very small. Wordsworth and his sister went alone on a walking tour in the Wye Valley during which he composed the famous poem of which the scene is set as "a few miles above Tintern Abbey." Wordsworth's own note on it says, "I began it upon leaving Tintern, after crossing the Wye, and concluded it just as I was entering Bristol in the evening, after a ramble of four or five days with my sister. Not a line of it was altered, and not any part of it written down till I reached Bristol."

These two poems illustrate the two cardinal points of poetry on which the conversations of Wordsworth and Coleridge frequently turned: (1) the power of exciting the sympathy of the reader by a faithful adherence to the truth of nature; and (2) the power of giving the interest of novelty by the modifying colors of the imagination. It was accordingly agreed that a series of poems should be composed of two sorts: by Wordsworth on subjects to be chosen from ordinary life; and by Coleridge with incidents and agents which were to be in part supernatural, or at least romantic. In this idea originated the plan of *Lyrical Ballads,* published by a Bristol printer in 1798. Coleridge's contribution was the "Ancient Mariner"; Wordsworth's poems in the little volume included "We are Seven," "The Idiot Boy," "Goody Blake and Harry Gill," and others of an extremely simple character, which for many years excited the derision of the scoffers and still stir doubt in the minds of the faithful. Wordsworth had been urged to make a full statement of the purpose of the new movement, but had contented himself with a very short preface, stating that the authors aimed at "a natural delineation of human passions" in the language of ordinary life, with a protest against "the gaudiness and inane phraseol-

COLERIDGE AT TWENTY-THREE   WORDSWORTH

LYRICAL BALLADS,

WITH

A FEW OTHER POEMS.

BRISTOL:
PRINTED BY BIGGS AND COTTLE,
FOR T. N. LONGMAN, PATERNOSTER-ROW, LONDON.
1798.

LYRICAL BALLADS,

WITH

OTHER POEMS.

IN TWO VOLUMES.

By W. WORDSWORTH.

Quam nihil ad genium, Papiniane, tuum!

VOL. I.

SECOND EDITION.

LONDON:
PRINTED FOR T. N. LONGMAN AND O. REES, PATERNOSTER-ROW,
BY BIGGS AND CO. BRISTOL.
1800.

ogy of many modern writers." He thought it best to let the
poems speak for themselves, and he doubtless relied upon the
"Lines composed a few Miles above Tintern Abbey," in which
he had set forth his feeling for nature, as shown first in the "glad
animal movements" of his boyhood and later in the passion of
his youth. Since then he had passed through the great spiritual
crisis of his life, and the ardors of youth with all its aching
joys and dizzy raptures were no more.

I have learned
To look on nature, not as in the hour
Of thoughtless youth, but hearing oftentimes
The still, sad music of humanity,
Nor harsh nor grating, though of ample power
To chasten and subdue. And I have felt
A presence that disturbs me with the joy
Of elevated thoughts; a sense sublime
Of something far more deeply interfused,
Whose dwelling is the light of setting suns,
And the round ocean and the living air,
And the blue sky, and in the mind of man:
A motion and a spirit, that impels
All thinking things, all objects of all thought,
And rolls through all things.

It is strange that at the time so few recognized in these lines,
quite apart from any question of poetic theory, a new accent of
power and beauty; but Mrs. Coleridge (doubtless regarding the
volume as mainly Wordsworth's affair) reported cheerfully:
"The Lyrical Ballads are not liked at all by any." This was an
exaggeration, for Wordsworth had a few stanch friends and
admirers, but it is a fact that when Cottle sold his business to
Longmans in 1799, the copyright of the volume, for which he
had paid $150, was valued at *nil*. It is, however, significant of
the interest excited that the first edition was very soon exhausted,
and Longmans offered Wordsworth $500 for a new edition, in
two volumes, with additional poems, and a systematic defense
of the theory upon which the poems were written.

TINTERN ABBEY

LINES

WRITTEN A FEW MILES ABOVE

TINTERN ABBEY,

ON REVISITING THE BANKS OF THE WYE DURING

A TOUR,

July 13, 1798.

Five years have passed ; five summers, with the length
Of five long winters ! and again I hear
These waters, rolling from their mountain-springs
With a sweet inland murmur.

This was the occasion of the famous Preface placed at the end of the second volume of the edition of 1800. In it Wordsworth sets forth the principal objects of the poems: (1) To choose incidents and situations from common life; (2) to relate or describe them, throughout, as far as possible, in a selection of language really used by men; (3) to throw over them a certain coloring of imagination whereby ordinary things should be presented to the mind in an unusual aspect; (4) to make these incidents and situations interesting by tracing in them the primary laws of our nature.

In support of his first position Wordsworth draws attention to the increasing accumulation of men in cities, where the uniformity of their occupations produces a craving for extraordinary incident, which the rapid communication of intelligence hourly justifies. These are his own words, and it is interesting to find him, at the end of the eighteenth century, making a protest against sensational journalism, "frantic novels," and a corrupt stage, such as we are inclined to regard as peculiar to our own time. It was, however, his second position, protesting against the artificialities and trivialities of conventional poetic diction, that provoked the most opposition and resentment. Less attention was paid to his answers to the questions: What is a poet? What is poetry? Starting from the position that "poetry is the spontaneous overflow of powerful feelings," Wordsworth argues that it takes its origin from "emotion recollected in tranquillity." "The emotion is contemplated, till, by a species of reaction, the tranquillity gradually disappears, and an emotion, kindred to that which was before the subject of contemplation, is gradually produced, and does itself actually exist in the mind." This bears a remarkable affinity with the theory of subconscious reminiscence propounded recently by the French novelist Marcel Proust.

Lyrical Ballads passed into a third edition in 1802 and through a fourth in 1805. Coleridge, who was with Wordsworth at Grasmere when the Preface to the 1800 edition was written, and had made himself familiar with Wordsworth's ideas by

DOVE COTTAGE

GRASMERE

frequent discussion, restated them in 1817 in *Biographia Literaria,* not with any serious modification but with some difference in emphasis. Up to that time they seem to have made little progress except in the practice of Wordsworth himself; according to De Quincey, in the decade 1820-30 the theory was still "militant"; it was not till 1830-40 that it was "triumphant." Certainly many years elapsed before Wordsworth gained any real hold on the public. From 1800, when he had five hundred dollars for the second edition of *Lyrical Ballads* till 1835, when he sold his copyrights for five thousand dollars for the six-volume edition of his works, he did not receive for his poems, as he put it himself, "enough to buy his shoestrings." It was fortunate for English poetry, as well as for Wordsworth himself, that he had not to depend upon poetry for his livelihood.

In 1798 the inseparable three went to Germany. They all liked to travel, but the contact with German philosophy (which was a great intellectual stimulus to Coleridge) made Wordsworth homesick. He wrote the "Lucy" poems, perhaps his finest lyrics; among them:

> I traveled among unknown men
> In lands beyond the sea;
> Nor, England! did I know till then
> What love I bore to thee.
>
> 'Tis past, that melancholy dream!
> Nor will I quit thy shore
> A second time; for still I seem
> To love thee more and more.

On his return to England in 1799, Wordsworth settled down in the Lake District, and he lived there till his death: his first house was Dove Cottage at Townend, Grasmere, and his later, more commodious residence Rydal Mount, in the same neighborhood. In 1802 he married an old friend of the family, Mary Hutchison, who is the subject of "She was a phantom of delight," and possibly of other poems. The conclusion of the Peace

RYDAL MOUNT

RYDAL WATER

of Amiens in the same year enabled him to return to France; the Westminster sonnet, his sister Dorothy tells us, was composed after they crossed the Bridge outside the Dover coach on their way from London to the coast on July 30. In August, on the sands of Calais, he wrote another beautiful sonnet, including the lines he addressed to his daughter by Annette Vallon, from whom he had been so long separated:

> Dear Child! dear Girl! that walkest with me here,
> If thou appear untouched by solemn thought,
> Thy nature is not therefore less divine:
> Thou liest in Abraham's bosom all the year,
> And worshipp'st at the Temple's inner shrine,
> God being with thee when we know it not.

Wordsworth, it should be said, not only acknowledged his illegitimate daughter, but contributed to her support for many years. It was the Victorian biographers who attempted to conceal the fact, which was brought to light again in the last few years.

The resumption of the Napoleonic War inspired some of Wordsworth's best sonnets, including those on the extinction of the Venetian Republic and on the subjugation of Switzerland: the *Character of the Happy Warrior* may have been suggested by the death of Nelson at Trafalgar (1805). These and many other of his finest efforts, including the *Ode on Intimations of Immortality from Recollections of early childhood,* were published in the volume of 1807.

After 1807 the poetic inspiration of Wordsworth seemed to decline—or, at any rate, to return at rare intervals. On his return to the Lake District in 1799 he had planned a great philosophical poem on "Man, Nature and Society," to be entitled *The Recluse,* and having as its principal subject "the sensations and opinions of a poet living in retirement." He felt such a poem should be written, but doubted whether he was qualified to write it. Accordingly, as a sort of "ante-chapel" to the greater edifice, he entered upon an account of his own poetical develop-

Wm Wordsworth

ment. This grew into a long blank-verse poem in fourteen books, which was completed in 1805, but on account of its autobiographical character was not published till after the poet's death in 1850, when it appeared under the title, *The Prelude, or Growth of a Poet's Mind*. It is now regarded as the most important of his longer works. Its completion encouraged him to go on with his main scheme, and he succeeded in bringing to a close the second of its three great divisions, published in 1814 as *The Excursion*. This gave occasion for a very severe condemnation by Jeffrey, the leading critic of the time, in an article beginning "This will never do," which he followed up by another stating that Wordsworth's *White Doe of Rylstone* (1815) was "the very worst poem ever written." Another long poem, *Peter Bell,* written in 1798 but not published till 1819, lent itself to parody and subjected the poet to painful ridicule. *The River Duddon,* a series of sonnets published in 1820, had a better reception, but the series of *Ecclesiastical Sonnets* which followed was less successful. Wordsworth's fame, however, continued to grow as his earlier work became more known and better understood. In 1843, when the laureateship, which had been held by his friend Southey, was offered to him, he was induced to accept it, in spite of his advanced years, by the insistence of Queen Victoria. His reputation increased up to the dictum of Matthew Arnold that "the poetical performance of Wordsworth is, after that of Shakspere and Milton, undoubtedly the most considerable in our language"; and though that verdict might now be challenged, it is hard to see what name could be substituted.

The life of S. T. COLERIDGE (1772-1834) is inextricably entangled with that of Wordsworth, to which it offers a striking and painful contrast. Wordsworth, by constant prudence and diligence (if we except the few years of youthful wildness) made the most of his great capacities; Coleridge wasted brilliant talents by weakness of character and irresolution. His troubles began when he was a child—sensitive, delicate, and imaginative to the point of dreaminess. Son of a Devonshire clergyman and schoolmaster, he was sent at the age of ten to the ancient foundation of Christ's Hospital, whose boys in their traditional costume of blue coat and yellow stockings used, up to recent times, to lend color to the London streets. There he stayed eight years and enjoyed the friendship of a gifted fellow-pupil, Charles Lamb. In 1791 he went up to Jesus College, Cambridge, and began to interest himself in the political questions of the day, especially Burke's pamphlets on the French Revolution; a fellow of the college was expelled for heresy and sedition, and Coleridge became one of his zealous defenders. In a rebellious mood against college discipline, he enlisted as a common soldier in a dragoon regiment, under the name of Silas Tomkyn Comberback—probably in allusion to his inability to ride. A Latin quotation he wrote up in his horse's stable attracted an officer's attention and his family secured his release. He went back to college, but left in 1794 without taking his degree. In the same year he visited Oxford, and made the acquaintance of a student there, Robert Southey, who shared his revolutionary enthusiasm. Southey came from Bristol and was acquainted with a family of three girls there, all dress-makers and all lovely. Coleridge had a novel scheme for founding a community on the principles of Liberty, Equality, and Fraternity, on the banks of the Susquehanna. It was proposed to take two of the Fricker girls as wives. The Pantisocracy fell through, because they could not raise the passage money, but in 1795 Coleridge married Sarah Fricker and Southey married Edith.

Coleridge's marriage was not a success. He took his young wife to a little house near Bristol, unprovided with groceries or kitchenware, and she complained that he "would walk up and down composing poetry, when he ought to have been in bed," so that they did not make a good start. By way of earning a living, Coleridge gave lectures to the Bristol public, but they did not like either his revolutionary politics or his transcendental philosophy; he printed the lectures, but the public did not like them any better. A friendly Bristol publisher gave him

$150 for his *Juvenile Poems* (1796) and Coleridge edited a periodical, *The Watchman,* which ran for only two months. He thought of becoming a Unitarian minister, and occasionally occupied the pulpit. This gives point to the story of his question, years after, to Charles Lamb, "Did you ever hear me preach?" The jest of Lamb's stammering reply, "I n-n-never heard you do anything else," lies in Coleridge's habit of interminable conversation, mostly one-sided, which he began as a school-boy at Christ's Hospital and ended only with his death. In 1796 the Coleridges took a cottage at Nether Stowey in Somersetshire and they made it their home till 1800. It was there that they were joined by Wordsworth and his sister, and that the plan of *Lyrical Ballads* took shape. It was originally intended that each author should do an equal number of poems, Wordsworth's dealing with the natural and Coleridge's with the supernatural. But even with Wordsworth's constant encouragement and the example of his industry, Coleridge completed only *The Rime of the Ancient Mariner,* to which Wordsworth contributed the albatross, the navigation of the ship by dead men, and two or three lines at the beginning. The companion poem, *Christabel,* begun at the same time, was continued in 1800, and published as a fragment in 1816; meanwhile Scott had heard a friend recite part of it and had been so struck by the melody of the verse that he adopted the meter for *The Lay of the Last Minstrel* (1805). In 1821 Coleridge said, "Of my poetic works I would fain finish *Christabel,*" but he never did. He pronounced the following lines from *Christabel* among "the best and sweetest I ever wrote" (they refer, perhaps, to an early difference with Southey, but Coleridge managed to quarrel with nearly all his friends at one time or another) :

> Alas! they had been friends in youth;
> But whispering tongues can poison truth;
> And constancy lives in realms above;
> And life is thorny; and youth is vain;
> And to be wroth with one we love
> Doth work like madness in the brain.

S. T. Coleridge

Another magnificent fragment, also published in 1816 but written much earlier, was *Kubla Khan*. The first line "In Xanadu did Kubla Khan" is taken word for word from a seventeenth-century travel book which Coleridge, according to his own account, was reading in a lonely farm-house, when, having taken an anodyne, he fell into a profound sleep. Waking up three hours after, he realized that, in his sleep, without any sensation or consciousness of effort, he had composed a poem of two or three hundred lines, and he at once proceeded to write it down. He had written fifty-four lines—all that are preserved—when he was interrupted by a person on business, and when the hour's interview was over, he found that the rest had faded from his memory and he was quite unable to recall it.

The "anodyne" to which Coleridge refers above was laudanum, and he had begun to take it, owing to his weak health, in 1796. He became increasingly addicted to it and in 1816 had to be placed under medical care near London, his family being looked after by Southey at Greta Hall, Keswick—where, indeed, they had already been for some years. Coleridge continued his literary activities and became something of a lion in London society. The Wedgewoods had allowed him a pension of $750 a year since 1798, and though half of this was withdrawn in 1812, Byron persuaded the managers of the new Drury Lane Theatre to produce Coleridge's tragedy *Remorse,* which brought him in $2,000 and was the most substantial sum he ever received for any of his literary efforts. He wrote extensively on religious and philosophical subjects, but had to acknowledge that his writings did not bring in "even bread"; his publisher, as a matter of fact, became bankrupt. As a lecturer he was more successful, and his criticisms—or, rather, analytic eulogiums—of Shakspere were perhaps his most solid contribution to the Romantic Revival, though his imaginative poems of the supernatural, the *Ancient Mariner* and *Christabel,* were as important in one way as Wordsworth's poems on nature-worship and common life were in another. With Wordsworth's philosophy of nature he was not, indeed, in agreement; he wrote in the *Ode to Dejection:*

> O William! we receive but what we give
> And in our life alone does nature live.

Of the later phase of Coleridge's life there is little to be said, except by way of excuse. Lamb described him as "an archangel—a little damaged," and Carlyle wrote of him as "a sage escaped from the inanity of life's battle." His own epitaph, written by himself the year before he died, is perhaps his best defense:

> Stop, Christian passerby!—Stop, child of God,
> And read with gentle breast. Beneath this sod
> A poet lies, or that which once seemed he.—
> O, lift one thought in prayer for S.T.C.;
> That he who many a year with toil of breath
> Found death in life, may here find life in death!
> Mercy for praise—to be forgiven for fame
> He asked, and hoped, through Christ. Do thou the same!

KESWICK BRIDGE AND GRETA HALL

ROBERT SOUTHEY (1774-1843) was a most industrious man of letters, leaving as a legacy to posterity ten volumes of verse and forty volumes of prose; of these some half-dozen pages of verse and perhaps three volumes of prose—the lives of Cowper, Nelson, and Wesley—have been saved from oblivion. Something has already been said of his friendship and family relationship with Coleridge. Like Wordsworth and Coleridge, Southey lost his revolutionary French sympathies when his own country was in danger, and became a solid conservative English patriot. In 1813 he was appointed poet laureate, and on the death of George III wrote:

> Such the proud, the virtuous story,
> Such the great, the endless glory

of his "splendid reign." As a man Southey was of exemplary virtue; as a student, he was of exemplary diligence. There is a story that he was telling a Quaker friend of his how he husbanded his time, learning Spanish while he was shaving, Portuguese in his bath, and so on. "And when," asked the Quaker, "does thee do thy thinking?" It is a question which might seem unanswerable, and yet when Southey and Macaulay in 1829 had a famous discussion as to the merits and defects of contemporary civilization, Macaulay by no means carried off the honors of the encounter. Dr. Richard Garnett judiciously observed that the view of social evils taken by Southey (and condemned with scathing ridicule by his doughty antagonist) often anticipated Ruskin, and "was in many respects deeper and truer than that of his optimistic critic." Probably Macaulay's temper was roused by Southey's advocacy of remedial measures which seemed in contravention of Macaulay's Liberal principles. His Lives of Nelson and of Wesley were held in high esteem throughout the nineteenth century, but hardly come up to the standard of epigrammatic discrimination set by recent practitioners of the biographical art. Some of his short lyrics still find their way into the anthologies on account of their simplicity of form and excellence of sentiment.

NEWSTEAD ABBEY, NOTTS

With GEORGE GORDON, LORD BYRON (1788-1824) the Romantic Revival enters upon a new phase—the expression in poetry of the poet's own romantic personality. Byron's personality and his power of expressing it were of extraordinary vigor. We cannot understand the power of his personality without a frank and careful consideration of the circumstances of his life, such as was not possible until recently. Only when these circumstances are weighed can we judge of Byron's character or of the force of public indignation which drove him out of England.

The Byron family was both famous and notorious. Newstead Abbey (now a public trust) came to them through the dissolution of the monasteries by Henry VIII, but the Byrons had previously distinguished themselves in the Crusades and in the French wars. In the seventeenth century the first baron's wife was the seventeenth mistress of Charles II; in the eighteenth, the fifth baron, the poet's immediate predecessor, was tried for the murder of his cousin, whom he had killed in a duel, and escaped punishment only by pleading privilege as a peer of the realm; he was known as the "Wicked Lord," having driven his wife from the Abbey and replaced her by a servant-girl whom the villagers called "Lady Betty." His nephew (the poet's father) was known as "Mad Jack" for his wild escapades and reckless debauchery. Returning as a youth from the American war, he eloped with the wife of the Lord Chamberlain, Lady Carmarthen, spent her money, and, so it is said, broke her heart. Before dying in 1784 she gave birth to a daughter, Augusta, who was brought up by her mother's relatives, and did not meet the poet till she was twenty, but after that played the principal part in his stormy career. Captain Byron was promptly married again, this time to a Scottish heiress, Catherine Gordon of Gight, whose ancestral line was even more plentifully marked with murders and suicides than that of the Byrons. He ran through her money and left an impoverished widow in 1791.

Byron remembered his father just enough to realize that the family life of his parents was impossible. He inherited from both sides a proud, violent, vindictive temper and unrestrained

HARROW

TRINITY COLLEGE, CAMBRIDGE

passions. His mother said to him, "You little dog, you're a thorough Byron; you are just as bad as your father," but between Byron and Gordon there was not much to choose. Mrs. Byron grew fat, she was vulgar and hysterical; the little boy soon came to be ashamed of her, and to hate her. With fair curling hair and beautiful features, he had a weakness of the tendons of the ankle which made him obviously lame; he suffered tortures in vain attemps at a cure and all his life he had to wear a specially constructed boot, which gave him a limping gait. Passionately fond of exercise, he became a magnificent rider and swimmer, but the ordinary boyish sports were too difficult for him, and the sense of his deformity rankled his proud sensitive spirit. The feeling of embitterment was increased when he overheard Mary Chaworth, the first girl he was seriously in love with, say "Do you think I could care anything for that lame boy?"

At the age of six Byron became heir presumptive to the barony and at ten he succeeded to the title. But the boy and his mother did not succeed to affluence, for the "Wicked Uncle" had done all he could to ruin the Abbey estate before he died, cutting down the timber, killing off the deer, and leaving the house in a general state of dilapidation. There was no money to keep up an establishment and the house was let to another noble-man. Mrs. Byron obtained a pension of $1,500 from the Government, and Byron was sent to Harrow, one of the great so-called "public" schools, which were at that time the private preserve of the English aristocracy.

Byron was happy at Harrow on the Hill, taking an active part in such games as were possible for him, and, though not a diligent student, a wide reader; he was already remarked as out of the common, and allowances were made for his haughty mien and violent temper. When he went up to Trinity College, Cambridge, in 1805, he was allowed an income of $2,500 from the estate and was able to keep a horse and a man-servant. With the help of Augusta, who backed his notes, he borrowed money, took rooms in Piccadilly, and kept a mistress, a private pugilist, and a fencing master, all of whom he brought from

HOURS OF IDLENESS,

A

SERIES OF POEMS,

ORIGINAL

AND

TRANSLATED,

By GEORGE GORDON, LORD BYRON,

A MINOR.

Μητ' αρ με μαλ' αινει μητε τι νεικει.
HOMER. Iliad, 10.
Virginibus puerisque Canto.
HORACE.
He whistled as he went for want of thought.
DRYDEN.

Newark:

Printed and sold by S. and J. RIDGE;
SOLD ALSO BY B. CROSBY AND CO. STATIONER'S COURT;
LONGMAN, HURST, REES, AND ORME, PATERNOSTER-
ROW; F. AND C. RIVINGTON, ST. PAUL'S CHURCH-
YARD; AND J. MAWMAN, IN THE POULTRY;
LONDON.

1807.

ENGLISH BARDS,

AND

Scotch Reviewers,

——

A SATIRE.

——

I had rather be a kitten, and cry, mew!
Than one of these same metre ballad-mongers.
SHAKSPEARE.

Such shameless Bards we have; and yet 'tis true,
There are as mad, abandon'd Critics too.
POPE.

LONDON:

PRINTED FOR JAMES CAWTHORN, BRITISH LIBRARY,
No. 24, COCKSPUR STREET.

Childe Harold's Pilgrimage.

A ROMAUNT.

BY

LORD BYRON.

———

L'univers est une espèce de livre, dont on n'a lu que la première page quand on n'a vu que son pays.
J'en ai feuilleté un assez grand nombre, que j'ai trouvé également mauvaises. Cet examen ne m'a point
été infructueux. Je haïssais ma patrie. Toutes les impertinences des peuples divers, parmi lesquels j'ai vécu,
m'ont réconcilié avec elle. Quand je n'aurais tiré d'autre bénéfice de mes voyages que celui-là, je n'en re-
gretterais ni les frais, ni les fatigues.
LE COSMOPOLITE.

LONDON:

PRINTED FOR JOHN MURRAY, 32, FLEET-STREET;
WILLIAM BLACKWOOD, EDINBURGH; AND JOHN CUMMING, DUBLIN.
By Thomas Davison, White-Friars.
1812.

DON JUAN.

———

" Difficile est proprie communia dicere."
HOR. Epist. ad Pison.

———

LONDON:

PRINTED BY THOMAS DAVISON, WHITEFRIARS.
1819.

London to Cambridge. But he was already beginning to take himself seriously as a poet. He had a local printer run off a few copies of his *Fugitive Pieces* and sent the first two that came from the press to personal friends; they were horrified at one of the love-poems, and Byron was persuaded to destroy the whole edition. But he at once set to work to print another edition, with the offending poem omitted and guaranteed by himself to be "vastly correct and miraculously chaste." His friends gave it a mixed reception, but he determined to secure for it a wider circulation and in June, 1807, published an enlarged edition under the title *Hours of Idleness*. In February, 1808, there appeared a scathing onslaught in the "Edinburgh Review," savagely attacking the production and its author, "George Gordon, Lord Byron, a Minor": such verses could be written by "nine men in ten" educated in England; and "the tenth man writes better verse than Lord Byron." Byron was intensely annoyed and humiliated: he waited for a year and retorted in March, 1809, with *English Bards and Scotch Reviewers,* in which he satirized not only the "Edinburgh Review" and its contributors but contemporary poets in general, including Tom Moore, whose verses Byron as a youth at Harrow had admired. In a letter which Byron did not receive till long after, Moore challenged him to a duel. By that time Moore's wrath had evaporated: a luncheon was substituted for the more deadly meeting and the two men became fast friends.

Meanwhile Byron left Cambridge with an M.A. degree, and being now over twenty years of age, took possession of his dilapidated estate at Newstead, with some fifty thousand dollars of personal debts. He fitted up a few rooms in the Abbey for the entertainment of his Cambridge friends, and on the site of the altar in the ruined chapel built a tomb to his favorite Newfoundland dog, with a cynical inscription. When he came of age on January 22, 1809, an ox was roasted whole in the courtyard and there was a ball for the tenants, but the young lord was in London. Two months later he took his seat in the House of Lords, and haughtily refused to associate himself with either

side in politics, though three years later he made a speech in a tone which might fairly be described as radical.

The summer of 1809 he spent at Newstead, engaging the prettiest girls he could find in the neighborhood to wait upon his guests:

> Monastic dome! condemned to uses vile!
> Where superstition once had made her den,
> Now Paphian girls were known to sing and smile.

To complete the contrast, the young guests wore the monastic habit at their revels, and drank from the skull of a monk dug up in the Abbey garden.

Byron left England for his first long Continental pilgrimage in June, 1809. He made his way to Lisbon, through Portugal and Spain to Malta, and by way of Albania to Athens, where he fell in love, after a fashion, with a young Greek girl to whom he wrote:

> Maid of Athens, ere we part
> Give, oh, give me back my heart!

The girl's mother tactlessly suggested marriage, but the poet had "better amusement"; he went to Constantinople, swam the Hellespont, returned to Greece, contracted malaria, and arrived in England in July, 1811.

Byron on his return prepared for publication a romantic and sentimental account of his travels, in Spenserian stanzas, which appeared at the end of February, 1812, as Cantos I and II of *Childe Harold's Pilgrimage;* it was originally to have been called *Childe Burun,* the name under which his progenitor had come over from Normandy at the time of the Conquest, but Byron thought better of the idea. He remained, however, his own hero, and he was very soon everybody's hero; it was on a morning in March that, as he himself put it, "I awoke and found myself famous." In fashionable circles he became the only topic of conversation—"the men jealous of him, the women of each other"; at dinner-tables there could be heard the ceaseless hum

LADY BYRON

LADY CAROLINE LAMB

of his name: *Byr'n, Byr'n, Byr'n*. Elizabeth Barrett (later Mrs. Browning) thought of dressing as a boy and becoming his page; and Lady Caroline Lamb did so. Before she met him, she was "dying to see him"; when she saw him, she avoided an introduction and entered him in her diary as "mad, bad, and dangerous to know." Two days later he was presented to her, and she added the words: "That beautiful pale face is my fate." The lady's husband, William Lamb, afterward Lord Melbourne, offered no particular obstacle to the prosecution of the intrigue, which was quickly consummated. But by the time the summer was over, Byron was wearied of her disguises and other follies, and only too ready to break off. She pursued him, and when her family expostulated with her, she fled—it was thought, to her lover. The family appealed to Byron for help; he discovered where she had taken refuge, and induced her to return home. The story went the rounds, and even the profligate regent (afterward George IV) was scandalized. Lady Caroline allowed herself to be taken to Ireland.

Before long, society was convulsed with a far worse scandal. Byron's mother died soon after his return from abroad, and he was keeping bachelor quarters in London when he was not pursuing amours at country houses. His half-sister, Augusta, was a married woman with three children, and he had not seen her since his return. In June, 1813, she wrote that she was obliged to leave home (her marriage had not been a success) and that she was coming to stay with Byron in London. She was four years older than Byron, but had had far less experience of the world, and was apparently as lacking in moral sense as in intelligence. She was fond of Byron, and he found in her an easy victim. His own passion was expressed in the lines to Leila, added to the romantic Oriental story in verse, *The Giaour,* he had published earlier in 1813. He returned to the theme of incest in another Turkish tale, *The Bride of Abydos,* published the same year, and talked and wrote about the illicit connection with an extraordinary boldness. He spoke of a woman passionately loved and with child by him, "and if a daughter, it shall

BYRON IN 1814

be called Medora." Augusta bore a child on April 15, 1814, called Elizabeth Medora Leigh. Byron acknowledged the child as his own, gave the mother fifteen thousand dollars, and made further provision for them in his will. It was at this time that he wrote the following lines:

> I speak not, I trace not, I breathe not thy name,
> There is grief in the sound, there is guilt in the fame:
> But the tear which now burns on my cheek may impart
> The deep thoughts that dwell in that silence of heart.
>
> Too brief for our passion, too long for our peace
> Were those hours—can their joy or their bitterness cease?
> We repent, we abjure, we will break from our chain,
> We will part, we will fly to—unite it again.
>
> Oh! thine be the gladness, and mine be the guilt!
> Forgive me, adored one!—forsake if thou wilt;—
> But the heart which is thine shall expire undebased,
> And *man* shall not break it—whatever *thou* mayst.

The months of August and September, 1814, Byron and Augusta spent together at the seaside; and in the latter month, Byron, doubtless with Augusta's consent, wrote making a formal proposal for the hand of Miss Milbanke, a well-known heiress, of strict and even puritanical principles. As she was a cousin of Lady Caroline Lamb, and had moved in London society, she could not have been ignorant of Byron's reputation, and the presumption is that she hoped to reform him. In any case, the marriage, which took place early in 1815, was a ghastly failure from the start; Byron's moodiness, ill-temper, and covert allusions to his relations with Augusta were intolerable, and after the birth of a daughter, early in 1816, Lady Byron took the baby home to her parents, and told them she thought Byron was mad. A doctor who was consulted failed to discover anything like settled lunacy—merely irritability. But Lady Byron was inexorable in her determination not to return to her husband,

and a legal separation was arranged. Byron bent to the inevitable and wrote for his wife the lines beginning:

> Fare thee well! and if for ever,
> Still for ever, fare thee well.

When his romantic poem *The Corsair* was published in 1814, fourteen thousand copies were sold the first day, and he appeared to be at the peak of his popularity. But now, in 1816, he was hissed on his way to the House of Lords, and inside the House only one peer spoke to him; at a farewell party given to him and Augusta in April by a courageous hostess everyone turned the cold shoulder to them. He said good-by to Augusta a week later, and on April 25 left England for ever.

But before leaving, Byron had begun a new love-affair. As frequently happened, the first advances came from the other side; Clara Mary Jane Clairmont (she called herself "Claire") was the stepdaughter of the radical philosopher William Godwin, who did not believe in marriage as an institution, but had been twice married. Of this philosophic household Claire (now eighteen) had been a member for fifteen years, and her mode of attack upon Byron was more vigorous and direct than that of a fashionable lady. She wrote to him repeatedly, asking for an interview, and, having obtained an interview, proposed a night in the country together. She was a new type of girl in Byron's varied experience and he accepted the adventure.

All this took place just before Byron was driven from England by a storm of public opprobrium, and it happened that Mary Godwin and her poet-lover Shelley were also on the point of leaving England for the Continent. What more natural than that Claire should travel with them and rejoin Byron on the Lake of Geneva? So it was arranged, and before the end of May the meeting took place: the Shelleys rented a small cottage on the other side of the lake from Geneva, and Byron with his suite occupied the Villa Diodati, where Claire came to see him every evening, the two houses being conveniently near. She became the mother of Byron's daughter Allegra, but long before the baby was born Byron had tired of his new mistress and refused ever to see her again.

Claire did a real service to Byron by bringing him under the influence of Shelley. Byron had left England with a heart full of passionate resentment and defiance. Just before sailing from Dover he had penned the lines:

> Here's a sigh to those who love me,
> And a smile to those who hate;
> And, whatever sky's above me,
> Here's a heart for every fate!

But his real feeling was much more embittered, and Shelley, the richest as well as the purest spirit he had yet encountered, cheered and quietened him. They had long excursions on the lake together, and long discussions ashore. Byron had already plunged into the third canto of *Childe Harold,* who now wandered forth again "with nought of hope left but with less of gloom." Shelley's pantheism and Wordsworth's nature-worship, which Byron learned from Shelley, reëcho in the third canto, which was finished before Shelley and the two stepsisters left for England in August. But Byron had not forgotten Augusta; he wrote to her constantly, composed the *Stanzas to Augusta,* and idealized her as the Astarte of *Manfred,* which he began in the Swiss Alps and finished in Italy:

> She was like me in lineaments; her eyes,
> Her hair, her features, all, to the very tone
> Even of her voice, they said were like to mine;
> But softened all, and tempered into beauty . . .
> Her faults were mine—her virtues were her own—
> I loved her, and destroyed her.

Canto IV of *Childe Harold's Pilgrimage,* which deals largely with Rome, was written at Venice, where Byron rode on the Lido, swam in the lagoon, and indulged recklessly in other delights, which had eventually to be stopped by the doctor's orders. From this career of promiscuous sensuality Byron was permanently rescued by the Countess Guiccioli, a seventeen-year-old bride with a husband over sixty. In the spring of 1819, after a wooing of respectable length (according to the standards of the time and place), she accepted him as her *cavaliere servente*. He followed her from Venice to Ravenna, and from Ravenna to Bologna; in the autumn she left her husband, and lived with Byron near Venice. Shelley, who visited them in 1820, thought the connection an inestimable benefit to Byron, whom he found greatly improved "in genius, in temper, in moral views, in health, in happiness." It was at Shelley's suggestion that Byron and his countess, having become involved in political troubles, removed in 1821 to Pisa and installed themselves in the Palazzo Lanfranchi. They were still there in July, 1822, when news was brought that Shelley had been drowned on the neighboring coast; Byron said of him that he "was, without exception, the best and least selfish man I ever knew. I never knew one who was not a beast in comparison."

Byron's own days were drawing near their close. He remained faithful to La Guiccioli; she was, as he had promised she should be, his last *amica*. He worked steadily at *Don Juan,* a mock-heroic epic in the Italian eight-line stanza called *ottava rima,* which gave ample room for his descriptive and narrative powers, potent rhetoric, and cynical humor. He had begun in 1817 with the promise of twelve books, and in five years he had completed eleven of them. But about a year from the death of Shelley, he cast *Don Juan* aside, sent the Countess Guiccioli home to her father, and plunged heart and soul into the struggle for Greek independence. To this cause he gave freely not only his money but his personal service, enlisting under the banner of the Greek revolutionary leader Mavrocordato, at Missolonghi, where he arrived in January, 1824. The situation was malarial, the weather was bad, and Byron was overwhelmed by work and worry; his health broke down under the strain, and he died from fever on April 19.

His sacrifice was not in vain. The Greeks proved unequal to the task of gaining their own freedom, but Byron's death drew the attention of Europe to their cause, and the combined fleets of Great Britain, France, and Russia achieved Greek independence by the Battle of Navarino in 1827. More than a century later, in July, 1931, when Newstead Abbey became public property, the Greek premier Venizelos paid a special visit to England to acknowledge what Byron had done for the Greek nation.

Byron had sold his Memoirs to a London publisher, but at Augusta's insistence they were destroyed unread, and the secret of his relations with her remained at any rate in doubt for over a hundred years. But apart from that, Byron's known excesses were enough to blacken his reputation with the British public, and his name has always been the occasion for keen controversy.

Even those who judged him from a literary point of view, apart from conventional standards of morality, have condemned him for sentimentalism or cynicism or insincerity. But when all reasonable objections are taken into account, he remains one of the outstanding figures of the Romantic Revival, not only in English but in European literature. Goethe to the end of his life regarded Byron as a poetical genius of the first rank, and this has remained the accepted opinion ever since among the critics of Continental Europe, who cannot understand the squeamishness of British and American opinion about his character and achievements. They appreciate his intellectual vigor and independence, and are perhaps less sensitive to his lack of subtlety and refinement, not only in his poetic diction and versification, but in his whole mode of life and thought.

PERCY BYSSHE SHELLEY (1792-1822), whose fate was so strangely interwoven with that of Byron, came, like him, of aristocratic descent, and, like him, was educated at one of the great public schools. But while Byron could trace his descent back to the Conquest and was the sixth baron when he first met Shelley, the latter was only the eldest son of the second baronet —facts which the elder poet never forgot. Besides, when Shelley was born, his grandfather, Bysshe Shelley, was not yet a baronet, but merely a very successful member of an old Sussex family who had made his own fortune, after committing the original

MAGDALEN COLLEGE AND BRIDGE

HIGH STREET, OXFORD

indiscretion of being born in America. Shelley's father, Timothy Shelley, represented the county in Parliament, was a man of obstinate conventional prejudices and limited intelligence. How this quiet nest of barnyard fowls produced such a wild eagle as Shelley is one of the mysteries beyond explanation.

At Eton the poet—he published a romance and a volume of poems before he left school—became known as "Mad Shelley" or "Shelley the Atheist," and made himself conspicuous by a revolt against the system of "fagging," which compelled the younger boys to do menial services for their elders. He had been at University College, Oxford, only a few months when he printed a pamphlet entitled *The Necessity of Atheism,* for which he was promptly expelled by the college authorities, together with his friend Hogg, who also had advanced opinions and refused to answer questions about the pamphlet. Hogg's father sent him off to study law, and Shelley, now only eighteen, solitary and penniless in London lodgings (for his father had cut off his allowance) received consolation and support from his sisters, who were at school in a London suburb, and gave him the pocket money and cakes intended for their own consumption. When the direct channel of supply became difficult, they made use of a pretty schoolfellow named Harriet Westbrook, with whom Shelley struck up an acquaintance and correspondence. This came to the ears of the head mistress, and Harriet fell into disgrace; but the summer holidays came round and relieved her from the tyranny of a system which would not allow a girl of sixteen to exchange letters with a young philosopher a little older than herself.

Meanwhile, through Shelley's uncle, who appealed to a local county magnate, the Duke of Norfolk, Timothy Shelley was induced to permit his son and heir to return home, and to allow him an income of a thousand dollars a year. Harriet's father, a retired publican, had rather encouraged Shelley's friendship with his daughter, and so did her sister Eliza; he was now invited to spend the summer with them in Wales, but he was prudent enough to decline the invitation. He kept up the cor-

Percy B Shelley

respondence with her, however, and she appealed to him to rescue her from the odious necessity of returning to school. Shelley consulted Hogg, and Hogg, who was not without shrewdness, advised him that rescue meant marriage. So Shelley carried Harriet off by stage-coach to Edinburgh, married her with money borrowed from the landlord of the hotel, and after a brief honeymoon went with Hogg to York. The poet was driven from York because Harriet complained that Hogg made love to her, and they went to the Lake District. There they called upon the Duke of Norfolk, whose duchess found Harriet "quite charming," and the hearts of the obdurate fathers of the young people were melted; each undertook to provide Shelley with a thousand dollars a year.

For the next two or three years Shelley and Harriet wandered about England, Wales, and Ireland, settling into a place with the intention of staying "for ever," and leaving next month, or next week, or next day. Shelley printed privately a revolutionary poem entitled *Queen Mab* (1813) and Harriet gave birth to her first child, Ianthe, in June of the same year. On her recovery it became evident that the relations between her and Shelley were strained, and each began to look for consolation elsewhere. Shelley found it in the household of the radical philosopher Godwin, with whom he had opened a correspondence soon after his marriage. It was a strange household. William Godwin, the head of it, had in 1793 published the *Enquiry concerning Political Justice,* which was the foundation of English theoretical radicalism. Following in the footsteps of Rousseau, he believed that man was naturally good, and capable of the highest perfection if his nature were not thwarted by political institutions; marriage should not be a binding tie, but a free union dissoluble at the will of either party. Nevertheless, he had been legally married to another advanced thinker of the time, Mary Wollstonecraft, whose *Vindication of the Rights of Women* was published the year before his own radical treatise. She brought with her into the Godwin household her natural daughter Fanny Imlay, and died in giving birth to Mary God-

MARY GODWIN SHELLEY

win, the first year of her marriage. Four years later Godwin married a Mrs. Clairmont, who added a third girl to the family, her daughter by her first marriage, the "Claire" who followed Byron in his final flight to the Continent. When Shelley first visited the Godwin household in 1813, Mary was away, but the other two girls became his devoted admirers and no doubt expatiated upon his charms to Mary, upon her return; besides, he had given financial help to Godwin, who was always in money difficulties, so that there was every reason for speaking well of him. Mary, now seventeen years of age, was unhappy with her stepmother, and confided her troubles to the young poet, who had possibly invited her confidence by the recital of his own. In any case, within a week of meeting each other, in June, 1814, they had fallen desperately in love, and within a month Shelley proposed to Godwin that they should be allowed to go away together. The philosopher was astonished that this favorite pupil should propose to put Godwin's own theories into practice with Godwin's own daughter, expostulated energetically with Shelley, and thought he had succeeded in dissuading him; but before the end of July, Mary and her lover were on their way to France. Claire, equally sick of life in the Godwin household, accompanied them. Before leaving England, Shelley had made financial provision for Harriet's wants, and his father's succession to the title and estate in 1815 gave him an income of five thousand dollars, out of which he allotted Harriet an income of one thousand in addition to the thousand she received from her father. Now, with his mind more at ease, he was able to turn his thoughts to poetry, and wrote *Alastor, or the Spirit of Solitude* (1816), which breathes the quiet beauty of the upper Thames, adopted by Shelley as his favorite haunt after his return from the Continent. Mary gave birth to a boy in January, 1816, and in the spring the lovers set out for Switzerland, accompanied by Claire, to meet Byron on the Lake of Geneva.

Returning to England in the autumn of 1816, Shelley met sorrow upon sorrow. Fanny Imlay, disheartened by an existence apparently futile, and perhaps in love with Shelley, committed suicide. This tragedy was quickly followed by the suicide of Harriet, who, leaving her two children to the care of her father, and deserted by her new lover, drowned herself in the Serpentine. Shelley's grief was embittered by a lawsuit on the part of Harriet's father to retain possession of the children, and in 1817 the Lord Chancellor, deeming both parties undesirable, assigned them to a guardian. Meanwhile Shelley bought a house in the Thames valley (Mary had now two children and there was the daughter of Claire and Byron, little Allegra), and wrote *The Revolt of Islam,* a romantic story of an ideal revolution, which has as its leaders and martyrs two young lovers, Laon and Cythna (in the first version brother and sister, but Shelley's publishers made him change it). Shelley was afraid that his children by Mary might also be taken away from him, though he was now married to her, and Mary had had the children baptized.

Mary was anxious also to be separated from Claire and her baby, whose presence in the household encouraged malignant gossip. So the babies, with their nurse-maids and the parents made their way to Venice to seek Byron, and Allegra was handed over to her father—to die, not many years after, in an Italian convent. Byron refused to have anything more to do with Claire, and the whole problem gave the Shelleys great anxiety. But soon they had keener anxieties of their own: first the little girl, then the little boy died, and Mary sank into the deepest depression. She recovered her spirits to some extent, however, in the friendlier social atmosphere of Florence, and the birth there of a son, Percy Florence (who afterward succeeded to the baronetcy), did much to console her.

Nearly all the work that placed Shelley in the first rank of English lyric poets was done in the short three years left to him. His study of Greek tragedy found a magnificently romantic outcome in *Prometheus Unbound,* which was written in 1819 and published in 1820. In it he expressed his philosophy in its noblest form:

To suffer woes which Hope thinks infinite;
To forgive wrongs darker than death or night;
　To defy Power, which seems omnipotent;
To love, and bear; to hope till Hope creates
From its own wreck the thing it contemplates;
　Neither to change, nor falter, nor repent;
This, like thy glory, Titan, is to be
Good, great and joyous, beautiful and free;
This is alone Life, Joy, Empire, and Victory.

About the same time he wrote some of his best independent
lyrics, including the *Ode to the West Wind* and *To a Skylark*.
His residence in Pisa brought him into contact with a young
(and, as he thought, wronged) Italian beauty, Emilia Viviani,
who inspired *Epipsychidion* (1821)—a poem far transcending
its occasion. The death of Keats in the same year and the story
that it had been hastened by a savage article in the "Quarterly
Review" roused Shelley to a pitch of feeling which gave us in
Adonais the finest elegy ever written by one poet for another.
The visit of Prince Mavrocordato, the Greek revolutionary
leader under whom Byron was to serve later, stirred Shelley to
a dream of enthusiasm which found vent in *Hellas* with its
beautiful choruses.

In the spring of 1822 the Shelleys moved from Pisa to the
neighboring coast to avoid the summer heat. They shared a
house at Lerici on the Gulf of Spezzia with Mr. and Mrs.
Williams—the last of the Platonic attachments in which Shelley's poetic soul strove to find more than can be realized in
human form. His adoration for her is expressed in the lines:

I can give not what men call love,
　But wilt thou accept not
The worship the heart lifts above
　And the Heavens reject not,
The desire of the moth for the star,
　Of the night for the morrow,
The devotion to something afar
　From the sphere of our sorrow?

SHELLEY'S VILLA AT LERICI

THE BURNING OF SHELLEY'S BODY

She was a musician, and Shelley sent her the lines "With a Guitar—to Jane," which are probably the last he ever wrote. Williams and Shelley had built for themselves at Genoa a small yacht, first named *Don Juan* in honor of Byron, but afterward rechristened *Ariel* by Shelley, who was offended by Byron's behavior to Claire at the time of the death of their daughter Allegra. On July 8, Shelley and Williams, with a young English sailor, left Leghorn in the yacht for Lerici; a storm came on and nothing was seen of them again until some days later, when the bodies of all three were washed up on the beach near Viareggio. Shelley had in one pocket a volume of Sophocles and in the other a volume of Keats, "doubled back as if the reader, in the act of reading, had hastily thrust it away." Owing to the extreme heat, the municipal regulations required the bodies to be buried at once in the sands. As that of Shelley was being burned, the heart was snatched from the flames. Byron and another friend of Shelley's, Trelawny, who were present at the cremation, had it sent for burial in the Protestant cemetery at Rome, under a stone bearing the inscription "Cor Cordium" (Heart of Hearts) and the lines:

> Nothing of him that doth fade
> But doth suffer a sea-change
> Into something rich and strange.

The lives of all this group of romantic poets were lamentably short, and that of JOHN KEATS (1795-1821) was the shortest of the three. Fortunately, Keats arrived very quickly at poetic maturity and was able to create a body of imperishable verse which has been a constant source not only of delight to lovers of poetry but of stimulus to poets from his own time to the present day. He was born in a London suburb and lived in or near the metropolis until his last journey to Rome. At sixteen he was apprenticed for five years to a "surgeon and apothecary"—considered at that time a lower order of the medical profession than the "physician"—and in the last year of his apprenticeship became a student at Guy's Hospital. At this time Keats, though

PROTESTANT CEMETERY AT ROME

short (a little over five feet), was robust and lively, with "golden red" hair, popular with his fellows, and a fair but not a diligent student (except of poetry) ; in July, 1816, he received his license to practise.

Earlier in the year Keats had made the acquaintance of Leigh Hunt, a leading journalist and man of letters, who in 1813 had been sent to prison for two years for an attack upon the Prince of Wales (afterward George IV) in his paper, the "Examiner." On Hunt's liberation, Keats wrote a sonnet in celebration of the event; it was in the "Examiner" that Keats saw his first poem in print (May 5, 1816), and it was through Hunt that he met Shelley, Lamb, and Hazlitt during the following winter. In a laudatory article on *Young Poets* (December 1) Hunt quoted the Sonnet *On first looking into Chapman's Homer,* included in the first volume of *Poems* by Keats (1817). All this had a good deal to do with Keats's abandonment of surgery for poetry, and also with his ultimate establishment at Hampstead, where Leigh Hunt had a house, which Keats frequently visited. The friendship had later repercussions which were not so agreeable.

When Keats published his first long poem, *Endymion,* in the spring of 1818, the newly established Blackwood's "Edinburgh Magazine" had already begun to publish a series of articles on "The Cockney School of Poetry," announcing as its first victims Leigh Hunt and John Keats. The magazine was Tory in politics and attacked Hunt because he was a leading Radical; although by opinion Keats was Liberal, he had taken no overt part in politics, and the only excuse for the attack upon him (for which the publication of *Endymion* offered a convenient occasion) was that he was known as Hunt's friend and protégé. Even if we take into account the violence of literary criticism and political partizanship of the time, the onslaught upon Keats in the August number of Blackwood's is of extraordinary virulence. The writer (probably John Gibson Lockhart, afterward son-in-law and biographer of Sir Walter Scott) opened fire with the statement, "The frenzy of the *Poems* was bad enough in its way; but it did not alarm us half so seriously as the calm, settled, imperturbable drivelling idiocy of *Endymion.*" In conclusion, Keats received this advice: "It is a better and a wiser thing to be a starved apothecary than a starved poet; so back to the shop, Mr. John, back to 'plasters, pills, and ointment boxes.'" In the following month, the London "Quarterly," not to be outdone by its more sensational Edinburgh contemporary, published a review in which *Endymion* was torn not merely limb from limb but line from line and word from word. Keats was quite aware that his juvenile poems (he was not yet twenty-three) had defects; he wrote to a friend: "Praise or blame has but a momentary effect on the man whose love of beauty in the abstract makes him a severe critic of his own works. My own domestic criticism has given me pain without comparison beyond what Blackwood's or the 'Quarterly' could possibly inflict." Keats was far too courageous as a man and too independent as an artist to be (as Byron put it in *Don Juan*) "snuffed out by an article." But there can be no doubt that the attacks caused him deep distress. During the past winter he had met Wordsworth in London and had at his request recited to him the "Ode to Pan" from *Endymion,* then in the hands of the printers; the older poet made the cold comment, "A very pretty piece of paganism," and Keats was deeply hurt. Shelley thought poorly of *Endymion,* and closer friends of Keats were not slow to point out its faults.

During the summer of 1818, Keats had other and more serious causes for concern. His younger brother Tom was dying of consumption and his own health was far from satisfactory. In an attempt to reëstablish it, he went with a Hampstead friend, Charles Brown, on a walking tour, beginning in the Lake District, chiefly notable for his conception there of one of his finest sonnets, long known as "the last sonnet," beginning, "Bright star! would I were steadfast as thou art." In its final form Keats undoubtedly wrote the poem out on his last voyage to Italy; but a copy of it exists in the handwriting of his friend Brown with the date "1819," and the idea underlying the opening lines is contained in a letter written by the poet to his brother George (then on his way to America) on June 26, 1818; he speaks of Lake Windermere as enough to "refine one's sensual vision into a sort of north star which can never cease to be open-lidded and steadfast over the wonders of the great Power."

Tom Keats died in December, 1818, and the poet, being left alone (he had lost his father and mother in his childhood), accepted the invitation of his friend Brown to share with him his semi-detached villa at Wentworth Place. Here Keats did his finest work, and Wentworth Place is now preserved as the Keats Memorial House. During the summer, when Brown and Keats were on their walking tour, Brown let his house to a widow named Brawne, with whose daughter, Fanny, Keats fell desperately in love. In the spring of 1819 (after Fanny's engagement to Keats) the Brawnes took the other semi-detached house, so that the poet had his fiancée next door—virtually under the same roof.

Stimulated by his successful wooing of Fanny Brawne, Keats rose at a bound to the height of his achievement and composed in rapid succession the "Eve of St. Agnes," "La Belle Dame sans Merci," and the odes "To a Nightingale" and "On a Grecian Urn." Of these and the other poems published by him in his last volume (1820), Swinburne wrote: "Greater lyrical poetry the world may have seen—lovelier surely it has never seen, nor ever can it possibly see. . . . They are the absolute expression of absolute natural beauty," and with them Keats reached "the foremost rank in the highest class of English poets."

But already, although Keats did not know it, the shades of death were beginning to close around him. In the spring of 1819 (Keats himself noted the date as Sunday, April 11) he took a walk toward Highgate along Millfield Lane, where in 1817 he had met Leigh Hunt and handed him a copy of the first volume of his poems. In the lane he met Coleridge in company with a man who was known to Keats as a demonstrator at Guy's Hospital and who now introduced the two poets to each other. The three men walked along together for a mile or so, at

Bright Star would I were stedfast as thou art —
  Not in lone splendor hung aloft the night
And watching, with eternal lids apart,
  Like nature's patient sleepless Eremite,
The moving waters at their priestlike task
  Of pure ablution round earth's human shores,
Or gazing on the new soft fallen masque
  Of snow upon the mountains and the moors.
No — yet still stedfast, still unchangeable,
  Pillow'd upon my fair love's ripening breast,
To feel for ever its soft swell and fall,
  Awake for ever in a sweet unrest,
Still, still to hear her tender taken breath,
And so live ever — or else swoon to death.

John Keats.

Coleridge's "alderman-after-dinner" pace, and the philosopher talked after his manner on a thousand things. When they parted Keats said, "Mr. Coleridge, allow me the honor of shaking your hand." Coleridge shook hands and invited the younger poet to visit him at Highgate; but when Keats had gone, Coleridge turned to his companion and said, "There is death in that hand."

Keats had lost his mother and brother from consumption, but the medical science of his day could do nothing for him, not even find out what was the matter. It was left to him to make the dread discovery himself. On a mild day in February, 1820, he went into town without overcoat, and returning late at night on the outside of the stage-coach, caught a severe chill. As he was getting into bed, he coughed slightly, and saw a single drop of blood on the sheet. After examining it by the light of a candle, he said to Brown, who was with him, "I know the color of that blood; it is arterial blood, I cannot be deceived in that color; that drop of blood is my death-warrant, I must die."

Keats was right in his diagnosis. He went to Rome, but only to write his own epitaph: "Here lies one whose name was writ in water." By the end of the following February his body was lying in the Protestant Cemetery where the heart of Shelley was so soon to be laid by his side.

Although it was said of Jeffrey, the first editor of the "Edinburgh Review" (1802-1929) that he regarded authors as criminals who appeared before him with ropes already round their necks, the revival of periodical literature early in the nineteenth century produced something more than the sneering at Wordsworth and the bludgeoning of Keats. It was to the columns of the "London Magazine," founded in 120, that CHARLES LAMB (1775-1834) contributed the *Essays of Elia,* which not only gave new life to the occasional essay but brought it to a perfection which has never since been equaled. Lamb was one of the most charming and amusing of letter-writers and he tried most forms of literary composition. Of his poems only one is found in the anthologies, with its haunting refrain "All, all are gone, the old familiar faces." He wrote a comedy (which failed), and a

Yours ratherish unwell

Chs Lamb.

tragedy (which never reached the stage) ; he was even reduced
to writing "witty paragraphs" for the morning papers at the
rate of "sixpence a joke, and it was thought pretty high too."
Yet he is dearer to us than many greater writers and perhaps
better men, whether we think of him as the lifelong friend with
whom Coleridge found it impossible to quarrel, or as the affectionate guardian of his mad sister, or as the inimitable wit of
the convivial gatherings of graver pundits. There is no picture
of the literary life of the time that gives more joy in the remembering than Haydon's story of Lamb's not altogether sober behavior at the dinner party attended by Wordsworth and the
unknown gentleman who insisted on meeting him because he
also was a distributor of stamps. As the other guests thought it
an intrusion, there was a painful silence, broken by the stranger's
asking Wordsworth, "Don't you think, sir, Milton was a great
genius?" Lamb, who was dozing by the fire, turned round and
said, "Pray, sir, did you say Milton was a great genius?" "No,
sir, I asked Mr. Wordsworth if he were not." "Oh," said Lamb,
"then you are a silly fellow." After an awful pause, the Comptroller of Stamps said, "Don't you think Newton a great
genius?" Lamb got up, and taking a candle said, "Sir, will you
allow me to look at your phrenological development?" He then
turned his back on the poor man, and at every question of the
Comptroller he chanted :

'Diddle, diddle, dumpling, my son John
Went to bed with his breeches on.'

"My dear Charles!" said Wordsworth. "Diddle, diddle, dumpling, my son John," chanted Lamb; and then rising, exclaimed,
"Do let me have another look at that gentleman's organs." Keats
and Haydon hurried Lamb into the painting-room, shut the
door and gave way to inextinguishable laughter.

Among the people of a hundred years ago whom one would
like to meet, the first choice of many readers would be Charles
Lamb.

HAZLITT   DE QUINCEY

WILLIAM HAZLITT (1778-1830) was second only to Lamb
in making a literary work out of an occasional essay, whether
for the "London Magazine" or the "Edinburgh Review"; he
achieved what was even more remarkable, in giving permanent
value to series of popular lectures. His lectures on the *Dramatic
Literature of the Age of Elizabeth* were an important contribution to literary criticism and are still valuable in their printed
form.

Unlike Lamb, Hazlitt was much less attractive in real life
than on the printed page. Like Coleridge, he quarreled with all
his friends except Lamb, and it was said of him that he spoke
well of nobody except the dead. When he had been married for
a dozen years, he scandalized his contemporaries by publishing
a detailed account of his infatuation for the daughter of a
London lodging-house keeper, *Liber Amoris* (1823); the girl
refused to have him when he had obtained a Scotch divorce
from his wife, and he married a wealthy widow, who had had
all she could stand of him when the honeymoon trip was over.

He did not even gratify the virtuous by a death-bed repentance, for his last words were, "Well, I have had a happy life."

THOMAS DE QUINCEY (1785-1859) wrote his *Confessions of an English Opium-Eater* (1821) for the "London Magazine" and *Murder as one of the Fine Arts* (1827) for Blackwood's. He attempted, not very successfully, to popularize German philosophy in England; but his revival of the gorgeously rhetorical, periodic style of seventeenth-century English prose had considerable influence. He was, all through his life, a good deal of a Bohemian, and his most interesting writings were about his own adventures. He ran away from the famous Grammar School of Manchester at the age of seventeen, wandered for a while in Wales (where a chance acquaintance with a German tourist enabled him to pick up the language), and made his way to London, where he suffered painful privations and was befriended by a street girl. After a year of this wandering life, he was found, and induced to become a student at Worcester College, Oxford. He refused, however, to submit to discipline, and left the university without taking his degree. In 1807 he made the acquaintance of Coleridge at Bridgewater and escorted Mrs. Coleridge and the children to the Lake District, where he met Wordsworth; and when Wordsworth gave up Dove Cottage, De Quincey moved into it. There he freed himself from his dependence upon opium, to which he had become addicted, married the daughter of a neighboring farmer, and settled down to domestic life.

De Quincey had a family of eight children, but he never became more than partially domesticated. The daughter who kept house for him in his latter years, which were spent mainly in the neighborhood of Edinburgh, said: "He was not a reassuring man for nervous people to live with, as those nights were exceptions on which he did not set something on fire, the commonest incident being for someone to look up from a book or work to say casually: 'Papa, your hair is on fire,' of which a calm, 'Is it, my love?' and a hand rubbing out the blaze was all the notice taken."

SIR WALTER SCOTT

If we had to choose one writer who would represent more phases of the Romantic Revival than any other, it would be SIR WALTER SCOTT (1771-1832), who combines the romantic love of nature, liking for the marvelous, interest in medieval life and literature, affectionate sympathy with the lowly and defeated, with qualities that are all his own—humor, unequaled powers to tell an entrancing story, to describe natural beauty "especially when combined with ancient ruins," or (within limits) to give life and reality to a character.

Scott said his birth was "neither distinguished nor sordid," but he was proud of his great-grandfather, who was a laird, and of the latter's grandfather, who was an ancient chieftain; it was true that the chief's livestock was at one time reduced to a single cow, but he regained his position by "lifting" the cattle of his English neighbors; when Scott built Abbotsford he adorned his entrance hall with the coats of arms of a dozen Border families with which he was connected. His father was an Edinburgh lawyer, or "writer to the signet," as the Scotch phrase still has it, and he was a delicate boy with a limp caused by the arrested growth of his right leg in infancy. He was an idle pupil in the sense that he paid little attention to the regular curriculum of Greek and Latin, but was much given as a child to the reading of chapbooks and ballads, was so enthralled at thirteen with Percy's *Reliques of Ancient English Poetry* that he forgot the dinner hour, and before he was out of his teens had learned enough French to read the old romances, enough Italian to read Ariosto and his successors, and enough Spanish to read Cervantes. He studied for the Scottish bar and became in 1792 a qualified advocate, but obtained very little business. He was still mainly interested in balladry and folklore, and, his health being now restored, he rode about the country collecting material. A lecture on German literature set him studying that language and he published translations of Bürger's *Lenore* (1796) and Goethe's *Götz von Berlichingen* (1799). In the latter year he was appointed deputy sheriff for Selkirkshire; this post encouraged him to still wider researches into ballad literature, which eventually found an outcome in the publication of three volumes of *Minstrelsy of the Scottish Border* (1802-1803).

The impulse to original composition came to Scott, in the first place, from a meeting with "Monk" Lewis, for whose *Tales of Wonder* (1801) he composed or adapted a few ballads. About this time he heard a friend recite some lines from Coleridge's *Christabel* (still in manuscript), which suggested to him the adoption (with some modifications) of its four-beat measure as the metrical medium for which he had been searching. Finally, the Countess of Dalkeith, wife of the heir apparent to the Duke of Buccleuch, who was the head of the Scott clan, suggested a subject in a legend of that great house. The upshot of all this was the *Lay of the last Minstrel,* which was published in 1805 and became enormously popular. Its success encouraged Scott to devote more of his time to literature, especially as he had begun to despair of success as an advocate; but as he had no intention of depending upon literary work for a livelihood (it was a favorite saying of his that "literature should be a staff and not a crutch"), he entered into a silent partnership in the printing business of an old school-fellow and personal friend, James Ballantyne. Scott's secrecy in this affair (which had social and professional considerations as its excuse) has been criticized and even condemned, but if he erred (and he was guilty of nothing more than an error of judgment), he paid most dearly for it in the sequel.

For some years Scott prospered exceedingly. *Marmion* (1808) and *The Lady of the Lake* (1810) were received with increasing enthusiasm. He obtained the reversion of a clerkship of session (an office in the law-court), and from 1812 on was in receipt of the salary, which brought his professional emoluments up to eight thousand dollars a year. Scott was handsome and popular and had a fair share of social ambition, though he was essentially a modest man; when the laureateship was offered to him, he declined it and nominated Southey. But he wanted to found a family and to build a great house (which alas! his son Walter did not live long enough to inhabit). In 1811 the lease of the small house he was living in at Ashestiel on the Tweed expired, and he seemed justified in buying a hundred acres of land with a farm-house upon it a few miles farther down the river at Abbotsford, with the intention of laying out an extensive estate by the acquisition of the adjoining property and erecting a large new house upon it, planned in the Scottish baronial style.

After Scott moved to Abbotsford in 1812 it very soon became evident that he would need more money. The estate, like other undertakings of the same kind, cost more than had been anticipated; Ballantyne and Company got into difficulties and had to be helped out; the later narrative poems did not do so well, perhaps owing to the competition of the more exciting metrical romances of Byron, just now at the height of his first popularity. It was therefore not surprising that Scott should turn his attention in another direction; he had already completed an unfinished historical romance by Joseph Strutt, and had indeed begun one of his own, but on the advice of a friend had not gone on with it. He now took up again the rejected manuscript, continued and completed it, and published it anonymously in 1814 under the title of *Waverley,* which was afterward attached to the whole series of twenty-nine novels which Scott poured out with astonishing industry and facility.

It is difficult for the present generation to realize the reasons for the elaborate secrecy Scott maintained until secrecy became impossible. The mystery of the authorship was certainly no hindrance to the sale, and Scott encouraged it by reviewing the successive issues of the Great Unknown, sometimes favorably, sometimes unfavorably. But it was more than a whim on his part, and to understand it we must remember the conditions of the time and place in which he was situated. He was a leading member of Edinburgh society, and though Edinburgh was beginning to call itself the modern Athens, it was still a provincial and conventional society, which had treated a literary genius like Burns as little more than a curiosity. Scott had no revolutionary feeling and no inclination to take himself seriously as a high priest of literature; he was profoundly conservative and

ABBOTSFORD

conventional. His main income came from his duties in court, which occupied him for some hours daily, and he was "not sure that it would be considered quite decorous for a Clerk of Session to write novels." The historical background of the romances in vogue was contemptible, and their use of the supernatural either crude or cynical; the best examples were those left over from the eighteenth century—Horace Walpole's *Castle of Otranto,* Mrs. Radcliffe's *Romance of the Forest* and *Mysteries of Udolpho,* and Lewis's *Ambrosio the Monk,* the indiscretion of a young attaché which supplanted his baptismal name of Matthew Gregory and made him go by the half-derisive pseudonym of "Monk Lewis" for his own generation and for posterity; besides these there was the tribe of imitators ridiculed by Jane Austen in *Northanger Abbey* and deplored by Wordsworth in the Preface to *Lyrical Ballads.* It was Scott's genius that lifted the historical romance from a popular diversion to a form of art imitated and respected not only in great Britain but in every country in the civilized world.

Scott continued his official duties as Clerk of Session till within two years of his death. He was doing a vast amount of planning and executing extensions and improvements at Abbotsford, where the walls of the baronial mansion rose from year to year; he entertained lavishly and took a reasonable share in sports and other social pastimes; he was doing a considerable amount of editorial work and producing an occasional poem or article. In addition to all this he published *Guy Mannering* and *The Antiquary* in 1815, *The Black Dwarf* and *Old Mortality* in 1816, *Rob Roy* in 1817, *Heart of Midlothian* in 1818, *The Bride of Lammermoor, A Legend of Montrose,* and *Ivanhoe* in 1819. When George IV came to the throne in 1820, the first honor he awarded any one was a baronetcy conferred upon Scott. Scott paid a visit to court to receive his title, and two years later entertained the king at Abbotsford with profuse hospitality.

The turreted walls of Abbotsford were hardly finished and the grounds all laid out before Scott became aware that his financial position was insecure. In addition to his official income, he earned by his pen in the course of his lifetime over a million dollars, but he had spent a great deal of money on the building and upkeep of Abbotsford, where he had many dependents and sometimes entertained as many as forty guests at a time. The publishing enterprises in which he was interested were not all as successful as the Waverley novels, and the business had been badly managed; it is no wonder that Scott, with his multifarious interests and occupations, kept no strict control over it. It was a complex affair in which the Ballantyne brothers, the great Edinburgh publisher Constable, and Constable's London agent were all concerned; it was the failure of the last-named in 1825 that brought about the crash. Scott found himself involved in personal liabilities of over half a million dollars; his assets were Abbottsford and his literary ability.

The creditors were merciful: they left Scott in possession of Abbotsford on condition that he restricted himself to his official income for his personal use and applied his literary gifts to the payment of his debts. Scott was fifty-four years of age, and he had already had serious warnings of a physical breakdown; but he set manfully to work; he lost his wife in 1826, he had an attack of apoplexy in 1828, and was stricken with paralysis in 1830. He strove on, but it soon became evident that the struggle was in vain; his mind fell into a state in which it appeared to him that the struggle was over and the debts had been paid. As a matter of fact, he had paid off about half of them, and the balance was extinguished after his death by the sale of his copyrights. Abbottsford remains in the possession of his descendants and is still a shrine to be visited by the curious; but the Waverley novels, begun with such high ambition and finished with such grim determination, are the real monument to Scott's fame.

CHAPTER IX

THE VICTORIAN AGE

"The Victorian age" is a convenient term, but so far as Queen Victoria is personally concerned it implies very little more than a complex of changes which roughly coincided with the period of her reign (1837-1901). Its predominant feature was the rise into political power and social influence of the middle class with its Puritan standards of conduct and view of life. Even so, the coincidence is not exact, for it is more convenient to date the beginning of the Victorian era from 1832 (the year of Sir Walter Scott's death and of the passing of the First Reform Act). Moreover, the main factors of change—puritanism, industrialism, and science—were at work long before Victoria's reign began and continued long after it was finished. With these qualifications, however, the term "Victorian" is advantageous not as an opprobrious epithet or as a term of appreciation but as indicative of certain social, political, and industrial changes which vitally affected both the people who wrote and the people who read, and therefore had great influence upon the literature that resulted from the unusual combinations of personalities and conditions then prevailing.

The most obvious characteristic of the Victorian age was its extraordinary expansive vigor. The colonial empire which had been lost in the eighteenth century was built up again in the nineteenth; and in spite of sending out thousands of emigrants to Canada, Australia, New Zealand, and South Africa, the English nation increased enormously, both in population and in wealth. Before the turn of the century no official statistics are available, but it is estimated that from the time of Elizabeth the increase in population had been very gradual, amounting only to two or three millions. In the first three decades of the nineteenth cen-

QUEEN VICTORIA IN 1837

tury a greater advance was made than in the previous three centuries, and by 1851 the population had doubled itself within the half-century, to double itself again before the century was over.

Along with the increase in population came a great increase in wealth, but the main point to be noted is that both increases were distributed in the same uneven way; that is, the increased population, along with the increased wealth, went to the urban centers. The agricultural areas stood still or actually lost wealth and population; it was the cities and towns that gained, until in the North of England, where the gain was greatest, the manufacturing districts formed almost continuous urban areas within which it was impossible to get out of sight of a factory chimney, though one might go for miles in the vain hope of getting into the real country. Even at the beginning of the Victorian age, England was still mainly agricultural, and as late as the new Doomsday Book of 1873 two thirds of the land in England and Wales was held by 10,207 landlords—known as the "upper ten thousand." But early in the century the inhabitants of the manufacturing areas began to resent the government of England by the landowning aristocracy, which held nearly all the seats in the House of Lords and controlled a great many of those in the House of Commons by the influence they exerted in the elections at what were known as "nomination" or "pocket" boroughs; these were Parliamentary constituencies with few or no electors and therefore in the "pocket" of some great landowner, who regarded them as his own property, and regularly "nominated" the Parliamentary member or members. The Reform Act of 1832 disfranchised fifty-six of these boroughs and gave increased representation to the manufacturing towns; the right to vote, which had been subject to vexatious restrictions, was now enlarged to include male householders on the basis of a small yearly rental. This was the beginning of the transformation of England into a modern democracy, with the balance of power transferred first from the great landowners to the middle class and later to the working class. The change was a very gradual one—more gradual even than is indicated by the successive

A. FORESTIER
Cimiez 1897

Victoria R I 1897

reform acts which marked its accomplishment, for the aristocracy and the middle class continued to exercise great influence and to hold most of the seats in Parliament and the principal posts in the Government long after their control of the electorate had theoretically passed away; but the fact remains that at the end of the Victorian age democracy was politically triumphant. It was an educated democracy, largely organized in trades-unions and coöperative societies, living in towns and cities which were easily accessible—very different from the ignorant agricultural laborers passing all their lives in isolated villages at the beginning of the Victorian era. Machines, factories, and workshops, steamboats and railroads, telegraphs, telephones, and wireless, electric street-cars (soon to be followed by the automobile and the airplane) had made a new England and a new world.

These industrial and political changes were accompanied by intellectual and spiritual changes that were no less remarkable. The Nonconformists, reinforced by the organization of various Methodist denominations in the first half of the century, came to count more adherents than the Established Church, and as they had a large following in the manufacturing and mercantile towns, they exercised a strong political influence. The village parson shared with the village squire in the loss of social prestige and intellectual leadership; traditional authority no longer had the same weight. The agricultural laborer, admitted to educational opportunity, the Parliamentary franchise, and the responsibilities of local government, began to read the newspapers and to do a little thinking for himself. He was no longer willing to accept as divinely ordered a social system in which he submitted to a scanty wage and primitive living conditions eked out with Christmas gifts of food and flannel from his superiors (with a certain amount of good advice and condescending kindness) and the prospect of the local poorhouse or an almshouse in which to end his days. That ideal figure "Honest John Tomkins, the hedger and ditcher, Who, though he was poor, never wished to be richer," disappeared from the English country-side. The agricultural laborer and still more the artisan in the towns, about the middle of the Victorian era, became aware that not only the clergy but the creed did not stand in their ancient position of assured authority.

The change in opinion may be illustrated by the fact that the publication of *The Rights of Man* and *The Age of Reason* made Thomas Paine an exile from England in the last decade of the eighteenth century; in the last decade of the nineteenth century views similar to his were commonly held among the English intellectuals and excited no remark. Once the country had recovered from the reaction caused by the Napoleonic wars, the advance of radical views in both political and religious matters was gradual but continuous. Religious orthodoxy found itself attacked on two sides—from within and from without. The inside attack rested upon a reëxamination of the Bible by the methods of modern scientific criticism applied to other works of ancient literature. *Essays and Reviews* (1860), which embodied some of the results of recent Biblical research, excited a hot discussion and the authors were violently criticized, but one of them, Frederick Temple, before the end of the century became Archbishop of Canterbury. Bishop Colenso of Natal was driven to a reëxamination of the early books of the Bible by his contacts with the African Zulus, and it seemed as if, instead of his converting these primitive people to evangelical Christianity, they converted him. His *Critical Examination of the Pentateuch* (1862-79) published his conclusions that these books were pious frauds, composed long after the dates to which they were assigned; he was deposed and excommunicated, but reinstated by the law-courts.

About the same time a controversy arose which was even more damaging to the authority of the ecclesiastical leaders of the time—the conflict with modern science, with regard not to literary documents but to the facts and theories of geology and biology. The British Association for the Advancement of Science (founded in 1831) provoked a pamphlet from an eminent divine, *The Bible defended against the British Association* (1844), which had a considerable sale. Charles Lyell in his *Principles of Geology* (1830-33) discredited the views of the "catastrophic" school which accounted for the discoveries in the earth's crust by a series of "catastrophes" similar to Noah's flood; Lyell argued that the development of the world had been uniform and continuous, extending over long periods of time; most of the theologians, however, were willing to grant that the "day" of the first chapter of Genesis might be more than twenty-four hours long, and the discussion of Lyell's views was mainly confined to scientific circles. But when Charles Darwin in 1859 published the *Origin of Species,* Samuel Wilberforce, Bishop of Oxford, who led the attack on *Essays and Reviews,* was put up at the meeting of the British Association for the Advancement of Science, to condemn the theory of evolution by means of natural selection, not because it was contrary to the facts, but because it was contrary to Holy Scripture. His arguments, which were mainly appeals to popular prejudice, were confuted by a leading young scientist of the time, Professor Thomas Henry Huxley, who took a prominent part in the controversy which raged for many years afterward. The outcome was a signal victory for the evolutionists and a proportionate loss of prestige for their opponents.

The effect upon religious faith was generally disturbing and in many cases disastrous. Sir Edmund Gosse (1849-1928) in his *Father and Son* (1907) told with intelligence and sympathy the gradual disintegration of orthodox belief in his own youth; in other minds of the period there were more painful conflicts and disillusions. The upshot was a general growth of skepticism, particularly among the intellectual leaders who made most of the permanent contributions to literature. This decay of religious belief affected not only the writers but the public for which they wrote. Early in the nineteenth century Wordsworth could take it for granted that his readers held in common with him—

> an assured belief
> That the procession of our fates, howe'er

LORD MACAULAY

Sad and disturbed, is ordered by a Being
Of infinite benevolence and power,
Whose everlasting purposes embrace
All accidents, converting them to good.

At the end of the century no writer could appeal with confidence to any such simple faith in the providential order of the universe. "The faith in God and Immortality" seemed, as Professor Henry Sidgwick remarked at the time, to be *"in the air,"* that is, subject to discussion and sustained by no secure basis of generally accepted belief.

It was natural that the first sensation accompanying these momentous changes should be a consciousness of progress. Expanding trade, increasing population; abolition of ancient privileges, prejudices, and superstitions; the extension of educational opportunities to all classes and the gradual betterment of the condition of the poor—all this gave to those who were concerned or interested in one or other of these movements the impression that the world in general and England in particular were moving rapidly onward. Later, there arose prophets of evil to come, and severe critics of the insufficiency of the progress actually accomplished; but in the early stages—extending in general to the first half of the Victorian age—the predominant feeling was one of buoyant confidence in the future and almost smug satisfaction with the present. A characteristic representative of this early Victorian view is THOMAS BABINGTON MACAULAY (1800-59) who became Lord Macaulay two years before his death and was buried in Westminster Abbey. His grandfather was a Scotch Presbyterian minister, his father an active journalist, publicist, and philanthropist, who did much for the curbing of the slave-trade and the abolition of slavery in the British Dominions. Young Macaulay was therefore deeply imbued with the ideas of the Puritan middle class, of which he became one of the leading spokesmen. A precocious youth gifted with a prodigious memory, he carried off all the prizes in literature at Trinity College, Cambridge, and left the university with a fellowship which gave him fifteen hundred dollars a year for the next seven years, to make his way in life. At twenty-five he wrote an essay on Milton for the "Edinburgh Review" which astonished both the editor and the public. "The more I think," said the great critical potentate Jeffrey, "the less I can conceive where you picked up that style." The new recruit to literature and the Whig cause was at once welcomed into the highest social and political circles; his reputation as a talker had preceded him, and at that time the art of conversation was still valued. With his wide reading and unfailing memory (he knew *Paradise Lost* and *Pilgrim's Progress* by heart) Macaulay could illustrate any subject with an apt quotation or an appropriate incident, and his powers of conversation soon became famous. His nephew and biographer, Sir George O. Trevelyan, gives us his own recollection of how it was done: "Sitting bolt upright, his hands resting on the arms of his chair, or folded over the handle of his walking-stick, knitting his eyebrows if the subject was one which had to be thought out as he went along, or brightening from the forehead downwards when a burst of humor was coming, his massive features and honest glance suited well with the manly sagacious sentiments which he set forth in his sonorous voice and in his racy and intelligible language. To get at his meaning people had never the need to think twice, and they certainly had seldom the time." With Macaulay, as with most great talkers, the weakness was that he liked an audience and did not know when to stop. When the young lady he took down to dinner asked him a question which gave him a conversational opening (and very few did not), he would turn to the company and say, "Miss Smith asks me—and I reply." Then would follow a monologue which sometimes ran to such lengths that the great Whig hostess, Lady Holland, would send a footman round to "tell Mr. Macaulay to stop talking."

At the outset of his career all went swimmingly. At twenty-eight he was made a commissioner in bankruptcy, which gave him two thousand dollars a year with nominal duties; he was making another thousand by writing for the reviews; and at thirty he had a seat in the House of Commons presented to him by the Whig Lord Lansdowne for the "pocket" borough of Calne. Macaulay made a brilliant speech for the abolition of "pocket" boroughs, and his eloquence helped materially in the passage of the Reform Act. In the next parliament he sat for the newly enfranchised borough of Leeds, one of the great manufacturing centers in the North which had been hitherto unrepresented. But among other reforms his commissionership in bankruptcy had been swept away, with his entire approval; he had undertaken the payment of his father's debts; and he had to sell his university medals; "he did not know where to turn for a morsel of bread," as he put it in his picturesque, perhaps rather extravagant way. When Lord Lansdowne urged him to make money by his pen, he replied: "Hitherto, literature has been merely my relaxation—the amusement of perhaps a month in the year. I have never considered it as the means of support. I have chosen my own topics, taken my own time, and dictated my own terms. The thought of becoming a bookseller's hack; of writing to relieve, not the fulness of the mind, but the emptiness of the pocket; of spurring a jaded fancy to reluctant exertion; of filling sheets with trash merely that sheets may be filled; of bearing from publishers and editors what Dryden bore from Tonson, what, to my own knowledge, Mackintosh bore from Lardner, is horrible to me." He accordingly accepted the offer of membership in the newly established Indian Council, which gave him fifty thousand a year for five years, with the deliberate intention of setting aside more than half his yearly salary to establish his independence.

On his return from India in 1838, he reëntered Parliament as member for Edinburgh, and became Secretary for War with a seat in the Cabinet. His party went out of office in 1841, and in 1847 he lost his constituency. On hearing of his defeat, Macaulay sat down and wrote a poem to the effect that his devotion to literature had been his consolation in all his misfortunes, of which, a friendly biographer remarks, "it was rather difficult to make a respectable list." As a matter of fact, Macaulay had before this realized that literary work was his true vocation, and had found political life increasingly irksome; he was glad to retire from it and was, fortunately, in a position to follow his natural bent.

In 1841 he had scored a great popular success with the *Lays of Ancient Rome* and his collected essays also had a large sale, first in America and afterward in England. But neither of these successes was comparable to that of the first two volumes of his *History of England* (1848)—a design suggested by him in one of his university essays and seriously begun by him on his return from India; written in brilliant and popular style, it sold like a novel, and the publishers sent the historian a check for $100,000. "I am half afraid of this strange prosperity," he said; but he took it calmly, built himself a comfortable house in a London suburb, and worked there at the history till his death. He brought it almost to the end of the reign of William III, and from that point it may be said to have been continued in *England under Queen Anne,* by his grandnephew, George Macaulay Trevelyan, now professor of history at Oxford.

Macaulay's merits and defects are obvious. His style is an admirable medium of popular communication, but it lacks delicacy, and is often not only rhetorical but mechanical. His mind was powerful but lacking in subtlety; he exaggerates accepted commonplaces until they offend by overemphasis, the process that Sir Leslie Stephen described as "blackening the chimney." The virtues which commended him to his own time—his English, Protestant, Puritan, Whig, middle-class prejudices—are no longer popular, and Macaulay was not only emphatic but dogmatic. "I wish I were as cocksure of any one thing as Macaulay is of everything," said his Prime Minister, Lord Melbourne. In literature Macaulay read widely, but his range of interest was limited; he knew little of modern science (apart from its application to industry), disliked speculation, and despised metaphysics. Macaulay's good, as Emerson remarked, means material good—good to eat, good to wear. In this he is not altogether out of harmony with the modern temper and the industrial age, which, in spite of the critics, still reveres and reads him.

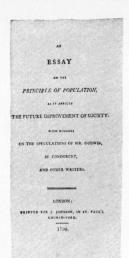

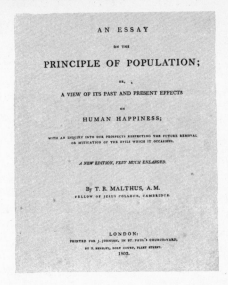

JOHN STUART MILL (1806-73), like Macaulay, was of humble Scottish ancestry; his grandfather was a shoemaker, and his father, although "licensed to preach," gave his energies to philosophy, political economy, and writing for periodicals. James Mill (the father) belonged to the "utilitarian" school, to which his son gave distinction and a name; it was founded by the successors of Adam Smith, among whom the most notable before the Victorian age were Jeremy Bentham, inventor of the formula "the greatest good of the greatest number," and the Anglican clergyman and economist, Malthus, author of the famous *Essay on the Principle of Population, or a View of its past and present Effects on human Happiness, with an Enquiry into our Prospects respecting the future Removal or Mitigation of the Evils which it occasions;* this had gone into six editions before the author's death in 1834, and has had an important influence on opinion and policy ever since. Malthus argued that while population increases in geometrical progression (by process of multiplication), the means of subsistence increase only by arithmetical progression (by addition), and that therefore the natural growth of the population should be held in check by "moral restraint."

To both Bentham and Malthus, John Stuart Mill was greatly indebted, but the predominant influence in shaping his opinions was James Mill, who took the boy's education into his own hands at a very early age. As a child of three, John Stuart learnt the Greek alphabet, at seven he was reading Plato's dialogues in the original, at eight he had had a good general education and was able to undertake the schooling of the younger children; at ten he knew more classics than the ordinary classical graduate of his time, and had, besides, a sound knowledge of history (including thirty volumes of the *Annual Register*); at twelve he went on to logic, and at thirteen to political economy, so that at fourteen he was ready to go abroad to acquire a knowledge of modern languages, with the study of mathematics and botany as side issues. His father thought one of the main objects of education should be to "generate a constant and anxious concern about evidence," and therefore left his son free to form his own opinions; but he could not help communicating to the boy his own intellectual and unemotional view of life, and he deliberately impressed upon him the duty of preparing himself for and devoting himself to public service. James Mill held a high position at the India House, and in this office at seventeen John Stuart obtained a junior clerkship with the understanding that he was to have the opportunity of fitting himself for a position of responsibility; this he obtained at twenty-two and proceeded by degrees to the highest position in the office after his father vacated it.

To the young Mill, the philosophy of Bentham was a religion, and he was still in his teens when he gave this philosophy the name of "utilitarianism" by founding the Utilitarian Club; but from the beginning the test of "utility" which he applied to all human endeavors included imaginative and spiritual elements such as poetry and religion. Under the strenuous discipline of his father's training he was not unhappy, but at the age of twenty he felt that his education had been very deficient on the side of the affections, and that if all the intellectual objects he had then in view were accomplished he would not be satisfied. For three or four years he suffered from deep despondency, but eventually found consolation in the poetry of Wordsworth and an ardent attachment to a Mrs. Taylor, whom, after a friendship of twenty years, he married.

Mill wrote steadily for radical periodicals and for some years edited the chief radical organ, the "Westminster Review." From twenty to thirty he schooled himself in the habit of thinking things out, never avoiding difficulties, never accepting half-solutions. It seemed to him that the system of logic then prevailing would be improved by combining with it the methods of physical science, and that by the systematic application of the scientific method to the moral world, the same degree of general acceptance might be gained as modern science was obtaining in the physical world. These ideas he developed through years of investigation and study in his *System of Logic* (1843) and *Principles of Political Economy* (1848). To the latter science he made important contributions. The older economists had laid down inexorable economic laws which apparently condemned thousands of laborers to a cramped and miserable existence and thousands more to semi-starvation; Mill pointed out that it was only the laws of production that rested upon a physical basis; the laws of distribution rested not upon nature but upon custom, upon human institutions and legislation. So far as England was concerned, he regarded with indifference the "mere increase of production and accumulation"; the important point was to see that "neither the increase of population nor anything else prevents the mass of the population from reaping any part of the benefit"; "what is economically needed is a better distribution, of which one indispensable means is a stricter restraint on population." He suggests therefore "a limitation of the sum which any person may acquire by gift or inheritance to the amount sufficient to maintain a modern independence," and he looked forward not only to a more equal distribution of the produce of labor, but to a distant future permitting such changes in human

JOHN STUART MILL

character as might render a state of society possible without the institution of private property.

It is significant that Mill turned aside from the completion of his *Political Economy* to urge peasant proprietorship as a remedy for the Irish famine of 1846-47. His marriage with Mrs. Taylor in 1851 gave him a fresh incentive and capacity by her constant companionship and collaboration; with her he produced some of his best works, *On Liberty, Representative Government, Utilitarianism,* and *The Subjection of Women*—the last a plea for woman suffrage, in which Mrs. Taylor was very much interested.

When the Government of India was transferred from the East India Company to the Crown in 1858, Mill declined the offer of a seat on the Council at fifty thousand dollars a year, which formed the foundation of Macaulay's fortune; he accepted a pension and retired to Avignon, where he continued to write after the death of his wife with the help and companionship of her daughter, Helen Taylor, who edited his *Autobiography*—one of the best books of its kind. His last years were serene, and though his health was greatly impaired, he interested himself in public affairs, especially the Irish land question and the struggle between capital and labor, which he foresaw would be the great issue of the future. For three years he represented Westminster in the House of Commons, but he was glad to escape from political life to the seclusion of his cottage at Avignon. Helen (he wrote to a friend) had carried out her long-cherished scheme of a "vibratory" for him, a pleasant covered walk, some thirty feet long, in which he took exercise in cold or rainy weather. He had also a "semi-circumgyratory"—a terrace going round two sides of the house—and a herbarium, a little room fitted up for botanical work. "Thus, you see, with my herbarium, my vibratory and my semi-circumgyratory, I am in clover; and you may imagine with what scorn I think of the House of Commons, which, comfortable club as it is said to be, could offer me none of these comforts, or more, perfectly speaking, these necessaries of life."

CARLYLE'S HOUSE IN CHELSEA

THE FRONT DOOR

THE SOUND-PROOF ROOM

THE GARDEN DOOR

A curious literary anecdote connects Mill with THOMAS CAR-LYLE (1795-1881). Born at Ecclefechan in Dumfriesshire, the son of a Scottish stone-mason, Carlyle had already established himself in Cheyne Row, Chelsea, when he read one of Mill's articles in a review and hailed him as "a new mystic." Although Carlyle was eleven years older than Mill, the latter's precocious development put them at about the same level of intellectual maturity and they became close friends. When Carlyle had finished the first book of *The French Revolution* in March, 1835, he gave the manuscript to Mill to read. Mill lent it to his devoted friend Mrs. Taylor, and Mrs. Taylor, sitting up late at night to read it, left it on the table when she went to bed. In the morning the housemaid lit the fire with it. Mill confessed the catastrophe to Carlyle, who was overwhelmed by it; he was poor, he had put months of work into the manuscript, and he had no second copy. Mill insisted on compensating Carlyle for his lost labor; but it was three months before Carlyle could bring himself to the task of doing the work over again.

Carlyle had known hard times from his youth as a poor man's son, a struggling student at Edinburgh University, an ill-paid schoolmaster who tried in vain to obtain a professorship, and an unsuccessful writer. German transcendental philosophy, in which he was chiefly interested, was not a popular subject, and he made the task of his readers more difficult by an extraordinary style, full of strange words and curiously constructed phrases. He earned some money by writing articles on German literature for the reviews, but a sort of spiritual autobiography published under the title of *Sartor Resartus* in "Fraser's Magazine" met with "universal disapprobation." Emerson was apparently the only reader who understood and appreciated it; he procured its publication in book form at Boston, Massachusetts (1835). It is still hard going for most readers. Nevertheless, Carlyle became a great source of inspiration for his own generation and the leading prose-writer of his time. He is now chiefly admired for his two shorter works *Past and Present* (1843), in which he preaches his Gospel of Work, and *Heroes and Hero*

Thomas Carlyle (Chelsea, 1865)

Worship (1841), a series of lectures delivered in London, in which he expounds his theory that history consists of the lives and influence of the few great men who made it. His greatest historical work in exemplification of this theory, *Frederick the Great* (1858-65), is now little read in England and America, though it is still popular in Germany.

Carlyle's fervent idealism, his exaltation of work for its own sake, the scorn he poured upon materialism, democracy, the selfish economics of the Manchester school, and other beliefs popular in his day, gave him a considerable following and a still more considerable reputation. His biting and often vitriolic verdicts upon the character and achievements of his contemporaries are often amusing, but sometimes seem merely ill-tempered. Owing to the privations of his youth, he suffered all his life from severe indigestion and insomnia, and his rooms had to be hermetically sealed from noise. He was not an easy man to live with, and though he and his wife, a high-spirited woman hardly less gifted than himself, were devoted to each other, they did not get on well together. Their differences were discussed in detail, with great frankness, by Carlyle's friend and biographer, James Anthony Froude, and the echoes raised by the controversy that broke out in consequence have not yet died down in literary circles. The common verdict of the time is expressed in the words of a contemporary wit to whom some one remarked that it was a pity that Carlyle and Jane Welsh did not each marry some one else. "No," he retorted, "there would have been four unhappy people in the world instead of two."

It seems idle at this date to discuss the recondite theories offered as an explanation of matrimonial friction common enough among people who are not geniuses. Jane Welsh was superior to her husband in social station and as the heiress of Craigenputtock (where the ill-assorted pair lived from 1828 to 1834), she no doubt thought herself entitled to greater consideration than the dyspeptic transcendentalist was able to give her. He, on his side, expected too much from her, and, as the survivor, repented his ill-temper when it was too late.

RUSKIN AS A YOUNG MAN

Equally unhappy in his domestic life and equally unpopular in his views of public policy was Carlyle's younger contemporary and disciple, JOHN RUSKIN (1819-1900). The master of a magnificent but voluble prose style, Ruskin was extraordinarily prolific with tongue and pen, and left to posterity more literary baggage than his reputation in his own time—great as it was—has been able to carry. Like Carlyle, he had no offspring except children of the brain, and the wife of his youth left him, in 1855, to be married to John Millais, a famous portrait-painter. A later attachment to a beautiful young girl, Rose de la Touche, proved equally disappointing.

Ruskin was the son of a London wine-merchant, and in his early travels about England in his father's carriage acquired a love of natural scenery which was the abiding passion of his life. In his teens he conceived an ardent admiration for the landscapes of Turner, and this youthful enthusiasm found expression in the first volume of *Modern Painters, by a Graduate of Oxford* (1843); the last volume (the fifth) appeared in 1860 and in the meantime Ruskin had published *The Seven Lamps of Architecture* (1849), *The Stones of Venice* (1851-53), and numerous writings in defense of the work of the Pre-Raphaelite Brotherhood (P. R. B.), of which Dante Gabriel Rossetti, Millais, Holman Hunt, William Morris, Burne-Jones, and other young painters were the leading exponents. They advocated a return to the style of naturalness and simplicity prevailing in Italian art before Raphael, and their leading interpreter to the public was Ruskin, who was by this time regarded as the principal English authority on all matters of art.

Before 1860, however, Ruskin turned his attention less to artistic questions and more to practical and, above all, economic problems. The kind of painting needed in London, he said, was "painting cheeks red with health." The squalor of the London slums, the ugliness of the factory towns, the ignorance and degradation of the laboring class awoke in his heart a volcanic indignation which poured forth torrents of fiery prose. Naturally these violent attacks upon the commercial and mechanical civ-

RUSKIN IN OLD AGE

ilization of the mid-Victorian age received little welcome from public opinion or the press. A series of articles in the "Cornhill Magazine" (published in book form as *Unto this Last*) was cut short by the editor; and the same fate befell *Munera Pulveris* on its first appearance in "Fraser's Magazine." Ruskin was invited to Manchester to lecture on art and lectured on political economy, which he defined as "a system of conduct founded on the sciences and impossible, except under certain conditions of moral culture." He was invited to Bradford to lecture on architecture in connection with the opening of a new Exchange and gave the Yorkshire woolen-manufacturers a sermon on their duties to their work-people. He was appointed professor of fine art at Oxford, and told the undergraduates that they ought to do something to improve the condition of the farmers in the surrounding country. So the class went out to the neighboring village of Hinksey and began to make a road under Ruskin's superintendence. As none of them knew anything about road-making, their efforts were not particularly successful and afforded the farmers whom they intended to benefit more amusement than material help; the site is still known as the "Hinksey diggings," but it is not a thoroughfare.

Ruskin's campaign for a more beautiful England in which the good things of life were more evenly distributed was continued for about twenty years, at the end of which his brain broke down under the strain. During that period he wrote and lectured incessantly, gave generously, and interested himself in the production of goods which afforded artistic satisfaction to the craftsmen who produced them. On his eightieth birthday the most distinguished men of the time united under the leadership of the Prince of Wales (afterward Edward VII) to assure him of their "deepest respect and continued affection." His last years were spent in retirement at Brantwood, a house he built for himself in a secluded spot on the shore of Coniston Water in the Lake District.

Of the great Victorians hitherto discussed, Macaulay was in sympathy with the main current of thought in his time and Mill

John H Newman

was rather ahead of it. Carlyle was in a sense a reactionary, harking back to aristocratic leadership without any practical suggestion for the discovery of the leaders. Ruskin, with a keen sense of the defects of the new industrial civilization, had no very practical remedies unless his Guild of St. George and village crafts can be counted as such. The qualities of beauty, quiet, and order which Carlyle and Ruskin found lacking in modern industry, JOHN HENRY (afterward Cardinal) NEWMAN (1801-90) found lacking in the English Church of his time, in which the evangelical movement and the liberalizing or modernist tendencies (afterward developed in *Essays and Reviews*) were the predominant influences; his mind accordingly turned back to the Church of England of the Middle Ages before it was separated from the Roman Catholic Church. In his earlier history there was no indication of his later point of view. Born and brought up in an orthodox Protestant household, he won first a scholarship and then a fellowship at Oxford, became a college tutor, vicar of the university church of St. Mary's, and leader of "the Oxford movement" to restore the pre-Reformation doctrines and practices of the Church of England. But long study and meditation convinced him that his position in that church was untenable, and in 1843 he retracted all that he had said against the Church of Rome. He resigned the Vicarage of St. Mary's, and was admitted, first to the communion and then to the priesthood of the Roman Catholic Church. His withdrawal from the Church of England caused consternation among his followers and roused his adversaries to bitter condemnation. For a long time he kept silence, but when Canon Kingsley, better known as a man of letters than as an ecclesiastic, attacked Newman's personal character, Newman made a dignified but effective defense of himself in his *Apologia pro Vita sua* (1864), which has become a classic of English prose. Newman wrote extensively on religious topics, was a novelist and a poet; his hymn "Lead, Kindly Light," written while he was still a member of the Church of England but already troubled by doubt, has long been a favorite with English-speaking Christians of all denominations.

Faithfully yours
Charles Dickens

CHARLES DICKENS (1812-70) has stood the test of time better than most of the great Victorians, though none of them was more subject to the Victorian limitations: among the sentimentalists, he was the arch-sentimentalist, cried out upon by the critics of his own time; he was extremely conventional, paying abject (because sincere) tribute to Mrs. Grundy in all her demands for decorum and respectability. He was dear to the hearts of the Victorian public for his defects as well as for his merits. They implored him "not to let little Nell die" and wept with him long and profusely at her death-bed. They enjoyed his hearty appreciation of eating and drinking, his extravagant burlesque and sometimes almost mechanical humor. They were not offended by his lack of artistic restraint, by his carelessness of artistic form, by his overt and direct approach to the fountains of tears and laughter, by his appeals to popular prejudice, or by his incessant laudation of such simple virtues as humility, cheerfulness, kindliness, simplicity, and truth. Yet it is Dickens whom the most recent critics have singled out among the Victorian novelists—not, it is true, for his intellectual insight or for his literary craftsmanship, but for the genius and vital energy which have transcended and overcome all his defects and limitations.

The Victorian populace loved Dickens because he was one of them and had known their simple joys and bitter sorrows by personal experience. He had suffered the pangs of disappointed ambition and the humiliations of grinding poverty when the oppression of circumstances is most painful, in early youth, even in childhood. His parents belonged to the shiftless, helpless stratum of the lowest middle class which suffers as much from its outraged susceptibilities and respectabilities as from actual privation. His father was the prototype of his eternal creation Mr. Micawber, his mother the original of Mrs. Nickleby. Born at Portsmouth, where his father held a small clerical post in the British Navy, Dickens drifted with his family to the metropolis, and made a direct acquaintance with the London slums and the Marshalsea debtors' prison in which his father was for some months confined. A delicate, sensitive child, eager to become

SECOND SERIES

OF

SKETCHES
BY
BOZ

George Cruikshank

"learned and distinguished," the boy Charles keenly resented his lack of educational opportunities and his enforced contacts with squalid surroundings. Never, in the days of his dizziest triumphs as a popular favorite, did he forget the hours he had spent in a London factory as a child, pasting labels on blacking bottles to earn a dollar and a half a week. At the very top of fame and fortune he wrote: "It is wonderful to me how I could have been so easily cast away at such an age. It is wonderful to me that, even after my descent into the poor little drudge I had been since we came to London, no one had compassion enough on me—a child of singular abilities, quick, eager, delicate, and soon hurt, bodily or mentally—to suggest that something might have been spared, as certainly it might have been, to place me in a common school. Our friends, I take it, were tired out. No one made any sign. My father and mother were quite satisfied. They could hardly have been more so if I had been twenty years of age, distinguished at a grammar school, and going to Cambridge."

It is an open question whether the conventional education at an English school and college would have been as useful to the future novelist as his actual experience; painful and humiliating as this undoubtedly was, it gave him a knowledge of life, especially the life of the London poor, that he could not have obtained in any other way. The London of his novels is the London of his childhood and youth, though he refreshed his memory in after-life by occasional visits to the mean streets, the cheap restaurants, the law-courts and offices he had frequented as a boy. At fifteen he was working in a lawyer's office at Gray's Inn for about three dollars and a half a week, and it was at this time that he went through the tribulations of learning shorthand as described in *David Copperfield,* to the joy of all subsequent stenographers: "The changes that were rung upon dots, which in such a position meant such a thing, and in such another position something else, entirely different; the wonderful vagaries that were played by circles; the unaccountable consequences that resulted from marks like flies' legs; the tremendous effects of a curve in a wrong place, not only troubled my waking hours, but

George Cruikshank

appeared before me in my sleep. When I had groped my way, blindly, through these difficulties, and had mastered the alphabet, which was an Egyptian Temple in itself, there then appeared a procession of new horrors, called arbitrary characters; the most despotic characters I have ever known; who insisted, for instance, that a thing like the beginning of a cobweb, meant expectation, and that a pen and ink sky-rocket stood for disadvantageous. When I had fixed these wretches in my mind, I found that they had driven everything else out of it; then beginning again, I forgot them; while I was picking them up, I dropped the other fragments of the system; in short, it was almost heart-breaking."

Yet at sixteen Dickens had picked up enough shorthand to be employed as a law reporter in Doctors' Commons, described in *David Copperfield* as "a little out-of-the-way place, where they administer what is called ecclesiastical law and play all kinds of tricks with obsolete old monsters of Acts of Parliament." At nineteen Dickens was reporting the Parliamentary debates for a London newspaper, recording (again to quote *Copperfield*) "predictions that never come to pass, professions that are never fulfilled, explanations that are only meant to mystify." His duties as a reporter, from 1831 to 1836, took him all about the country near London in the days of the stagecoaches, post-chaises, and old inns which it is his delight to describe in his novels. As a recent French critic observes, a railway train is for Dickens a phenomenon.

It was in 1834 that Dickens (with the young David Copperfield still following in his track) took "with fear and trembling to authorship. I wrote a little something in secret, and sent it to a magazine, and it was published in the magazine." This was the first of the *Sketches by Boz,* gathered into a volume two years later and published with illustrations by the famous engraver George Cruikshank. Within six months a second edition was called for, but more important was the fact that the book drew the attention of the great publishing firm of Chapman and Hall, who had arranged for a monthly serial to be illustrated

DICKENS, HIS WIFE, AND HER SISTER

by Seymour and were on the lookout for some one to write the letterpress. The first idea was that of a "Nimrod Club," with sporting incidents of hunting and fishing; but after Dickens accepted the invitation to contribute the text, the title was changed to *Posthumous Papers of the Pickwick Club*. The first number was published in April, 1836, and the early issues went off rather slowly, but before the end of the year Mr. Pickwick and his faithful attendant, Sam Weller, had become popular favorites, and pipes, cigars, pens, and other articles of general consumption began to be called by their names; the last monthly number, published in November, 1837, reached a sale of forty thousand, which for that time was a very large figure. This was immediately followed by *Oliver Twist* (1837-39)—an attack upon poor-law administration and a revelation of the criminal life of the metropolis—and *Nicholas Nickleby* (1838-39), an exposure of the abuses of private schools. *Pickwick* made no pretense of having a plot; there was merely a framework "for the introduction of diverting characters and incidents." The two subsequent novels followed the biographical "life and adventures" style of Defoe and Smollett, with which Dickens had long been familiar in his reading of eighteenth-century fiction.

In the first tide of success Dickens married and began housekeeping in London at Furnival's Inn, removing later to larger houses in the metropolis and ultimately to an estate in the country, Gadshill Place near Rochester, about thirty miles from London. In the earlier years of his married life he had children, one of whom, Sir Henry Dickens, became a successful lawyer and magistrate and is at this time of writing still alive.

The task of writing two novels at the same time, to be published by monthly instalments, each of which was printed before the following one was written, proved very exhausting, and in order to escape from it Dickens in 1840 started an illustrated weekly journal, "Master Humphrey's Clock," which he hoped would give him greater leisure; as it turned out, it gave him less, for the public refused to buy the paper if it had not part of a serial by Dickens in it, so that he had escaped from monthly

DICKENS READING *THE CHIMES* TO HIS FRIENDS

instalments only to subject himself to the bondage of weekly parts; *Old Curiosity Shop* and *Barnaby Rudge* appeared in this way, and then *Master Humphrey's Clock* came to a stop.

At thirty years of age Dickens stood at the pinnacle of literary fame and was invited to visit the United States as the guest of the nation. He was there (and in Canada) during the first half of 1842 and was received everywhere with the most lavish hospitality and the greatest enthusiasm. Two subjects occupied prominent places in the numerous addresses the novelist delivered during his extensive tour—the need for an American copyright law to prevent American publishers from reprinting the works of British authors without payment, and the abolition of negro slavery. The latter subject was still prominent in his mind when on his return to England he wrote *American Notes* and *Martin Chuzzlewit,* in which he pictured the Southern planter as "dreaming of Freedom in a slave's embrace and waking to sell her offspring and his own in public markets." Other comments on what Dickens conceived to be representative features of American life at that date were equally exaggerated, and the American public, although accustomed to his severe satire of English institutions, resented the application of the lash to a country which had shown itself most hospitable to and appreciative of a foreign visitor. There was heated feeling on both sides, but when Dickens visited the United States again in 1867-68, he made honorable and generous amends to the American public.

In spite of his enormous success, Dickens suffered from "intolerable anxiety and disappointment," partly due to an uncongenial atmosphere in his own home. In 1843 he left England for Italy and settled for some time at Genoa, where in 1844 he finished *Martin Chuzzlewit,* of which the first instalment was published in January, 1843. Meanwhile Dickens had discovered a new outlet for his prolific energy in a yearly succession of Christmas stories, of which the first and perhaps the best was *The Christmas Carol* (1843). He returned to England in 1844 to read to a gathering of his friends his second Christmas story, *The Chimes* (1844); the third, *The Cricket on the Hearth*

DICKENS IN 1868

(1845), was enormously popular. But Dickens still felt discontented with his position, and sought in vain a London magistracy, which would make him financially secure. In the beginning of 1846 he undertook the editorship of the London "Daily News," but two weeks of it was enough to convince him that the treadmill of daily journalism did not suit his mercurial temperament. Living still a good deal abroad, he produced *Dombey and Son* in 1848; and in 1849-50 *David Copperfield,* generally regarded as his greatest achievement.

In 1850, Dickens started a new weekly periodical, "Household Words," succeeded by still another, "All the Year Round." The novels continued to appear—*Bleak House* (1852-53), *Hard Times* (1854), a study of industrialism in the North of England; *Little Dorrit* (1857), revealing once more the sufferings of the London poor, the iniquities of the debtors' prison, and the law's delay; in all of these the critics discerned some falling off in the author's vital energy. This was not surprising when one realizes the varied and engrossing occupations in which Dickens was at that time engaged. Besides editing magazines and writing novels, he was the enthusiastic manager of a dramatic company which acted Elizabethan tragedies and modern comedies not only in London but in the chief provincial towns, and in 1858-59 he gave the first series of dramatic readings from his novels. These were repeated in subsequent years and were enormously successful from every point of view; but they proved in the end to be a fatal drain on the novelist's wonderful vitality.

For the time being, however, Dickens seemed to gain new energy. Through his friendship with Wilkie Collins, who wrote for "All the Year Round" the first and perhaps the best of all mystery novels, *The Woman in White,* Dickens recognized the potency of an exciting plot, and used the new form to advantage in *A Tale of Two Cities* (1859), cast in the stirring scene of Paris during the French Revolution. In the same year in which this was published Dickens moved into Gadshill Place, which he had bought a year or two before; the change into the country, with ample opportunity for his favorite diversion of taking long

GADSHILL PLACE, KENT

THE EMPTY CHAIR

walks, did him good. His next novel *Great Expectations* (published in "All the Year Round" 1860-61) combined a complicated plot with his old fertile invention of humorous and pathetic characters and situations. At Gadshill, where his sister-in-law kept house for him after his final separation from his wife, his domestic life became more peaceful and harmonious, but he continued to exhaust his physical resources by histrionic readings from his novels, not only all over England but in the United States. His American tour (1867-68) was a great popular triumph, but each evening's performance was followed by a sort of fainting fit, in which the novelist lay in a state of complete exhaustion; he earned a hundred thousand dollars by the tour, but it was at the price of his life. On his return to England he rested for a while, but soon returned to the stage and died suddenly on June 9, 1870, from an effusion of blood on the brain while engaged in writing *The Mystery of Edwin Drood,* of which publication had been begun in the previous April. Various attempts have been made to finish it, but no other novelist could use the wizard's pen.

The question has often been asked why Dickens, with his remarkable histrionic powers and interest in the drama, did not write plays. The answer is that he did. At the beginning of his literary career he wrote a farce, *The Strange Gentleman,* and a musical comedy, *The Village Coquettes;* and it is obvious that innumerable scenes in his novels are first-rate melodrama. But he found a much more remunerative and a much more reputable mode of reaching his middle-class audience through the novel than through the drama. Throughout his literary career the popular drama and the popular stage were regarded with contempt by intelligent people, and for reasons of propriety or prejudice the middle class stayed away from the theater on principle. Dickens could have written better melodrama than Sheridan Knowles or Lord Lytton, but it was not worth his while. Probably he could not have done the polite comedy with which Robertson, Jones, and Pinero opened the way for Barrie and Shaw.

For polite comedy, even in the novel form, the early Vic-

OLD PORCH, CHARTERHOUSE

PENSIONERS' HALL, CHARTERHOUSE

torian intellectuals looked not to Dickens but to Thackeray, whom they held to be the superior artist. It was quite customary all through the Victorian age for superior persons to exalt Thackeray at the expense of Dickens, and few critics had the discernment to see that in the long run the latter's creative ability would more than hold its own as against the very different talents of his great contemporary. One of the few, Professor W. Minto of Aberdeen University, pointed out not long after the death of Dickens that Thackeray's kind of novel "is much less sure of enduring fame, because the sentiments on which it rests, being the product of a particular knot of circumstances, are more fugitive, and pass sooner into the province of the historian. The novels of Dickens will live longer because they take hold of the permanent and universal sentiments of the race—sentiments which pervade all classes, and which no culture can ever eradicate. His fun may be too boisterous for the refined tastes of his own time, or, for the matter of that, of posterity; his pathos may appear maudlin; but they carried everything before them when they burst upon our literature, because, however much exaggerated, they were exaggerations of what our race feels in its inner heart; and unless culture in the future works a miracle, and carries its changes beneath the surface, we may be certain that Dickens will keep his hold."

So far, posterity has agreed with this view.

WILLIAM MAKEPEACE THACKERAY (1811-63) presents a remarkable contrast to Dickens, not only in the nature of his genius and the character of his achievement, but in his family connections and the circumstances of his early life. His father and grandfather, belonging to an old Yorkshire family, were in the service of the East India Company, and he was born at Calcutta. At six years of age he was sent to England to be educated, and at eleven entered the famous old Charterhouse School, then situated near the Smithfield Cattle Market in London, but now removed to Godalming in Surrey; in his earlier works Thackeray refers to it as the Slaughterhouse or Smithfield, and in *The Newcomes* (more sympathetically) as Grey Friars, in allusion

W M Thackeray

to the Carthusian monks whose sequestrated monastery furnished the original school building in the seventeenth century. From the Charterhouse, Thackeray went to another famous ancient foundation, Trinity College, Cambridge; he was an idle student and left without taking his degree. Later, he enrolled at the Middle Temple in London as a law student, but found the law not to his liking. Meanwhile he had traveled abroad in Germany (where he saw Goethe at Weimar) and in France, where, in a somewhat desultory fashion, he studied drawing. At twenty-one he came into an income of five hundred pounds a year, but managed to get rid of it. He married, but after a few years separated from his wife on account of her mental derangement; of the two daughters, the elder became Lady Ritchie, herself well known as a novelist and woman of letters; the younger married Sir Leslie Stephen, one of the leading critics and literary historians of the later Victorian period.

By ill luck or good fortune, through infirmity of character or uncertainty of purpose, Thackeray's youthful contacts with life were in one way more restricted, in another more various than those of Dickens. He saw the upper middle class in several European centers; but at close quarters he saw little else. He had no pressing reason to exert himself, and took things easily. Dickens was the younger man, but he was already celebrated and had been earning his own living for some years while Thackeray was still hesitating between the pencil and the pen; in fact, Thackeray applied to Dickens for permission to illustrate one of his earlier novels—an offer which Dickens did not accept. It was ten years after the latter had established his position by *Pickwick* that Thackeray made his first hit with *Vanity Fair* (1847-48); in the meantime he had done a good deal of journalism, not always successful, and had only gradually won a moderate reputation by his contributions to "Fraser's Magazine" and to "Punch," which was established in 1842.

In their attitude to their work the two men differed very widely. To Dickens the creations of his brain were real people, whose sorrows he wept over and whose foibles he laughed at in the very act of creation; to Thackeray even his best characters are only "puppets." In the preface to *Vanity Fair,* when it was published in book form, he says: "The famous little Becky Puppet has been pronounced to be uncommonly flexible in the joints, and lively on the wire; the Amelia Doll, though it has had a smaller circle of admirers, has yet been carved and dressed with the greatest care by the artist; the Dobbin Figure, though apparently clumsy, yet dances in a very amusing and natural manner; the Little Boys' Dance has been liked by some; and please to remark the richly dressed figure of the Wicked Nobleman, on which no expense has been spared, and which Old Nick will fetch away at the end of this singular performance." And at the end of the book he writes (commenting on the disappointment of his hero and heroine in each other after they are married): "Which of us is happy in this world? Which of us has his desire? or having it, is satisfied?—Come, children, let us shut up the box and the puppets, for our play is played out."

It is because of Thackeray's continual sense of himself as the showman that he claims the right in the course of the performance to step now and then from behind the scenes and comment on the characters: "if they are good and kindly, to love and shake them by the hand; if they are silly, to laugh at them confidentially in the reader's sleeve; if they are wicked and heartless, to abuse them in the strongest terms politeness admits of." He has in mind the combination of the essay and the novel attempted by his master Fielding.

His conception of life also is different from that of Dickens. The ideal of Thackeray is a class ideal—that of gentlemanliness: "Be each, pray God, a gentleman." Dickens was never, either in the world of the imagination or in the actual world, entirely at his ease in gentlemanly society; Thackeray was never at his ease anywhere else. This lies at the basis of the accusation that although he is continually satirizing snobbery, he is himself snobbish. His emphasis is on manners, while that of Dickens is on morals. The heroes Dickens takes to his heart are Tom Pinch, Mark Tapley, Joe Gargery, and a hundred other simple folk of humble life; Thackeray has a sneaking admiration for his Wicked Nobleman (Lord Steyn), his Adventuress and her gambling husband, the foolish Amelia and her two foolish husbands—for if some of them lack morals and others lack brains, have they not all good manners?

Thackeray was further hampered by his inability to portray his "gentlemen" as they really were on account of the Victorian taboo against frankness in matters of sex. When Dickens relates the betrayal of little Emily by Steerforth, he sentimentalizes the whole episode, but he does it sincerely, because he accepts the Victorian attitude as to seduction. When Thackeray has to deal with the relations between Pendennis and Fanny Bolton, he consciously and deliberately falsifies them in accordance with the Victorian convention. In the preface to *Pendennis,* he admits that he cannot tell the truth about the gentlemen of his own age as Fielding did in the eighteenth century: "Even the gentlemen of our age—this is an attempt to describe one of them, no better nor worse than most educated men—even these we cannot show as they are, with the notorious foibles and selfishness of their lives and their education. Since the author of *Tom Jones* was buried, no writer of fiction among us has been permitted to depict to his utmost power a MAN. We must drape him, and give him a certain conventional simper—Society will not tolerate the Natural in our Art. Many ladies have remonstrated and subscribers left me, because in the course of the story I described a young man resisting and affected by temptation. My object was to say that he had the passions to feel and the manliness and generosity to overcome them. You will not hear—it is best to know it—what moves in the real world, what passes in society, in your clubs, colleges, mess rooms,—what is the life and talk of your sons."

It was perhaps for this reason that Thackeray achieved his greatest artistic success in *Esmond* (1852), in which he transferred his scene into the eighteenth century and told the whole story through the mouth of an eighteenth-century narrator. *The Newcomes,* which followed, is overweighted with Victorian sentiment; *The Virginians* (1857-59) is a continuation of *Esmond* and, like most sequels, obviously inferior to it.

Besides novel-writing Thackeray had many other intellectual activities. His lectures on *The English Humorists of the Eighteenth Century* and on *The Four Georges* made for him a great platform reputation both in England and the United States; like Dickens, he was much concerned about international copyright, and when he was in New York as the guest of a leading American publisher—perhaps with more humor than tact—he greeted his host as "the pirate chief." He was for a year or two, not long before his death, editor of "Cornhill Magazine," but he was too easy-going and good-natured to deal firmly with contributors or would-be contributors. His burly figure, six feet four in height, was familiar in London clubs and literary circles in the middle of the nineteenth century; "with his flowing hair, already nearly gray, and his broken nose, his broad forehead and ample chest" he was greeted everywhere with affection and respect, and his sudden death on Christmas Eve, 1862, caused universal regret.

Thackeray's ideal was that of the Christian gentleman and by that ideal his conception of life must stand or fall. It is a class as well as a religious ideal, and the two sides are not always consistent with each other; there is, therefore, sometimes a sense, not only of compromise but of confusion in Thackeray's presentation of life and character. His experience of life perhaps tended to increase that confusion; and his superficial cheerfulness overlaid an inward pessimism. We get something of the conflicting elements in his mind in the lines he wrote for a Christmas Eve not very long before that on which he died.

> My song, save this, is little worth;
>   I lay the weary pen aside,
> And wish you health, and love and mirth,
>   As fits the solemn Christmas-tide.
> As fits the holy Christmas birth,
>   Be this, good friends, our carol still:
> Be peace on earth, be peace on earth,
>   To men of gentle will.'

ANTHONY TROLLOPE

ANTHONY TROLLOPE (1815-82) was born in Keppel Street, in the west-central district of London and lived for many years in the West End on Montagu Square. He belonged to a good English family, and went to two public schools, Winchester and Harrow, but he was miserable at both, owing to the slovenly and poverty-stricken state in which he was kept by a spendthrift and unpractical father. His mother, however, was a woman of energy and intelligence, and in 1827 came out to Cincinnati, Ohio, to try fortune as a seller of fancy goods. The adventure failing, she retrieved herself on her return to England by writing a scathing account of *The Domestic Manners of the Americans*. She was a diligent maker of books, and maintained her worthless husband (in Bruges) until his death. Family connections found Anthony a place in the post-office at nineteen (after he had failed in the civil-service examination), and, being transferred to Ireland, he made his beginning in fiction with two novels of Irish life, *The Macdermots of Ballycloran* (1847) and *The Kellys and the O'Kellys* (1849): they were unsuccessful, and Trollope cannot be said to have gained much from his stay in Ireland beyond a taste for whist, fox-hunting, and the life of the country gentry. Returning to England, he was appointed to inspect and extend rural postal deliveries, which enabled him to keep up his hunting and to acquire as thorough a knowledge of the English country-side as he had of the Irish. In 1855 he published the first novel of what afterward became known as the Barsetshire series, *The Warden,* continued in *Barchester Towers,* and brought to a reluctant close in *The Last Chronicle of Barset* (1867). Meanwhile he had been induced by Thackeray to write *Framley Parsonage* for "Cornhill Magazine," and it was this study of the life of the rural clergy that established his reputation. Between 1859 and 1879 he earned $350,000 by his pen, though no single novel brought him in more than $17,000. All this he tells in full detail in his *Autobiography* (1883), in which he confided to the public his methodical way of working—so many words an hour, so many hours a day. The public was rather taken aback at the revelation of this mechanical system of authorship, and Trollope's reputation fell off; but in recent years it has recovered ground, and the novels—especially those of the Barsetshire series—are again read for their lively and humorous representation of the Victorian compromise between piety and worldly ambition which Trollope depicted unflinchingly but not unkindly, as he fully sympathized with it himself. About Trollope's personality, as about his work, there is a quality of downright honesty and love of fair play which has been described as peculiarly English. His characters are thoroughly Victorian, conforming to the author's Victorian standards of virtue and common sense, but rarely touched by religious devotion or any other kind of passionate excess. When they show such qualities, the author makes it quite clear that they are exceptions to the rule of life among the clergy, the gentry, or any other class of society with which he was acquainted. Yet his wordly clergyman and prejudiced or ignorant country gentleman are not held up to scorn; they are made not only human but likeable.

CHARLES READE (1814-84) an Oxford don and in his own time a famous dramatist and novelist, is now remembered chiefly as the author of the historical romance *The Cloister and the Hearth*—a study of the emergence of Europe from the medieval period into the Renaissance during the youth of the hero of the story, who is the father of Erasmus.

CHARLES KINGSLEY (1819-75) is now best known for his stirring Elizabethan romance *Westward Ho!* (1855), though its violent Protestant patriotism is out of fashion. His unfortunate attack upon Cardinal Newman has already been mentioned. He was prominent in his own time as a leader of the rather sentimental "Christian Socialism" of the mid-nineteenth century, and wrote two novels expressive of the spirit of the movement, *Yeast* and *Alton Locke,* as well as numerous articles. He was also identified with what was then known as "muscular Christianity," being a great sportsman and devoted to physical exercise in the open air. Besides all this, he was one of Queen Victoria's chaplains, professor of modern history at the University

KINGSLEY

CHARLES READE

of Cambridge, and a canon of Westminster. He was very active in many causes—the reconciliation of religion and science was another of his undertakings—and it is not surprising that he accomplished comparatively little with any one of them. But he was a striking and impressive figure, tall and active, with a dark complexion and "fiery and hawklike eyes," full of humor and animal spirits, bubbling over with enthusiasm for whatever cause was at the moment uppermost in his mind; and his name was often on the lips of his own generation. In spite of his numerous crusades and activities in London and elsewhere, his real occupation in life was that of a country parson. From 1842 till his death he was first curate and then rector of the remote but beautifully situated parish of Eversley in Hampshire, where his love of country life found its natural outlet and setting. It is this side of his character and work that appeals to posterity rather than his fulminations on contemporary issues which have now largely lost their significance. He was a man of vigorous personality rather than of deep or subtle intelligence.

The BRONTË SISTERS Charlotte (1816-55) and Emily (1818-48), with their younger sister Anne, were the authors of the *Poems by Currer, Ellis, and Acton Bell,* published in 1846. The publication was without effect so far as the public was concerned, for within a year only two copies were sold and the remainder of the edition was distributed gratuitously by the sisters (who preserved their anonymity and the secret of their sex) to contemporary authors whose work they admired. Undeterred by their failure, the young writers turned to prose fiction, with better success. Lonely spinsters, daughters of an eccentric Irish Protestant clergyman who had obtained the "perpetual curacy" of Howarth—a desolate factory village on the Yorkshire moors—few people seemed more unlikely to be afflicted with the desire for literary renown, or to have any chance of achieving it. Charlotte, the third of six children, had lost her mother at the age of five and become the oldest daughter of the house at the age of nine, her two elder sisters having died, apparently in consequence of the hardships and privations they suffered at a boarding-school for clergymen's daughters to which the four elder children were sent on their mother's death. After some years at home, during which the children educated themselves by their own devices (chiefly literary), Charlotte was sent at fifteen to another boarding-school, where she was much happier and made rapid progress in the studies she had neglected; at nineteen she returned to the school as a teacher, bringing with her Emily and Anne as pupils. Charlotte left when she was twenty-two, to take a place as a governess in a private family, and in 1842 she and Emily—now twenty-six and twenty-four respectively—went to Brussels to enlarge their educational resources as pupil-teachers in the boarding-school of M. and Mme. Héger. Emily was unhappy in the foreign surroundings and pined for the seclusion of the Yorkshire moors, to which she was glad to return when the school year was over. Charlotte went back the following year as a teacher, and, continuing her studies in French literature under the direction of M. Héger, fell in love with her professor; her

a single woman and likely to remain a single
woman — but because I am a lonely woman
and likely to be lonely. But it cannot be
helped and therefore imperatively must be
borne — and borne too with as few words
about it as may be.

I write all this just to prove to you that
whatever you would freely say to me — you
may just as freely write.

Understand — that I remain just as resolved
as ever not to allow myself the holiday
of a visit from you — till I have
done my work. After labour — pleasure — but
while work was lying at the mill undone —
I never yet could enjoy recreation
    Yours very faithfully
           C Brontë

FACSIMILE LETTER FROM CHARLOTTE BRONTË

intense devotion caused M. Héger more embarrassment than pleasure and excited the jealousy of his wife, so that Charlotte was very unhappy, both before she left Brussels and after her return home. Her passionate letters to him and his prudent replies were published long after, when both were dead. She tried to turn her Brussels experiences to account by idealizing them in a novel called *The Professor,* but this also did not see the light during her lifetime; submitted by her to various publishers, it "found acceptance nowhere, nor any acknowledgment of merit, so that something like the chill of despair began to invade her heart." Her only brother was dying from repeated debauches, and her father added blindness to his other defects; he used to waken up the family in the morning by firing a pistol out of his bedroom window. But at last the sun shone on the gloomy household. The three novels the sisters had written separately were all accepted: *Jane Eyre* by Currer Bell (1847) achieved immediate success, and, its authorship being revealed by a North-country reader who recognized some of the places and incidents, Charlotte went to London and met Thackeray and other celebrities. But fame and fortune came too late. Emily's *Wuthering Heights* and Anne's *Agnes Gray* appeared soon after *Jane Eyre,* but before the year of 1848 was out, Emily was dead and Anne sick unto death. In 1849, Charlotte, now famous, was the only survivor of the family of six children; and within six years her own life ended. Meanwhile, she had published two other novels, *Shirley,* a study of Yorkshire manufacturing life, and *Villette,* a reminiscence of her life at Brussels.

It was strange that these two sisters, with no more experience of life than falls to the lot of the average school-mistress, should have attained an intensity in the portrayal of passion beyond the reach of any other novelist of their time. *Jane Eyre* and *Wuthering Heights* have limitations which are not surprising in view of the secluded lives led by their young authors, but they still live by a flame of passion which animates their Victorian dust.

CHARLOTTE BRONTË   EMILY BRONTË

ANNE BRONTË   MRS. GASKELL

Among the literary friends made by Charlotte Brontë in the brief years of her success was ELIZABETH CLEGHORN GASKELL, the wife of a Manchester Unitarian minister, whose anonymous novel *Mary Barton* was published the year after *Jane Eyre,* and won almost equal success. A study of the life of the Lancashire cotton operative founded on much more intimate knowledge of the working class than Disraeli's *Sybil,* which preceded it, or *Hard Times* by Dickens, which followed it, *Mary Barton* aroused violent controversy by its picture of suffering and privation. Mrs. Gaskell offered a solatium to the offended cotton-spinners in a later novel, *North and South,* but no one acquainted with subsequent studies of the facts of the cotton industry in sober histories and Parliamentary reports now doubts the fairness and substantial truth of her portrayal in fiction. Beautiful, lively, and accomplished, an affectionate wife and a devoted mother, the friend of Dickens, Carlyle, and Thackeray and the author of several popular novels, she was nevertheless fated to become involved in bitter controversies. Her *Life of Charlotte Brontë* shows an admirable discretion, compared with the achievements of some modern biographers, concerning the private life of the subject and her family, but it fell under severe criticism for revelations at that time thought too personal. Her one book which escaped adverse comment and is still enjoyed without reservation is *Cranford,* a charming picture of the idyllic life she had herself lived in the Cheshire village of Knutsford during her girlhood before Queen Victoria came to the throne. Knutsford is (or was, when the writer last visited it to see the girls of the village dance round the Maypole) an attractive bit of the old rural world untouched by modern industrialism, and a hundred years ago it still maintained the quaint manners and customs of the previous century. Mrs. Gaskell brought these to life again in *Cranford* with unfailing sympathy and humor, and the book is still cherished, both in England and the United States, as preserving the charm of a day that has gone.

At the beginning of the nineteenth century, authorship was

COVENTRY

thought hardly becoming in a woman, and Jane Austen was hiding her manuscript under embroidery; in mid-century, as we have just seen, Charlotte Brontë and Mrs. Gaskell published their first novels anonymously. Mary Ann (or, as she preferred to call herself, Marian) Evans (1819-80) chose to write under the masculine pseudonym of GEORGE ELIOT, and under that name has come down to posterity, though for many years in private life she was known as Mrs. George Henry Lewes and she died the wife of J. W. Cross, a New York banker. No one, however, led more devotedly the intellectual life and lived in every sense by the labor of her pen, so that for present-day readers all names but that of George Eliot have rightly fallen into oblivion.

She was born at Arbury Farm, on a Warwickshire estate of which her father was steward. She went to school at the neighboring town of Coventry, to which, after some years of residence at Griff, she and her father (for whom she kept house) removed when she was twenty-one. Her family was orthodox and she grew up under strong evangelical influences; but coming at Coventry into contact with a local manufacturer named Charles Bray, who was a student of sociology and philosophy, she gave up the faith of her earlier years. Her first publication was an anonymous translation of Strauss's *Life of Jesus* (1846), paid for by Radical subscribers and at that time regarded as extremely skeptical in its tendencies. After nursing her father through a long and painful illness, which ended in his death in 1849, she suffered a physical breakdown and was taken by the Brays to Switzerland, where she took up the study of physical science. Returning to England, she contributed to the leading Radical organ, the "Westminster Review," of which she was for two years assistant editor; living in London, she came into contact with Herbert Spencer and other advanced thinkers of the mid-nineteenth century. One of these, George Henry Lewes, particularly attracted her, and as he was living apart from his wife, from whom he could not obtain a divorce, she agreed to unite her life with his and look after his children. They lived and worked together abroad, especially in Germany, where Lewes completed his *Life of Goethe* (1855), and returned to England the same year. Encouraged by Lewes, she wrote for "Blackwood's Magazine" the short story of *Amos Barton,* afterward included, with two or three others of the same type, in *Scenes of Clerical Life* (1858) by George Eliot— a signature which caused some confusion, as several men laid claim to the authorship. These stories of rural life in the Midlands, regarded mainly on its moral and religious sides, were but a prologue to the more elaborate and profound study of moral and religious issues in *Adam Bede* (1859). Relying mainly on her own recollections of Midland life during her youth, she dealt sympathetically with the religious faith she had abandoned, whether Methodist or Anglican, High- or Low-church, and enriched her pictures of rural life with lively humor and pungent criticism of human nature, expressed or implied. In her next novel, *The Mill on the Floss* (1860), she followed even more closely her remembrance of her childish affection for her

GEORGE ELIOT

brother, and in the picture of the ardent and aspiring Maggie Tulliver gave a vivid account of certain sides of her own nature. *Silas Marner* (1861) treats a simple theme with exquisite art, and marks, perhaps, the climax of her first and best period. After completing it, she went to Italy and spent some months there, acquiring material for a historical romance of Florence in the time of Savanarola, which was published n 1862-63 as *Romola*. It made an immense impression upon the contemporary public and brought her in a large sum of money, but later generations have thought it overweighted with learning and falsified by Puritan prejudice. From now on for fifteen years George Eliot and Lewes occupied a house at North Bank, Regent's Park, which became an intellectual center for the literary and scientific world of the English metropolis. The novelist presided over the afternoon tea-table with the impressiveness of an oracle. Her conversation tended to be philosophical and, above all, ethical in tone. F. W. H. Myers, a Trinity College don, in the following description, recalls a talk he had with her in the beautiful walk of the fellows' garden when she visited Cambridge:

"She, stirred somewhat beyond her wont, and taking as her text the three words which have been used so often as the inspiring trumpet call of men—the words God, Immortality, Duty —pronounced with terrible earnestness how inconceivable was the first, how unbelievable the second, and yet how peremptory and absolute the third. Never, perhaps, have sterner accents affirmed the sovereignty of impersonal and unrecompensing Law. I listened, and night fell; her grave, majestic countenance turned towards me like a sibyl's in the gloom; it was as though she withdrew from my grasp, one by one, the two scrolls of promise, and left me the third scroll only, awful with inevitable fates."

In George Eliot's later novels, ethical, social, or political philosophy was likely to be the dominating theme. *Felix Holt the Radical* (1866), a study of provincial town life about the beginning of the Victorian period, combines the simple story of the Radical agitator's love for the Nonconformist minister's daughter with the complicated problem of an ancient love-intrigue and a testamentary lawsuit; it is an attempt, not altogether successful, to make use of the mystery plots brought into fashion by Wilkie Collins. *Middlemarch* (1871-72), another study of provincial town life at a somewhat earlier period, is an ambitious attempt to realize a whole community in its various social, political, and commercial ramifications; it is, not only in size but in scope, George Eliot's biggest book, and is thought by many of her admirers to be her greatest work; but it is too involved and elaborate to be easily absorbed by the modern novel-reader. Her last novel, *Daniel Deronda* (1874-76), with a Jewish idealist as its hero, was too philosophical and alien in theme even for the later Victorian public.

Although George Eliot's life and her work from the beginning of her literary career were permeated by the spirit of modern science, her novels are studiously conservative from the moral point of view; as she had outraged the conventions by her union with Lewes, she seemed to feel it incumbent upon her not to swerve, in her novels, from the most rigid requirements of Victorian morality. The seduction of Hetty Sorrel in *Adam Bede* is treated with the utmost reticence, and Maggie's innocent escapade with her cousin's lover in *The Mill on the Floss* is regarded as a grave offense against the proprieties. This Victorian attitude, and George Eliot's rather heavy-handed insistence upon moral issues, have made it difficult for youthful readers of the twentieth century to recognize her real merits —her artistic gifts, her humor, and her emotional power. The final verdict on her work has not yet been agreed upon.

The difficulties of the Victorian transition involved not only the novelists but also the poets. The impulse to change came mainly from the philosophers, such as John Stuart Mill and Herbert Spencer, who early adopted the evolutionary theory; from men of science like Lyell, Darwin, Huxley, and Tyndall; or from Biblical critics like Bishop Colenso, as set forth in the opening pages of this chapter. But the poets incorporated the new ideas in their own systems of thought, and gave them harmonious expression which found ready access to a wider audience than the philosophers and scientists could command. No writer expressed the Victorian ideas more melodiously or more completely than ALFRED TENNYSON (1809-92).

Born in Lincolnshire, where his father was rector of Somersby, "a mere hamlet of sixty souls," for nearly thirty years Tennyson regarded the rectory as his home and spent most of his time there. He was away for a few years at school, but came home to be prepared by his father for the University of Cambridge, where he entered Trinity College in 1828. Two years before, he had published, along with his older brother Charles, *Poems by Two Brothers,* and while still a freshman he won the English poetry prize with a blank-verse poem on the assigned subject of *Timbuctoo;* later in life, Tennyson remarked that it was the first poem ever written in blank verse that took the Chancellor's Medal and he "could wish that it had never been written at all." Even at the time he attached no great importance to these juvenile effusions, written before he was twenty, but when, at twenty-one, he published *Poems, chiefly Lyrical,* he recognized that poetry was to be his vocation in life, and never afterwards wavered.

He was recalled home from Cambridge before he finished his degree course, by the death of his father, but he had already made friendships that materially affected his future career and way of looking at things. Twenty years after, he looked back fondly to the college rooms—

> Where once we held debate, a band
>   Of youthful friends, on mind and art,
>   And labor, and the changing mart,
> And all the framework of the land.

He was one of the group of undergraduates known as "the Apostles," who took life seriously and discussed not only social and political questions but problems of theology and philosophy, of which they knew, no doubt, very little. The leading member

TENNYSON

of the group was Arthur Hallam, son of the well-known historian and man of letters; he was two years older than Tennyson, and had had a much wider experience, of both men and books; all his friends regarded him as a youth of brilliant promise. Tennyson conceived a deep affection for him, and the bond of friendship was drawn closer by Hallam's engagement to Tennyson's sister. In 1833 young Hallam, whose health was precarious, left England with his father for a tour on the Continent, and Tennyson went to London to see him off; the two friends never saw each other again, for three months later, at Vienna, Arthur Hallam died suddenly in his sleep.

The death of Hallam caused Tennyson more than the pang of personal bereavement; his whole view of life (including his religious beliefs) was clouded by doubt and he sank into deep depression. This mood was intensified by the reception of a volume of poems published the year before, which called forth severe criticism. For some months after Hallam's death he wrote nothing, and for ten years he published no new volume. Until 1837 he was still living in seclusion at Somersby, wrestling with religious and philosophic problems, and embodying his meditations in a long poem which enshrined Hallam's memory and was not published till seventeen years after his death. Meanwhile Tennyson became a recognized figure in London literary society. He would have been a conspicuous figure in any society, being six feet high, broad-chested, strong-limbed, and beautifully proportioned; his head finely poised, and his forehead ample, crowned with dark wavy hair. Carlyle, who formed a close friendship with Tennyson, described him as "one of the finest-looking men in the world. A great shock of rough, dusky-dark hair, bright, laughing hazel eyes, massive, aquiline face, most massive yet most delicate, of sallow brown complexion, almost Indian looking, clothes cynically loose, free and easy, smokes infinite tobacco. His voice is musical, metallic, fit for loud laughter and piercing wail, and all that may lie between; speech and speculation free and plenteous; I do not meet in these late decades such company over a pipe!" In later years he

SOMERSBY CHURCH

SOMERSBY RECTORY

increased the impressiveness of his appearance by wearing a long cloak and a broad-brimmed felt hat.

After a silence of nearly ten years Tennyson was induced to issue his poems in two volumes, including carefully revised versions of those previously published and such new compositions as *Ulysses, Locksley Hall,* and *Morte d'Arthur*—his first and perhaps his best handling of the Arthurian legend. There was still a good deal of hostile criticism, but the volumes of 1842 caught the public taste and several editions were called for in the next few years.

Tennyson was steadily gaining ground in public favor, but he did not yet feel able to marry, although he had been engaged for many years. Unfortunately, in an attempt to increase his little capital by a commercial speculation, he lost it all, and was for some time again extremely depressed. This was made up to him to some extent by the grant of a government pension of a thousand dollars a year. *The Princess* (1847), a long poem on the subject of the higher education of women, rather puzzled the public by its fantastic story and setting, but it contained some of his most exquisite lyrics—"The splendor falls on castle walls," "Home they brought her warrior dead," "Ask me no more," and, above all, "Tears, idle tears," from which two stanzas may be quoted as examples of Tennyson's power to make melodious words (even without the aid of rhyme) convey an emotional effect.

> Tears, idle tears, I know not what they mean,
> Tears from the depth of some divine despair
> Rise in the heart, and gather to the eyes,
> In looking on the happy autumn-fields,
> And thinking of the days that are no more.
>
> *   *   *   *
>
> Dear as remembered kisses after death,
> And sweet as those by hopeless fancy feigned
> On lips that are for others; deep as love,
> Deep as first love, and wild with all regret;
> O Death in Life, the days that are no more!

It was not, however, till 1850 that Tennyson's place as the leading figure in contemporary poetry was established by the publication of *In Memoriam*. It had a somewhat mixed reception, but there could be no denial of its poetic beauty or of its power as an interpretation of the transition in religious thought which was then going on. The sympathetic but questioning attitude toward modern scientific theories, the defense of "honest doubt," the positive but undogmatic belief in the immortality of the soul—

> I stretch lame hands of faith, and grope,
>   And gather dust and chaff, and call
>   To what I feel is Lord of all,
> And faintly trust the larger hope—

all this encouraged the more liberal spirits in the religious world as much as it alarmed the orthodox. In its conclusion the poem is optimistic, looking forward to the coming of a nobler race:

> Of those that, eye to eye, shall look
>   On knowledge; under whose command
>   Is Earth and Earth's, and in their hand
> Is Nature like an open book;
>
> No longer half-akin to brute,
>   For all we thought and loved and did,
>   And hoped, and suffered, is but seed
> Of what in them is flower and fruit;
>
> Whereof the man that with me trod
>   This planet was a noble type
>   Appearing ere the times were ripe,
> That friend of mine who lives in God,
>
> That God, which ever lives and loves,
>   One God, one law, one element,
>   And one far-off divine event,
> To which the whole creation moves.

Among the admirers of the poem was the Prince Consort, and this no doubt was an element in the appointment of Tennyson as poet laureate on the death of Wordsworth the same year; the salary was hardly an important consideration, being only five hundred dollars a year, but the position was an official acknowledgment of the place the poet already occupied in the affections of the public. A substantial advance by his publishers enabled Tennyson to marry Emily Selwood, who had been waiting for him for over a dozen years. "The peace of God came into my soul before the altar when I wedded her," was the poet's verdict long afterward, and for over forty years they lived most happily together.

From 1850 on, the poet's mind was at rest on spiritual issues, and he continued to prosper in the enjoyment of the income his popularity brought with it. He gradually became one of the best established of national institutions and received with dignity (and not without enjoyment) a great deal of public attention. He was able to buy a house (Farringford) in the Isle of Wight, and when this seemed too accessible to the populace and not entirely suited to his wife's health, he was in a position to build another near Haslemere in Surrey (Aldworth). He was on friendly terms with Queen Victoria and was always able to provide the ceremonial poetry expected from the laureate. His *Ode on the Death of the Duke of Wellington* gave fitting recognition to a national hero, and *The Charge of the Light Brigade,* celebrating an incident in the Crimean War, was widely popular. A longer poem in connection with the war, *Maud; a Monodrama,* was less liked, perhaps on account of its disrespectful language about cotton-spinners and commercialism in general.

Is it peace or war? better, war! loud war by land and by sea,
War with a thousand battles, and shaking a hundred thrones.

The period of his greatest popularity may be dated from the beginning of the long series of the *Idylls of the King* in 1859; the successive issues were greeted with almost universal

TENNYSON IN OLD AGE

applause, though a few of the more independent critics shook their heads over the sentimentalizing of the medieval stories and the distorting of the main figures and events into accordance with the Victorian proprieties. A less successful effort on his part was to revive the glories of Shaksperean historical drama, begun in 1875 with *Queen Mary,* and continued in *Harold* and *Becket;* all these elaborate compositions remained closet dramas, unsuited for presentation on the modern stage, the requirements of which Tennyson quietly ignored. He was writing for the stage of Shakspere in the Shaksperean manner, and he knew his Shakspere well; but it was a copy, not an original creation.

Tennyson, however, kept his lyrical gift to the end of his life, and each successive volume up to the last, in 1889, was warmly welcomed by an ever-respectful public. After twice declining a peerage, he was induced at seventy-five years of age to accept and to take his seat in the House of Lords, but he voted only twice. At his funeral in Westminster Abbey, one of his latest lyrics, "Crossing the Bar," was sung as an anthem:

> Sunset and evening star,
>   And one clear call for me!
> And may there be no moaning of the bar,
>   When I put out to sea,
>
> But such a tide as moving seems asleep,
>   Too full for sound and foam,
> When that which drew from out the boundless deep
>   Turns again home.
>
> Twilight and evening bell,
>   And after that the dark!
> And may there be no sadness of farewell,
>   When I embark;
>
> For though from out our bourne of Time and Place
>   The flood may bear me far,
> I hope to see my Pilot face to face
>   When I have crossed the bar.

To their contemporaries ROBERT BROWNING (1812-89) offered a marked contrast to Tennyson in his outlook on life and the character of his poetic genius. To readers of a century later they seem to have much in common—their religious faith, their limited sympathy with modern science, their romantic fervor, and their general acceptance of the Victorian compromises with science and with romanticism. Browning, it is true, approached religion from a liberal Nonconformist point of view, Tennyson from that of a conservative Churchman, but they both clung to the essentials of the Christian faith. Browning's orthodoxy is perhaps even more unquestioning than that of Tennyson. *Christmas Eve* and *Easter Day* (1850) constitute together a poetical statement, as the poet himself put it, of "what is to be believed *now*," and the gist of it is the necessity of accepting the evangelical doctrine of the incarnation and resurrection of Jesus as held by a country congregation of English Nonconformists in Browning's youth. In *Saul* (1845-55), *An Epistle of Karshish* (1855), *Bishop Blougram's Apology* (1855), and *A Death in the Desert* (1864), he reaffirmed his belief in these doctrines. *La Saisiaz* (1878) is wholly devoted to a development of the theme that without a belief in the Christian doctrine of immortality, human life is meaningless. In this belief the poet lived and died. His last message to his generation in the Epilogue to *Asolando,* published on the day of his death, was that only fools would think of him as "imprisoned" by death: he looked forward to a future life of free activity in which he would fight on, "strive and thrive," being

One who never turned his back but marched breast forward,
    Never doubted clouds would break,
Never dreamed, though right were worsted, wrong would triumph,
    Held we fall to rise, are baffled to fight better,
        Sleep to wake.

Browning came of Nonconformist middle-class stock; his father was a clerk in the Bank of England, and sent him first to a private school and later to University College, London,

BROWNING AT FORTY-SEVEN

founded not long before to afford opportunities of higher education to Nonconformists, who were still excluded from the universities of Oxford and Cambridge. The poetic gods of his youth were Byron, Shelley, and Keats, and his first published poem *Pauline* (1833) was Shelleyan in spirit as well as in form. A poetic drama, *Paracelsus* (1835) induced the leading actor of the time, Macready, to say to him, "Write me a play, and save me from going to America." In response Browning wrote the tragedy of *Strafford,* which was put on the stage of Covent Garden Theatre in 1837, but ran only for a few nights; further dramatic attempts by Browning, of which the most notable were *A Blot in the 'Scutcheon* (Drury Lane, 1843) and *Colombe's Birthday* (Haymarket, 1853), are of interest as poetry, but none succeeded in holding a place on the stage.

Meanwhile Browning had tempted fortune by the publication of a long narrative poem, *Sordello* (1840), which reduced both critics and public to utter bewilderment; it was reported that Tennyson said he understood only two lines of it; one was the first, "Who will, may hear Sordello's story told," and the other was the last, "Who would has heard Sordello's story told"—and they were both lies. Douglas Jerrold, recovering from an illness and picking up the volume to amuse his convalescence, thought he had taken leave of his senses, and was convinced that he was still in his right mind only by the assurances of his wife and her sister that they could make nothing of it either. Such were the stories with which literary pundits amused themselves and one another in the forties. But the consequences to the author were serious; he entered upon "a period of general neglect which covered nearly twenty years of his life."

Browning's reputation was still in this state of depression when he was cheered by a complimentary reference in a poem by ELIZABETH BARRETT (1806-61) to his *Bells and Pomegranates,* a cheap series of pamphlet-like volumes in which his shorter poems were offered to the public after the failure of *Sordello.* Miss Barrett was an invalid and a recluse, not personally known

ELIZABETH BARRETT BROWNING

to Browning, but well known to the public, with whom her work was exceedingly popular. Another poetess of that time, her friend Miss Mitford, described her figure as slight and delicate (she was unusually small) "with a shower of dark curls falling on each side of a most expressive face, large tender eyes, richly fringed. with dark eyelashes, and a smile like a sunbeam." Browning took advantage of her reference to his work and wrote to her at her home, 50 Wimpole Street, London, not very far from New Cross, Surrey, where he was then living. "I love your verses, dear Miss Barrett," he wrote in January, 1845, and he added, later in the same letter, "I love you too." When he asked to be allowed to see her (she received very few friends), she protested: "There is nothing to see in me, nor to hear in me. If my poetry is worth anything to any eye, it is the flower of me. . . . The rest of me is nothing but a root, fit for the ground and the dark." Their correspondence, kept secret for years but published after both were dead, is one of the most remarkable known to literature.

After the interchange of several letters, he did see her in May and wrote almost immediately after the interview, proposing marriage; he was refused and reprimanded, bidden never to mention the subject again. But they continued "the truest of friends," and by September they had come to a satisfactory understanding. By this time Miss Barrett's health had sufficiently improved for there to be talk of a voyage to Italy. The one obstacle in the way was her father, a religious monomaniac, who regarded any inclination on the part of his daughters to leave the parental roof as "undutifulness and rebellion"; marriage or an engagement to marry was a matter that could not even be mentioned. It took a year's correspondence and much personal persuasion before Miss Barrett could be induced to get away from her invalid couch (on September 12, 1846) long enough to be married in a neighboring church, and a week later she was sufficiently rested to leave the house secretly and escape with her husband to Paris. Her father's comment to an intercessor on her behalf was "I have no objection to the young man;

I can have little doubt but that my
writing has been, in the main, too hard
for many I should have been pleased
to communicate with: but I never
designedly tried to puzzle people, as
some of my critics have supposed. On
the other hand, I never pretended to
offer such literature as should be
a substitute for a cigar, or game
at dominoes to an idle man. So, perhaps on the whole I get my deserts and
something over — not a crowd but
a few I value more.

but my daughter ought to have been thinking of another world."
He refused ever to see her again and never forgave her.

The eloping couple went on from Paris to Italy, and after
some wanderings settled down in apartments in the Casa Guidi,
near the Pitti Palace in Florence. Mrs. Browning's health
greatly improved and in 1849 she gave birth to a son. The poet-
lovers continued to be both lovers and poets, and did their best
work during their married life in Florence, which continued to
be their home until Mrs. Browning's death. She was buried in
the Protestant cemetery there, and on Casa Guidi the grateful
Florentines placed an inscription: "Here wrote and died Elizabeth Barrett Browning, who made of her verse a golden ring to
unite Italy and England."

The two poets worked independently and showed each other
the result only when it was in its finished state. Soon after their
arrival in Italy she showed him for the first time a series of
sonnets she had addressed to him during his courtship; they
are her finest work and among the noblest love-poems in the
language; they were published in 1850 under the title *Sonnets
from the Portuguese*. She was intensely interested in the Italian
struggle for unity and independence and expressed her sympathy in *Casa Guidi Windows* (1851). Her next poetic venture
was a modern novel in verse, *Aurora Leigh* (1856), which was
well received at the time, but has failed to hold its reputation,
except as a curiosity. *Poems before Congress* (1860) and *Last
Poems* (1862) showed that the love of Italy possessed her up to
the time of her death, which was ascribed in part to the shock
caused by the death of Cavour the Italian liberator, whom she
greatly admired.

Browning shared his wife's enthusiasm for the liberation of
Italy and it inspired some of his best poems. In the *Bells and
Pomegranates* series, published before he left England, he had
already developed the form of dramatic monologue which was
to become his most abiding and characteristic mode of expression. It is a form developed from the most difficult but convenient of dramatic conventions—the soliloquy, in which a char-

acter sets forth for the benefit of the audience the innermost thoughts of his heart. Browning's main interest lay in the analysis of the soul; "little else," he said, "is worth study." The limitations of the dramatic monologue are obvious; how many men analyze themselves, discuss with themselves the motives of their actions, or acknowledge, even to themselves, the secret thoughts of their hearts? But Browning adapted his genius to the form with astonishing versatility, and his wide knowledge gave him an extraordinary range of subjects and personalities, from David harping before Saul to people of his own time, of various classes and nationalities. *Men and Women* (1855), the chief work of his Florentine period, contains some of the best of these character studies, and was accompanied by a charming poem 'One Word More,' addressed to "E.B.B."—a fitting pendant to the *Sonnets from the Portuguese*.

After Mrs. Browning's death Browning left Florence, never to return, and, almost to the end of his life, made his home in London. His first effort was to complete the works he had begun with the help of his wife's companionship and inspiration—a new series of dramatic monologues, *Dramatis Personæ* (1864), and *The Ring and the Book*. The latter was published in the last two months of 1868 and the first two of 1869, in four volumes. By its very size and the evidence of metrical and intellectual versatility it displayed, this enormous work impressed the British public, even if they did not read it, and some of his shorter pieces had by this time become even popular. It is an elaborate treatment, from various points of view, mainly by the method of psychological analysis, of a seventeenth-century Roman murder case, the particulars of which, including the evidence and pleadings at the trial, the poet obtained from an old parchment-covered volume at a second-hand book-stall as he was passing through the Piazza San Lorenzo in Florence. It was a good enough story, as handled by Browning, to afford a basis for a romantic melodrama acted with great success in New York City in 1929-30. Browning tells the story, in some twenty-four thousand lines, first from the point of view of the half-

BROWNING IN OLD AGE

Rome favorable to the murderer Guido; secondly, from that of the other half-Rome in favor of Pompilia his wife; thirdly, from that of "a tertium quid," leaning sometimes to one side, sometimes to the other; next, we hear the accused; then the hero, Caponsacchi, who helped Pompilia to escape from the brutal and tyrannical husband. The finest book is that given to the heroine herself; but we must listen also to counsel for the prosecution and counsel for the defense, with their pitiless jargon of legal lore; the Pope sums up, and Guido, convicted and sentenced, makes a last dying speech and confession to the extent of nearly three thousand lines, about the length of a Shaksperean play. Finally, in Book XII, the author tells the final state of the story, expressing the pious hope that the British public, "Ye who like me not," as he had said at the beginning, "may like me yet."

The British public never came really to like Browning, but they accepted him as a phenomenon they did not pretend to understand. For some months after his wife's death he lived in seclusion, but, deeming it his duty to make social contacts, he came out into London society and became one of the best-known figures of the literary world. He frequented afternoon teas and knew all the literary and artistic gossip. "Everybody wished him to come and dine; and he did his utmost to gratify everybody. He said everything; read all the notable books; kept himself acquainted with the leading contents of the journals and magazines; conducted a large correspondence; read new French, German, and Italian books of mark; read and translated Euripides and Æschylus." In physique, says Sir Edmund Gosse, who knew him well, he was "short and thick-set, of a very muscular build; his temper was ardent and optimistic; he was appreciative, sympathetic, and full of curiosity; prudent in affairs, and rather 'close' about money; robust, active, loud of speech, cordial in manner, gracious and conciliatory in address, but subject to sudden fits of indignation."

In spite of multifarious social activities, Browning wrote and published a great deal in the latter part of his life. *The Ring and the Book* is his central and supreme achievement; but so

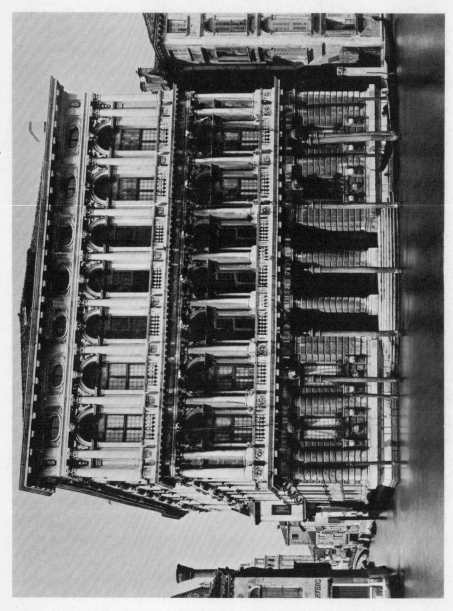

PALAZZO REZZONICO

far as quantity is concerned, he published as much poetry after he had finished it (when he was nearly sixty) as before he began it, at about fifty. The work of these last years, though it consolidated his position with his contemporaries, added little to his permanent fame. There were the Greek studies already referred to—*Balaustion's Adventure, Aristophanes' Apology,* and the translation of the *Agamemnon* of Æschylus—of which it was said that no one could understand it without constant reference to the original; all these were done in the seventies. Having spent several summers on the French coast and narrowly escaped entanglement in the disturbance caused by the Franco-German War of 1870, he devoted the proceeds of one of his best ballads, *Hervé Riel,* to the relief of sufferers from the siege of Paris. A longer poem of the same period was an analysis, keen rather than sympathetic, of the character of the fallen Emperor Napoleon III, published under the title of *Prince Hohenstiel-Schwangau.* His visits to Brittany gave occasion for other long poems, *Fifine at the Fair, Red Cotton Nightcap Country,* and *The Two Poets of Croisic. La Saisiaz,* a philosophical discussion of the immortality of the soul, was occasioned by the death in 1878 of Miss Anne Egerton Smith, a great lover of music, with whom he had spent much of his time in London, attending the principal concerts. In later years, an American lady, Mrs. Arthur Bronson, revived his interest in the Northern Italian haunts of his youth, especially Venice and Asolo. The latter especially interested him as the home of Sordello, the hero of the great poetic enterprise of his youth, and from the word Asolo was taken the Italian title of his last volume of short poems, *Asolando.* Browning thought of building a villa there for himself, for at seventy-five he was still vigorous. He left his rather humdrum house at 19 Warwick Crescent, in which he had lived for a quarter of a century, for more agreeable quarters in De Vere Gardens at the West End of London, and he bought a Venetian palace on the Grand Canal, the Palazzo Rezzonico, where he died on December 12, 1889, after hearing, on his sickbed, news of the favorable reviews of *Asolando.*

RUGBY SCHOOL

RUGBY CHAPEL

With the death of Browning and Tennyson, their contemporaries felt that the lights of Victorian poetry had gone out; and even in retrospect the two seem the great poetic luminaries of that era. But there were smaller stars, of a more subdued radiance and of gentler warmth, yet not unworthy of attention. MATTHEW ARNOLD (1822-88) was an influential and characteristic figure in the middle period, which differed greatly in spirit from the early Victorian age; instead of the buoyant optimism and sometimes smug self-satisfaction of the earlier years, we find, beginning about 1860, an inclination to self-examination, self-questioning, self-criticism, and often distrust. The world, once "so various, so beautiful, so new," Arnold cried:

> Hath really neither joy, nor love, nor light,
> Nor certitude, nor peace, nor help for pain;
> And we are here as on a darkling plain
> Swept with confused alarms of struggle and flight,
> Where ignorant armies clash by night.

And if Arnold found no lasting satisfaction in mortal life, his faith in immortality was far from vigorous. In the lines on the death of his father, "Rugby Chapel, November, 1857," he writes:

> O strong soul, by what shore
> Tarriest thou now? For that force,
> Surely, has not been left vain!
> Somewhere, surely, afar,
> In the sounding labor-house vast
> Of being, is practised that strength,
> Zealous, beneficent, firm!

The sure faith of Tennyson and Browning was gone. Arnold maintained throughout life this reserved, doubtful, critical spirit, tinged with melancholy, though in social relations he was cheerful, even gay, and enjoyed a fair degree of success in the matters in which he was chiefly interested. At Rugby School, of which his father was headmaster, he wrote a prize poem which he considered superior to his later performance at Oxford,

MATTHEW ARNOLD

where he won the Newdigate prize and a fellowship. After teaching for a year or two at Rugby, he became secretary to Lord Lansdowne, and in 1851 an inspector of schools. This post occupied his main attention until he was able to retire with a pension in 1883. His poetry, published in two volumes in 1853-55 and in three in 1885, was written mainly in the earlier part of his career, of which the latter part was given rather to critical lectures and prose writing. He was for ten years professor of poetry at Oxford, and made two lecture tours in the United States—as he frankly acknowledged, to make provision for his family. In connection with his school inspectorship, he traveled much on the European Continent, and was appalled by the somberness and narrowness of life in Mid-Victorian England. Thus, while his earlier lectures and essays were on literary topics, his later subjects were more often the social and religious conditions of contemporary life. He criticized sharply the combination of Puritanism and commercialism which he thought responsible for the drabness of life in England and the United States, with its excessive stress upon morals, its lack of beauty, and its horizons limited by the fear of hell and the bankruptcy court. He condemned with equal emphasis the "barbarous" English aristocracy, the "philistine" middle class, and the ignorant and degraded proletariat. He preached the gospel of "sweetness and light" (a phrase he borrowed from Swift), advocated "culture" against the prevailing "anarchy," and suggested a greater degree of equality in English class relations. All this was said (and frequently repeated) not with deadly seriousness, but in a tone of light banter, often reinforced with irony. He was often reproached on account of his attitude of superiority, but his counsels were not without effect. Nor have the evils to which he drew attention entirely passed away.

After living for some years at Harrow, Arnold made his home for the last fifteen years of his life at Pains Hill Cottage, Cobham, Surrey. He died suddenly from heart disease at Liverpool, whither he had gone to meet a married daughter (Mrs. Whitcombe) then living in New York City.

DANTE GABRIEL ROSSETTI IN 1847

DANTE GABRIEL ROSSETTI (1828-82) was the leader of the artistic group known as the Pre-Raphaelite Brotherhood, whose sponsorship by Ruskin has been already mentioned. These young artists gave their first exhibition of pictures in 1849, and in 1850 established a magazine, "The Germ," to "encourage and enforce an entire adherence to the simplicity of nature." To this Rossetti, who was born in London, the son of an Italian refugee, and educated there at King's College and the Royal Academy, contributed a dozen poems, among them "The Blessèd Damozel." But for the next ten years he continued to devote his main attention to pictorial art. He fell in love with a beautiful model, a London tradesman's daughter, became engaged to her in 1853, and married her in 1860. Two years later she died under mysterious circumstances, and on the day of the funeral Rossetti thrust into the coffin the MS. of the poems he had written to her.

Not long after, he set up housekeeping at 16 Cheyne Walk, Chelsea, along with George Meredith and Algernon Swinburne, but three poets under one roof were too many, and Meredith and Swinburne soon left. Rossetti developed curious fads, including a menagerie of pets, of which one was to have been a small white elephant which he saw advertised for sale in the newspapers; according to the story, Rossetti said he intended to teach it to clean the windows, and so advertise his paintings. He was suffering from extreme nervous strain, insomnia, and the threat of blindness, which obliged him to give less attention to painting and more to poetry. His friends urged him to publish, but his best work had been buried in his wife's coffin. An order for exhumation was obtained from the Home Secretary, and in 1870 the poems were published. They made a considerable stir, and were the subject of a violent attack by an anonymous critic (afterward known to be Robert Buchanan), entitled *The Fleshly School in Poetry*. This caused the poet great pain, in his nervous state of health, and he began to take chloral for the relief of his insomnia; in 1872 he suffered so severely from depression that he attempted suicide, although only a year before he had completed one of his best pictures, "Dante's Dream," now in the

DANTE GABRIEL ROSSETTI   CHRISTINA ROSSETTI AND HER MOTHER
IN 1855

WILLIAM MORRIS   SWINBURNE

Walker Art Gallery, Liverpool. Although he recovered to some extent, he became a chloral-addict and a recluse at 16 Cheyne Walk; it is said that for four years he never left the house except at night, and even on these exceptional occasions did not go beyond the walls of his own garden.

CHRISTINA GEORGINA ROSSETTI (1830-94) younger sister of Dante Gabriel, began to write at the age of twelve, and at seventeen printed a collection of her verses privately at the expense of an uncle. At twenty she was a precociously mature contributor to "The Germ," but it was not until 1862 that she made her first real appeal to the public in a volume entitled *Goblin Market, and other Poems*. The public response was immediate and has been ratified by posterity; modern critics now give Christina Rossetti pride of place as the leading woman poet of the nineteenth century, although during her lifetime Mrs. Browning and others, whom it is needless to mention, had a greater reputation. Although not lacking in the sensuous charm which is characteristic of her brother's poetry, her work has, to a much greater extent than his, an intensity of religious devotion which sometimes gives it the power of a mystical revelation. She was from her girlhood a devout Anglican, and her religious faith grew with years, so that toward the end of her life she lived in a state of seclusion from which she rarely emerged except to attend the services of the neighboring church in Woburn Square, where after her death Sir Edward Burne-Jones of the Pre-Raphaelite Brotherhood, placed a reredos to her memory. This may still be seen in the interesting London quarter known as Bloomsbury, including the British Museum, the University of London, and many houses of present and former celebrities. Christina's nature was from the beginning inclined to melancholy, and this tendency was encouraged by frequent and serious illnesses. She was twice engaged to be married, but in each case on coming to know her lover better and finding his religious convictions not in strict accord with her own, she broke off the engagement. Her life was one long tissue of illnesses and disappointments, to which was often added the gloom of mental depression.

WILLIAM MORRIS (1834-96), though not so greatly gifted as the forementioned members of the P.R.B., was more robust, both in body and mind. Dante Gabriel Rossetti was inclined in later life to an unhealthy stoutness, and Christina had from her girlhood a melancholy cast of countenance; William Morris, short and thick-set, with a noble head adorned with plenteous brown hair, and a brown beard which turned to gray in later years, had a berserker appearance which agreed well with his skill as an interpreter of Icelandic sagas. The son of a wealthy London broker, he went to Marlborough School and Exeter College, Oxford, where Burne-Jones also was an undergraduate. With the help of D. G. Rossetti and others, in 1856 they adorned the debating hall of the Oxford Union with frescoes—which, alas! quickly faded. In 1858, Morris published his first long poem, *The Defence of Guinevere,* the forerunner of many other narratives in verse, taken from various sources. In 1862 he founded the business firm of Morris & Co. (in which Rossetti and Burne-Jones were partners) for bringing back art into house-furnishing and decorating and later into typography (the Kelmscott Press). Meanwhile, Morris was taking a great interest in public affairs, and from being a Radical in politics he developed into an active Socialist. He was the leader of the Social Democratic Federation up to 1884, when it was dissolved, and as head of the more extreme members of it formed the Socialist League. The labor troubles of 1886, culminating in the Trafalgar Square riots, provoked jealousy and suspicion between him and his followers, and he was formally deposed from the leadership in 1889. His socialistic theories were set forth in *A Dream of John Ball* (1888) and *News from Nowhere* (1891). A disciple of Ruskin, Morris directed his efforts more to restoring to the worker an interest in craftsmanship, and to placing him in right relations to his fellows and the community, than to the establishment of any hard and fast economic plan for the equal distribution of goods or state control of capitalism. He was a man of wide interests, of great energy and enthusiasm, and made his mark on the way of thinking and living of his generation.

ALGERNON CHARLES SWINBURNE (1837-1909) came of an aristocratic family and was educated at Eton and Balliol College, Oxford, where he made friends of William Morris, Rossetti, and Burne-Jones. With the Pre-Raphaelite movement he had no very substantial connection, though he owed to it, probably, the development of the sensuous element in his poetry which gave such serious offense on the publication of *Poems and Ballads* in 1866; according to recent biographers, a Balliol undergraduate, John Nichol (afterward professor of English at Glasgow) exercised a deleterious influence upon Swinburne in their student days, teaching him "republicanism and a good deal that was less worthy to be learned." Swinburne was throughout his life very impressionable, and his poetry echoes many influences to which he was from time to time subjected. The son of a British admiral and brought up on the Isle of Wight, he acquired during his boyhood that passionate love of the sea which he shares in generous measure with many English poets, from *Beowulf* to the present day. At Oxford he was swept away with enthusiasm for the liberation of Italy and wrote an ode to the Italian patriot Mazzini, then a refugee in England. He took a classical degree and the influence of Greek tragedy is plainly seen in his poetic dramas, though he is thoroughly romantic in spirit. He won prizes at Eton and also at Oxford for proficiency in French and Italian, and conceived a passionate admiration for Victor Hugo, whom he met in Paris in 1882; he was also indebted to later French poets, including Gautier and Baudelaire. He was a diligent student of Elizabethan drama and wrote eloquent critical eulogies of Shakspere, Ben Jonson, and Chapman; he could flash forth in defense of his friends Rossetti and Meredith when they were assailed by ignorant reviewers, and he was not without words of praise for more alien spirits among his contemporaries, such as Carlyle, Charlotte Brontë, and George Eliot. In later years he could even hymn the jubilees of Queen Victoria and the new imperialism. Amid all these external influences, it may be asked, What of the man himself? And that is a question hard to answer. He was a delicate, wayward spirit, often the victim of his own excesses, and obliged to live for the last thirty years of his life under the personal care of his friend Theodore Watts-Dunton at the Pines, Putney Hill, near London.

In his earlier life he was an ardent republican and skeptic, a declared rebel aginst most of the Victorian conventions, sexual and other. He expressed open disbelief in the immortality of the soul:

> From too much love of living,
>   From hope and fear set free,
> We thank with brief thanksgiving,
>   Whatever gods may be
> That no life lives for ever;
> That dead men rise up never;
> That even the weariest river
>   Winds somewhere safe to sea.

He adopted Shelley's pantheism without Shelley's aërial music, and made it a dogmatic creed, as in *Hertha*:

> Mother, not maker,
>   Born, and not made;
> Though her children forsake her,
>   Allured or afraid,
> Praying prayers to the God of their fashion, she
>   stirs not for all that have prayed.
>
> A creed is a rod,
>   And a crown is of night;
> But this thing is God,
>   To be man with thy might,
> To grow straight in the strength of thy spirit,
>   and live out thy life as the light.

In the *Songs before Sunrise,* from which the last lines are quoted, some have thought that we have the authentic Swinburne; but a recent critic (London "Times," July 1931) doubts whether he uttered anything that was indefeasibly his own. Of his command over meter and poetic expression, there is no question.

HUXLEY

THOMAS HENRY HUXLEY (1825-95) marks the dividing line between the pre-scientific and the evolutionary periods of the Victorian age. It fell to his lot to be the protagonist on behalf of the evolution theory, and he was well fitted for the task, having, in addition to the necessary scientific knowledge, a wide acquaintance with literature, a love of controversy, and a clear and trenchant style, with either tongue or pen. Darwin, who was not fond of either controversy or publicity, was obliged to publish the *Origin of Species* in 1859, because a young naturalist, A. R. Wallace, had hit upon the theory of natural selection upon which Darwin had been working for over fifteen years and had sent Darwin for publication a paper embodying the theory. Wallace's paper and a previous statement by Darwin of his own views were submitted together to the Linnæan Society in 1858, and attracted no general attention. But it happened that the advance sheets of the *Origin of Species* sent to the London "Times" for review were forwarded, by the reviewer to whom they were assigned, to Huxley, who was at that time lecturer on natural history at South Kensington and naturalist to the geological survey. Huxley had already some familiarity with the work through discussions with Darwin, and was able to present in the "Times" a long and able exposition of the new theory on the day the *Origin of Species* was published. A lively controversy at once arose, not only among the scientists but among the clergy, who were inclined to regard evolution as contradicting the first chapter of Genesis and therefore denying the authority of Holy Scripture. At the Oxford meeting of the British Association for the Advancement of Science in 1860 the Bishop of Oxford, Samuel Wilberforce, familiarly known on account of his persuasive oratory as "Soapy Sam," was put up to lead the attack upon Darwin and did so in a jesting personal spirit with particular reference to the popular version of evolution as tracing man's descent from a monkey. Darwin had purposely absented himself from the meeting, and Huxley accordingly replied on behalf of the scientists who espoused the new doctrine; he completely turned the tables upon his ecclesiastical

DARWIN

antagonist, and was recognized by the public, during the long controversy that followed, as the leading champion of evolution.

Darwin had as far as possible avoided the question of human descent in the *Origin of Species,* but when it was forced upon him, he met the issue squarely in *The Descent of Man* (1871). Meanwhile Huxley had published *Zoölogical Evidences as to Man's Place in Nature* (1863) and had made numerous addresses on the subject at scientific and popular gatherings. Huxley had also given many popular expositions on the effects of the evolution theory on ethics, and these "lay sermons" and other essays on similar subjects were collected in nine volumes not long before his death. He was keenly interested in the introduction of scientific teaching into elementary and high-school education, and assisted greatly in the organization of zoölogical instruction in colleges and universities on both sides of the Atlantic. He gave the inaugural address at the opening of Johns Hopkins University in 1876, and was elected president of the English Royal Society in 1883. At a meeting of the British Association for the Advancement of Science, held at Oxford in 1894, he had the satisfaction of hearing Lord Salisbury, then leader of the Conservative party and president of the association, state that the evolution theory, which Huxley had spent the best years of his life in establishing and defending, had won the universal assent of the scientific world. In recognition of his services to science, literature, and education, he was appointed, not long before his death, an honorary member of the privy council.

Darwin lived the retired life of a research student in his country house at Down in Kent, which in 1928 was given to the nation as a memorial to his fame; he died there in 1882 at the age of seventy-three, and was buried in Westminster Abbey. Both Darwin and Huxley were of singularly impressive appearance in old age, with dignified bearing, white hair, and keenly intelligent faces. They brought to the study of science the Victorian earnestness, faith in law, and something perhaps of the Victorian dogmatism.

MEREDITH

GEORGE MEREDITH (1828-1909) contributed to "The Germ" and lived for a while at Chelsea with Rossetti, but his main literary activities belong to a later date and he was influenced more by the scientific than by the Pre-Raphaelite movement. He frankly accepted the theory of evolution and incorporated it with ideas formed by his previous religious and philosophical training. The son of a Portsmouth tailor, educated at a Moravian school at Neuwied in the Rhine Valley, Meredith was greatly impressed by the religious teaching of the Moravian Brothers, and though in after-life he entirely gave up the evangelical dogma, he kept firm hold of the Christian ethics. His small inheritance was dissipated by his trustees, who articled him to a London solicitor, a man more given to literary interests than to the practice of the law. Thus, though young Meredith made no progress toward the legal profession, he was introduced by his employer into literary circles, where he met and married the daughter of Thomas Love Peacock, an eccentric novelist of the time, now better known as the friend of Shelley. She was a widow, thirty years of age, and he was only twenty-one. They were both gifted but excitable to the point of nervous tension, they had no regular income, and no settled home; the marriage was not a success, and after a few years she fled with a lover, leaving to Meredith the care of their son. After her death he married in 1864 a lady of French origin, Marie Vulliamy, and a few years later took a house at Box Hill, Surrey, where he lived happily to the day of his death.

When he was left alone with a young son to look after, Meredith's thoughts were directed to the subject of education, and this is the main theme of his first important novel, *The Ordeal of Richard Feverel* (1859). He dealt more freely than was at that time the custom with the sex question, and was accordingly condemned by the reviewers and neglected by the public. This was the more serious because Meredith had taken to novel-writing as a means of livelihood, renouncing for the time being what seemed to him his real vocation as a poet. He was driven to journalism, to a position in the publishing firm of

Feby 20th

Miss Nellie!

We violets are
modest flowers. but not the
Queenly Rose is surer of
welcome where she appears.
So, pray withold acknowledgements
of our transmission to you,
... shall be flattered
the more by knowing you
pleased of course.

Chapman and Hall, and even to reading aloud to an old lady for so much an hour. His consciousness of the inferiority of his social station in the county society which he frequented and depicted in his novels was the inspiration of *Evan Harrington* (1860-61), which may be commended to younger readers as free from the difficulties of style and thought which make much of his work hard going for the uninitiated. His service as a war correspondent in Italy in 1866 is associated with *Vittoria,* which passed (as he wrote to Swinburne) "to the limbo where the rest of my works repose."

The unhappy experiences of his first marriage formed the suggestion for a series of connected poems published under the title of *Modern Love* in 1862; but again Meredith had the experience, not only of losing money, but of being (as he put it) "kicked, cuffed, and spat upon for my pains." Meredith fiercely resented this lack of appreciation on the part of the British public, and he was correspondingly grateful when the success of *Diana of the Crossways* (1884-85) opened the way for the sale of his previous work, especially in the United States. "The run of my novels," he wrote later, "started from American appreciation." It was a moderate run, and in 1902 he described himself as "an unpopular novelist and an unaccepted poet."

By this time, however, he was highly esteemed by the critics, by the younger writers, and by aspiring intellectuals at the leading universities in Great Britain and the United States. Following up the theme of the emancipation of women he had successfully broached in *Diana,* he wrote three other novels in the last decade of the century, all warmly welcomed. In 1905 he was awarded the greatest literary distinction the British Government has to give, the Order of Merit, and on his eightieth birthday he received an address of congratulation from the leading writers of the English-speaking world. His fame, both as a novelist and as a poet, has diminished since his death, and in view of the difficulties his style, form, and matter present to the ordinary reader, the probability of a Meredithian revival is not great. His poetry is, perhaps, more likely to last than his prose.

Thomas Hardy

THOMAS HARDY (1840-1928) held his place in the affections of the novel-reading public and the esteem of the critics better than his great contemporary, whose vacant place in the Order of Merit and the leadership of English letters in the twentieth century he filled. Perhaps it was in part that Hardy was less arrogant in his attitude to the public than Meredith, and even went out of his way, sometimes, to please it, though he by no means always yielded to its prejudices. Oddly enough, it was Meredith who as "reader" for Chapman and Hall gave to Hardy at the very outset of his career as a novelist the advice that to be successful a novel should have an exciting plot. It was at the time when the mystery stories of Wilkie Collins were exceedingly popular, and Hardy took the advice to heart. We find in most of the Hardy novels two kinds of interest—an idyllic strain reproducing the tender charm of country life in Hardy's native Dorsetshire, and a more sensational melodramatic element. The second of these is stressed in Hardy's first novel, *Desperate Remedies* (1871), the first in his second novel, *Under the Greenwood Tree* (1872), and both are combined in *Far from the Madding Crowd,* which was published in the "Cornhill Magazine" in 1874 and laid the foundation for the novelist's successful career; he was able to retire to the neighborhood of Dorchester, where he was born and brought up, and to work there in comfortable seclusion for the rest of his days.

To the two elements in Hardy's novels suggested above may be added a third characteristic of those he wrote after his position as a writer of fiction was established—a pessimistic philosophy which gives a tragic ending to the masterpieces of this later period: *The Return of the Native* (1878), *The Mayor of Casterbridge* (1886), *The Woodlanders* (1887), *Tess of the D'Urbervilles* (1891), and *Jude the Obscure* (1895). Hardy denied the pessimism, contending that he portrayed life as he saw it, but it is undeniable that in these later novels the author did sometimes load the dice against the unfortunate victims who figure as hero and heroine.

This dark view of human life and destiny was probably ab-

He resolves to say no more.

O my ~~heart~~ soul, keep the rest unknown!
It is too like a sound of moan
    When the charnel-eyed
    Pale Horse has nighed:
Yea, none shall gather what I hide!

———

Why load men's minds with more to bear
That bear already ails to spare?
    From now alway
    Till my last day
What I discern I will not say.

———

Let Time roll backward if it will;
(Magians who drive the midnight quill
    With brain aglow
    Can see it so,)
What I have learnt no man shall know.

———

And if my vision range beyond
The blinkered sight of souls in bond,
    — By truth made free —
    I'll let all be,
And show to no man what I see.

sorbed from the soil rather than due to the influence of scientific teaching or the philosophy of Schopenhauer. Hardy's family had been living in and about Dorsetshire for many generations, and the country folk who inhabited the little village of High Bockhampton, where he was born, and worshiped at Stinstead Church, where his heart is buried, were no doubt like the peasants of his novels; they may have sung (or played) in the church choir, but there was a good deal of primitive paganism left in their view of life; they were too near the inexorable cruelty of nature and the ill luck that produces bad harvests and other calamities to have any deep faith in a beneficent order of Providence. There is apparently no reason for pessimism to be found in Hardy's personal experiences. His wants were few and he was not socially ambitious. He married the girl of his youthful choice, and it was through her encouragement that he gave up architecture (at which he had been reasonably successful) and followed the pursuit of literature. His merits as a writer of popular fiction were speedily recognized, and his reputation grew continuously throughout a long life. When he discontinued novel-writing because of the hostile criticism of *Jude the Obscure,* he was able, a year or two later, to begin the publication of a succession of volumes of poetry which reached their climax in the epic-drama of *The Dynasts* (1904-1908).

The atmosphere of Hardy's poems is even darker than that of his novels; in the novels we get a richness of color and humor, sometimes in the descriptions of natural scenery, sometimes in the clash of temperaments, sometimes in the quaint sayings and odd doings of people who have the savor of life in them. In the poems is set forth in bare, stark phrases a rather grim philosophy. This is especially noticeable in *The Dynasts,* where the greatest leaders in the Napoleonic struggle are but marionettes under the control of a heedless God, the Immanent Will working "like a knitter drowsed, Whose fingers play in skilled unmindfulness." The Will winds up Napoleon and other "flesh-hinged manikins" "to click-clack off Its preadjusted laws," but all are merely puppets, pulled by invisible strings.

BUTLER   15, CLIFFORD'S INN

The life of SAMUEL BUTLER (1835-1902) coincided almost exactly with the Victorian age, and most of its ideas and achievements are exhibited in his works—in a distorting mirror. He was the original inventor of the method attributed to Bernard Shaw (who had much in common with him) of seeing things from a detached point of view by standing them on their heads. He was a student of Scripture (from a skeptical point of view), a musical critic (who preferred Handel to Beethoven), a worshiper of Mrs. Grundy (in a reversed position), an admirer of Homer (he thought Nausicaa wrote the *Odyssey*), a believer in evolution (who quarreled with Darwin), an expander of the empire (who ridiculed the colonies), a praiser of money (who lived on very little), and a lover of mechanism (who believed man was becoming the slave of machinery). In short, he was a Victorian Jack Horner who put his thumb into every pie, to call attention not to his virtue but to his perversity. He was a professional "bad boy" and produced the effect usually produced: those who suffered from his pranks were very much annoyed, and those who did not were considerably amused. The suffering has passed, and the amusement, which was very great when Victorianism was out of fashion, is somewhat diminished now that it seems to be coming in again. But a taste for Butler's peculiar humor is not given to everyone.

Of his external life there is little to tell. Born into an ecclesiastical family, he refused to become a clergyman, because he did not believe in the efficacy of infant baptism: the unbaptized boys in the parish club seemed to him no more troublesome than the baptized ones. Accordingly, on attaining manhood he went out to New Zealand, and in the course of five years made enough to save a competency, which (with the aid of one or two legacies) was enough to maintain him in modest comfort for the rest of his life. Returning to England in 1864, he settled down to bachelor life in rooms at 15 Clifford's Inn, London, and spent much of his time in the British Museum Library, where are now preserved his famous Notebooks—not the garnerings of other men's wit but his own satirical reflections on men and things, sometimes made use of in his books but often left to be saved from oblivion by a conscientious and discerning editor.

His first novel, *Erewhon* (1872), is a satire on Victorian institutions. His last novel, *The Way of All Flesh,* published after his death, is a satire on the family as an institution, illustrated mainly from the deficiencies of his father, his mother, his sisters, and to some extent himself. He wrote in the Notebooks, under the heading "The Family": "I believe that more unhappiness comes from this source than from any other—I mean from the attempt to prolong family connection unduly and to make people hang together who would never naturally do so." He said he wrote his books (out of which he made little money) in order to have some amusing reading in his old age; and he certainly afforded a good deal of amusement and intellectual stimulus to the following generation. Much of what passes for revolutionary novelty in doctrine in the twentieth century finds its source in the Victorian paradoxes of Samuel Butler. Bernard Shaw was greatly indebted to Butler, not only for his epigrammatic style, but for much of his thought, and made full acknowledgment of his obligations to Butler's "extraordinarily fresh, free, and future-piercing suggestions" as to "the necessity and morality of a conscientious Laodiceanism in religion and of an earnest and constant sense of the importance of money."

GILBERT

SULLIVAN

H. A. JONES

A. W. PINERO

The early Victorians, for the most part, stayed away from the theater, and it took several decades to bring the respectable middle class back to it. A beginning was made with T. W. Robertson's *Caste* in 1867, but to the modern playgoer this "cup-and-saucer" comedy now appears so hopelessly old-fashioned that it has little more than historical interest. A firmer hold on the stage was taken by the comic operas of Gilbert and Sullivan, beginning with *H.M.S. Pinafore* (1878) and ending with *The Gondoliers* (1889). The partnership was severed through a financial disagreement, and though it was afterward patched up again, it did not work with the old enthusiasm and "go." Gilbert's clever rimes and satirical hits at Victorian foibles and some more serious follies, combined with Sullivan's melodious airs and pretty dances to convince even the puritanically inclined that the stage could offer a delightful form of entertainment which would not offend the most delicate sensibilities. Through half a century of revivals they have kept their hold on the popular taste, both in England and America.

Two other Victorian dramatists, HENRY ARTHUR JONES (1851-1929) and ARTHUR PINERO (1855-   ), contributed to the reconciliation of the later Victorian public and the theater. When Jones came to New York early in the present century, a tactless millionaire book-collector took three little volumes from his shelves and said, "That's all the harvest of your British drama for the last two hundred years." The three plays were by Goldsmith and Sheridan. Few would now accept the American bibliophile's dictum, but he may have been right in the unkind suggestion that the polite comedies and successful melodramas of his guest were not literary masterpieces. Whenever Jones tried to write for posterity, the contemporary British public stayed away from the theater or even hissed his ambitious efforts off the stage. Something like the same fate befell the later and more expert playwright Pinero. Their successes had their day of popular esteem, but have now "ceased to be," so far as the stage is concerned. They paved the way, however, for Shaw and Barrie.

WALTER PATER   OSCAR WILDE

WALTER HORATIO PATER (1839-94) was an Oxford human-
ist who from an early association with the Pre-Raphaelites developed later in life into the leader of the esthetic movement
which attracted attention in the last two decades of the nineteenth century. His subtle hedonism was set forth in *Studies in
the History of the Renaissance* and in *Marius the Epicurean,*
which were much admired for their scholarship and critical insight, and for the elegance of their style. The more external
features of the movement were ridiculed by Gilbert and Sullivan in *Patience* and were developed into a cult among the Oxford undergraduates by OSCAR WILDE (1856-1900), who in 1882
gave lectures on esthetic philosophy in the United States. In the
nineties Wilde sprang into sudden fame as the author of the
brilliant but highly artificial comedies, *Lady Windermere's
Fan, A Woman of No Importance,* and *The Importance of Being Earnest.* In 1895 he was subjected to a criminal prosecution
for immoral conduct and sentenced to two years' imprisonment,
from which he emerged broken in health and spirits.

Neither the estheticism of the eighties nor the cynicism of the nineties ever caught the general taste, which responded to the older fashion of romanticism as presented to them in the closing years of the century, under modern guises, by Stevenson, Conrad, Barrie, and Kipling.

ROBERT LOUIS STEVENSON (1850-94) was from his childhood an invalid, and his invalidism has been the principal bone of contention among his recent critics. Born at Edinburgh, the son of a leading Scottish engineer and meteorologist, he rejected the family profession of building harbors and lighthouses, and took very lightly the training for the law imposed upon him by an anxious parent. Though to the strict religious circle in which he was brought up, his youth must have seemed given over to bohemianism, he was from his teens a diligent student of the writer's craft. At the expense of an indulgent aunt, he printed when only sixteen *The Pentland Rising of 1666,* written as a romance but reduced to the more modest proportions of a historical essay. Contributions to the "Edinburgh University Magazine," a student enterprise which "ran four months in undisturbed obscurity and died without a gasp," helped to give an outlet to his literary ambitions during his student days, and a canoe trip in France and Belgium provided material for a small travel book, *An Inland Voyage* (1878), followed by another, *Travels with a Donkey in the Cévennes* (1879) ; but at the age of thirty he had done very little toward getting any real footing in the literary world.

In 1876, when in the Forest of Fontainebleau for the sake of his health, Stevenson met in the artist colony at Barbizon an American lady, Mrs. Fanny Osbourne, with whom he promptly fell in love. She was a married woman with two children, and even if there had been no such incumbrances, the lovers had no financial resources. But they felt in course of time that the position was intolerable and, in 1878, Mrs. Osbourne returned to California to obtain a divorce from her husband. Thither, in 1879, Stevenson followed her, and as he knew that his parents would not approve of the expedition, he went on his own re-

R. L. STEVENSON

sources, in the cheapest possible way. In his delicate health, the privations he suffered on the journey were all but fatal; Mrs. Osbourne, however, nursed him back to life, and having gained her divorce, married him, his father having now assured him of a regular income of $1250 a year. Their honeymoon in the mountains north of San Francisco gave occasion for another book, *The Silverado Squatters* (1883). Meanwhile, two volumes of essays had appeared, *Virginibus Puerisque* and *Familiar Studies of Men and Books*.

Success first came to Stevenson in 1883 with the publication in book form of *Treasure Island,* a romantic story of adventure which had previously appeared as a serial in a boys' magazine. Before this, Stevenson had brought his wife home to Edinburgh, and lived there when his health made the climate endurable; but most of his time during these years he passed at a sanatorium in the Alps or on the southern English coast at Bournemouth. He established his position in the public favor by a story of double personality which came to him in a dream—*The Strange Case of Dr. Jekyll and Mr. Hyde* (1886). It was dramatized and won enormous success, especially in the United States. Stevenson paid his last visit to Edinburgh on account of his father's serious illness in 1887, and when this ended fatally, he was so ill and exhausted that he set out for Saranac in the Adirondacks. But his fame had preceded him, and at New York he found himself besieged by reporters and publishers' agents. It was a new and exhilarating experience, and he enjoyed the excitement—and the increased income. He was still at Saranac when his wife telegraphed him from San Francisco that the yacht *Casco* was for sale, and the telegraph boy who brought the message took back an answer telling her to buy it. Three years' cruising on the Pacific followed, and gave opportunity for a good deal of journalism and two novels done in collaboration with his stepson Lloyd Osbourne, *The Wrecker* and *The Ebb Tide*. In 1891 he bought an estate of 350 acres near Apia in Samoa, called it Vailima, "the five waters," and built a house on it, the whole costing him about $20,000; he kept a consider-

R. L. STEVENSON

able retinue of native servants, clad in a special uniform composed mainly of a white coat, straw hat, and a Samoan lavalava (a kind of kilt) in Stuart tartan. The combination of Samoan chief and Highland chieftain amused Stevenson and kept him in good health and spirits; he continued *Kidnapped* (1886), which in Europe he had failed to complete on account of physical weakness, and at the time of his sudden death of effusion of blood on the brain he was working on two novels, *St. Ives,* a romance of the Napoleonic wars, and *Weir of Hermiston,* a study of Scottish life which promised to be better than anything he had yet done. The exaggerated reputation he enjoyed during the latter years of the nineteenth century was not maintained in the twentieth, and his real merits have perhaps been unduly depreciated. He had great personal charm and by dint of long study and practice had won command of a graceful but rather mannered style.

GEORGE GISSING (1859-1903) was a contemporary of Stevenson, with perhaps greater literary ability but with less personal charm and less power to please the public. The apostle of conscientious realism, he has been held in high esteem by twentieth-century realistic novelists and critics, and his books continue to have the regular but limited sale they had during his lifetime. His personal history is a painful story of privation and humiliation. Coming of North of England middle-class stock, as a boy of sixteen he went to the recently founded Owens College (now the University of Manchester). He was a brilliant scholar but a shy and lonely youth. Having picked up acquaintance with a girl of the streets, to meet her demands he stole from his fellow-students. He was detected, convicted, and imprisoned. It was the year of the Centennial Exhibition at Philadelphia, and, all avenues in England being closed to him, he tried his fortunes in the United States. He earned a precarious living by writing short stories for the newspapers in Chicago and Troy, New York, but took the first opportunity of returning to England. In London he kept his soul alive in the British Museum Library and by starving in squalid lodgings obtained a first-hand

GISSING

CONRAD

BARRIE

KIPLING

knowledge of the degraded lives of the London poor. A legacy of five hundred dollars enabled him to print his first novel, *Workers in the Dawn* (1880), which did not sell but brought him to the notice of people in the literary world who were able to befriend him. He was a difficult man to help: he hated teaching and despised journalism. All he really wished to do was to sit in a garden and read books. He was persuaded, however, to undertake some private teaching and he began to make something of a reputation by his stories of working-class life in London. *Demos* (1886) went into a second edition. His behavior and his account of the matter are characteristic: "There came into my hands a sum of money (such a poor little sum) for a book I had written. It was early autumn. I chanced to hear some one speak of Naples—and only death would have held me back."

If Gissing had been able to remain single, he would have been beyond the reach of want. The girl who had ruined his career in Manchester, and whom, having married her, he continued to support, freed him from this burden by drinking herself to death; but in his desperate loneliness in London he married again. The second Mrs. Gissing, who was at least respectable, has been described by H. G. Wells as "a poor, tormented, miserable, angry, servant girl." After the birth of two children there came the inevitable separation.

Wearying of the study of the London poor, for whom he had little sympathy or admiration, Gissing turned to the class immediately above them—the people of the lowest middle class with sensibilities and aspirations above the material conditions of their station. He imagined personalities "wholly unfitted for the rough and tumble of the world's labor-market," and he realized them sympathetically, for it was the class to which he himself belonged. His best novel of this type is *New Grub Street* (1891), which deals with the life of the struggling and unsuccessful author, and is largely autobiographical.

It is pleasant to record that the last years of Gissing's life were spent in more congenial surroundings. A French lady who translated some of his later novels was able to give him the sympathetic companionship and simple but comfortable quarters in the South of France that enabled him to work with some enjoyment, notwithstanding the breakdown of his health. He made an excellent critical study of *Dickens* (1898), and his personal meditations, cast in a semi-autobiographic form and entitled *The Private Papers of Henry Ryecroft* (1903), have had a considerable sale. There is something attractive and sympathetic in Gissing's character, despite or because of its strain of weakness. His chief fault, as he himself put it, was the "inability to earn money; but indeed, that inability does not call for unmingled disdain."

JOSEPH CONRAD (1856-1924) began his literary career just about the time when that of Stevenson came to an end, and upheld the romantic tradition with some modifications and additions of his own. When Stevenson was manufacturing the adventures of *Treasure Island* out of previous stories of adventure, in the early eighties, Conrad was still having adventures in the British merchant marine service, in which he took his certificate as master mariner and became a British subject in 1884.

Born in the Ukraine of a Polish family which was aristocratic but liberal, and had suffered for its convictions, Feodor Jozef Konrad Korzeniowski was educated at Warsaw and was just ready to enter the university there when he decided to devote himself to the life of seafaring adventure. Still earlier he had put his finger on the then uncharted part of a map of Central Africa and said, "I want to go there." He had traveled as a sailor on many seas before that dream of his youth was fulfilled, to the destruction of his health and the ending of his seafaring career. It was then that he bethought himself of a manuscript written to beguile the tedium of a long voyage. He completed it and sent it to the publisher, a story of English and Dutch adventurers among Arabs and Malays, entitled *Almayer's Folly*. Somewhat to his astonishment it was immediately accepted and published, and he followed it the next year with *An Outcast of the Islands* (1896). Both these were tales of the Malay Peninsula which had come within Conrad's experience or invention during his voyages there, and the local types and scenery were etched in with extraordinary impressiveness. They revealed also a brilliant and sonorous style, perhaps a little exotic in its emphasis, but showing a remarkable command of English idiom. The analysis of character was keen, and there was a Slavic background of pessimism, of yielding to destiny; the whole combination was strangely effective and was welcomed by the critics as new in romantic fiction. With the public, Conrad made his way more slowly; he had married an Englishwoman and settled down in the South of England. His style lost something of its foreign resonance and gained in simplicity and power. By so distinguished an authority as Henry James he was recognized as a master of the technique of the novel, and the public saw in him an expert in the romance of life at sea. *The Nigger of the Narcissus* (1898), *Lord Jim* (1900), and *Nostromo* (1903) enlarged and established his reputation, but it was not until the publication of *Victory,* in 1915, that he achieved a great popular success, especially in the United States. His subsequent novels had a large sale, but only one, *The Rescue* (1920), which he had begun twenty years before, seemed to reach the level of power and artistic finish which he had so easily attained at the beginning of his career. Conrad's style will always be admired by a few discerning critics, but it seems doubtful whether the popularity of his romances with the general reader will continue as long as that of the work of Scott or even of R. L. Stevenson.

Although Conrad's son fought in the World War as a British officer, his own sympathies were naturally Polish, and he was on a visit to his native country when the war broke out. The loyalties of his novels are not national loyalties, though they are sometimes racial. More often, however, he appeals to the sense of solidarity which brave men realize everywhere as a bond of fellowship—the fidelity of one comrade to another, whatever may be his color or creed, his place of birth or social station. It is man's duty of faithfulness to mankind that he stresses, no local or patriotic virtue.

RUDYARD KIPLING (1865-   ) was the first to bring home to the popular imagination the idea of the empire. In Elizabethan days Raleigh, Spenser, and Shakspere had saluted the queen with the imperial title, and in the eighteenth century the American colonists who took the losing side in the Revolutionary War and found refuge in Canada were proud to call themselves United Empire Loyalists. In the nineteenth century Benjamin Disraeli persuaded Queen Victoria to assume the title of Empress of India in the same year (1876) that she persuaded him to accept the title of Earl of Beaconsfield. Sir John Seeley, professor of modern history at Cambridge University 1869-95, exhorted successive generations of undergraduates to "think imperially," and in *The Expansion of England* preached the same doctrine to the public at large. In the political arena Joseph Chamberlain and Cecil Rhodes strove, each in his own way, to strengthen the bonds of empire, but none of these made the imperial idea familiar to the consciousness of the common people as Rudyard Kipling did, not only in Great Britain but in the outlying parts of the British Empire and in the United States. The Americans, it is true, paid little heed to the exhortation he addressed to them to "take up the white man's burden," but they read his stories and his ballads with keen enjoyment and had a full share in establishing and maintaining his popularity, which lasted, indeed, longer in the United States than in England.

Kipling was born in Bombay, the son of a gifted and intelligent Anglo-Indian official. He was sent to England to school and returned to India at the age of eighteen to work as a reporter on the "Civil and Military Gazette" at Lahore, where his father was head of the museum. By special permission of the Duke of Connaught, then commander of the Northwestern Division of the Indian Army, Kipling was enabled to visit the Afghan frontier, and "write up Tommy Atkins." This was the origin of *Departmental Ditties* (1886) and *Soldiers Three* (1888); the first was printed on brown paper and tied up with red tape to imitate a government publication, and the second was the first issue in *Plain Tales from the Hills,* published in seven small paper-bound volumes as part of the Indian Railway Library, intended to amuse passengers on the trains. Some of Kipling's best stories were thus in print before he was twenty-three, when he left the Lahore "Gazette" for the Allahabad "Pioneer."

The latter paper in 1889 sent him as its correspondent to England by way of San Francisco and New York. His offers of stories already printed or still in manuscript received no encouragement from New York publishers, who thought the American public cared nothing about India. The London publishers and the British public seemed equally indifferent, until a "World" interview and a "Times" review drew attention to the new author; and before the end of 1890, Kipling had one of his finest stories, "The Incarnation of Krishna Mulvaney," and "A Ballad of East and West" (perhaps the best verses he ever wrote) published in one issue of "Macmillan's Magazine." From this time to the end of the decade Kipling never looked behind him as a popular writer, producing in rapid succession *Barrack Room Ballads, Many Inventions,* the two *Jungle Books, The Seven Seas, Stalky and Co., Kim* and *Just So Stories* (1901). It was an astonishing achievement for a man between the ages of twenty-five and thirty-five, and those who reproach Kipling for his failure to maintain this extraordinary burst of energy in the twentieth century should remember the precocity of his early performance. Many a brilliant writer had produced much less at seventy than Kipling had published at thirty-five.

It must be admitted that in the second half of his life Kipling produced nothing to surpass what he had done in the first half; and his total product in the second half seemed much inferior to that of the first. This was, of course, due in part to the fact that his ideas had become familiar and his artistic methods were no longer novelites. The hard brilliance of his style, so taking at first, became much less effective after frequent repetition, and the imperialistic doctrine he preached has gone out of fashion. The India of to-day is no longer the India of Kipling: it does not look to British officials for leadership and instruction. It asks nothing better than the opportunity to go its own way.

The work of JAMES M. BARRIE (1860-   ) was a domestic
product, very popular in the English-speaking world but hardly
suitable for exportation to the European Continent. Though
Barrie was five years older than Kipling, the literary careers
of the two men began at about the same time, the road from
Kirriemuir to London being apparently longer than that from
Bombay. Both began with newspaper work, and both left it,
as soon as they could, for fiction. At first Barrie was associated
with the "kailyard" (cabbage patch) school of Scottish novelists,
but as most of the other members of it have been lost to memory,
he is better considered on his own merits. His original impulse
in fiction seems to have been toward realism, and the title of his
first collection of sketches of Scottish small town life, *Auld
Licht Idylls,* was probably meant to be ironical; but the public
insisted on his being idyllic and sentimental and the author had
to submit. With the help of his mother's memories of the more
romantic phases of his native town (idealized into "Thrums")
he produced a long array of romantic sketches and novels up
to *Sentimental Tommy* (1896), in which the sugary flavor was
combined with a dash of cynicism. The cynical dosage was increased in *Tommy and Grizel* (1900), and both author and public apparently had enough of that vein, for it was not continued.

Before the end of the century Barrie had turned his attention to the stage. *The Professor's Love-Story* (1894) and *The
Little Minister* (1897), the latter dramatized from a successful novel of the same title, were saccharine enough to be im-
mensely popular with the Victorian public on both sides of the
Atlantic, but it was not until *The Admirable Crichton* (1902)
that Barrie hit on his own special blend of sugar and vinegar,
a curious combination of sentiment with irony that sometimes
leaves a rather bitter taste in the mouth. The invariable in-
gredient of humor pleased the public mightily and the touch of
cynicism kept the critics guessing. Did Barrie really mean that
English butlers were superior in character and intelligence to
the peers who employed them, and that the English aristocracy
was without wit or courage or sportsmanship or a sense of

shame? Was *What Every Woman Knows* the fact that her husband was a fool but she must not let him find it out? Does *The Twelve-Pound Look* suggest that every married woman would leave her husband if she had the courage (and the money) to buy a typewriter, or is it only Barrie's fun? At any rate, the British and American public liked it, and *The Admirable Crichton,* thirty years after its first production, still held the stage.

Barrie's best work belongs to the twentieth century, and indeed Bernard Shaw gave him credit for "the final relegation of the nineteenth century London theatre to the dust bin." But he is essentially Victorian in spirit, and it is still a question whether his plays will pass in their turn into the limbo in which his sentimental novels and smaller sketches repose. He is not all "whimsy," though no doubt that is the main source of his popularity. He has an admirable sense of the theater, and an astonishing gift for creating an atmosphere in which the impossible appears almost probable. Who but Barrie would dare to show us a middle-class household in which a railway porter commits burglary in pursuit of knowledge and is forthwith bribed by the two brothers who capture him to marry the plain-looking daughter of the family at the end of his college course? The foundations of several of his plays are equally fantastic, but he succeeds in giving them enough verisimilitude to carry the momentary conviction that is all that is necessary for comedy. He showed no less deftness of touch in turning his plays (which he long refused to publish) into dramatic dialogues which many enjoyed by the fireside with the aid of introductions and elaborate stage directions which Barrie supplied with marvelous ingenuity. He is, above all, an engaging personality and has endeared himself to the public by the modesty with which he has accepted success and the shyness with which he has avoided publicity. Essentially he is a lonely man, but no man has more personal friends among the vast public which is scattered all over the British Empire and the United States.

CHAPTER X

THE TWENTIETH CENTURY

The main occupation of the younger writers during some of the earlier years of the twentieth century seemed to be violent criticism of the literary methods, standards, and achievements of their immediate predecessors, but when we look back on the literature actually produced during the first quarter of the present century, we are struck by the fact that most of it was produced by writers who were not only born in the Victorian era, but grew up and began their literary career in it. The leading literary figure of the twentieth century, so far as it has gone, is undoubtedly Bernard Shaw, and though he was the leader of the rebellion against many Victorian institutions, it must always be remembered that he was part of the system against which he revolted. No man can rebel against all the conventions of his own epoch, and Shaw accepted (as all revolutionists must) much more than he rejected. The literary forms he adopts, whether as pamphleteer, dramatist, or novelist, are those established by years and even centuries of usage; the standards of literary excellence and logical reasoning to which he appeals are familiar standards and his literary achievements must stand or fall by the same kind of judgment that we apply to Swift and Sheridan in the eighteenth century, to Milton and Dryden in the seventeenth, and to Shakspere and his Elizabethan contemporaries. Literary fashions change and they affect the transitory features of a work of literature, but not its permanent significance.

As literature performs a social function, part of its office is to criticize human institutions, and to attempt by argument, persuasion or ridicule to promote or retard changes of which the writer approves or disapproves; even when a writer neither condemns nor defends, he often records social changes of which we become conscious in these days more through the

BERNARD SHAW

written than through the spoken word. This is especially true of comedy and the novel, which depend for their main interest upon the representation and criticism of contemporary life. Changes in the prevailing attitude toward great human interests such as property and sex; new features in civilized life, such as industrial organization and mechanical inventions taking the place of human labor; increased rapidity of means of transportation and communication; the transfer of political power from one class to another; the extension of educational and other opportunities to the whole population; the weakening of religious and other conventions through the teaching of science —all these things come home to most of us through reading and hearing more than from personal observation.

Most of these changes, beginning in the nineteenth century and continuing with increasing velocity in the twentieth, found their apostle and prophet, or at least a keenly sympathetic observer, in GEORGE BERNARD SHAW (1856-   ). He is one of that distinguished band of English writers who were born in Ireland. "I am a typical Irishman," he said: "my family come from Yorkshire." He belonged to that Protestant minority which fought so persistently to maintain its ascendency in politics, religion, education, and social life, and was driven from its last stronghold only by the establishment of the Irish Free State after the World War. He came from a ruling class, but from a depressed and struggling section of it—a position by which a strong nature is stimulated and a weak one is submerged. He had relatives in high official positions and connections in the Anglo-Irish aristocracy; but his own family was poverty-stricken and humiliated. His father was (to use Shaw's own words) "an ineffective, unsuccessful man, in theory a vehement teetotaler, but in practice often a furtive drinker." He drank not only furtively but to excess, and the household eventually broke up. The mother, who had musical gifts, went to London to make an independent living as a teacher of singing, and thither before he was twenty-one Bernard Shaw followed her.

To most people it would have seemed that Bernard Shaw on

his arrival in London was singularly ill equipped to make his way in the English metropolis. In his own opinion, his school-days were "the most completely wasted and mischievous" part of his life, and had taught him nothing. At home he had picked up a desultory knowledge of modern music, which afterward proved of advantage, and a total disregard of the dreary evangel-icalism professed by his father—which might also be put to the credit side of the account. He had spent five years as a clerk in a Dublin real-estate agency; and that was all he had to offer in the London labor market. In nine years he earned by his pen thirty dollars, of which twenty-five were paid for writing the advertisement of a patent medicine. Not that he was idle: he was studying Henry George's *Progress and Poverty* and Karl Marx's *Capital*. He was a Socialist agitator, discoursing at street cor-ners and on the free-for-all platforms in Hyde Park; he was making up the deficiencies in his education; and during the pe-riod 1880-83 he wrote five novels, four of which were published serially in a Socialist periodical after nearly ruining the author in paying postage on them in manuscript to various publishers. He did not seem to fit in anywhere: he had "no respect for popu-lar morality, no belief in popular religion"; he was a pacifist, a vegetarian, a teetotaler, and a Socialist, "detesting our anarch-ical scramble for money and believing in equality as the only possible permanent basis of social organization, discipline, sub-ordination, good manners, and selection of fit persons for high functions."

It was by journalism that Shaw established his position and obtained a hearing. He wrote pamphlets for the organization of the young Socialist intellectuals known as the Fabian Society, founded in 1884, and thus became sufficiently known as an au-thority on economic subjects to get articles published in the re-views. As book-reviewer for the "Pall Mall Gazette," art critic for the London "World," musical critic first for the "Star," then for the "World," dramatic critic for the "Saturday Review," the author of books on Ibsen and on Wagner, he made himself known in the literary world as a brilliant satirist and paradoxical epigrammatist. But he was over forty before he had won an assured position or a reliable income. His marriage at forty-two, to Miss Payne-Townshend, who, if not "an Irish millionairess," was at any rate "very comfortably circumstanced," must have helped to secure an independence of financial considerations which, as a matter of principle, he had always assumed.

Shaw's first attempt at writing a play was made in 1885, in collaboration with William Archer, who was at that time, as a dramatic critic and translator of Ibsen, much better known than Shaw himself. Archer provided the scenario—borrowed from a French play—and Shaw was to do the dialogue. At the end of the first act, Shaw had used up all the scenario, and Archer was thoroughly dissatisfied with the dialogue; but Shaw insisted on reading more dialogue to Archer, who thereupon went to sleep. Shaw was discouraged, put the manuscript away, and forgot about it. But in 1891, when the Independent Theatre was started in London, there was a call for new plays, and Shaw remembered his discarded effort. He completed it and put it on the stage as *Widowers' Houses;* it is an attack upon slum-landlordism and the profits made out of it by "nice" people. Shaw's Socialist friends applauded, the opponents of Socialism hooted; and as the latter were in a majority, the play was booed off the stage.

Undeterred by failure—indeed, now "quite sure of himself as a writer for the stage"—Shaw immediately wrote another social satire in the form of a play, *The Philanderer,* which could not make its way to performance, and then a third, *Mrs. Warren's Profession,* which used the white-slave traffic as a mode of attack on modern capitalistic organization and was accordingly banned by the censor. These three made up the volume of *Unpleasant Plays* with which Shaw appealed from the theater to the reading public in 1898.

In the meantime Shaw had realized that to a theater audience he must administer propaganda in smaller doses and had written *Arms and the Man,* which is mildly pacifist and antiromantic in temper; besides, it was the Bulgarian, not the British Army that was ridiculed, and the British public saw no objection to that. The play ran for three months in 1894 at the Avenue Theatre in London, and appeared to make a distinct success; only those behind the scenes knew that the loss of the run to the management was $25,000, and even Shaw was at the time unaware that the "angel" who provided the money was Miss Horniman, who, having inherited a fortune from the sale of a popular tea, chose to spend it on the modern English drama rather than on a college or a hospital.

Richard Mansfield, then the most gifted actor on the American stage, made a hit with *Arms and the Man* in the United States in 1894, but Shaw's next play, *Candida* (one of his best), again went begging for a producer. Cyril Maude, then manager of the London Haymarket Theatre, heard that Richard Mansfield, for whom it was written, did not like it, and asked Shaw if he might read it. Shaw, with his usual independence, said it would not suit the Haymarket, but he undertook to write one that would. The result was *You Never Can Tell,* which was accordingly put into rehearsal in 1897; it is a clever compound of smart talk, smart dresses and dances, a wife who can cow her husband but has no control of her children, a comic waiter, who has an equally comic barrister for a son, a dental chair, and some novelites in the way of thought—not many, but apparently too many for the capable company who had it in hand; they rebelled, and the play was withdrawn from the stage before it reached the public. It joined the three previous efforts Shaw had made at being "pleasant" and the four comedies were published the following year as the second volume of *Plays Pleasant and Unpleasant.*

At the time when Shaw was still known mainly as a musical critic and socialist pamphleteer, he had begun an ardent courtship (entirely on paper) of the leading romantic actress of the day, Ellen Terry, whose talents he wished to enlist in the service of the modern drama, and whose character and personal charm he greatly admired. She was the inspiration of *The Man of Destiny,* written in 1895, and the model for the heroine of

Candida; Captain Brassbound's Conversion was written specially for her. But Ellen Terry, despite all her efforts, was unable to persuade Sir Henry Irving, who controlled the Lyceum
Theatre, to put any of Shaw's plays on the stage. Shaw's first
real box-office success was *The Devil's Disciple* as produced
in America by Richard Mansfield in October, 1897, first at Al-
bany and then at the Fifth Avenue Theatre, New York City. At
the end of that year Shaw reported to Ellen Terry that he had
received over $4,000 in author's fees and had become "a man of
wealth and consideration"; two years later the amount had gone
over $10,000, and Shaw had been enabled to free himself from
the grind of weekly journalism. The London Stage Society
(perhaps encouraged by Shaw's American success) gave single
performances during 1899-1900 of *You Never Can Tell, Candida,* and *Captain Brassbound's Conversion.* These performances brought no money to Shaw's pocket, but they helped to
convince the British public—or, at any rate, the intellectuals—
of Shaw's abilities as a dramatist. Still, he had, at the turn of
the century, no hold on the London stage. In 1901, *The Devil's
Disciple, Cæsar and Cleopatra,* and *Captain Brassbound's Conversion* came to general knowledge of the reading public on both
sides of the Atlantic in print as *Three Plays for Puritans.*

Shaw's friendship for Ellen Terry was affected by important
changes in his life and hers—his marriage in 1898; their first
meeting face to face at the Stage Society's production of *Captain
Brassbound's Conversion* in 1900; Sir Henry Irving's death in
1905, which Shaw made the occasion for an untimely attack
upon Irving's character and achievements; the production of
Captain Brassbound's Conversion at the Court Theatre in 1906,
with Ellen Terry in the principal part, and her marriage to one
of the actors in that production soon after. But none of these
things lessened the affection they felt for each other; and at her
death, in 1928, Shaw's name was the first (among those of the living) on the list the actress made of the friends of her lifetime.

It was on all accounts to be regretted that the publication of
the Shaw-Terry letters in 1931 should have been the occasion for

controversy between the dramatist and Ellen Terry's son, Gordon Craig. The correspondence is of high interest, not only as an interchange of ideas and opinions, affectionate flattery and no less affectionate criticism between two people of most unusual wit and charm; it is a valuable contribution to the history of the modern English drama.

Decisive success as a dramatist came to Shaw in New York during the season of 1903-1904 when *Arms and the Man, Candida, The Man of Destiny,* and *You Never Can Tell* were all put on the stage to the delight of the public; there was a similar revival at the Court Theatre in London, where seven hundred performances of Shaw plays were given in three seasons, beginning in 1904. German translations of his plays were acted about the same time at Vienna and Berlin, and the rest of the Continent (except France) quickly followed suit, so that in a very short time Shaw sprang from being almost unknown, to the leadership of the world stage.

In *Man and Superman,* which was the success of the dramatic season of 1904-1905, both in London and New York, Shaw concentrated the propaganda in the third act; nothing was easier for the producer than to drop this act out. Shaw had intended, he said later, to make the play a dramatic parable of Creative Evolution, the religion of which mankind stood in need, but "being then at the height of my inventive and comedic talent, I decorated it too brilliantly and lavishly." The audiences at its first production laughed at the illustrations and did not take the doctrine seriously; in fact, much of the doctrine never reached them. It is significant that twenty years later, when the play was performed as a whole, beginning at five in the afternoon and going on till eleven, the Gospel of the Life Force was received with respectful attention.

Having at last succeeded in gaining the attention of the public, Shaw proceeded to make ample use of the opportunity to propound his ideas. He delivered dramatic dissertations on Irish politics (*John Bull's Other Island*), on poverty (*Major Barbara*), on medical ethics (*The Doctor's Dilemma*), on marriage (*Getting Married*), on English politics (*Press Cuttings*), on parents and children (*Misalliance*) ; and all of these found their way to the stage without much difficulty or delay, though none of them made any great success on it. Shaw apparently concluded that he had done more propaganda than the traffic would bear, and tried the public with what he called a "pot-boiler," *Fanny's First Play* (1911), which had enormous success, especially in the United States, but, as he himself admitted, had no particular significance. In 1913 he was at the height of his power and popularity, and both the plays of this year, *Androcles and the Lion* and *Pygmalion,* were abrim with comic exuberance and intellectual suggestion.

The next year was the year of the World War and Shaw plunged into his former activity as a pamphleteer and journalist. The British public, in its first burst of war enthusiasm, was in no mood to receive dispassionate suggestions that there was very little to choose between the German Junkers and the British Jingoes and that the moral responsibility for the war was not all to be credited to the German account. Always somewhat blind to the emotional side of life and inclined to judge things from a purely intellectual point of view, Shaw merely gave offense by offering cold reason where moral support was called for, and the nation with singular unanimity "sent him to Coventry": his plays disappeared from the boards and his name from the newspapers. It must be said that his *Playlets of the War* offered little inducement to the public to change its mind, either from a national or an artistic point of view, and *Heartbreak House,* a more elaborate study of war psychology in the dramatic manner of Chekhov, published in 1919, sought in vain for a chance of stage production in Great Britain.

It was in this crisis of Shaw's stage fortunes that the recently organized New York Theatre Guild came to the rescue, and in 1920 put on *Heartbreak House* with satisfactory results; the audiences were somewhat bewildered, but they were pleased and amused. The Guild asked permission to produce *Back to Methuselah, A Metabiological Pentateuch,* a volume of 350 pages comprising five plays in one, which Shaw had printed in 1921, apparently with little hope of stage representation; he replied to the Guild cable, "You are quite mad, but go ahead." The five dramatic episodes were spread over three performances, and as they covered about 35,000 years (from *The Garden of Eden* to *As Far as Thought Can Reach*), this was enough to test the endurance of the Theatre Guild subscribers; but they stood the strain. The promoters lost $20,000, but Shaw pointed out that they had expected a loss of $30,000, so that they were really $10,000 to the good. Meanwhile he had regained his position with the British public; *Back to Methuselah,* produced in New York in 1922, reached the stage of the Birmingham Repertory Theatre in 1923, and London in 1924. A revival of several of his pre-war plays had already begun.

In the winter of 1923-24, *Saint Joan* was produced, first in New York, then in London. It was an effective play, both emotionally and intellectually, and aroused widespread interest on both sides of the Atlantic. *The Applecart,* a political extravaganza, poking good humored fun at democracy and the Labor governments of the future, had its first hearing in England at the Malvern Festival of 1929; it had previously been produced in Polish at Warsaw. The Festival of 1932 saw another new play at Malvern, *Too True to be Good,* which pleased the audience but not the critics.

Shaw's reputation (officially recognized by the award of the Nobel Prize of 1926) was gained very slowly, in the face of much adverse criticism and persistent neglect by the public; there seems no reason to believe that it will be quickly lost. Of his keen intelligence and possession of the genuine spirit of comedy, there can be no question. The subjects of many of his plays will no doubt become superannuated; his Socialistic propaganda may become out of date, either by adoption or by relegation to the dust-bin. But this will have to be a very different world before men and women cease to be interested in questions of property, poverty, and sex. So far as the immediate future is concerned, his fame seems to stand secure.

An interesting movement which began in the last decade of the nineteenth century and came to fuller fruition in the twentieth was the IRISH RENAISSANCE. Leaving aside on the one hand all political aspirations and on the other the attempt to bring the old Irish language to life again, small groups of enthusiasts in London and Dublin set themselves to interpret the Irish spirit in English versions of the ancient myths and lyrics. Dr. Douglas Hyde in *Love Songs of Connaught* (1893) revealed the effective use of a diction founded on the Anglo-Irish of the peasants—a curious combination of the English of the seventeenth and eighteenth centuries with Celtic constructions and idioms. Lady Gregory used the same medium in her versions of Irish legends entitled *Cuchulain of Muirthemne,* and it was later brought to perfection in the plays of JOHN MILLINGTON SYNGE (1871-1909). A writer on the Irish revival in 1894 spoke of the Irish drama as "a thing unknown" and it was in that year that a young Irish poet, WILLIAM BUTLER YEATS (1865-   ), born in Dublin but educated in England, made an attempt to bring it to life with a lyric play, *The Land of Heart's Desire,* which was acted, with no great success, at the Avenue Theatre, London. Yeats then joined forces with Lady Gregory in Ireland, and they called to their aid GEORGE MOORE (1852-1933), who already had a considerable reputation as an art critic and author of several realistic novels (*Esther Waters,* 1894). The Boer War had disgusted him with England, and he was ready for a new venture. Yeats and Moore (according to the latter's account) met at Lady Gregory's to collaborate on a lyric drama *Diarmuid and Grania.* There was really no hope of successful coöperation, for Yeats was ardent, mystical, and romantic, while Moore was realistic, skeptical, and satiric. Yeats was left to organize the Irish drama as best he could, and Moore went off to write a highly diverting account of the new Irish literary movement in *Ave, Salve,* and *Vale.* "A literary movement," he explained, "consists of five or six people, who live in the same town and hate each other cordially." Moore barbed the shaft by ascribing this definition to another Irish poet "A. E." (G. W. Russell).

W. B. YEATS   J. M. SYNGE

GEORGE MOORE   SEAN O'CASEY

In 1903, Yeats organized the Irish National Theatre Society with himself as President, and induced Miss Horniman to help them financially in the acquisition and management of the Abbey Theatre in Dublin. But his greatest service to the Irish Theatre was the discovery in a Paris attic of Synge, who belonged, like himself, to the Irish Protestant minority and had come under the influence of modern French literature. Yeats persuaded Synge to abandon his French studies and devote himself to a study of Irish peasant life in the desolate Aran Islands. Synge's first play *In the Shadow of the Glen* was part of the initial repertory of the Irish players at the opening season of the Abbey Theatre in 1903. Its romantic atmosphere, tense dramatic interest, and incisive but poetic dialogue was something new—quite different from the lyric drama Yeats had planned, but something he was able to appreciate. This and the dramas that followed in the few years left to Synge—*Riders to the Sea, The Well of the Saints,* and *The Playboy of the Western World*—constituted the main dramatic capital of the Abbey Theatre Company on its successful tours in England and America, though Yeats and Lady Gregory added valuable contributions.

A graduate of Trinity College, Dublin, who had wandered wide on the Continent and had spent three years in the sophisticated literary atmosphere of Paris, Synge was far removed from any real sympathy with the primitive Catholicism of the Irish peasant, and his freely humorous treatment of the character of the Irish priest in *The Tinker's Wedding* prevented that play from being performed in Ireland. Some passages in *The Playboy of the Western World* aroused resentment both at the first performance in Dublin and at the representations in New York and Philadelphia; the particular expressions objected to now appear of trivial moment, but the Irish audiences no doubt felt that the portrayal of Irish peasant life was not entirely to their taste. It was certainly an odd combination of circumstances that made so detached and ironic a genius as Synge the interpreter of the Irish peasantry.

Just before his death, Synge had tired of the Irish peasant as a theme and was considering the dramatic possibilities of life in the Dublin slums. This rich vein was, however, left undeveloped for many years. It was in 1923 that the Abbey Theatre put on *The Shadow of a Gunman,* followed the next year by *Juno and the Paycock,* and in 1926 by *The Plough and the Stars.* The author was as great a discovery as Synge—SEAN O'CASEY, born in 1884 in a Dublin tenement-house and still living in one in 1925 when the success of the London production of *Juno and the Paycock* enabled him to leave the slums forever. In his case there could be no accusation of unfamiliarity with the life he dealt with, for he had been steeped in it to the brink of submergence. A London correspondent who interviewed him when he was still living in a tenement described him as "a slim hatchet-faced man with pointed nose and chin, and brown twinkling weak eyes" so that he had to hold his manuscript six inches or so from his nose to read what he had written. His father died when he was three, and his mother brought up the family on tea and dry bread; he was half starved until in his early teens he began to earn his living by selling papers. Then he worked as a navvy for many years, frequented the Abbey Theatre, studied Shakspere, and began to write plays. Although he served with the Citizen Army in the Irish revolution, O'Casey has a good share of Synge's almost cynical detachment, and the last play of the group mentioned above, *The Plough and the Stars,* which deals with the Easter Rising of 1916, provoked a riot when it was first presented at the Abbey Theatre. His next play *The Silver Tassie* also had an unfavorable reception. A New York critic commented: "Dear, dear, but the Irish are quare. They consistently produce genius and as consistently rotten-egg it." O'Casey lacks Synge's literary sureness of touch in the use of words or the handling of a situation, but he has genuine dramatic gifts, and it would be a calamity if his fellow-countrymen were to judge him according to the political feeling of the moment rather than in accordance with his real artistic merits.

HERBERT GEORGE WELLS (1866-   ) at one time threatened to outrank Shaw as the instructor and interpreter of post-Victorian England, but was in the last few years outstripped by his older but apparently more vigorous colleague. Both were Socialists and were members of the Fabian Society as originally organized; both supported the Labor party from the side-lines, with an occasional scoff or sneer at the Labor leaders for not going far enough. They looked at things, however, from different points of view, and arrived at conclusions by different ways. Shaw's way was individualistic and intellectual; Wells was more positive and experimental. Divorce, for instance, to Shaw was merely a resource of reason, to be resorted to at the will of either party. Wells, looking at the matter not as an intellectual problem but in the light of the warm realities of the home and the nursery, described marriage organized according to Shaw's theory as not a social bond, but merely an encounter.

The differences between the two men no doubt arose mainly from a fundamental difference in nature, but they were encouraged by differences in origin and upbringing. Shaw suffered from no sense of social inferiority; he had always belonged to the great republic of cultivated people and men of letters. Wells had to fight from the beginning for recognition and opportunity. He was the son of a professional cricketer who kept a small store in Bromley, Kent, and when his father died his mother returned as housekeeper to the service of the family in which she had been a lady's maid. His struggling youth as assistant in a drugstore, a dry-good's store, and a small private school gave him experience of a variety of social humiliations which he turned to account in two of his first real novels, *The Wheels of Chance* and *Love and Mr. Lewisham,* and two of his best novels, *Kipps* and *Tono-Bungay.* He broke out of the bondage of middle-class servility by gaining a scholarship in the Royal College of Science at South Kensington, in which Huxley was professor of biology, and from Huxley's teaching he gained an inspiration and an interest in science which he never lost, and which has been a most important element in his whole view of life.

H. G. WELLS　　　　　　　ARNOLD BENNETT

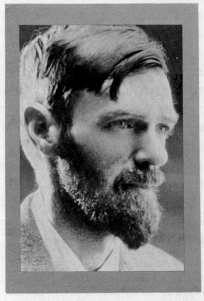

JOHN GALSWORTHY　　　　　D. H. LAWRENCE

After taking his degree, Wells experienced the usual difficulties of the youth without influential friends or social connections to help him in making a living. He turned again to
teaching, from that to writing for educational periodicals, then
to writing for the reviews, and finally to publishing articles,
short stories, and scientific romances in book form. Despite
severe overwork and resulting ill health, at the age of thirty he
had established himself as a writer of fiction.

From a writer of romances of scientific theory which he himself compared to the "monstrous experimental imaginings" of
children, he developed by the turn of the century into a novelist
after the standard Victorian pattern, dealing with social issues
under the new conditions of an industrial and democratic age.
He dealt first (in the novels mentioned above) with the attempts
of the newly enfranchised to conquer social as well as political
barriers. But he soon claimed "the whole of human life" as the
scope of the novel; a free hand to deal with political, religious,
and social questions. In a series of novels beginning with *Ann
Veronica* (1909) he put aside the Victorian taboo on discussions
of sex and marriage, and set forth various phases of coöperation
and antagonism between men and women until he had worn
out the theme.

The outbreak of the World War stirred him deeply, and in
Mr. Britling Sees It Through he wrote the best of contemporary accounts of the emotional and intellectual reactions of the
average Englishman to the great struggle. His attention was increasingly directed to the need not only for the socialistic internal organization of each nation, but for some international
world organization, especially for industrial, financial, and
other economic ends. He was for some time interested in the
League of Nations, but as ultimately organized, it was far from
meeting his aspirations. His ideas are best expressed in *The
Salvaging of Civilization* (1921)—a series of discourses he was
prevented, by ill health, from delivering in the United States—
and *The World of William Clissold* (1926), a huge, chaotic
novel almost entirely given over, once the story is well started,

to propaganda. In 1921, Wells attended the International Conference on Armament Limitation in Washington, D. C., as the representative of the New York "World," and in 1922 paid a visit of investigation to Russia.

Three of his most recent undertakings—the *Outline of History* (1921), *The Science of Life* (1931, in collaboration with his son and Professor Julian Huxley), and *The Work, Wealth and Happiness of Mankind*—are educational in character, though the first and the last are not free from the desire to deduce certain political theories from the facts. The will to teach is, indeed, a strongly marked characteristic of the mind of H. G. Wells, and has interfered seriously with the artistic effectiveness of the novels of his later years. His best imaginative work seems to have been done in the series of novels beginning with *Kipps* in 1905 and ending with *The New Machiavelli* in 1911. Soon after that, didacticism began to creep in, and though there was a magnificent recovery in *Mr. Britling Sees It Through,* the novels written since the war have been increasingly overloaded with the author's opinions on world issues. Wells had a mind of extraordinary energy and unusual powers of exposition and narrative, but it is doubtful whether the combination of the novel with political argument can be carried on without injury to both. The argumentation has certainly injured the reputation Wells acquired by the social novels of his middle period, and posterity can hardly be expected to take more interest in his later work than has been shown by contemporary readers.

It is hard to say whether Shaw's cool intellectual analysis of the inequalities of the Victorian social and industrial system or the passionate attacks of Wells upon its abuses did more to upset the minds of English and American readers; it is certain that both did a great deal. Shaw may be set aside by the prudent as merely a jester, a skilled performer with intellectual conceptions which have very little relation to real life; but the downright earnestness of Wells is not so easily put off. Wells has never lost his ardor for intelligent organization or his faith in science.

JOHN GALSWORTHY (1866-1933) has no specific to offer for the ills of mankind, but he brings to their consideration and presentation a sincere and generous sympathy, restrained by his artistic sense of form from slopping over into sentimentality. Some think that he has not always escaped this danger, and Max Beerbohm accused him of "selling his birthright for a pot of message." In general, however, he has a keen perception of the golden mean, and does not often transgress, either on the side of didacticism or on that of sentimentality.

Among his contemporaries he was a striking and characteristic figure, the typical "gentleman" of tradition, with easy, gracious manners, courteous address, perfect self-possession, and a certain reserve made agreeable by a touch of shyness. The son of a successful London lawyer, he was educated at Harrow and Oxford, enlarged his outlook by a year's travel, read for the bar and passed his examinations, but never practised law. His approaches to literature were gradual; he was never under any financial compulsion to publish immature or hasty work. After some tentative essays and stories, he established himself in the front rank of contemporary literature at the age of forty with a successful novel *The Man of Property,* and a successful play *The Silver Box.* He pursued both these kinds of composition with patient and consistent industry, but with varying success, so that it was still a question whether he was better as a novelist or as a dramatist when the World War checked his literary activities; characteristically enough, while Wells was agitating for the League of Nations, and Bennett was holding a prominent position in the War Department of Publicity, Galsworthy was working quietly as a masseur in a French hospital. The publication of *The Forsyte Saga* in one volume in 1922 seemed to establish the supremacy of the novel in his literary work, and it will be convenient to discuss his novels first.

The first volume of the Forsyte series, *The Man of Property,* was apparently first planned and executed as an independent work, complete in itself. It sets forth, chiefly in the person of the principal character, Soames Forsyte, but also in the subordinate figures of the story, "the sense of property" as a motive force in life, regarding the acquisition and retention of wealth as superior to all other interests. "The Forsytes are the middlemen, the commercials, the pillars of society, the cornerstones of convention, everything that is admirable," at the time of the Victorian Jubilee—the date at which the story opens. Art, literature, religion, the public welfare, beauty, passion have their places, in moderation; but the Forsytes never give themselves up to anything "soul and body" except to the acquisition and possession of wealth. The people who pursue love or beauty or art are brought up against the power of money and beaten by it; at the end of the story Irene, whom Galsworthy afterward interpreted as a "concretion of disturbing Beauty impinging on a possessive world," is left at the mercy of the superior power of property, embodied in her husband, Soames; her lover, the young architect who stands for art and passion, is swept out of life, defeated.

For ten years Galsworthy left the beautiful Irene baffled and degraded by "the man of property." He showed us in *The Country House* the "crassness" of life among the unintelligent county gentry, and in *Fraternity* the impassable gulf that divides the intellectual and artistic society of London from the masses whom they interest themselves in and hope to benefit. In *The Dark Flower* he exhibited the power of passionate love; and in *The Freelands,* the tyranny of the landowning squire. Then, apparently, he remembered Irene, and decided that youth and beauty were perhaps not so easily defeated by "the sense of property" as he had thought. So in the *Indian Summer of a Forsyte* (1917), one of his most charming sketches, we see Irene relieved from submission to Soames by her own efforts and the benevolent help of old Jolyon Forsyte. *In Chancery* (1920) shows Soames abandoned but still pursuing, and finally defeated. In *The Awakening,* a second connective interlude, Irene is triumphant, married to young Jolyon and the mother of a son. In *To Let* (1921), the third novel, (with the two intervening sketches making up the *Saga* proper), we have the spectacle of "the man of property" realizing that he is beaten: *"To Let*—the Forsyte age and way of life, when a man owned his soul, his investments, and his woman, without check or question. And now the State had, or would have, his investments, his woman had herself, and God knew who had his soul. *To Let*—that sane and simple creed!"

The Forsyte Saga, covering a whole generation and equal in size to one of the great Victorian novels, was a bigger success as a whole than any of its component parts, and it is not surprising that Galsworthy was encouraged to continue the series. Having rescued Irene, he proceeded to rehabilitate Soames; as the Victorian Age receded, the post-war generation, which appeared to substitute the headlong pursuit of pleasure for the acquisition of wealth, offered an unfavorable contrast. The second series, published as a whole in 1929 under the title *A Modern Comedy,* consisted, like the first, of three novels and two connecting links, but it was less effective than the *Saga.*

As a dramatist, Galsworthy had the advantage of a more regular traditional structure and a more concentrated literary form, which helped to correct both the diffuseness one sometimes notices in the novels and a certain thinness in the presentation of minor characters. He was from the beginning admirably served by excellent companies of actors, both in London and New York, and his plays were well put on. In their composition he was at first inclined to an even stricter symmetry than was required by dramatic tradition. "A drama," he holds, "must be so shaped as to have a spire of meaning," and the easiest way to secure this shaping is by the balance of one set of characters against another. Thus, in his first play, *The Silver Box,* Jones the drunken out-of-work who has stolen the cigarette-case, has taken it from an idle and dissolute young man about town who has, in a state of intoxication, stolen a crimson silk purse from "an unknown lady, from beyond." Jack gets off with a scolding from a wealthy father, who gives the scarlet lady money compensation for her loss; Jones, whose wife is charwoman in the wealthy family, gets a month's hard labor and his children are left to starve.

Similarly in *Strife,* which deals with a labor dispute culminating in a strike, the chairman of the directors is balanced against the workman's leader, the directors against the workman's committee, the manager against the walking delegate sent down by the trade union. This enables Galsworthy to present the case of both sides, though always with sympathy for the under dog. Sometimes this careful balancing of parts gives an impression of artificiality, as in *The Pigeon,* in which three "wild birds" are contrasted with three domesticated fowl. The French vagabond is put under the care of the professor, the drunken cabman is allotted to the magistrate, and the loose-living flower-girl placed under the guidance of the clergyman —all to no purpose, for you cannot make wild birds tame, however tame the birds may be who are appointed to look after them.

The Skin Game is another balanced play—the Hillcrists, a Southern county family rather down on its luck, are pitted against an intruding business family from the North very much swollen with success, the Hornblowers. Again Galsworthy tries to hold the balance even, but he cannot help making it dip a little now and then on the side of the people who have gentle manners and an ancient tradition which gives them some sense of social responsibility.

Loyalties, another after-war play, carries the principle of balance still farther, but succeeds by dint of extreme tact and delicacy of adjustment on the part of the dramatist. On one side is the Jew, De Levis, who is robbed of a thousand pounds in a country house, by a fellow-guest; on the other are all the social forces arrayed against him by the friends of the young officer who is suspected of the theft—rightly suspected, as it turns out in the end. But meanwhile Galsworthy has cunningly interested all the prejudices of class, race, regiment, club, and profession on the wrong side. The Jew wins, but, as he was socially ambitious, he might better have lost his thousand pounds at the beginning quietly, without making an ungentlemanly fuss about it.

ARNOLD BENNETT (1867-1931) told us, himself, the story of his early career, in *The Truth about an Author,* published at first anonymously but afterward openly acknowledged. Born near Hanley in the pottery district which he was afterward to make famous as "the Five Towns," he had some experience as a reporter on a local newspaper before leaving home; but according to his own account it was a natural gift for preparing a lawyer's bill of costs that found him a position in London at a salary of five dollars a week when he was twenty-one, and secured his advance in the office. But he saw no future for himself as a lawyer's clerk, and he began to do free-lance work in journalism at the same time that he was having a grand gorge in English, French, and Russian fiction. On the strength of a few published articles and short stories, he was able to leave the law for the office of a woman's magazine, of which he became first assistant editor and then editor.

When he was a year over thirty, he had published his first novel, *A Man from the North;* with the proceeds, after paying for typewriting, he was able to buy a new hat. His next year's record of writing totaled 335,340 words, including 224 published articles and stories, a volume of *Polite Farces,* a newspaper serial, and a draft (80,000 words) of a novel of Staffordshire life published in 1902 as *Anna of the Five Towns.* Success did not enable Bennett to lay aside his self-imposed habit of dire industry and he produced a great deal that was merely competent journalism; but at his best he is a fine artist and a few of his novels have permanent value. Retiring to France when he had made his financial position sufficiently secure, he married a French wife and settled down for several years in a cottage in the forest of Fontainebleau. *The Old Wives' Tale* (1908), the first of his novels to win the admiration of English and American critics, was suggested by an eccentric old woman whom he saw in a Paris restaurant. The thought came to him: "This woman was once young, slim, perhaps beautiful. Very probably she is unconscious of her singularities. Her case is a tragedy. One ought to be able to make a heart-rending novel out of a woman such as she." The thing had already been done by Guy de Maupassant in *Une Vie,* and by way of bravado Bennett decided to have two commonplace heroines instead of one. But it took him five years to bring his first conception of the theme to the form in which we now have it.

The Old Wives' Tale remains Arnold Bennett's greatest achievement. He did almost as good work in the trilogy of Five Town life, consisting of *Clayhanger, Hilda Lessways,* and *These Twain* (1910-16), and seven years later he was able to apply the same methods to similar material in a dismal quarter of London in *Riceyman Steps* with conspicuous success. His choice of material is as characteristic of him as his method. He did not choose his heroes and heroines from the toiling masses whom Dickens idealized and sentimentalized as the Stephen Blackpool and Rachel of *Hard Times* or brutalized as Stephen's wife; Bennett virtually confined his personages to the shop-keepers immediately above the laboring class, the people whom Gissing defined as the "ignobly decent," weighed down with petty cares, absurd conventions, sordid ambitions, and grotesque but lifeless religious creeds. Out of this unpromising material Bennett undertook to reveal to us the pathos and tragedy, as well as the humor, of commonplace life; and he achieved his purpose, not by satirizing such life but by painting it with scrupulous and loving fidelity.

Unlike Sinclair Lewis, who carried on the study of provincialism in the United States, Bennett was in sympathy with the life he portrayed. He was aware of its shortcomings, and often ridiculed them; but he made fun of the quaint foibles of his characters with affection. He had a sincere admiration for their virtues—their industry and steadfastness, their self-restraint and courage. He shared their lack of spirituality; or it might be more correct to say that they shared his, for he made them in his own image, being himself created out of the same Midland clay. They are, as he himself was, profoundly English, though they have the characteristic virtues and failings of the provincial type, as it is to be found all the world over.

D. H. LAWRENCE (1887-1931) belonged to a later generation than the group of three novelists last discussed (all of whom were born in 1866-67); after the World War, the younger group for a while threatened to win the supremacy, but none of them seemed able to stand the course except Lawrence. Hugh Walpole, Gilbert Cannan, Compton Mackenzie were great names in the second decade of the century, but had dropped almost out of sight again by the end of the third decade. Lawrence's work had something more distinctive about it and seems more likely to endure. The others were clever young university men who wrote pleasing stories—mainly, it would seem, of their childhood and youth—and reflected the waves of French or Russian influence then current; Lawrence had apparently more in himself to interest the critics, though he never gained the favor of any large public. The son of a Nottinghamshire coal-miner, he won scholarships which enabled him to go, first to Nottingham High School, and then to the neighboring Day Training College (or Normal School). He taught until the publication of two novels enabled him to give his whole time to literary work, though his life, to the end, was something of a struggle. It was his third novel, *Sons and Lovers* (1913), which first attracted wide attention; it is mainly the story of his own family life in a mining village, and showed remarkable powers both of psychological insight and literary expression. Unfortunately for his own material comfort and peace of mind, he was swept away by the prevailing interest in the problem of sex, which took up so much space and attention in subsequent novels as to appear an obsession from which he could not escape. This theme was made prominent in his fourth novel, *The Rainbow* (1915), which brought his publishers into the police court; the whole edition —or as much of it as could be recovered—was burnt by order of the London magistrate, though it continued to circulate in the United States. Lawrence kept silence for five years before he returned to further exploration of his pessimistic philosophy of sex. He lived for some years abroad, but not long before his death he was again in conflict with the British authorities.

JOHN MASEFIELD

RUPERT BROOKE

MAY SINCLAIR

VIRGINIA WOOLF

At the turn of the century English poetry seemed to be under a cloud. Tennyson was succeeded as laureate by Sir Alfred Austin, and Sir Alfred Austin by Sir Robert Bridges. In the long roll of English laureates there have been some who were less respectable but few who were less significant. Yet it was hard to say in 1892, or again in 1913, how the choice could have been bettered. Swinburne and Meredith were regarded, at the earlier date, as too old, or possibly too radical; Kipling was thought too flippant; and at the later date Masefield was apparently not thought sufficiently mature, for he had to wait for his turn till 1930. There are, however, others whose names ought not to be altogether forgotten.

Among these perhaps the most distinctive of the older group was the Cambridge professor ALFRED E. HOUSMAN (1859-   ) who was well known in academic circles as a scholar and would have been well known in wider circles as a poet if the quantity of his work had been larger. Two slim volumes, *The Shropshire Lad* (1896) and *Last Poems* (1922), constitute the whole of his published verse. The poems are short and few in number; they have a Greek perfection of phrasing, the clearness and sharpness of outline of an intaglio, and a spirit of almost cynical stoicism, generally regarded as characteristic of the young poets of a later date.

JOHN MASEFIELD (1873-   ) was clearly entitled to the laureateship by his devotion to literature and the variety of his achievement. His *August, 1914,* is the best of the numberless poems of the war, and his *Gallipoli* the finest piece of prose published about it while the struggle was in progress. He wrote also tales and novels, mainly of romantic adventure, a prose tragedy of domestic life, *Nan,* and several tragedies in verse on historical or scriptural subjects, *The Tragedy of Pompey the Great, Philip the King, Good Friday, The Trial of Jesus,* and *A King's Daughter.* The last named was first put on the stage for the opening in 1923 of the new Playhouse at Oxford. Near his house at Boar's Hill, Oxford, Masefield and his wife made a private theater and organized an amateur company for the production of poetic drama. He said in 1926, "So long as there remain two enthusiasts and a plank there will still be a poetical stage," and he devoted much of the energies of his later years to maintaining it.

Masefield's beginnings promised for him a very different career. Born in Herefordshire of farming stock, he kept his love for the English country-side in spite of wanderings all over the world and strange adventures as a sailor before the mast and a roving worker at many occupations. Report has it that he was a bartender in New York City and worked in a carpet factory at Yonkers. It is certain that his early poetry was characterized not only by the fondness for the sea, indicated in the title of his first publication, *Salt Water Ballads* (1902), but by a keen sympathy, and wide acquaintance with the humble toilers, on sea and shore, in many lands.

Others may sing of the wine and the wealth and the mirth,
The portly presence of potentates goodly in girth;
Mine be the dirt and the dross, the dust and scum of the earth.

Theirs be the music, the color, the glory, the gold;
Mine be a handful of ashes, a mouthful of mold.
Of the maimed, of the halt and the blind in the rain and the cold—
Of these shall my songs be fashioned, my tales be told.

With *The Widow in the Bye Street* he began a series of long narrative poems of humble life, which were very original and successful. After the war he gave his narrative gift a new turn in *Reynard the Fox,* a poem describing a hunting meet and the run of the hounds. It was obviously done in the manner of Chaucer—a poet Masefield greatly admired—and in its easy movement and lively humor was not unworthy of its model. Subsequent narrative poems or collections of poems (*Minnie Maylow's Story,* 1931) have maintained his reputation as a graceful and sympathetic teller of tales in verse and justified his official recognition as the leading representative of the best traditions in English poetry.

RUPERT BROOKE (1887-1915), partly by his personal charm, partly by his death on the ill-fated expedition to the Dardanelles, made a greater impression on the public mind than the other young poets who joined in the publication of *Georgian Poetry 1911-12* and of *New Numbers* (1914). In the last little volume, intended to be the first of a quarterly series, Wilfred Wilson Gibson, Lascelles Abercrombie, and John Drinkwater also participated, but in both enterprises Rupert Brooke was the leading spirit. His youthful beauty and ardent enthusiasm made him conspicuous in any society. His graceful figure, classical features, and golden hair, with his keen intelligence and engaging manner, made him appear to Henry James the "ideal image of English youth, at once radiant and reflective." Another admirer described him in the following lines:

> A young Apollo, golden-haired,
> Stands dreaming on the verge of strife,
> Magnificently unprepared
> For the long littleness of life.

A brilliant scholar as well as an accomplished athlete, Brooke won prizes at Rugby School (of which his father was a master) and a fellowship at King's College, Cambridge. Besides taking part in the collections of verse mentioned above, he had at the age of twenty-four already published an independent volume of his own poems. This youthful verse was extraordinarily precocious, flippant, satirical, and even cynical—with the superficial cynicism of exuberant youth. But in the last few years of his life he had already begun to mature. *The Great Lover, The Old Vicarage Grantchester,* and the war sonnets show a greater sincerity and depth of feeling. His metrical facility, even in the poems written when he was nineteen, was unique. What he might have become had he lived none can say, and in the monument placed in 1931 above the lonely grave on the Island of Skyros, England laments not only Brooke but many other poet comrades of his, slain in the war, "the inheritors of unfulfilled renown."

Among the younger poets who survived the war may be mentioned Robert Graves, Siegfried Sassoon, and Ralph Hodgson. The first is an Oxford graduate, the second a Cambridge man, and the third a London journalist, who writes mainly about sport and is the leading English authority on bull-terriers. Hodgson's poetry is in curious contrast with his professional prose—imaginative, even fanciful, melodious, and with a simple charm that makes one regret that the volume of his verse is so small.

In recent fiction the most striking feature is the achievement of women authors. The career of KATHERINE MANSFIELD (1890-1923) was cut short by consumption before she had fully realized the brilliant promise of her youth, but her accomplishment in the short story of a subtle and delicate type, approaching the work of Chekhov, was remarkable, and she wrote charming letters, published after her death by her husband, J. Middleton Murry, a leading London critic.

MAY SINCLAIR won early success by her study of a young poet in a London boarding-house, entitled *The Divine Fire* (1904). More recently she has interested herself in the time-space theories of Einstein and is credited with the authorship of a popular limerick giving the theory of relativity in a nutshell:

> There was a young lady named Bright,
> Whose speed was much faster than light,
> She went out one day
> In a relative way,
> And returned on the previous night.

Miss Sinclair was a serious student of the new psychology of Freud and other Vienna scientists, and made use of their ideas in her novels. *The Three Sisters* (1914), *Mary Olivier* (1919), *The Fieldings* (1922), and *The Allinghams* (1927) were notable examples of the combination of modern sex theories with artistic restraint. Her *Mr. Waddington of Wyck* (1921), a keenly humorous psychological analysis of masculine egotism, is not unworthy to be compared with Meredith's *Egoist*.

ROSE MACAULAY won favor with *Potterism* (1920) and *Dangerous Ages* (1921) before she ventured to make use of the psychological hypothesis of a double personality in *Daisy and Daphne,* published in England under the title *Keeping up Appearances.* The quick-witted reader may guess before he (more probably she) is half-way through the book that the two heroines are one, but the authoress very cleverly withholds her secret as long as possible.

Mrs. Henry Maxwell Andrews (born 1893), whose maiden name was Cicely Fairfield, is well known on both sides of the Atlantic for the acute and profound literary criticism written over the signature of REBECCA WEST; she has also succeeded, but perhaps not quite so well, as a novelist. *The Judge* began well, but tailed off into melodrama; and *Harriet Hume* (1929), another experiment in double personality, was sometimes too subtle for the ordinary reader to make out what the story was about.

The most brilliant of this group of women writers, and the most successful in imposing on the public a convention different from that of the traditional form of the novel, was VIRGINIA WOOLF, who in *Mrs. Dalloway* (1925) repeated in a simpler manner and in a much shorter form the experiment, tried a few years before by James Joyce in *Ulysses,* of restricting the period within which the action of the novel is confined to one day. Neither *Ulysses* nor *Mrs. Dalloway* encouraged the continuance of so great a strain on the novelist's invention and versatility, to say nothing of the demand made on the reader's attention, which, particularly in the case of *Ulysses,* was unmercifully taxed, often with no adequate return for the intellectual energy required. *To the Lighthouse* (1927) also dealt rather cavalierly with the element of time, but not so drastically; the continuity of the story is not too violently broken, and the central figure of the Scottish professor (plausibly identified with Mrs. Woolf's father, Sir Leslie Stephen) lends unity to the various threads of interest. In *Orlando,* which was the success of the season 1928-29, she was still more daring, for her hero is a multiple per-

sonality including male and female representatives of several
generations of the Sackville family, and the period of Orlando's
life is extended over more than three centuries. *The Waves*
(1931) also dealt, in a very indirect and subtle fashion, beyond
the grasp of the ordinary reader, with the effect of time and circumstance upon human character and destiny; but there is no
regular narrative and very little character study beyond the
self-analysis conveyed by introspective soliloquy. One critic hails
The Waves as a novel of first importance; another as "the multiple reflection of a dying race, the twilight of small souls."
The writer's command of a brilliant and elusive style is beyond
question; but her appeal is confined to a small intellectual circle.

While the novel by its eccentricities has proved, perhaps,
that its best days are over, other forms of prose show remarkable
vitality. If history, in the hands of the experts, has become
increasingly scientific and increasingly unreadable (except by
other experts), physical science has attempted, through the pens
of some of its most distinguished professors, to make itself understood by the ordinary reader. The number of war books of all
kinds—fiction, history, and military science—is enormous, but
few of them are of any permanent literary value. An exception
should be made in favor of *Revolt in the Desert* (1927) by
T. E. Lawrence, who combines unusual literary gifts with a very
exceptional personality and remarkable adventures.

Another unusual personality was that of W. H. HUDSON
(1841-1922). Born in the Argentine Republic at a time when
the country was being settled by English and Scottish land-
holders, he retained a vivid memory of the free and open life
of those pioneer days and accumulated a vast store of quaint
reminiscences, not only of the city of Buenos Aires in its more
primitive days, but of the wilder country not far away. For color
and sound, as well as for out-of-the-way characters and incidents, he had a keen eye and a keen ear, and his style is very easy
and agreeable. Of the many books he made out of the apparently
endless material he had at command, the best is probably his
autobiography, *Far Away and Long Ago* (1918).

ALDOUS HUXLEY

ALDOUS HUXLEY (1894-   ), grandson of the eminent biologist of Victorian times, Thomas H. Huxley, attracted the attention of a few by his early poems, published soon after the close of the World War, and won a much wider public for his novels; but he is probably seen at his best in his essays and observations of foreign travel. Of keen and often sardonic humor, he is an unsparing satirist of the follies and vices of the younger generation, whose antics he analyzed with so much particularity that some readers were inclined to believe that he sympathized with them. In his later work, however, he has shown himself a stern and constructive moralist, though he builds on other foundations than the Victorian tradition.

Biography has recently shown more revolutionary activity than any other kind of literature. The new movement marks both gains and losses: the conventional biography of the nineteenth century, in which the subject was posed and draped as for a funeral monument, has not yet entirely disappeared, but it is no longer treated with respect, and this is to the good. On the other hand, the new biography, as practised not by the discoverers of the art but by their baser imitators on both sides of the Atlantic, and on the Continent of Europe as well as in Great Britain, has flooded the market with cheap and flashy wares unworthy of any serious attention.

LYTTON STRACHEY (1880-1932) the founder of the new school, had a long and thorough training in literary method before he undertook biography, and came to it with not only the instincts but the habits of the scholar. Educated at Trinity College, Cambridge, he devoted some years after graduation to private study, and in 1912 published *Landmarks in French Literature*. His first biographical essays, *Eminent Victorians* (1918), included character studies of Thomas Arnold, Cardinal Manning, General Gordon, and Florence Nightingale. All of these were at that time still familiar figures to British thought, and the outlines of their characters and achievements were well known, not only through numerous biographies but by popular tradition and daily reference in conversation and the newspaper

LYTTON STRACHEY

press. It was in fact because these eminent persons had become established as part of the Victorian tradition that Strachey, in his short, concise sketches, pointed out that the standards by which they had been judged were not final, and that the general impression transmitted by the Victorians to the following generation was not in all particulars in accordance with the facts. T. H. Arnold, for example, had been idealized as the reformer of the public-school system; but how much reform had he really accomplished, and was the public school education really fitted to modern requirements? General Gordon had been made a national hero, but had he not human failings as well as sublime virtues? So with Cardinal Manning and Florence Nightingale, whose substantial achievements no one would question. In his next book, *Queen Victoria* (1921), Strachey was faced with a rather different problem. He was able, as before, to bring to bear a considerable amount of evidence not hitherto available—or at any rate, accessible to the ordinary reader—but his main task, in the fuller space now at his disposal, was to give a rounded estimate of what kind of person Victoria really was, and what she had done, as well as to indicate what she was not and what she had not done. Without telling all over again the story of the Victorian era and its accomplishments, Strachey was able to convey an adequate idea of the queen's share in them and of her personal attitude toward her successive ministers; and, above all, to her distinguished consort, Prince Albert, who in knowledge and intelligence was greatly her superior. While Strachey got in many satiric touches at the expense of both, his estimate of Prince Albert's character is higher than that generally received in the past, and his picture of the queen, though it destroys many popular illusions, is on the whole sympathetic. *Elizabeth and Essex* (1929), despite many brilliant character sketches, was less successful, probably on account of its historical remoteness, for, while Queen Victoria was only a generation back, Elizabeth belongs to an age long past. *Essays in Miniature* (1931) were thumb-nail sketches, which hardly gave sufficient scope for the author's power of ironical suggestion.

Among the countless host who have adopted Strachey's methods, few have his scholarship, and still fewer his satiric power. Perhaps his cleverest disciple in England is Philip Guedalla, whose *Palmerston* (1927) is a brilliant performance. *Wellington* (1931) has many amusing touches, but gives less opportunity for the realization of an epoch not too remote to be of general interest.

INDEX OF ILLUSTRATIONS

INDEX OF NAMES AND TITLES

In accordance with the practice of the Congressional Library, A's and The's at the beginning of a title are omitted.

INDEX OF ILLUSTRATIONS

Abbotsford, 258.
Addison, 118.
Ann Hathaway's Cottage, 45.
Arbuthnot, 140.
Areopagitica, 79.
Arnold, Matthew, 346.
Austen, Jane, 168.

Bacon, 60.
Bacon's *Instauratio,* 64.
Barrie, 377.
Beaumont, 57.
Bennett, Arnold, 400.
Blake, 184.
Blount, Martha, 136.
Bodleian Library, Oxford, 6.
Bolingbroke, 140.
Boswell, 158.
Boswell's *Johnson,* 160.
British Museum Reading Room, ii.
Brontë, Charlotte, Facsimile, 314.
Brontë Sisters, 316.
Brooke, Rupert, 410.
Browning, 333. 340.
Browning Facsimile, 337.
Browning, Mrs., 335.
Bunyan, 88.
Bunyan's Birthplace, 94.
Burke, 158.
Burney, Fanny, 166.
Burning of Shelley's Body, 242.
Burns, 193.
Burns, Kilmarnock edition, 191.
Butler and 15 Clifford's Inn, 367.
Byron, 224, 228.
Byron, Lady, 226.

Carlyle, 280.
Carlyle's House, 278.
Caxton's Dictes, 26.
Chapman, 57.
Charterhouse, Old Porch, 302.
Charterhouse, Pensioners' Hall, 302.
Chaucer, 19.
Childe Harold, 222.
Clarissa, 146.
Coffee House, 108.
Coleridge, 202, 214.
Congreve, 140.
Conrad, 377.
Coventry, 318.
Cowper, 179.
Cowper's House at Weston, 182.
Cromwell, Thomas, 28.

Darwin, 357.
De Quincey, 252.
Dickens, 288, 292, 296, 298.
Dickens, his Wife, and her Sister, 294.
Defoe, 112.
Defoe's *Review,* 110.
Don Juan, 222.
Donne, 98.
Dorset, 105.
Dove Cottage, 206.
Dryden, 96.
Dumfries, 189.

Edgeworth, Maria, 171.
Elizabeth, Queen, 67.
Elstow Church, 94.
English Bards and Scotch Reviewers, 222.
Essay on Population, 273.
Eton, 176.
Exeter Cathedral Chapter House, xxxii.

Faerie Queene, 36.
Fielding, 150.
First "Great Bible," 26.
Fletcher, 47.
Frank's Casket, 3.

Gadshill Place, 300.
Galsworthy, 400.
Gascoigne and Queen Elizabeth, 32.
Gaskell, Mrs., 316.
Gay, 140.
Geoffrey's Window, Monmouth, 10.
George Eliot, 320.
Gilbert, 369.
Gissing, 377.
Globe Theater (1616), 50.
Goldsmith, 158.
Gower, 17.
Grasmere, 206.
Gray, 174.
Greta Hall, 216.
Gulliver's Travels, 124.

Hamlet, 48.
Hardy, 363.
Hardy Facsimile, 365.
Harrow, 220.
Hawkshead School, 196.
Hazlitt, 252.
Henry IV, 48.
Henry VIII, 28.
Herrick, 102.
High St., Oxford, 234.

Hours of Idleness, 222.
Huxley, Aldous, 417.
Huxley, T. H., 355.

Johnson, 158.
Jones, H. A., 369.
Jonson, 57.
Journal to Stella, 126.

Keats, 248.
Keswick Bridge, 216.
Kingsley, 312.
Kipling, 377.

Lamb, Lady Caroline, 226.
Lamb, 250.
Lawrence, D. H., 400.
Lerici, 242.
Lindisfarne Gospel, 24.
Lines written above Tintern Abbey, 204.
London Gazette, 110.
Lovelace, 105.
Lyrical Ballads, 202.

Macaulay, 268.
Magdalen College and Bridge, 234.
Marvell, 102.
Masefield, 410.
Meredith, 359.
Meredith Facsimile, 361.
Mill, John Stuart, 276.
Milton, 72, 76.
Milton's Poems, 74.
Montagu, Lady Mary Wortley, 136.
Moore, George, 396.
Moral Tales, 171.
More, Sir Thomas, 28.
Morris, William, 350.
Mossgiel, 189.

Newman, 286.
Newstead Abbey, 218.

O'Casey, Sean, 396.

Palazzo Rezzonico, 342.
Paradise Lost, 84.
Pater, 371.
Pilgrim's Progress, 91.
Pinero, Sir Arthur, 369.
Pope, 132.
Pope's Villa at Twickenham, 136.
Printing Office (16th century), 30.
Protestant Cemetery at Rome, 244.

Raleigh, 36.
Reade, 312.
Richard II's Bible, 24.
Richard III, 48.
Richardson, 142.
Robinson Crusoe, 114.
Roderick Random, 155.

Romeo and Juliet, 48.
Rossetti, D. G., 348, 350.
Rossetti, Christina, 350.
Rugby School and Chapel, 344.
Ruskin, 282, 284.
Rydal Mount, 208.
Rydal Water, 208.

Scott, 254.
Shakspere's Birthplace, 43.
Shakspere's Bust, 54.
Shakspere's Portrait in First Folio, 55.
Shaw, Bernard, 386.
Shelley, 236.
Shelley, Mary Godwin, 238.
Sidney, 36.
Sinclair, May, 410.
Sketches by Boz, 290.
Smith, Adam, 162.
Smollett, 155.
Somersby Church and Rectory, 326.
Spectator, 118.
Spenser, 34.
Steele, 118.
Stella, 126.
Sterne, 155.
Stevenson, 373, 375.
Stoke Poges Churchyard, 176.
Strachey, Lytton, 419.
Stratford Church, 45.
Suckling, 105.
Sullivan, 369.
Sumer is icumen in, 14.
Swan Theater, 41.
Swift, 122.
Swinburne, 350.
Synge, J. M., 396.

Tatler, 118.
Tennyson, 324, 330.
Thackeray, 304.
Tintern Abbey, 204.
Tom Jones, 152.
Trinity College, Cambridge, 220.
Tristram Shandy, 155.
Trollope, 309.
Tyndale, 30.
Tyndale and Coverdale Bible, 26.

Vanhomrigh, Hester, 126.
Victoria, Queen, 262, 264.

Wealth of Nations, 162.
Wells, H. G., 400.
Whitby Abbey, 6.
Wilde, 371.
Windermere and Esthwaite, 196.
Wolsey, 28.
Woolf, Virginia, 410.
Wordsworth, 202, 210.
Wycliffite Bible, 24.

Yeats, W. B., 396.

INDEX OF NAMES AND TITLES

Abbess Hilda, 7.
Abbotsford, 257, 259.
Absentee, 172.
Adam Bede, 319, 322.
Addison, 116, 119, 121, 135, 143.
Address to the De'il, 194.
Admirable Crichton, 383, 384.
Adonais, 75, 241.
Advancement of Learning, 61, 66.
Agamemnon, 343.
Age of Reason, 266.
Agnes Gray, 315.
Alastor, 239.
Alchemist, 56.
Alcuin, 8.
Alexander, Prince of Rhodes, 133.
Alexander the Great, 11.
Alfoxden Manor, 200.
Alfred, King, 8, 25.
All's Well that Ends Well, 46.
All the Year Round, 299, 301.
Allen, Edward, 42.
Allinghams, 414.
Almayer's Folly, 379.
Alton Locke, 311.
Alysoun, 15.
Ambrosio the Monk, 259.
American Notes, 297.
Amyot, 51.
Androcles and the Lion, 172, 393.
Anglo-Saxon Chronicle, 8.
Ann Veronica, 401.
Anna of the Five Towns, 407.
Anne, Queen, 113, 120, 125.
Annual Register, 274.
Antiquary, 259.
Antony and Cleopatra, 51.
Apologia pro Vita sua, 287.
Applecart, 394.
Arbuthnot, 131.
Arcades, 73.
Archer, William, 389.
Arden, Mary, 42.
Areopagitica, 80.
Argument to prove that the Abolishing of Christianity, &c., 125.
Ariel, 243.
Ariosto, 31, 37.
Aristophanes' Apology, 343.
Aristotle, 18, 37, 59, 61.
Armour, Jean, 188, 194.
Arms and the Man, 389, 390, 392.
Arnold, Matthew, 211, 345-347.
Arthur, King, 11-13.

As Far as Thought Can Reach, 394.
As You Like It, 49, 52.
Asolando, 332, 343.
August, 1914, 411.
Auld Lang Syne, 194.
Auld Licht Idylls, 383.
Aurora Leigh, 338.
Austen, Jane, 165-170, 259, 318.
Austen, Lady, 181, 183.
Austin, Sir Alfred, 411.
Authorized Version, 59.
Autobiography (Mill), 277.
Autobiography (Trollope), 310.
Ave, Salve and Vale, 395.
Awakening, 404.

Back to Methuselah, 393, 394.
Bacon, 59-66.
Balaustion's Adventure, 343.
Ballantyne, James, 256, 257.
Balliol College, Oxford, 353.
Barchester Towers, 310.
Barrack Room Ballads, 382.
Barrett, Elizabeth, 334-339, 351.
Barrie, 301, 372, 383-384.
Barry Lyndon, 156.
Bartholomew Fair, 56.
Battle of Maldon, 8-9.
Beaduhild, 2.
Beaumont, 52, 56, 58.
Becket, 331.
Bede, 7-8, 22, 25.
Beggar's Opera, 141.
Bells and Pomegranates, 334, 338.
Bennett, Arnold, 407-408.
Bentham, Jeremy, 273, 274.
Beowulf, 4.
Bible, 29, 30, 59.
Bishop Blougram's Apology, 332.
Bishop Colenso, 266.
Bishops' Bible, 29.
Black Dwarf, 259.
Blackwood's Edinburgh Magazine, 245, 319.
Blake, William, 185-187.
Bleak House, 299.
Blessèd Damozel, 349.
Blot on the 'Scutcheon, 334.
Blount, Martha, 137.
Boccaccio, 31.
Bodley, Sir Thomas, 62.
Bolingbroke (Henry IV), 47, 49.
Bolingbroke (Henry St. John), 123, 138.
Boswell, 159, 165.

Boyle, Elizabeth, 35.
Bradshaigh, Lady, 148.
Brawne, Fanny, 247.
Bray, Charles, 319.
Bride of Abydos, 227.
Bride of Lammermoor, 259.
Bridges, Sir Robert, 411.
British Association for the Advancement of Science, 266, 267, 356.
Broken Heart, 58.
Brontë, Anne, 313.
Brontë, Charlotte, 313-317, 318, 353.
Brontë, Emily, 313-315.
Brooke, Rupert, 413.
Browning, 332-343.
Bunyan, 87-95.
Burbage, Richard, 42, 46, 49.
Bürger's *Lenore,* 255.
Burghley, 61.
Burke, 161, 165, 212.
Burne-Jones, 283, 351, 352, 353.
Burney, Fanny, 165, 167.
Burns, Robert, 187-195.
Butler, Samuel, 367-368.
Byron, 139, 219-233, 334.

Cadenus and Vanessa, 127.
Cædmon's Hymn, 7-8.
Cæsar and Cleopatra, 391.
Cæsar, Julius, 1.
Caliban, 52.
Calvert, Raisley, 199.
Calvin, 29.
Campaign, 120.
Campbell, Mary, 190.
Candida, 390, 391, 392.
Cannan, Gilbert, 409.
Canterbury Tales, 27.
Canute, 9.
Capital, 388.
Captain Brassbound's Conversion, 391.
Carew, Thomas, 103.
Carlyle, 187, 216, 279-281, 283, 287, 317, 325, 353.
Casa Guidi Windows, 338.
Caste, 370.
Castle of Otranto, 259.
Castle Rackreut, 172.
Catiline, 56.
Caxton, 25.
Cervantes, 151.
Chapman, George, 58, 353.
Chapman and Hall, 293, 364.
Character of the Happy Warrior, 209.
Charge of the Light Brigade, 329.
Charlemagne, 8, 11.
Charles I, 70, 81, 103.
Charles II, 111, 117.
Charles V, 27.
Charterhouse School, 119, 303, 305.
Chatterton, 175.
Chaucer, 16, 18, 35, 68, 73, 135.
Childe Harold's Pilgrimage, 225, 231.

Chimes, 297.
Christ's College, Cambridge, 71.
Christ's Hospital, 213.
Christabel, 213, 215, 256.
"Christian Socialism," 311.
Christmas Carol, 297.
Christmas Eve and Easter Day, 332.
Cibber, Colley, 138, 151.
Clairmont, Clara Mary Jane, 230.
Clarissa, 147, 148, 154.
Clayhanger, 408.
"Cockney School of Poetry," 245.
Cloister and the Hearth, 311.
Coleridge, Samuel Taylor, 200-216, 247, 253, 256.
Collier, Jeremy, 117.
Collins, Wilkie, 299.
Colombe's Birthday, 334.
Comedy of Errors, 46.
Complete English Gentleman, 115.
Complete English Tradesman, 115.
Comus, 73.
Confessions of an English Opium-Eater, 253.
Congreve, 139.
Conrad, 372, 379-380.
Copernicus, 21.
Coriolanus, 51.
Cornhill Magazine, 285, 308, 310, 364.
Corsair, 230.
Cotter's Saturday Night, 190.
Cotton, Sir Robert, 5.
Country House, 404.
Coverdale, 27-29.
Cowper, Ashley, 180.
Cowper, William, 178-183.
Craigenputtock, 281.
Cranford, 317.
Cranmer's Bible, 29.
Crashaw, 104.
Cricket on the Hearth, 297.
Critical Examination of the Pentateuch, 266.
Cromwell, Oliver, 85.
Cromwell, Thomas, 27.
Crossing the Bar, 331.
Cruikshank, George, 293.
Cuthbert, 22.
Cuthwin, 22.
Cymbeline, 52.

Daily News, 299.
Daisy and Daphne, 415.
Dangerous Ages, 415.
Daniel Deronda, 322.
Dante, 30, 31, 63.
Dark Flower, 404.
Darwin, Charles, 267, 356.
David Copperfield, 291, 293, 299.
Day, Thomas, 172.
Death and Dr. Hornbrook, 190.
Death in the Desert, 332.
Debits and Credits, 170.

Decline and Fall of the Roman Empire, 162.
Defence of Guinevere, 352.
Defoe, 111-116, 143.
Dekker, 58.
Demos, 378.
Dennis, John, 135.
Departmental Ditties, 381.
De Quincey, 207, 253.
Descent of Man, 358.
Descriptive Sketches, 197.
Deserted Village, 157.
Desperate Remedies, 364.
Devil's Disciple, 391.
Diana of the Crossways, 362.
Diarmuid and Grania, 395.
Dickens, 22, 156, 289-303, 305, 306, 317.
Dickens (Gissing), 379.
Dictes and Sayings (Caxton), 25.
Disraeli, 317.
Doctor's Dilemma, 392.
Dombey and Son, 299.
Domestic Manners of the Americans, 310.
Don Juan, 232, 246.
Don Quixote, 151, 153, 154.
Donne, 97, 99, 103.
Douai Bible, 29.
Dove Cottage, Grasmere, 207, 253.
Dramatic Literature of the Age of Elizabeth, 252.
Dramatis Personæ, 339.
Dr. Donne and Gargantua, 99.
Dream of John Ball, 352.
Drinkwater, 151.
Dryden, 86, 119, 133, 271.
Duchess of Malfi, 58.
Dunciad, 131, 138.
Dynasts, 366.

East India Company, 277.
Eastward Ho, 58.
Ebb Tide, 374.
Ecclesiastical History, 7-8.
Ecclesiastical Sonnets, 211.
Eclogues (Virgil), 135.
Edgeworth, Maria, 171.
Edinburgh Review, 249, 270.
Edinburgh University, 279.
Edward II, 39.
Edward VII, 285.
Egoist, 414.
Elegy written in a Country Churchyard, 177.
Elizabeth, Queen, 29, 33, 69-70.
Elizabeth and Essex, 420.
Elizabethan Age, 33, 68.
Elizabethan Drama, 353.
Elton, Professor Oliver, 5.
Emerson, 279.
Eminent Victorians, 418.
Emma, 170.
Endymion, 245, 246.
England under Queen Anne, 272.

English Bards and Scotch Reviewers, 223.
English Humorists, 308.
Enquiry concerning Political Justice, 237.
Epipsychidion, 241.
Epistle of Eloisa, 137.
Epistle of Karshish, 332.
Epithalamium, 37.
Erasmus, 27, 31.
Erewhon, 368.
Esmond, 307, 308.
Essay on Criticism, 135.
Essay on Man, 139.
Essay on the Principle of Population, 273.
Essays (Bacon), 59, 61.
Essays and Reviews, 266, 267, 287.
Essays of Elia, 249.
Esther Waters, 395.
Euphues, 40, 147.
Evan Harrington, 362.
Evans, Marian, 318.
Eve of St. Agnes, 247.
Evelina, 165.
Evelyn, John, 117.
Evening Walk, 197.
Every Man in his Humour, 53.
Examiner, 123, 245.
Excursion, 211.
Exeter Book, 1.
Expansion of England, 381.

Faerie Queene, 35, 37, 87.
Familiar Studies of Men and Books, 374.
Fanny's First Play, 393.
Far Away and Long Ago, 416.
Far from the Madding Crowd, 364.
Father and Son, 267.
Felix Holt, 321.
Fielding, 149-151, 154, 161, 167, 170, 306, 307.
Fieldings, 414.
Fifine at the Fair, 343.
First Reform Act, 261, 263, 271.
Flaxman, 185.
Fleshly School in Poetry, 349.
Fletcher, 52, 56, 58.
Forsyte Saga, 403, 404.
Four Georges, 308.
Fox, 161.
Framley Parsonage, 310.
Frank's Casket, 3-4.
Fraser's Magazine, 279, 285, 305.
Fraternity, 404.
Frederick the Great, 281.
Freeholder, 120.
Freelands, 404.
French Revolution, 279.
Fugitive Pieces, 223.
Fuseli, 185.

Gadshill Place, 299, 301.
Gallipoli, 411.
Galsworthy, John, 403-406.
Garden of Eden, 394.

Garnett, Dr. Richard, 217.
Garrick, David, 159, 165.
Gascoigne, George, 33.
Gaskell, Elizabeth Cleghorn, 317, 318.
Gay, 141.
Geneva Bible, 29.
Geoffrey of Monmouth, 11.
George I, 107, 120.
George II, 129.
George IV, 170, 245, 259.
George Eliot, 22, 170, 318, 353.
George, Henry, 388.
Georgian Poetry 1911-1912, 413.
Getting Married, 393.
Giaour, 227.
Gibbon, Edward, 162.
Gil Blas, 154.
Gissing, George, 376-379.
Goblin Market, 351.
Godwin, Mary, 230.
Godwin, William, 230, 237, 239.
Goethe, 173, 305.
Götz von Berlichingen, 255.
Goldsmith, 116, 157-161.
Gondoliers, 370.
Good Companions, 156.
Good Friday, 411.
Goody Blake and Harry Gill, 201.
Gosse, Sir Edmund, 267, 341.
Gower, 16.
Grace Abounding, 93, 95.
Gray, Thomas, 175, 177.
"Great" Bible, 29.
Great Expectations, 301.
Great Lover, 413.
Greene, Robert, 40, 44.
Gregory, Matthew, 259.
Greta Hall, Keswick, 215.
Groatsworth of Wit bought with a Million of Repentance, 44.
Guedalla, Philip, 421.
Gulliver's Travels, 128, 130, 131, 170.
Guardian, 120.
Guiccioli, Countess, 231.
Guy Mannering, 259.
Guy's Hospital, 243, 247.

Hakluyt's *Voyages*, 58.
Hall, Joseph, 99.
Hallam, Arthur, 325.
Hallowe'en, 190.
Hamlet, 39, 49.
Hard Times, 299, 317, 408.
Hardy, Thomas, 364-366.
Harley, 120, 123.
Harold, 331.
Harriet Hume, 415.
Harrow, 221, 310, 347.
Harvard College, 111.
Hathaway, Ann, 44.
Haydon, 251.
Hazlitt, William, 252.
Heart of Midlothian, 259.

Heartbreak House, 393.
Hellas, 241.
Hemetes the Hermit, 33.
Henry IV, 46, 47.
Henry V, 49.
Henry VI, 49.
Henry VII, 21.
Henry VIII, 27, 78.
Herbert, George, 104.
Herrick, 101.
Heroes and Hero Worship, 281.
Hertha, 354.
Hervé Riel, 343.
Hesketh, Lady, 183.
Heywood, Thomas, 58.
Hilda Lessways, 408.
"Hinksey diggings," 285.
History of England (Macaulay), 272.
History of John Bull, 131.
H. M. S. Pinafore, 370.
Holy Willie's Prayer, 190.
Homer, 138.
Horace, 135.
Hours of Idleness, 223.
Household Words, 299.
Housman, Alfred E., 411.
Hudson, W. H., 416.
Hugo, 173, 353.
Hunt, Holman, 283.
Hunt, Leigh, 245, 247.
Hutchinson, Mary, 207.
Huxley, Aldous, 418.
Huxley, T. H., 267, 356-358, 418.
Hyde, Douglas, 395.
Hymn to the Pillory, 113.

Ibsen, 388.
Idiot Boy, 201.
Idylls of the King, 329.
Iliad, 137, 138.
Il Penseroso, 73.
Imlay, Fanny, 239.
Importance of Being Earnest, 371.
In Chancery, 404.
In Memoriam, 328.
Indian Summer of a Forsyte, 404.
Industrialism, 261.
Inland Voyage, 372.
Instauratio, 62.
Irish Renaissance, 395.
Ivanhoe, 259.

James I, 70.
Jane Eyre, 315, 317.
Jefferson, 107.
Jesus College, Cambridge, 212.
Jew of Malta, 39.
John Bull's Other Island, 392.
Johnson, Dr., 116, 159, 161, 164, 165, 175.
Johnson, Esther, 123, 125, 127.
Jolly Beggars, 190.
Jones, H. A., 301, 370.
Jonson, 35, 53, 58, 353.

Joseph Andrews, 151, 153.
Journal of the Plague Year, 115.
Journal to Stella, 127.
Joyce, James, 415.
Jude the Obscure, 364, 366.
Judge, 415.
Judith, 5.
Julius Cæsar, 51.
Jungle Books, 382.
Junius, 5-7.
Juno and the Paycock, 398.
Just So Stories, 382.
Juvenile Poems, 213.

Keats, 75, 243-249, 334.
Keats Memorial House, 247.
Keeping up Appearances, 415.
Kellys and the O'Kellys, 310.
Kidnapped, 376.
Kim, 382.
King, Edward, 73.
King John, 46.
King Lear, 51.
King's Daughter, 411.
Kingsley, Canon, 287, 311.
Kipling, 170, 372, 381-382.
Kipps, 399, 402.
Kneller, Sir Godfrey, 138.
Knight of the Burning Pestle, 56.
Knowles, Sheridan, 301.
Kubla Khan, 215.
Kyd, 39.

La Belle Dame sans Merci, 247.
L'Allegro, 73.
La Saisiaz, 332, 343.
Lady of the Lake, 256.
Lady Windermere's Fan, 371.
Lamb, Charles, 212, 213, 216, 249, 251.
Langland, William, 16.
Land of Heart's Desire, 395.
Landmarks in French Literature, 418.
Landowning aristocracy, 164, 263.
Last Chronicle of Barset, 310.
Last Poems (Housman), 411.
Laud, Archbishop, 77.
Lawrence, D. H., 409.
Lay of the Last Minstrel, 213, 256.
Layamon, 11-12.
Lays of Ancient Rome, 272.
Lead, Kindly Light, 287.
Legend of Montrose, 259.
Leicester, Earl of, 35.
Leigh, Elizabeth Medora, 229.
Lerici, 241, 243.
Lessing, 173.
Lewes, 170, 319.
Liber Amoris, 252.
Liberty of Prophesying, 80.
Life of Charlotte Brontë, 317.
Life of Goethe, 319.
Life of Jesus (Strauss), 319.
Life of Johnson, 159.

Life of Swift, 123.
Lincoln, Abraham, 75.
Lines composed a few miles above Tintern Abbey, 203.
Literary Club, 159, 164.
Little Dorrit, 299.
Little Minister, 383.
Lloyd, Edward, 111.
Locke, 106.
Lockhart, John Gibson, 245.
Locksley Hall, 327.
London Gazette, 111, 119.
London Magazine, 249, 253.
Lonsdale, Earl of, 195, 199.
Lord Jim, 380.
Love and Mr. Lewisham, 399.
Love's Labor's Lost, 46.
Love's Labor's Won, 46.
Love Songs of Connaught, 395.
Lovelace, 103, 104.
Lowther, Sir James, 195.
Loyalties, 406.
Lucy poems, 207.
Luther, 22, 27.
Lycidas, 73, 75.
Lyell, Charles, 267.
Lyly, John, 40, 47, 59, 147.
Lyrical Ballads, 201, 203, 205, 207, 213, 259.
Lytton, Lord, 301.

Macaulay, 170, 171, 269-272, 285.
Macaulay, Rose, 415.
Macbeth, 51.
Macdermots of Ballycloran, 310.
Machiavelli, 31.
Mackenzie, Compton, 409.
Macpherson, 173, 175.
Magdalen College, 119.
Major Barbara, 392.
Malory, 27.
Malthus, 273, 274.
Malvern Hills, 16.
Man and Superman, 392.
Man from the North, 407.
Man of Destiny, 390, 392.
Man of Property, 403.
Man's Place in Nature, 358.
Manchester Grammar School, 253.
Mansfield, Katherine, 414.
Mansfield Park, 170.
Many Inventions, 382.
Marius the Epicurean, 371.
Marlborough, Duke of, 113, 120.
Marlowe, 38, 39, 47.
Marmion, 256.
Marshalsea prison, 289.
Marston, John, 99.
Martin Chuzzlewit, 156, 297.
Martin Scriblerus, 131.
Mary Barton, 317.
Mary Morison, 188.
Mary Olivier, 414.

Mary, Queen, 29.
Marvell, 103.
Marx, Karl, 388.
Masefield, John, 411-412.
Master Humphrey's Clock, 295.
Maud; a Monodrama, 329.
Maupassant, 408.
Mayor of Casterbridge, 364.
Mazzini, 353.
Melbourne, Lord, 227, 272.
Melodies of Scotland, 194.
Menæchmi, 46.
Men and Women, 339.
Merchant of Venice, 39, 46, 47.
Meredith, George, 349, 353, 360-362, 411, 414.
Meres, 47.
Metabiological Pentateuch, 393.
"Metaphysical Poetry," 99.
Methodists, 265.
Middlemarch, 322.
Midsummer Night's Dream, 40, 46, 47.
Mill, James, 273, 274.
Mill, John Stuart, 273-277, 279, 285, 322.
Mill on the Floss, 319, 322.
Millais, John, 283.
Milton, 71-87, 270.
Milton (Blake), 185.
Minnie Maylow's Story, 412.
Misalliance, 393.
Mitford, Miss, 336.
Modern Comedy, 405.
Modern Love, 362.
Modern Painters, 283.
Modest Proposal, 129.
Moll Flanders, 115.
"Monk" Lewis, 256, 259.
Montaigne, 31, 52.
Montagu, Lady Mary Wortley, 137.
Moore, George, 395.
Moral Essays, 139.
Moral Tales, 172.
More, Sir Thomas, 27.
Morris, William, 283, 352, 353.
Morte d'Arthur, 27, 327.
Mr. Britling Sees It Through, 401, 402.
Mrs. Dalloway, 415.
Mrs. Warren's Profession, 389.
Mr. Waddington of Wyck, 414.
Much Ado about Nothing, 49.
Munera Pulveris, 285.
Murder as one of the Fine Arts, 253.
Murry, J. Middleton, 414.
Myers, F. W. H., 321.
Mysteries of Udolpho, 259.
Mystery of Edwin Drood, 301.

Nan, 411.
Necessity of Atheism, 235.
Nether Stowey, 200, 213.
New Grub Street, 378.
New Machiavelli, 402.
New Numbers, 413.

Newcomes, 303, 307.
Newman, Cardinal, 287, 311.
News from Nowhere, 352.
Newstead Abbey, 233.
Newton, Isaac, 63, 106, 128, 165.
Newton, Rev. John, 178, 181.
Nicholas Nickleby, 295.
Nichol, John, 353.
Nigger of the Narcissus, 380.
Nithhad, 2.
Nonconformists, 265.
North and South, 317.
North, Sir Thomas, 51.
Northanger Abbey, 169, 170, 259.
Northumbria, 4, 8.
Nostromo, 380.
Novum Organum, 62, 66.
Nowell, Laurence, 4.

O' a' the airts the wind can blaw, 194.
O'Casey, Sean, 398.
Ode on Intimations of Immortality, 106, 209.
Ode on the Death of the Duke of Wellington, 329.
Ode on the Morning of Christ's Nativity, 73.
Ode to Dejection, 216.
Ode to Pan, 246.
Ode to Solitude, 133.
Ode to the West Wind, 241.
Odyssey, 138, 367.
Of Reformation in England, 77.
Old Mortality, 259.
Old Vicarage, Grantchester, 413.
Old Wives' Tale, 407, 408.
Oliver Twist, 295.
Olney Hymns, 181.
On a Grecian Urn, 247.
On first looking into Chapman's Homer, 245.
On Liberty, 277.
Ordeal of Richard Feverel, 360.
Origin of Species, 267, 356, 358.
Orlando, 415.
Orlando Furioso, 37.
Ossian, 173, 175.
Osborne, Mrs. Fanny, 372.
Othello, 51.
Outcast of the Islands, 379.
Outline of History, 402.
Ovid, 16.
Oxford movement, 287.

Palmerston, 421.
Pamela, 144, 145, 148-153.
Pantisocracy, 212.
Paracelsus, 334.
Paradise Lost, 85, 86, 116, 270.
Paradise Regained, 71.
Parliamentarians, 70.
Parson Adams, 153.
Past and Present, 279.

Pastorals, 135.
Pater, Walter Horatio, 371.
Patience, 371.
Pauline, 334.
Payne-Townshend, Miss, 389.
Pearl, 15.
Pembroke College, 177.
Pentland Rising, 372.
Pepys, 117.
Percy, Bishop, 165, 173, 175.
Persuasion, 170.
Peter Bell, 211.
Peterhouse, Cambridge, 177.
Petrarch, 31.
Philanderer, 389.
Philanthropist, 198.
Philaster, 52, 56.
Philip the King, 411.
Pickwick, 156, 295, 305.
Piers Plowman, 16.
Pigeon, 406.
Pilgrim's Progress, 87-93, 95, 270.
Pinero, 301, 370.
Pitt, 161.
Plain Tales from the Hills, 381.
Playboy of the Western World, 397.
Playlets of the War, 393.
Plays Pleasant and Unpleasant, 390.
Plough and the Stars, 398.
Plutarch's Lives, 51.
Poems and Ballads, 353.
Poems before Congress, 338.
Poems by Currer, Ellis, and Acton Bell, 313.
Poems by Two Brothers, 323.
Poems, chiefly in the Scottish Dialect, 190.
Poems, chiefly Lyrical, 323.
Poetaster, 56.
Poetical Sketches, 185.
Polite Farces, 407.
Pompey the Great, 411.
Pope, Alexander, 116, 131-139, 175.
Population, Increase of, 261-263.
Posthumous Papers of the Pickwick Club, 295.
Powell, Mary, 78.
Pre-Raphaelite Brotherhood, (P.R.B.), 283, 349, 352, 353.
Prelude, 211.
Press Cuttings, 393.
Pride and Prejudice, 167, 169, 170.
Priestley, J. B., 156.
Prince Consort, 329.
Prince Hohenstiel-Schwangau, 343.
Princess, 327.
Principles of Geology, 267.
Principles of Political Economy, 275, 277.
Private Papers of Henry Ryecroft, 379.
Professor, 315.
Professor's Love Story, 383.
Progress and Poverty, 388.
Progress of Error, 181.
Prometheus Unbound, 240.

Prospero, 52.
Protestantism, 22.
Proust, Marcel, 205.
Punch, 305.
Puritans, 70, 77, 261.
Pygmalion, 393.

Quarterly, 246.
Queen Mab, 237.
Queen Mary, 331.
Queen Victoria, 420.

Rabelais, 31.
Radcliffe, Mrs., 259.
Rainbow, 409.
Raleigh, 35, 38.
Rape of Lucrece, 46.
Rape of the Lock, 135.
Rapture, 103.
Reade, Charles, 311.
Rebecca West, 415.
Recluse, 209.
Recuyell of the Histories of Troy, 25.
Red Cotton Nightcap Country, 343.
Reformation, 21, 66.
Reliques (Percy's) 173, 175, 255.
Religious Courtship, 115.
Remorse, 215.
Renaissance, 66.
Representative Government, 277.
Rescue, 380.
Return of the Native, 364.
Revenge, 59.
Review of the Affairs of France, 113.
Revival of Learning, 21, 31.
Revolt in the Desert, 416.
Revolt of Islam, 240.
Reynard the Fox, 412.
Reynolds, Sir Joshua, 159, 165.
Riceyman Steps, 408.
Richard II, 25.
Richard II, 46.
Richard III, 46, 47, 49.
Richardson, 143, 147-151, 154, 161, 167, 170.
Riders to the Sea, 397.
Rights of Man, 266.
Rime of the Ancient Mariner, 201, 213, 215.
Ring and the Book, 339, 341.
Ritchie, Lady, 305.
River Duddon, 211.
Rob Roy, 259.
Robertson, T. W., 370.
Robinson Crusoe, 116, 170.
Rochester, Earl of, 117.
Roderick Random, 154.
Romance of the Forest, 259.
Romantic Revival, 173-260.
Romeo and Juliet, 46, 47.
Romola, 321.
Rossetti, Christina Georgina, 351.
Rossetti, Dante Gabriel, 283, 349, 352, 353.

Rosetti, W. M., 187.
Rousseau, 173.
Royal Society, 63.
Royalists, 70.
Rugby Chapel, November 1857, 345.
Ruskin, John, 283-285.
Rydal Mount, 207.

Sackville, Charles, 104.
Saint Joan, 394.
Salisbury, Lord, 358.
Salt Water Ballads, 412.
Salvaging of Civilization, 401.
Sancho Panza, 153.
Sandford and Merton, 172.
Sartor Resartus, 279.
Scenes of Clerical Life, 319.
Schiller, 173.
Schlegels, 173.
School for Scandal, 157.
Science of Life, 402.
Scots Musical Museum, 194.
Scott, Sir Walter, 169, 170, 171, 245, 255-260, 261, 380.
Scriblerus Club, 131.
Seeley, Sir John, 381.
Sejanus, 56.
Selkirk, Alexander, 116.
Selwood, Emily, 329.
Sense and Sensibility, 167.
Sentimental Journey, 156, 157.
Sentimental Tommy, 383.
Septuagint, 31.
Seven Lamps of Architecture, 283.
Seven Seas, 382.
Shadow of a Gunman, 398.
Shadow of the Glen, 397.
Shakspere, 35, 39, 42, 46-58, 66, 68, 116, 215, 353.
Shamela, 151.
Shaw, Bernard, 172, 301, 387-394.
She Stoops to Conquer, 157.
She was a Phantom of Delight, 207.
Shelley, 75, 230-243, 334.
Shepherd's Calendar, 35.
Sheridan, 161.
Shirley, 315.
Shoemaker's Holiday, 58.
Short View of the Profaneness and Immorality of the English Stage, 117.
Shropshire Lad, 411.
Sidney, Sir Henry, 35.
Sidney, Sir Philip, 35, 38, 59.
Silas Marner, 321.
Silent Woman, 56.
Silver Box, 403, 405.
Silver Tassie, 398.
Silverado Squatters, 374.
Sinclair, May, 414.
Sir Charles Grandison, 148.
Sir Gawain and the Green Knight, 16.
Sir Thopas, 18.
Sitwell, Edith, 131.

Sitwell, Sacheverell, 99.
Sketches by Boz, 293.
Skin Game, 406.
Smith, Adam, 162-164, 273.
Smollett, 154.
Soldiers Three, 381.
Somers, Sir George, 52.
Song of Deor, 1-2.
Songs before Sunrise, 354.
Songs of Experience, 186.
Songs of Innocence, 186.
Sonnets from the Portuguese, 338, 339.
Sons and Lovers, 409.
Sophocles, 51.
Sordello, 334.
Southampton, Earl of, 46.
Southey, 211, 212, 217.
Southwark Cathedral, 16.
Spanish Tragedy, 39.
Spectator, 120.
Spencer, Herbert, 319, 322.
Spenser, 35-38, 86, 87.
Stalky & Co., 382.
Stanzas to Augusta, 231.
Steele, 116, 119, 120, 135, 143.
Stephen, Sir Leslie, 305, 415.
Sterne, 156.
Stevenson, 372-376, 379, 380.
St. Ives, 376.
St. John's College, Cambridge, 197.
St. Saviour's Church, 16.
Stoke Poges, 177.
Stones of Venice, 283.
Strachey, Lytton, 418.
Strafford, 334.
Strange Case of Dr. Jekyll and Mr. Hyde, 374.
Strange Gentleman, 301.
Strife, 406.
Studies in the History of the Renaissance, 371.
Subjection of Women, 277.
Suckling, Sir John, 103.
Sumer is icumen in, 13-14.
Surrey, Earl of, 33.
Swift, 116, 121-131, 141, 143.
Swinburne, 187, 247, 349, 353-354, 411.
Sybil, 317.
Synge, J. M., 395-398.

Taggard, Genevieve, 99.
Tale of a Tub, 131.
Tale of Two Cities, 299.
Tales of Wonder, 256.
Tamburlaine, 39.
Tam O'Shanter, 194.
Task, 183.
Tasso, 30.
Tatler, 119.
Taylor, Helen, 277.
Temple, Sir William, 123.
Taylor, Jeremy, 80.
Taylor, Mrs., 275, 277, 279.

Temple, Frederick, 266.
Tempest, 52.
Tennyson, 323-331, 411.
Tess of the D'Urbervilles, 364.
Thackeray, 22, 156, 170, 301-308, 317.
These Twain, 408.
Theobald, 138.
Three Plays for Puritans, 391.
Timbuctoo, 323.
Three Sisters, 414.
Tinker's Wedding, 397.
Tintern Abbey, 201.
Titus Andronicus, 39, 46.
To a Mouse, 190.
To a Mountain Daisy, 190.
To a Nightingale, 247.
To a Skylark, 241.
To Let, 404, 405.
To the Lighthouse, 415.
Toleration Act, 107.
Tom Jones, 154, 307.
Tommy and Grizel, 383.
Tono-Bungay, 399.
Tonson, Jacob, 135.
Too True to be Good, 394.
Tottel's Miscellany, 33.
Tragical History of Dr. Faustus, 39.
Travels with a Donkey, 372.
Treasure Island, 374, 379.
Trevelyan, George Otto, 270.
Trevelyan, G. M., 109-117, 272.
Trial of Jesus, 411.
Trinity College, Cambridge, 63, 221, 269, 305, 323.
Tristram Shandy, 156, 157.
Trollope, Anthony, 170, 310-311.
True Born Englishman, 111.
True Relation of the Apparition of one Mrs. Veal, 115.
Truth about an Author, 407.
Turner, 283.
Twelfth Night, 49, 52.
Twelve-Pound Look, 384.
Two Gentlemen of Verona, 46, 47, 52.
Two Poets of Croisic, 343.
Tyndale, 22, 27.

Ulysses (James Joyce), 415.
Ulysses (Tennyson), 327.
Under the Greenwood Tree, 364.
Une Vie, 408.
Unpleasant Plays, 389.
Unto this Last, 285.
Unwin, Mrs., 180-181.
Ussher, Archbishop, 5.
Utilitarianism, 277.

Vallon, Annette, 198, 199.
Vanhomrigh, Hester, 127.
Vanity Fair, 305, 306.
Vaughan, 104.
Venus and Adonis, 46.
Venizelos, 233.

Vicar of Wakefield, 157.
Victoria, Queen, 211, 261, 329, 353.
Victorian Age, 261-384.
Village Coquettes, 301.
Villette, 315.
Vindication of the Rights of Women, 237.
Virgil, 135.
Virginia, 52.
Virginibus Puerisque, 374.
Virginians, 308.
Vision of William concerning Piers the Plowman, 16.
Volpone, 56.
Voltaire, 139.
Vulgate, 31.
Vulliamy, Marie, 360.

Wace of Jersey, 11.
Wallace, A. R., 356.
Walpole, Horace, 259.
Walpole, Hugh, 409.
Walpole, Sir Robert, 128.
Walsh, William, 134.
Walton, Izaak, 101.
Warden, 310.
Warton, Thomas, 177.
Watchman, 213.
Watts-Dunton, Theodore, 354.
Waverley, 257.
Waves, 416.
Wayland the Smith, 2.
Way of All Flesh, 368.
We are Seven, 201.
Wealth of Nations, 162-164.
Webster, John, 58.
Weir of Hermiston, 376.
Wellington, 421.
Well of the Saints, 397.
Wells, H. G., 399-402.
Welsh, Jane, 281.
Wentworth Place, 247.
Wesley, Charles, 178.
Wesley, John, 178, 185.
Westbrook, Harriet, 235, 240.
Westminster Review, 275, 319.
Westminster School, 180.
Weston, Jessie, 16.
Westward Ho, 311.
What Every Woman Knows, 384.
Wheels of Chance, 399.
When Lilacs last in the Dooryard Bloomed, 75.
Whitby Abbey, 7.
White Devil, 58.
White Doe of Rylstone, 211.
Whitefield, George, 178.
Whitman, Walt, 75.
Whittingham, William, 29.
Widow in the Bye Street, 412.
Widowers' Houses, 389.
Wilberforce, Samuel, Bishop of Oxford, 267, 356.

Wilde, Oscar, 371.
William of Normandy, 11.
William of Orange, 107, 111, 117.
Windsor Forest, 135, 175.
Winter's Tale, 52.
With a Guitar—to Jane, 243.
Wit's Commonwealth, 46.
Wolfe, General, 177.
Wollstonecraft, Mary, 237.
Wolsey, 27.
Woman in White, 299.
Woman of No Importance, 371.
Woodlanders, 364.
Woolf, Virginia, 415.
Worcester College, Oxford, 253.
Wordsworth, Dorothy, 199.

Wordsworth, William, 106, 178, 195-211, 259, 329.
Workers in the Dawn, 378.
Work, Wealth and Happiness of Mankind, 402.
World of William Clissold, 401.
Wrecker, 374.
Wuthering Heights, 315.
Wyatt, 33.
Wycherley, 134.
Wyclif, 22.
Wye Valley, 201.

Yeast, 311.
Yeats, William Butler, 395.
You Never Can Tell, 390, 391, 392.

[1]